Advance Praise for

Health Care Choices for Today's Consumer

"*Health Care Choices for Today's Consumer* provides readers with a wealth of information about the various aspects of making health-care choices. It will be a valuable resource for consumers with questions about how to make the best decisions about their health care and how to be in control of their choices."

Arthur S. Flemming
Secretary of Health, Education and Welfare
under President Eisenhower

"With great clarity, *Health Care Choices for Today's Consumer* helps to demystify a health-care system that can be utterly confusing. Families USA has come to our aid by showing us what to look for—and what to look out for—in a health-care provider."

Ben Cohen
Founder and Chairman, Ben & Jerry's Homemade, Inc.

"As someone with personal experience in making complex health-care decisions and in dealing with the complexities of the system, I strongly recommend *Health Care Choices for Today's Consumer* as a valuable and objective guide for all of us."

The Honorable Paul E. Tsongas
Former U.S. Senator

"More than ever before, U.S. companies and their employees are pressed to spend health-care dollars wisely. *Health Care Choices for Today's Consumer* explains just how to go about it."

Arnold Hiatt
Former Chairman, Stride Rite

"*Health Care Choices for Today's Consumer* is a remarkable book that serves as a detailed road map—helping the consumer navigate in today's complex health-care system—and an encyclopedia of useful information about specific health issues. For those moving into a new community or a new stage of life, for those facing unfamiliar health-related problems, or for those simply seeking to reevaluate the treatment they have been getting, it will be a very valuable resource."

Jean A. Dowdall
President, Simmons College

"This book is a veritable treasure of essential, user-friendly information for the health-care consumer. I enthusiastically recommend it as an important part of the education of those who are or will be faced with health-care decisions—which includes us all. Elders and families—professionals and non-professionals alike—should get and read a copy now."

John R. Delfs, MD
Chief, Section of Geriatric Medicine and
Director, Deaconess ElderCare
New England Deaconess Hospital

"Nurses in America appreciate the role that consumers can play in decision-making about their health. This book will help consumers assume that role more effectively and thoughtfully."

Virginia Trotter Betts
President, American Nurses Association

HEALTH CARE CHOICES

For Today's Consumer

Families USA Guide to Quality & Cost

Marc S. Miller, Editor

LIVING PLANET
PRESS

Washington, DC

Published in the United States of America by
Living Planet Press, 2940 Newark St., NW, Washington, DC 20008

Distributed to bookstores by
Independent Publishers Group, Chicago, Illinois (800)888-4741

Design, layout, and original artwork by Hobbamock Design
Production by Anne Read
Marketing by Lee Phenner Marketing Communications

Grateful acknowledgment is made for permission to use the following material:
"Home Care" © 1994 United Seniors Health Cooperative
Consumers Union for excerpts from *Consumer Reports* © 1992, 1994

To order additional copies of *Health Care Choices for Today's Consumer,*
use the order form in this book or look in your local bookstore.

For information on bulk orders, contact Families USA Publications (617)338-6035 ext. 302.

Manufactured in the United States of America
ISBN 1-879326-23-X
10 9 8 7 6 5 4 3 2 1

Table of Contents

Acknowledgments

Literally countless people contributed to *Health Care Choices for Today's Consumer*. Two were critical throughout: Martha Grover, project associate and my close collaborator on every element of this book, and Philippe Villers, president and founder of Families USA Foundation and the guiding light for this project.

In addition, two groups of people have been invaluable: the authors and the project advisory board. The members of both groups contributed far and beyond their "official" roles. For example, many authors provided critical insight for chapters by other people, as well as guidance for the project as a whole. The advisory board, chaired by Mr. Villers, consists of J. Larry Brown, Michael Crump, Thomas Delbanco, MD, Barbara Ferrer, Norbert Goldfield, MD, Suzanne Mercure, Joseph Restuccia, DrPH, Richard Rockefeller, MD, Richard Rowe, Michael Segal, Rina Spence, and Harriet Tolpin. Of this number, Richard Rowe deserves special mention: he contributed the initial idea that Families USA Foundation issue a consumer's guide to health care.

Several colleagues at Families USA Foundation borrowed time from the intense demands of their jobs to assist this project, in particular executive director Ron Pollack and Kate Villers, director of the Massachusetts office. In addition, Phyllis Torda, Susan Sherry, Rena Murman, Arnold Bennett, Peggy Denker, and Barbara Campbell contributed, as did many others at Families USA, including board members Robert Kuttner, who played a major role in fleshing out the original concept, Robert Crittendon, and Velvet Miller. My apologies for not naming the entire organization.

Interns have been indispensable. Thanks to Doreen Balbuena, Sherrylyn Cotaco, David Cuttino, Joshua Dyckman, Shulamit Lewin, Kathryn McKinney, Jason Reblando, Deepika Reddy, and Magda Elise Schaler for volunteering their time and skills.

Many other individuals, organizations, and companies contributed time and expertise to *Health Care Choices*. In roughly alphabetical order, they are: Harris Allen, Dana Safran, and Alvin Tarlov, Health Institute; Myron Allukian, Boston Department of Health and Hospitals; Michael Bailit, Massachusetts Healthcare Purchasers Group; Elaine Barkley and Dan Bevins, Wheaton Regional Library; Charles Bell, Joel Gurin, and Rhoda Karpatkin, Consumers Union; James Bentley and Peter Kralovic, American Hospital Association; Robert Blendon and John Benson, Harvard School of Public Health; Nancy Bolduc, Dolores Mitchell, and Charles Slavin, Massachusetts Group Insurance Commission; Barbara Brown, Virginia Hospital Association; Stan Butler, Gay and Lesbian Advocates and Defenders; Thomas Chapman, George Washington University Hospital; Frank Coldiron and Andrew Dreyfus, Massachusetts Hospital Association; Frank Connolly, Martilla and Kiley; Thomas Crossman, Jean Delahanty, Lou Friedman, Paula Griswold, Scott

Osborne, Kevin Pryor, and Amy Simms, Massachusetts Rate Setting Commission; Linda deBenedictis and Ann Mueller, New England Patient Rights Group; John Delfs, Deaconess Hospital; Ellen Dombo, District of Columbia Office on Aging; Gail Douglas; Cathy Dunham, Robert Wood Johnson Foundation; Maria Durham; Susan Edgman-Levitan, Margaret Gerteis, and Jan Walker, Picker-Commonwealth Program for Patient-Centered Care; Roz Feldberg, Massachusetts Nurses Association; James Firman and Charles Mondin, United Seniors Health Cooperative; Barbara Giloth; Jennifer Frost and Rachel Benson Gold, Alan Guttmacher Institute; Fred Gardner, Virginia Medical Associates; Ben Gitterman; Suzanne Gordon; Carol Greenfield and Ken Phillips, New England Employees Benefits Council; Sarah Grigsby, Health Care Coalition; Julie Han, District of Columbia Hospital Association; the staff of Health Care for All, especially Marcia Hams, Meizhu Lui, Michael Miller, Kim Shellenberger, Rob Restuccia, and Mary Yeaton; James Hunt, Massachusetts League of Community Health Centers; Amy Hunter; Karen Ignani, Nina Lane, Sue Palsbo, and Susan Pisano, Group Health Association of America; Phil Kerth, Barbara Masters, Nancy Navin, and Matt Siegel, Massachusetts Division of Insurance; Jeffrey Kichen, Massachusetts Medical Society; Martha Kleinerman, Planned Parenthood Clinic of Greater Boston; Robert Krughoff, *Checkbook* magazine; Richard Laudon, New England Eye Institute; Jennifer Lederman, Word Designs; Teressa Lee, Maryland Health Services Commission; Francis Ludman, Maryland Attorney General's Office; Edward Madara, American Self-Help Clearinghouse; John May and Margaret Fearey, Massachusetts Association of HMOs; Jeanne McGee; Susan McTier, Medirisk, Inc.; Ken Melansen, Vinfen Corporation; Rebecca Morse, Women's Educational and Industrial Union; Judith Norsigian and Norma Swenson, Boston Women's Health Book Collective; Margaret O'Kane and Linda Shelton, National Committee for Quality Assurance; Patrick O'Reilly, Massachusetts Peer Review Organization; Lee Phenner; Barbara Popper, Children in Hospitals; Alan Raymond, Harvard Community Health Plan; Anne Read; Gail Ross, Lichtman, Trister, Singer, and Ross; Judith Schindul-Rothschild, Boston College; Martin Schneider, *Health Pages* magazine; Terry Shannon, Agency for Health Care Policy and Research; Gary Snyderman and Doug Steel, Joint Commission for the Accreditation of Health Care Organizations; Eliot Stone, Massachusetts Health Data Consortium; Virginia Sullivan, Massachusetts Department of Public Health; Rick Surpin, Cooperative Home Care Associates; Gillian Thomas, American Medical Women's Association; Deborah Wadsworth, Public Agenda Foundation; Gail Warner, Millipore Corp.; Karen Wong, Hobbamock Design; Richard Wurman; and Arnold Zide.

Thanks also to Lotus Development Corporation and Consumers Union for their support for this project.

Marc S. Miller
Jamaica Plain, Massachusetts

Foreword

by Hillary Rodham Clinton

For nearly two years, Americans from all walks of life have been engaged in an historic discussion about our nation's health-care system. No subject resonates so deeply with the American people. Our health-care system affects parents who worry about their children and aging relatives. It affects workers who worry about their livelihoods and business owners who worry about their companies' productivity. It affects every local, state, and federal official who worries about rising health-care costs consuming our budgets and exploding the deficit.

For all of these reasons, we have a collective responsibility as Americans to work for reform in the future. We also have a responsibility as individuals to take greater care of our own health.

We can start by becoming better informed health-care consumers. This publication provides consumers with valuable information they can use in making decisions about their own health care.

Each of us needs to be involved in the health-care decisions affecting our families. Each of us needs to be educated about the quality of the care we receive and how much we pay for it.

You may not agree with all of the advice here, but I think you will find it to be a helpful resource. As wiser health consumers, we can make better decisions about the health care we seek, and from whom we should seek it. When we confront choices about family doctors, specialists, dentists, insurance companies, managed care plans, hospitals, and mental health needs, we should be empowered with information to make effective and affordable decisions.

That is the purpose of this book. *Health Care Choices for Today's Consumer* is a comprehensive guide to help you and your family ensure that you receive the best and most affordable health care available. It comes to you from Families USA, an organization that is a thoughtful and effective advocate for the American health-care consumer. For many years, Families USA has provided national advocacy leadership for the improvement of our nation's health-care system. This Families USA book enables increasing numbers of consumers to become more confident and effective decision-makers in the health-care marketplace.

HEALTH CARE CHOICES

For Today's Consumer

Families
USA Guide to Quality & Cost

A User's Guide to Health Care Choices for Today's Consumer

By Marc S. Miller

Use Health Care Choices To . . .

◆ Become an active partner with health-care professionals;

◆ Find the answers to key health-care questions;

◆ Negotiate your path through the health-care maze;

◆ Make sure you receive high-quality health care; and

◆ Invest your health-care dollars wisely.

O nce upon a time, your doctor spoke and you obeyed. He told you what to do and how to do it—when to stay in bed, how often to take medicine, what hospital to use.

Of course, that picture is part fairy tale, part reality. And both doctors and patients now know that this approach to medicine fails you as well as the men and women you entrust with your health.

In other words, the world of health care is in the midst of a revolution:

• More and more people are recognizing that quality care goes far deeper than tending to the sick and injured.

• You are learning that doctors—and other health-care professionals—aren't the only ones responsible for your health. You, too, are central to the pursuit of a healthy life for yourself and your family.

• Hospitals are merging, HMOs are multiplying, health-care bills are soaring, and doctors are joining in widening networks—probably leaving you more confused and lost each day as you face the intricacies of access and quality.

As this revolution unfolds, uninformed and passive consumers will lose—in terms of their health, their happiness, and their bank balances. Americans are finding that they must either learn to be better consumers or do without

T I P

Write Here
Record your own notes as you read Health Care Choices. *Use the blank space in the narrow columns on each page.*

possibly essential care. The bottom line is that you play the starring role in your own health care. It's a role millions of Americans must learn to play to the fullest, day in and day out, in sickness *and* in health.

Health Care Choices is the script you'll follow to perform your role. Its theme is information: the aware consumer is a healthier consumer. According to researchers at New England Medical Center, patients with chronic diseases who communicate well with doctors benefit both medically *and* emotionally. They are physically healthier, recover faster, and can tolerate pain and handle stress better.

Marc S. Miller, project director for Health Care Choices for Today's Consumer, *is the author of* Irony of Victory *(University of Illinois Press, 1988). He is the editor of* State of the Peoples: A Global Human Rights Report on Societies in Danger *(Beacon Press, 1993) and* Working Lives *(Pantheon, 1981).*

The informed health-care consumer also saves money. For example, Dartmouth Medical School

researchers report that men who receive thorough, un-biased explanations of all the reasonable treatments for prostate cancer feel safer in *not* choosing expensive surgery. Instead, more men choose "watchful waiting," which is often more appropriate than facing the risks associated with surgery.

Partnerships and Good Health

The premise of *Health Care Choices* is that the aware consumer benefits from a full partnership with professional caregivers—and that you can lose big if you fail to accept this responsibility. In other words, *Health Care Choices* works best for the person who:

- Asks questions about treatment options and costs;
- Makes his or her own medical decisions; *and*
- Demands *evidence* of quality and expertise.

A strong partnership between you and health-care professionals rests on a number of principles. We invite you, as an aware health-care consumer, to keep these in mind as you read on:

- Learn what you can do for yourself, what professionals can do for you—and what you can do together.
- Plan ahead. Get care while you're healthy—and prepare for the time when you'll need professional assistance.
- Ignorance isn't bliss. A true partner in care accepts and deals with both bad news and good.
- Health care is both an art and a science, with few cut-and-dried "right" answers. Only you can decide among the many possible options for your own situation.
- Health care is also personal. No one plan of care works best for everybody.
- The vast majority of health-care professionals are com-petent and can serve you well—*if* you do your part.

- The health-care system contains some second-rate facilities and uninformed providers, as well as a few seedy characters. Know how to recognize and deal with them.

A Look Ahead

Access counts. Like the health-care system, *Health Care Choices* will serve you if you know how to use it. That's the thinking behind the unique format and writing style of this book. The authors purposely avoid fancy phrases, cute titles, and scientific-sounding jargon in favor of straightforward facts and advice. As a result, you'll find that the information is succinct and easy to understand and apply.

Each chapter focuses on a single facet of your health care. *Health Care Choices* starts with the foundation—consumer rights—and moves on to your first choice: an insurance or health plan for you and your family. A wise health-care consumer assembles a personal and family health-care system *now* to provide and finance comprehensive care over the years.

Throughout, the authors direct you to your next moves. We don't expect you to sit down and read every page of *Health Care Choices* at once (although you'll benefit if you do). Instead, scan the whole book today and then return to specific chapters and sections when you need them. Pay special attention to the bulleted items, which represent points to keep in mind and steps to take. And don't skip the fast-action "Tips" in every chapter or the sidebars that look deeper at individual topics.

Now it's time to commence. To get you going, here's the nickel tour through the highlights of *Health Care Choices*:

Chapter 2 *"Consumer Rights"* explains your rights as a buyer of health care.

- Your right to accept or refuse any treatment.
- Your right to emergency treatment.
- Your right to information about your condition and treatment alternatives
- Getting your medical records.
- Preventing and responding to medical malpractice.
- The rights of hospital patients.

Raising the New Standard

Aware consumers improve care for themselves—and for others. In fact, health-care providers now accept the informed consumer as normal—if not universal—and they're responding. From hospitals to insurance plans to nursing homes to doctors, health-care providers know that more and more consumers choose to work closely with physicians and other professional caregivers. The result is better health care.

On the other hand, some providers try to attract consumers in less favorable ways. You need to know how to recognize a good provider—and when to ignore slick advertisements, fast talkers, and the irrelevant bells and whistles in flashy brochures.

Chapter 3 *"Health Insurance"* explores the issues you confront when deciding about financing your health care.
- A buyer's guide to the varieties of medical insurance.
- Choosing a health plan best suited to you and your family.
- The meaning of managed care.
- Getting the best quality from the health plan you choose.

Chapter 4 *"Primary Care"* guides you in selecting and using a professional for your day-to-day, year-to-year care.
- Promoting health and preventing illness.
- A comprehensive approach to health care.
- Keeping you healthy at every stage of your life.
- Questions to ask a prospective primary-care provider.
- Where to go and who to see for primary care.

Chapter 5 *"Hospitals"* explores what you can expect from your hospital stay—and how you can improve it.
- What hospitals offer patients.
- The costs and quality of outpatient and inpatient care.
- Recognizing quality in a hospital.
- Choosing a hospital.
- Saving on your hospital bill.

Chapter 6 *"Women As Health Care Consumers"* presents an overview for women on providers at all levels of care.
- Your partnership with health-care providers.
- Your options for obtaining care.
- Choosing and using the best provider for you.
- Women's health issues, from young womanhood through old age.

Chapter 7 *"Parents As Health Care Consumers"* examines the role parents can play in working with health-care professionals for children.
- Your child and primary care.
- Children and hospitals: the family experience.
- Prenatal care and the search for children's caregivers.
- Maintaining a record of your child's medical history.
- Patient rights and children.
- Insurance coverage for the first two decades of life.

Chapter 8 *"Elders As Health Care Consumers"* deals with the issues of cost and access as they affect men and women

---

Ask Questions

A New England Medical Center team reports that patients ask an average of four questions in a 15-minute visit. That includes questions like, "Will you validate my parking?"

---

over the age of 60.
- Your changing health-care needs as you age.
- Healthy habits, improving your health, and living longer.
- Preparing a plan to cover *all* your health-care needs.
- Promoting independence through medicine, nursing, social work, and family supports.
- Paying for care: Medicare, Medigap, and more.

Chapter 9 *"Physician Specialists"* helps you collaborate with primary-care providers to find the best advanced care.
- Choosing and evaluating specialists.
- Discussing diagnosis and treatment with a specialist.
- Your right to a second opinion.
- Ensuring that your health plan pays for the type of specialized care you require.

Chapter 10 *"Alternative Health Care"* introduces you to a variety of non-traditional approaches to health care.
- The parallel histories of alternative and conventional medicine.
- Treating the whole person.
- Identifying the major alternative health-care providers.
- Reducing out-of-pocket costs.

Chapter 11 *"Mental Health"* reveals the range of mental health services that are open to families.
- The available providers and services.
- Measuring how well your care meets your goals.
- Recognizing and responding to the signs of depression.
- Services for people with severe mental illnesses.
- Your insurance and your mental health.
- Protecting the rights of the mentally ill.

Chapter 12 *"Long Term Care"* discusses how you can get information on health-care resources for extended needs.
- Defining long-term care.
- Preparing a plan for long-term care.
- What long-term care costs—and how to pay for it.
- Choosing a nursing home.
- The rights of nursing-home residents.

Chapter 13 *"Home Care"* reviews the many services that help you live at home instead of in a health-care facility.

The Unaware Majority

Four out of five Americans don't know enough about medical concepts to make intelligent choices about their own health care. That's the conclusion of a study by the International Center for the Advancement of Science Literacy.

To help Families USA Foundation correct this situation, send in your comments and suggestions for improving this book. Use the form at the end of *Health Care Choices* or write to Health Care Choices, Families USA Foundation, 30 Winter St., Boston, MA 02108.

- When home care is right for you.
- Home services outside the home.
- Interviewing a home-care provider.
- How to be an effective "employer" of home-care providers.
- Insurance coverage for home care.

Chapter 14 *"Caring for Your Teeth"* explains how to evaluate and use dentists.

- Oral hygiene and prevention.
- Fluoride, sealants, and other preventive measures.
- The advantages—and disadvantages—of the most common dental treatments.
- Recognizing quality in a dentist.
- What parents need to know.

Chapter 15 *"Eyeglasses and Contact Lens"* reviews your options for obtaining these crucial vision aids.

- Deciding between eyeglasses and contact lenses.
- Ensuring the comfort and durability of your eyeglasses.
- Choosing among the lens options.
- Picking an optician, optometrist, or an opthalmologist.
- Addressing problems with prescription eye wear.

Chapter 16 *"Workplace Illness and Injury"* instructs you in ways to prevent or respond to unhealthy jobs.

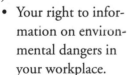

Use It or Lose It
Failing to make a choice about your own care is a choice in itself. But it's a choice you make to the detriment of your health.

- Your right to information on environmental dangers in your workplace.
- Health-care providers and workplace hazards.
- Sources of help when you encounter workplace risks to your health.
- Workers compensation.
- The common causes of occupational illness.

Chapter 17 *"Death With Dignity"* explores the human and legal issues faced by the millions of Americans with a terminal diagnosis.

- Hospice care for the last six months of life.
- Living wills, health-care proxies, and other "advance

directives."
- Your right to refuse *any* medical care, including life-saving treatments.

Chapter 18 *"Unreformed Health Care"* details the impact of the federal government's 1994 failure to reform the U.S. health-care system.
- The U.S. Health Care System: what it can and can't do today.
- Washington's role in improving your health care.
- When changes will affect you directly.

Chapter 19 *"Partners in Health"* lists the many resources available to help you be an informed health-care consumer.
- Finding and joining mutual-help groups.
- Going on-line with computers.
- Organizations that can assist you.
- Books, magazines, and other aids for the aware health-care consumer.

To get started as an aware health-care consumer, turn to Chapter **2**

Consumer Rights

By George J. Annas

Ⓞne of the most powerful forces shaping the practice of modern medicine is the recognition that patients have rights. Respect for these rights can transform the doctor-patient relationship from an authoritarian and paternalistic one into a partnership, simultaneously improving the quality of medical care.

Patients have only recently begun to recognize they have rights. Unlike virtually all other groups that have proclaimed or discovered their rights, patients are often sick, and thus "not themselves." Moreover, they hope to quickly become non-patients and are usually far less concerned about exercising their rights than about getting better.

Nonetheless, it's critical that you and your family know your rights when you see health-care providers and make decisions about your care. Most important is your *right to decide* about your treatment. You also have the *right to information* about all reasonable treatment alternatives and the *right to decide* among all the reasonable treatment options available, although you may have to go outside your health plan if you choose certain ones. And all competent adults have the *right to refuse* any treatment, even if such a refusal means you will likely get sicker or even die.

The doctrine of informed consent is founded on two fundamental propositions:

• It's your body—you should be able to decide what is done with it. This idea is sometimes referred to as "self-determination."

• You are likely to make a better decision about what is done with your body if you are provided with information on which to base a rational decision.

PART I: INFORMED CONSENT

As the words "informed consent" imply, no one can treat or even touch you until you make an educated decision to accept or reject treatment. Health-care providers must supply the necessary information, and do so in language you can understand. Many court decisions support your right to information, which rests on common sense: because you have to live with the consequences of treatment, you have

---

Technology and Rights

The sophistication of medical technology tends to distance health-care staff from patients and turn hospitals into alien and alienating places. The recognition of patient rights, on the other hand, humanizes both hospitals and encounters with health-care professionals.

George J. Annas is the Edward R. Utley Professor of Health Law at the Boston University School of Medicine and head of the Health Law Department at the Boston University School of Public Health. He is the author of The Rights of Patients *(Southern Illinois University Press, 1989) and* Standard of Care: The Law of American Bioethics *(Oxford University Press, 1993) and writes a regular feature on law for the* New England Journal of Medicine.

the greatest interest in deciding how your body will be treated.

When providers and patients take informed consent seriously, their relationship can be a true partnership, with shared authority, decision-making, and responsibility. Because of their special knowledge and the trust of patients, physicians have obligations to their patients that ordinary business people don't have to their customers. Among these obligations are to provide patients with at least the following information:

- A description of the recommended treatment or procedure;
- A description of the risks and benefits of the recommended treatment or procedure, with a special emphasis on the risk of death or serious disability;
- A description of alternative treatments and procedures, together with the risks and benefits of each;
- The likely results if you refuse any treatment;
- The probability of success, and what the physician means by success;
- The major problems anticipated in recuperation, including how long it will be until you can resume your normal activities; *and*
- Any other information patients in your situation generally receive, such as cost and how much of the cost your health plan will cover.

There is nothing profound or mysterious about this list. It's what you need to know to decide whether to accept or reject a recommended treatment plan.

Some physicians have argued that it's difficult to determine what risks to disclose. In general, physicians must tell you about *material* risks, those that might lead you or a reasonable person like you to reject a recommendation, choose an alternative, or decide on no treatment at all.

One way to think about the importance of a risk is to multiply its probability of occurring by its magnitude if it occurs. For example, a physician must tell you about even a small risk of death, but not necessarily about the possibility of a two-hour headache.

Keep Those Rights

You don't check your rights along with your other valuables when you enter a health-care institution. Human rights merit strong protection by their very nature, and respect for patient rights can improve the quality of life of both providers and patients—as well as the quality of care patients receive.

By custom, health-care personnel defer to the next of kin to speak for incompetent patients. By consenting to a treatment, relatives effectively waive their rights to sue a physician for failure to obtain consent.

Their consent also demonstrates that the doctor consulted someone likely to know the patient well and be concerned about his or her best interests. This will probably persuade a patient who recovers not to sue a doctor for failing to obtain consent.

Consent Must Be Competent and Voluntary

The idea of *voluntary* consent is simple. You must not be overly medicated, intoxicated, threatened by the physician, or under extreme duress. Obviously consent is involuntary if someone holds a gun to your head and says, "Sign!"

Competence is more complex. The key point is that the law presumes that every adult is competent. A person who tries to take away your right to decide must

T I P

When Your Consent Is Enough
If you are a competent adult, only you can consent to medical care. It is both unnecessary and inappropriate for your family—or anyone else—to give consent.

prove that you are "incompetent," and this usually must be done in a courtroom unless you are unconscious or incapable of communicating your decision.

Another important point is that you can't be labeled incompetent simply because you refuse treatment or disagree with your physician. Otherwise, informed consent would collapse into the "right" to agree with the doctor.

In health care, *you are competent if you understand the information needed to give informed consent for a proposed treatment.* Only a judge can *legally* declare you "incompetent" and appoint a guardian to act for you. Still, guardians must act in a way that is consistent with your best interests, and courts usually defer to your family's judgment. Thus,

A Test for Competence

No magic formula proves competence, but a person who can understand the answers to these informed consent-related questions generally passes the test:

◆ What is your present physical condition?

◆ What treatment is being recommended for you?

◆ What do you and your doctor think might happen if you accept the treatment?

◆ What do you and your doctor think might happen if you reject it?

◆ What alternatives are available? What are the probable consequences of each option—including no treatment?

rarely does anyone with a loving family gain by having a legal guardian appointed, a process that is time-consuming and expensive.

Because competence ultimately rests on your ability to understand the nature and consequences of your decisions, it's appropriate for health-care providers to conduct a basic informed consent discussion with you. In such discussions, medical personnel carefully explain the proposed treatment, its likely risks and benefits, the alternatives, their risks and benefits, and the likely consequences of refusing treatment.

Ideally, the discussion deter-mines if you understand this basic information *before* you are asked to consent. Making that determination beforehand avoids the "outcome approach" pitfall—that is, labeling a person incompetent solely based on a refusal to undergo a recommended treatment.

> **T I P**
>
> **Cross It Out**
> *Cross out any clauses in a consent form with which you disagree.*

The Consent Form

Consent is *not* a form, but doctors and hospitals usually want you to put your consent in writing for the same reason most contracts are written down: to preserve the exact terms in case of future disagreement. If you later sue a doctor alleging lack of informed consent, the doctor can use the form as evidence.

To be useful evidence of your informed consent, the written form must contain everything you need to know to grant consent: a description of the proposed procedure, its risks and benefits, the alternatives and their risks and benefits, the risks of nontreatment, success rates, problems of recuperation, and so on. In general, the form contains the names of the physicians involved, and it may also deal with such topics as the disposition and use of removed tissues, organs, and body parts.

You can limit a doctor's authority in the consent form. However, a surgeon, for example, who believes the limitations are too strict to proceed with an operation safely

> **Wake-Up Call**
>
> A patient who took a sleeping pill was awakened in the middle of the night and asked to sign a consent form. Later, the patient couldn't remember the event. His consent wasn't valid. Memory isn't a measure of valid consent, but the circumstances in which consent is requested can make it invalid.

Research and Consent

Very few situations legally require a written consent form. The most common situation requiring a form is when you consent to be a research subject.

might reasonably decide not to go ahead with it. The surgeon could also note the limitations you have placed on his or her authority in the medical record, together with the fact that you understand and consent to the associated increased risks.

You can withdraw your consent at any time before treatment. First, tell the physician about your change of mind. Then, either obtain and destroy the original consent form or write a "non-consent form," noting on it the date and time of day you are withdrawing consent. This is the rule, but there are practical limitations. For example, if you're under general anesthesia and on the operating table, it's obviously too late to change your mind.

THE INFORMED CONSENT CHECKLIST

Before you sign a consent form, make sure you completely understand everything about the proposed treatment:

- Know the name and nature of your injury, illness, or disability, as well as the dangers or disadvantages of not treating it.
- Understand the nature of the specific procedure recommended to deal with your problem.
- Know if there are other ways of treating the problem and their associated risks and benefits. Feel confident that the procedure proposed is the best one. *List the alternatives.*
- Know the advantages, risks, and side effects of this procedure. *List these if you can.*

- Know the probability of success. *What is it? What is meant by success?*
- Know the likely result if you aren't treated. *What is it?*
- Understand all you've been told and explain it in your own words. *Try to explain it to your closest friend or relative.*
- Make sure that your doctor has answered all your questions openly and offered to discuss any additional concerns with you. *Get satisfactory answers to your questions before you sign the consent form.*
- Understand the meaning of all the words in the consent form. *If you don't, have them explained.*
- Carefully read the consent form and add new

requirements or cross out points you disagree with. Make sure your doctor is aware of these changes. *If you don't agree to everything in the form, don't sign it.*
- Know the identity and qualifications of the people who will perform this procedure. *If you don't know, ask.*
- Have a clear head and an alert mind. Make sure you aren't too anxious or harassed to feel that this decision isn't your own free choice.
- Feel confident that the benefits to you of this procedure outweigh the risks. *If not, reconsider your decision.*
- Know that you don't have to consent to this procedure.

PART II: YOUR RIGHT TO EMERGENCY TREATMENT

An emergency is an injury or acute medical condition likely to cause death, disability, or serious illness if not attended to very quickly. If you have a medical emergency or are in labor, any hospital with emergency facilities must treat you if it can. If it can't, it must refer you elsewhere.

The physician's role is central. First, the physician has a duty to determine if an emergency exists. If one does, law and medical ethics require the physician to treat you or to find someone who can.

Conditions that require the immediate attention of a physician include:

- Heavy bleeding;
- Heart stoppage;
- Breathing stoppage;
- Profound shock from any cause;
- Ingestion or exposure to a rapidly acting poison;
- Labor;
- Severe head injuries;
- Sudden and complete changes in personality; *and*
- Anaphylactic reactions (allergic response).

An emergency can be less serious, however. It could include broken bones, fevers, and cuts that require stitches.

The Hospital Emergency Department

You have a legal right to be screened by competent personnel. *If* they determine that a medical emergency exists, you have a right to be examined by a physician. Both the federal government, in the Medicare Conditions of Participation, and the American College of Surgeons, in its Standards for Emergency Departments in Hospitals, go further and specify that a physician should see every applicant for treatment.

Usually a nurse does the screening, but occasionally it's done by a clerk. He or she determines your need for immediate care and decides how long you can reasonably wait to see a physician. A hospital must continue to treat you until it can transfer or discharge you safely.

For more information on emergency departments, turn to Chapter **5**

The Right to Emergency Treatment

The leading court case explicitly dealing with the right to emergency care involved a four-month-old baby with diarrhea. The family physician prescribed medication by phone on the second day of the illness and saw the child on the third day. The child didn't sleep that night, so the parents took the child to the emergency room in the morning, knowing the doctor wasn't in his office.

The nurse on duty refused to examine the child, saying the hospital couldn't treat anyone under a doctor's care without contacting the doctor first. The parents took the child home and made an appointment with their doctor for that night, but the child died of bronchial pneumonia in the afternoon.

The court ruled that the parents could recover damages from the hospital for refusal to treat an "unmistakable emergency" if the nurse should have spotted the child's emergency condition.

Daddy Doctors

Information is power, and some doctors simply don't want to share decision-making power with patients. Others view patients like children. They complain that patients will misunderstand the information or be upset by it.

Getting Your Medical Records

Medical Records: Getting Yours, by Bruce Samuels and Sidney M. Wolfe, is a comprehensive guide to state-by-state rules. To order, send $10 ($20 for businesses) plus $2 for postage and handling to Public Citizen, Publications Dept., 2000 P St., NW, Washington, DC 20036.

For help in obtaining your medical record, contact the American Health Information Management Association, 919 N. Michigan Ave., Chicago, IL 60611 (800)335-5535. Send $1.35 for the pamphlet, "Your Health Information Belongs to You."

Emergency-room personnel must also examine you within a reasonable time. In one case, a patient entered an emergency room bleeding from a shotgun wound in his arm. He was observed but not treated for two hours, then transferred to another hospital. He died shortly after arriving in the second hospital. A court understandably found the first hospital responsible.

PART III: YOUR RIGHT TO YOUR MEDICAL RECORDS

The *information* in your medical record is *your* information. Nonetheless, in general, the owner of the paper, computer file, or photographic film that contains the information owns the physical record itself, and thus has custody of the information in or on them.

Fortunately for you, this ownership is a limited right. Health-care providers have custody of records and strong interests in them, but you have even stronger privacy and confidentiality interests in their contents and in who else has access.

Your Right to See and Copy Your Medical Record

In most states, you have an explicit legal right to see and copy your medical records. In other states, you probably have this legal right even though no specific law exists on the subject. Regardless of the law, you deserve routine access to your medical record. You may need the information to decide on treatment, determine if and when to change physicians or health plans, and prepare for your future.

In some states, you only have legal access to your hospital records after leaving the hospital. Some states also limit access to psychiatric records, while others limit the types of records that are open to you. For example, some laws exclude access to lab reports, X-rays, prescriptions, and other technical information. A few states require you to show "good cause" before you can read the record, but this term is virtually meaningless. Other states either provide for access under specific circumstances or require you to go through an attorney, physician, or relative; these outmoded requirements should be rescinded. Physicians and health facilities can charge you a reasonable fee for making a copy of your medical record, but this should not exceed the actual cost of duplication.

What Your Record *Shouldn't* Contain

It's inappropriate for your medical record to include personal criticisms, such as "This patient is fat and sloppy." Nor should it contain offhand comments, such as "I love her perfume." Statements like these unfairly color the attitudes of others who read the record. They can also lead health-care providers to try to conceal the record from you out of fear of embarrassing the person who wrote the remarks.

Health-care providers should record *facts* about a patient (for example, "speech slurred, eyes bloodshot") rather than conclusions that may not be true ("patient is an alcoholic").

Why Read Your Medical Record?

The primary reason to read your medical record is to better understand your health condition and cooperate in improving it. Other reasons include:

- To check the accuracy of family and personal histories;
- To be informed about diagnoses and options when asked to consent to any procedures;

Be Selective
When asking for copies of your medical record, try to review the entire record first and order only the pages you need. You may have little interest in lab reports and many other parts of the record, which could cover hundreds of pages.

- To understand the role of the physician and others in treatment;
- To make sure you aren't unfairly denied insurance benefits; *and*
- To help prevent a recurrence of a disease or condition in the future.

Medical Records and Insurance

Health-insurance companies often report the contents of medical records to national databanks, such as the Medical Information Bureau. The largest such private databank in the United States, MIB holds records on more than 12 million Americans and Canadians. It releases data to its members—mostly insurance companies— to control fraud.

Check with MIB to see if it has a file on you. Because it affects your insurance claims, make sure that any information about you in the databank is accurate. The bureau will answer your request and correct errors you report at no charge. MIB reports that errors occur in fewer than 1 percent of the files.

For a free brochure, contact the MIB, P.O. Box 105, Essex Station, Boston, MA 02112 (617)426-3660.

For more information on hospitals, turn to Chapter **5**

If You are Denied Access to Your Record . . .

Raise hell! There is no valid ethical or legal reason to deny a competent patient access to his or her medical record. If you are in a hospital, don't consent to any treatment or testing until you can review your record. If you are denied access, complain to the hospital's patient representative, the hospital administrator, and the ethics committee.

And a Partridge

Physician Mark Siegler decided to find out how many people might read the medical record of one of his patients. As Siegler wrote in the *New England Journal of Medicine,* among the many people at the hospital with a *legitimate* need were: six attending physicians, twelve house officers, twenty nurses, six respiratory therapists, three nutritionists, two pharmacologists, four secretaries, fifteen students, four financial officers, and four chart reviewers.

Your medical record can be a powerful means of health education, of benefit to you both in a hospital and outside it. In one study, for example, a pregnant patient noted an incorrect blood typing in her record. In another study, half the patients found at least one factual error in their records.

> **T I P**
>
> **On the Move**
> *If you move out of town or go on a long trip, consider taking along a copy of your medical record or at least the discharge summary of your most recent hospital visit.*

PART IV: THE (LIMITED) RIGHT TO PRIVACY

All health-care practitioners have an ethical and legal duty to maintain confidentiality about you. The Hippocratic Oath sets out this duty: "Whatsoever things I see or hear concerning the life of man, in any attendance on the sick or even apart therefrom, which ought not to be noised about, I will keep silent thereon, counting such things to be professional secrets."

The American Medical Association Principles of Ethics reinterprets this oath: "A physician shall respect the rights of patients, of colleagues, and of other health professionals, and shall safeguard patient confidences within the constraints of the law."

The American Nurses Association Code provides that: "The nurse safeguards the clients right to privacy by judiciously protecting information of a confidential nature."

These rules arise from the fact that health-care providers often must know the most personal details of your life in order to help you. You are unlikely to speak freely unless you know that no one not directly involved in your care will learn of the information you provide.

Nevertheless, it isn't realistic to expect medical information to remain secret. The general rule is that everyone in the hospital—including you—has access. Information exchange in a hospital is essential to the "team" approach to health care. Moreover, medical records are central to education, financial decisions, and quality monitoring.

Thus, even on a "need-to-know" basis, many people have access to your medical record. That's why it's reasonable to fear that very sensitive information about you, such as a psychiatric diagnosis or an HIV infection, could spread rapidly in the hospital and damage the way members of the hospital staff treat you. It could also leak from the hospital, affecting your housing, employment, and insurance.

PART V: MEDICAL MALPRACTICE

The term "medical malpractice" denotes the basis for a lawsuit for injuries you suffer due to a health-care provider's negligence or carelessness. A trial or other adversary proceeding determines if the health-care provider is at fault. Usually a jury makes that decision, and if so, how much the provider should pay you as compensation.

What You Must Prove

To win a malpractice claim against a health-care provider, you must prove four things: duty, breach, damages, and causation.

- The health-care provider had a *duty* toward you. Duty is defined by the standard of care: what would a reasonably prudent practitioner do under the same or similar circumstances?
- The practitioner—by action or inaction—*breached* that duty. This is also measured by the standard of care.
- The breach of duty resulted in actual *damages,* usually physical harm. These are measured in monetary terms.
- The breach of duty was the act that specifically *caused* the harm.

Ordinarily, an expert medical witness must testify that the health-care provider failed to fulfill his or her duty, resulting in an injury to you. In most cases, only a physician with "expert" knowledge can legally establish that fact because a jury of lay people doesn't know what good medical practice is. The witness explains what the health-care community recognizes as the standard of care in the particular situation and gives an opinion on whether the defendant's conduct met that standard.

The Few Who Sue

About 1 percent of all hospitalized patients are treated negligently in a way that results in injury to them. However, a recent Harvard University study showed that fewer than one patient files a lawsuit for every eight patients injured by a physician's negligence. Of these, only half ever collect any money.

The reasons aren't well understood, but many injured patients may not know their injury results from the physician's mistake rather than their underlying illness or injury. Others may want to avoid litigation or may have difficulty finding a lawyer to take their case.

Complaining to the Licensing Board

All physicians and nurses, and most other health-care providers, are licensed by an agency of the state government, usually called a licensing board or board of registration. If you believe your health-care provider has acted unethically or negligently in your care, you can *and should* file a written complaint with this board. You should receive a written response, which is likely to include a request to see your medical records covering the care about which you are complaining.

The board should investigate your complaint. It may take action against the health-care provider, including reprimanding him or her, suspending her or his license to practice, or even revoking the license.

Even if the board finds your complaint was correct, you won't get any money. However, you'll be helping other patients by alerting the health-care practitioner and those responsible for licensing him or her. This may help prevent future injury.

Malpractice Litigation and Informed Consent

Informed consent is central to *preventing* both malpractice and malpractice litigation from occurring. Unrealistic expectations on the part of patients—and ritualistic silence and demands for blind faith on the part of physicians—only lead to more malpractice suits.

Arbitration, mediation, and other possible alternatives to a malpractice lawsuit deserve consideration, but all should serve three primary goals:
• Compensate victims for injury;
• Foster quality; *and*
• Respond to consumers' needs to have their grievances heard.

Only changes in the malpractice system that enhance these goals deserve serious consideration as an alternative to your right to sue unprofessional health-care personnel.

PART IV: ADVOCATES FOR YOUR RIGHTS

The ideal standard for the doctor-patient relationship is a *partnership*. When the relationship doesn't meet this standard, you need an advocate for your rights and dignity.

The Patient Rights Advocate

The job of a patient-rights advocate is to help you exercise your rights within the health-care system, whether these are outlined in state or federal law, an institution's Patient Bill of Rights, or simple common sense.

The employer of the advocate may be a health-care facility, health plan, insurance company, government agency, consumer group, or you. The critical factor is loyalty: *the advocate must represent you, the patient.* The goal of a true advocate of patient rights is to enhance your ability to make decisions, not to encourage you to "behave."

More than 3,000 hospitals and health plans employ at least one person with the job title "patient representative." Unfortunately, this title can be misleading, and true advocates are hard to find in many health-care institutions.

Keep a Record

If you file a complaint against a hospital, physician, HMO, or any other health-care provider, keep copies of all letters and other materials you send and receive that pertain to the complaint. Keep notes on phone conversations as well.

HOW CAN HEALTH CARE FACILITIES ENHANCE PATIENT RIGHTS?

Every health-care facility should immediately adopt a simple five-point agenda to greatly enhance patient rights:

◆ *Eliminate "Routine" Procedures:* Health-care personnel commonly answer the question, "Why are you doing this?" with "Don't worry, it's routine." This isn't acceptable. Procedures are acceptable only if they are specifically indicated for the patient.

◆ *Open Access to Medical Records:* Patient access to medical records remains difficult, despite many federal and state laws and regulations. A patient often asserts the right to see the record at the peril of being labeled a troublemaker.

◆ *Provide 24-Hour-a-Day Visitor Rights:* At least one person of the patient's choosing needs unlimited access to the patient's room at any time of day or night. This person also needs the right to stay with the patient during any procedure as long as this doesn't interfere with the care of other patients.

◆ *Require Full Disclosure of Practitioners' Experience Before Procedures are Performed:* Despite the almost universal acknowledgment of the need for informed consent, an important fact is still routinely withheld: the experience of the person doing the procedure. Patients have a right to know if the person asking permission to draw blood, do a bone-marrow aspiration, or do a spinal tap—to list just a few examples—has performed the procedure before, and if so, the rate of adverse effects. This applies to medical students and certified surgeons alike.

◆ *Implement an Effective Patient-Rights Advocate Program:* This would include a patient-centered bill of rights.

Often, their real assignment is to represent their employer, not you. In fact, many hospitals recruit patient representatives from the public-relations department, and even limit their duties to non-medical issues.

Despite this potential conflict of interest, some patient representatives do an excellent job on behalf of patients. Ask the nurse how to get in touch with the patient advocate or patient representative, or call the hospital switchboard. Give the representative a fair chance to help you, but explore other avenues of redress immediately if it becomes clear that he or she is more concerned with

A BILL OF RIGHTS FOR HOSPITAL PATIENTS

The American Hospital Association, of which most hospitals are members, has adopted the following Hospital Patient's Bill of Rights. It's a welcome move, but don't feel limited by this statement: it's the hospital's—not a consumer's—view of your rights. In addition, rights are only as good as a health-care facility's enforcement mechanism. In most cases, protecting your rights is up to you and your family.

Also, note that the AHA has prepared this "short version" of your rights. To get a copy of the full version, expanding on these points, call the AHA at (312)280-6263.

We consider you to be a partner in your hospital care. When you are well-informed, participate in treatment decisions, and communicate openly with your doctor and other health professional, you help make your care as effective as possible. The hospital encourages respect for the personal preferences and values of each individual.

While you are a patient in the hospital, your rights include the following:

◆ You have the right to considerate and respectful care.

◆ You have the right to be well-informed about your illness, possible treatments, and likely outcome and to discuss this information with your doctor. Your have the right to know the names and roles of people treating you.

◆ You have the right to consent to or refuse a treatment, as permitted by law, throughout your hospital stay. If you refuse a recommended treatment, you will receive other needed and available care.

◆ You have the right to have an advance directive, such as a living will or health-care proxy. These documents express your choices about your future care or name someone to decide if you cannot speak for yourself. If you have a written advance directive, you should provide a copy to the hospital, your family, and your doctor.

◆ You have the right to privacy. The hospital, your doctor, and others caring for you will protect your privacy as much as possible.

◆ You have the right to expect that treatment records are confidential unless you have given permission to release information or reporting is required or permitted by law. When the hospital releases records to others, such as insurers, it emphasizes that the records are confidential.

◆ You have the right to review your medical records and to have the information explained, except when restricted by law.

◆ You have the right to expect that the hospital

protecting the institution. If a hospital or any health-care facility doesn't supply you with a real advocate, find your own: a friend, lawyer, physician, nurse, social worker, or relative. In theory, all these people can help you exercise your rights.

Unfortunately, few health-care institutions have a *formal* advocate system, despite the potential benefit to patients. Formal advocates would have direct access to the hospital staff, administration, and relevant committees in the hospital structure, which would help them develop credibility as problem solvers.

A BILL OF RIGHTS *CONTINUED*

will give you necessary health services to the best of its ability. Treatment, referral, or transfer may be recommended. If transfer is recommended or requested, you will be informed of risks, benefits, and alternatives. You will not be transferred until the other institution agrees to accept you.

◆ You have the right to know if this hospital has relationships with outside parties that may influence your treatment and care. These relationships may be with educational institutions, other health-care providers, or insurers.

◆ You have the right to consent or decline to take part in research affecting your care. If you choose not to take part, you will receive the most effective care the hospital otherwise provides.

◆ You have the right to be told of realistic care alternatives when hospital

care is no longer appropriate.

◆ You have the right to know about hospital rules that affect you and your treatment and about charges and payment methods. You have the right to now about hospital resources, such as patient representatives or ethics committees, that can help you resolve problems and questions about your hospital stay and care.

You have responsibilities as a patient. You are responsible for providing information about your health, including past illness, hospital stays, use of medicine. You are responsible for asking questions when you do not understand information or instructions. If you believe you can't follow through with your treatment, your are responsible for telling your doctor.

The hospital works to provide care efficiently and

fairly to all patients and the community. You and your visitors are responsible for being considerate of the needs of other patients, staff, and the hospital. You are responsible for providing information for insurance and for working with the hospital to arrange payment, when needed.

Your health depends not just on your hospital care but, in the long-term, on the decisions you make in your daily life. You are responsible for recognizing the effect of life-style on your personal health.

A hospital serves many purposes. Hospitals work to improve people's health; treat people with injury and disease; educate doctors, health professionals, patients, and community members; and improve understanding of health and disease. In carrying out these activities, their institution works to respect your value and dignity.

RESOURCES

Organizations

American Civil Liberties Union
132 West 32nd St.
New York, NY 10036
(212)944-9800
This national organization and its state affiliates and local chapters actively protect people's constitutional rights. In the health field, the ACLU is most concerned about the right to privacy, confidentiality, access to records, and equal access to care. The ACLU may help you find legal assistance in exercising your rights.

People's Medical Society
462 Walnut St.
Allentown, PA 18102
(800)624-8773
(215)770-1670
Call or write for information on a variety of issues regarding patient rights, including *Your Medical Rights: How to Be an Empowered Consumer* ($14.95; $12.95 for members) and *Your Complete Medical Record* ($12.95; $11.95 for members).

Public Citizen Health Research Group
2000 P St., NW
Washington, DC 20036
(202)872-0320
This consumer advocacy group is a good source of basic information about medical care, drug safety, medical-device safety, physician competence, and health issues in general. It prepares many publications, offers testimony before Congress and regulatory agencies, participates in lawsuits on patient-rights issues, and publishes "Health Letter" monthly.

Publications

The Rights of Patients, by George J. Annas (Southern Illinois University Press, 1989). $8.95.

The Consumer's Legal Guide to Today's Health Care: Your Medical Rights and How to Assert Them, by Stephen Isaacs and Ava Swartz (Houghton Mifflin, 1992). $12.70.

Patient Power: How to Have a Say During Your Hospital Stay, by Iris Sneider (Betterway, 1986).

Take This Book to the Hospital With You: A Consumer Guide to Surviving Your Hospital Stay, by Charles B. Inlander and Ed Weiner (Outlet Book Co., 1993). $7.99.

Health Insurance

3

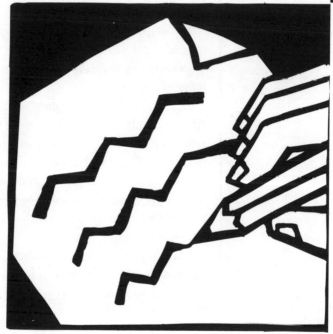

By Nancy Turnbull

You're just starting a new job. On your first day at work, the personnel department sends you a thick folder with descriptions of your options for health insurance. Your deadline to select a plan is the end of the week. *How do you pick one?*

The company where you work wants to reduce its health-insurance bill for its 20 employees without cutting benefits. Instead of offering several plans, the company will enroll everyone in a single HMO—and it's not the one where you've gotten your health care for years. *How will that affect your health care?*

You suspect your daughter has asthma, and you'd like to consult a specialist. Your health plan is denying your request to see a specialist outside its network of physicians. *What can you do?*

Navigating the "marketplace" of health plans can be difficult and bewildering these days. Consumers confront a dizzying array of unfamiliar acronyms and options: HMOs, PPOs, managed care, fee-for-service, managed indemnity.... The list grows almost daily. It's often hard to know *what* to ask—let alone *who* to ask—as you try to assemble the best personal health-care system for yourself and your family.

This chapter provides some practical ideas as you take the most common first step in health care: evaluating and selecting insurance. It explains the differences among the major types of health insurance plans and suggests a number of questions to ask yourself and others as you weigh the many options.

No matter what your situation, you do need health insurance. Medical bills are one of the major expenses for any family, and the costs are rising. At the very least, protect yourself and your family in case a serious accident

Nancy Turnbull is an instructor in health policy and management at the Harvard School of Public Health. As a former first deputy commissioner of insurance for the Massachusetts Division of Insurance, her responsibilities included regulating HMOs and other health plans. She also worked for five years for the Blue Cross Blue Shield system. After fifteen years of dealing with the private insurance system, she's a big fan of the single-payer approach to health care.

> **TIP**
>
> **Do It Now**
>
> *Buy health insurance when you are healthy. Besides the obvious reasons, many policies exclude coverage—either temporarily or permanently—for any health conditions you had before you signed up. For example, many plans don't pay for child birth in the first nine months a person is a member. During this "waiting period," you'll have to delay care related to these "pre-existing conditions," or pay for it yourself.*

or a major illness arises. And remember, you simply can't predict the size of your future medical bills.

PART I:
THIS THING CALLED "MANAGED CARE"

The two magic words in health care these days are "managed care." A phrase with many meanings, it generally

3

Hundreds of people answered surveys for *Health Care Choices,* providing insight on how medical insurance works *in practice.* Here are a few of the myriad pleasures and pitfalls other consumers have encountered:

"I have had outpatient surgery twice this past year. The doctors were great! I got to choose doctors—very important. I had almost no paperwork to be concerned about, which allowed me to focus completely on my health and how I was cared for."

"I spent twelve years with Plan A. I was short-changed for the full twelve years. Plan A denied or deflected problems and categorized them as typical ailments when in fact my family had several serious problems. I regret my time with them. We have physical scars as a result of their substandard attentions."

"I'm about to marry and would like to cover my husband. Because of the cost of the "family plan," which does not allow for a reduction in cost for childless couples, I cannot. I am

very upset about this."

"More professional staff of color needed ASAP! It seems that you have to be in crisis to see a mental-health therapist of your own gender and race."

"My plan does not cover dental visits and I wish it did."

"Overall, I'm pleased with Plan B. However, I've had to fight hard to get some bills paid and have ended up on collection lists with service providers. That's a big hassle."

"A routine gynecological exam and an emergency-room visit requiring three stitches are the only use I have tried to make of this HMO. They have refused to pay these claims on no particular grounds, and I have been unable to communicate with them. Consequently, I have been reported to collection agencies and lawyers. I cannot wait to choose a different HMO."

"I am treated like a number—mass confusion with regard to my file. I hate HMOs and wish I could afford a real doctor."

"The most inconvenient

component is making sure that lab tests performed by participating physicians end up at participating labs."

"The one glaring exception to generally satisfactory coverage is mental-health benefits. The current plan is biased against employees' mental health and discourages them from becoming mentally healthy."

"The amount of paperwork is absurd. Plan C appears to go out of its way not to make prompt full payment to doctors. I have to spend an inordinate amount of time on the phone trying to resolve payment issues between doctors and Plan C. It is very frustrating and aggravating, to the point where I now ignore all paperwork from this program."

"I really like the personal attention I get when I call with a question. Plan D has good follow-up and has resolved problems with billings from doctors. I'm very satisfied."

"All health plans fall short of providing preventive care and coverage."

describes health insurance that attempts to control the rising cost of medical care with one or more of the following methods:

Provider Networks: A group of doctors, hospitals, and other health-care providers treat plan members, often at reduced rates of payment. Members generally receive the most benefits at the lowest cost if they see a provider in the network.

Utilization Management: Medical professionals review proposed hospital admissions, surgery, and other procedures to determine if they are necessary and appropriate.

Case Management: In the case of very serious illnesses—AIDS or cancer, for example—the plan works with the member and his or her doctor to coordinate care and arrange for home care, hospice care, or some other alternative treatment that may enhance the person's quality of life and care while also reducing costs.

While managed care is not a new idea, its features are spreading rapidly as employers and other large purchasers of health insurance seek to contain soaring medical costs. In 1993, most insured Americans were enrolled in some

For information on home care, turn to Chapter **13**

For information on hospice care, turn to Chapter **17**

POWER IN NUMBERS

Buy group health insurance if you can, whether through your employer, a union, or an association. The volume of members allows group plans to provide more benefits with lower premiums than individual plans can.

If your only option is a non-group policy, look for one that is non-cancelable or guaranteed renewable as long as you keep paying the monthly premiums. At a minimum, it should be "conditionally renewable," meaning that the insurer

can't cancel your policy unless all policies like yours are being eliminated from the plan.

Also, make sure the policy explains clearly when and on what basis the insurer can raise your premiums. Ask the company about its rate increases over the past few years for a person of your age in your community. Don't buy a policy that can increase your rates based only on your medical costs.

Check for a policy that:

◆ Has a "free-look" clause that allows you at least 10 days during which you can cancel and get a full refund;

◆ Protects you from large medical costs; *and*

◆ Has the right coverage for you.

State insurance laws determine the kinds of policies and benefits that insurers can sell. Contact your state insurance department to find out about laws that protect you when you buy insurance.

type of managed-care health plan. And virtually every plan will include some features of managed care within just a few years.

Traditional Insurance and Managed Care: The Differences

The alternative to managed care is called indemnity insurance. In this traditional form of health insurance, you usually pay your health-care provider for each visit, and your insurer reimburses you if your policy covers the particular service you received. However, the provider will often bill the insurer directly, especially for hospital services. Only a few companies now market pure indemnity plans alone.

For you, the consumer of health care, many things distinguish traditional indemnity insurance from managed care—affecting cost, quality, and your well-being. Some of the most common and important differences to you are:

• Choice of Physician

Traditional plan: You can see any doctor you want, whenever you want.

Managed care: You must use providers in the plan's network, or you have a strong financial incentive to do so. In most plans, you select a primary-care provider—often called a "gatekeeper." He or she is almost always a general practitioner, family-practice physician, internist, or, for children, a pediatrician. This person handles all routine medical services, as well as authorizing and coordinating your care from other health-care providers. The purposes of this primary-care provider are to cut down on unnecessary visits to specialists and to make one physician responsible for managing your care. However, critics of the gatekeeper process believe it has the potential to introduce administrative burdens.

• How to See a Specialist

Traditional plan: You can consult any specialist at any time, although some specialists may refuse to see you unless your physician sends you to them.

Managed care: Your primary-care provider decides when

The Paperwork Difference

In a traditional plan, you usually pay your physician and then submit a claim form to the health plan for reimbursement.

3

With managed care, you usually pay a copayment and submit no forms when receiving care from a network provider. The provider handles any paperwork.

Key Words

Copayments: A fixed dollar amount you pay for health-care services. For example, you might have to pay $3 as a copayment at a doctor's office visit.

Deductibles: Amount you must pay before the insurer starts paying the health-care bills.

Coinsurance: A percentage you pay for health-care services. For example, you might have to pay 20 percent of a hospital bill.

Premiums: What you or your employer pay for insurance coverage

For more information on primary care, turn to Chapter **4**

For more information on specialists, turn to Chapter **9**

For more information on hospitals, turn to Chapter **5**

Contraception and Abortion

Two-thirds of indemnity plans routinely pay for abortions. The remainder either don't cover abortion services at all or restrict coverage, most often by requiring certification of a specific medical reason for the procedure.

About half of indemnity plans don't cover contraception, reflecting their traditional exclusions on preventive care. Only 22 percent routinely cover contraceptive counseling.

HMO coverage for abortions is roughly the same as that in indemnity plans, but contrace ptive coverage is considerably superior. About four in ten HMOs cover the most common methods of family planning. Nearly all cover contraceptive counseling

—*Source: Alan Guttmacher Institute*

you'll see a specialist and usually sends you to someone affiliated with the plan. Some plans let you see any specialist without a referral, but you may have to pay a larger share of the bill yourself.

• How You Are Admitted to a Hospital

Traditional plan: You and your doctor decide when you'll enter a hospital and which one.

Managed care: Except in an emergency, your doctor asks the plan to approve your hospitalization beforehand. The plan also approves the hospital to be used.

• What the Plan Covers—and What It Doesn't

Traditional plan: You pay an annual deductible—generally from $200 to $1,000—before insurance kicks in. You also pay some percentage of the bills—most often 20 percent. Your total maximum yearly out-of-pocket payment is generally limited, often to $1,000 or $2,000. In general, the plan doesn't cover prescription drugs or preventive services such as routine physicals, well-child visits, and immunizations.

Managed care: You pay a fixed amount—a "copayment" —for each office visit to network providers. Copayments vary but generally run $5 to $15. The plan usually includes preventive care and pays the full cost for most other covered services. It may also include prescription drugs. You may be responsible for a deductible before the plan pays anything.

The Varieties of Managed Care

"If you've seen one plan . . . you've seen one plan." In other words, it's risky to generalize about managed care. That said, you'll probably have to select among roughly three types of managed care:

• *Health Maintenance Organization (HMO):* HMOs have a network of health-care providers, sometimes located at the plan's own facilities. Except in an emergency, HMO members get care from affiliated providers. The plan rarely pays for care from non-HMO providers, unless the member gets approval for such services in advance. HMO members select a primary-care provider when they enroll. In general, HMOs cover preventive care, and members don't have to file claims.

• *Managed Indemnity:* As with traditional health insurance, a member of a managed-indemnity plan can see any medical provider. But you typically get prior approval from the plan for hospitalizations and some outpatient procedures. Such plans don't always cover preventive services, and you may have to file claim forms for some services.

• *Preferred Provider Organization (PPO):* A PPO borrows features from both traditional indemnity and HMO plans. Like an HMO, a PPO contracts with a network of providers. Unlike an HMO, a member may use *any* provider, although financial incentives—usually broader benefits and lower copayments—encourage the use of network providers. Members may have to select a primary-care provider and usually need prior approval for all in-patient care and selected outpatient procedures, regardless of whether the care is from network providers or not. Members usually submit claims forms to get reimbursed for services received from non-network providers.

CONSUMERS AND THE PRIMARY FORMS OF MEDICAL INSURANCE

Type of Plan	Advantages	Disadvantages	Out-of-Pocket Costs
Traditional Indemnity	Choice of any doctor or hospital	Claim forms to file; no quality monitoring; limited preventive care	Varies with plan
Managed Indemnity	Choice of any doctor and access to any hospital if the service is approved in advance	More paperwork to get approval for some services; little or no quality monitoring; limited preventive care	Varies with plan
PPO	Choice of any doctor or hospital; preventive care sometimes covered	More paperwork to get approval for some services; may have some quality monitoring; preventive care may be limited	Lower in network; higher outside the network
HMO	No claim forms; may have quality monitoring preventive care always covered	Only covers affiliated or approved doctors and hospitals	Low

In general, when you join a managed-care plan, particularly an HMO, you sacrifice the freedom to go to any provider. In return, you usually receive lower out-of-pocket costs, more comprehensive benefits, and often some initial screening of providers. It's up to you to weigh the pros and the cons.

Other Types of Medical Insurance

Besides general medical insurance, you may qualify for, or have need of, other types of coverage. Perhaps the most important is *Medicare,* the federal health insurance program for people 65 and older and for certain disabled Americans. It pays for many, though not all, of the health-care expenses of millions of Americans.

A second government program, *Medicaid,* provides health-care coverage for some low-income people. It's operated by the states; within federal guidelines, they decide who is eligible and determine the scope of services. You apply for Medicaid at welfare offices or, in some states, at senior-citizen centers and other locations. The Medicaid benefits are highly variable from state to state.

An additional type of private policy is Medigap insurance, which covers many aspects of health care for elders that Medicare doesn't cover or covers only partially. In addition, insurance companies are marketing a variety of policies, of varying value, for long-term care.

PART II: CHOOSING A HEALTH PLAN

The process of choosing—and using—a health plan is complicated, and at times very frustrating. Fortunately, a variety of resources can help you. Here are two to get you started:

• *Your Friends and Coworkers:* Ask people you know

Point of Service

Confused by the variety of health plans? Well, here's yet another.

A point of service (POS) plan is like a PPO offered by an HMO. A member can go outside the HMO's network by paying higher out-of pocket costs. In many POS plans, certain services —most commonly preventive care—are covered only if you go to an HMO.

For more information on these forms of medical insurance, refer to the following special topics:

For information on Medicare, Medigap, and elders as health-care consumers, turn to Chapter **8**

For information on long-term care, turn to Chapter **12**

For information on home care, turn to Chapter **13**

Travel Alert
Does your health insurance cover travel abroad? Under what conditions? Especially if you're planning a long trip, read your policy and consult your insurer and your employer's benefits manager. If your current policy isn't enough for your needs, consider buying special traveler's insurance.

TIP

Data Sources
A number of organizations, usually sponsored by coalitions of employers and other large health purchasers, compile, analyze, and publish data on how well health plans do their job. You can find these studies in some libraries or by contacting the organizations directly. Watch the newspaper for articles about these groups, especially when they release studies.

about their health plans. What do they think of the coverage and services provided by their plans?

• *Your Health-Care Providers:* Ask your present physician and other providers which health plans they rec-

Lack of Choice

Many people don't have a choice of plan. For example, their employers may offer only one plan or their health status may limit their options. If dissatisfied these consumers can use their plan's complaint procedure, contact state insurance departments, or consult a private attorney

3

ommend and why. If you want to continue seeing a particular provider, find out what plans cover his or her services.

In your search for a good health plan, the information you receive—from your friends and doctors and from the plans' representatives and written materials—will lead you toward a wiser choice. Use the questions in the checklist below to help you in your research. Some questions apply only to certain types of plans; others are important only to

CHECKLIST FOR CHOOSING A HEALTH PLAN

◆ Will you most often get to see a doctor, a nurse practitioner, or a physician's assistant?
◆ How easy is it to change your primary-care doctor if you're unhappy?
◆ Are you likely to need any services listed in the "exclusions" section of the description of benefits? What will this cost you?
◆ What is the procedure for getting second opinions?
◆ Is there a limit on your out-of-pocket copayments?
◆ Is there a lifetime limit on what the plan will pay

for your health care?
◆ Are your current medications covered? What pharmacies must you go to? Are they convenient? What are the drug copayments, and do they vary based on the drugs?
◆ What medical equipment is covered? Under what circumstances?
◆ What health-education and wellness programs are provided?
◆ Are the hours and location convenient? Are lab and other tests conducted in a convenient location? Is parking or public transportation available?

◆ Are the facilities clean?
◆ How long does it take to schedule a routine check up?
◆ Does the staff appear friendly, helpful, compassionate, patient?
◆ With which hospitals is the plan affiliated? Are certain ones only available to you for a limited range of conditions or services?
◆ How is emergency care provided?
◆ What is the procedure when you need a specialist?
◆ How does the plan pick its doctors?

certain families. Think about what's most relevant to your own situation and your potential health-care needs.

Cost + Coverage = Your Choice

What you pay and what you get are the obvious issues to consider when selecting a health plan.

Unfortunately, it's often hard to predict your future medical needs. Start by taking your recent health-care use as a rough guide. This will allow you to compare the coverage of different health plans and to estimate your total cost under each plan, including your share of the monthly premium or any out-of-pocket costs, like deductibles and copayments.

It's especially difficult to compare the benefits and costs of different plans because the coverage and copayments vary greatly from plan to plan. If you're lucky, your employer will provide a written comparison of your options. And if you're really fortunate, your employer will require all contracting health plans to provide exactly the same benefits at the same cost to you, making it easier for you to concentrate on finding the highest quality care. Unfortunately, this is far from the norm.

In any case, don't rely only on overviews from health plans *or* your employer, particularly if you have specific medical needs. You can't simply review the plan's marketing material or summary benefit descriptions and make an adequate comparison.

Overall, a 1994 study by the Congressional Budget Office found that managed care, especially the best HMOs, provide equivalent care at a cost about 9 percent less than traditional fee-for-service plans. However, the savings are a mere 4 percent for the average HMO. Even that gap is narrowing, and nearly all fee-for-service plans now include some element of managed care.

What Else Does the Plan Cover?

Health-insurance plans, whatever their general type, can cover a wide variety of services. Among the most important services you might need are: preventive care; inpatient hos-

Be Healthy!

The best health plans stress health promotion and disease prevention in addition to protecting you when you become seriously ill. In practical terms, this means that they educate their members about ways to stay healthy and cover child immunizations, Pap smears, cholesterol screenings, and other preventive services.

If "wellness" is a major concern for you, look for a plan that not only offers these services—almost all HMOs do—but actively promotes them as well. Do wellness or health promotion take a prominent place in the plan's advertising, member materials, and brochures and posters in waiting rooms? Ask other members if they are encouraged to use such services. Ask the providers about their attitudes toward prevention and about the

pital services; outpatient surgery; physician hospital visits; office visits, both routine and urgent; hospital emergency care; skilled nursing care; medical tests and X-rays; prescription drugs; mental health care; drug and alcohol treatment; home health care; rehabilitation facilities; physical therapy; hospice care; maternity care; experimental surgery or treatments; well-baby care; dental care, both routine and specialized; vision care; hearing aids; and alternative providers (chiropractic, acupuncture, homeopathy, etc.).

To make your consumer task even more difficult, the health plan might not provide many of these services directly. More and more health plans contract with specialized firms to provide certain services, most commonly mental health care, dental care, and prescription drugs. In fact, the specialty firm might contract directly with your employer. In other cases, the health plan contracts with the specialty firm and manages the use of covered services.

In other words, the specialty firm, rather than your health plan, could determine what care you'll receive and who will provide it. So you may need to contact the specialty firm, rather than the health plan, to obtain detailed information on the provider network and how to obtain care.

Your Choice of Providers

If you're considering a plan with a network of providers, review the list of providers—it's often called the "provider directory." If you join a plan that delivers care in health centers, you'll pick one center, probably near your work or home, and generally pick a primary-care physician who practices there. If the plan contracts with doctors practicing in private offices, you'll also probably pick a primary-care physician. In any case, check the directory to find out what providers and hospitals you'll use if you need specialty care.

The directory for some health plans only covers primary care. Nevertheless, before you decide to join, you have a right to know about *every* provider who contracts with the

The Typical Employer's Health Plan

In 1992, the health insurance that Americans received through their employers included:

◆ Mental health in 92 percent of plans;

◆ Substance abuse in 91 percent of plans;

◆ Home health care in 79 percent of plans;

◆ Hospice care in 71 percent of plans;

◆ Nursing-home care in 45 percent of plans;

◆ Well-baby care in 45 percent of plans; *and*

◆ Preventive care in 37 percent of plans.

Source: Bureau of National Affairs survey of employer-provided health benefits

plan. Ask for a comprehensive list. And if you want to know if a specific specialist, hospital, or other provider belongs to the plan, call the plan directly and ask.

Who's Available?

It's not enough to know that a particular provider belongs to a health plan. You need to find out if you can actually select the provider and what is required to do so.

• *Does the provider accept new patients from the health plan?* A doctor's practice may be full, so he or she won't take on new patients. As strange as it may seem, this could be true even if you now see the doctor through a different health plan. On the other hand, few practices are full under every circumstance. Call the provider to check.

• *Do you need a referral to see a particular provider?* In most managed-health plans, your primary-care physician must refer you to a specialist. Usually the specialist also contracts with the plan. However, if your primary-care physician refers you out of the network, the care is generally covered. Some plans even allow you to go out-of-network without a referral, but you pay a larger share of the specialist's bill.

• *Can your primary-care physician refer you to any network specialist or hospital?* While a health plan may contract with a seemingly large number of specialists and hospitals, some plans organize providers into subnetworks—often called "provider units," "referral circles," or "independent practice associations" (IPAs). In these cases, physicians usually refer you only to providers in their subnetwork or provider unit.

It may be important for you to check which specialists you could actually use. For example, if you select a primary-care physician in one provider unit, can you continue to use your obstetrician in another unit? Ask your doctor or the plan's member-services department to explain limits on your ability to see specific participating providers.

Similarly, you may want to look into restrictions on your use of network hospitals. A plan may advertise its contract with a particular hospital though it only uses that institution for certain services. Perhaps you want to take advantage of the outstanding maternity services at an affiliated hospital, but the plan only sends people there for cardiac surgery. Again, if this matters to you, check with your doctor or the health plan.

How Does the Plan Pay Primary-Care Physicians?

Health plans use a wide variety of methods to pay providers, and this could directly affect the type and amount of medical care you receive. Particularly important is how the plan pays your primary-care provider.

You might want to ask the plan:

• *Are physicians salaried employees?* Salary arrangements are less likely to induce physicians to skimp on services or to overtreat you. Doctors who earn a salary will make the same amount of money no matter how much or how little treatment you receive.

> **T I P**
>
> **Board Certification**
> *What percent of the doctors in a plan are certified by national boards to practice a specialty? If it's below 85 percent, get an explanation from the member-services department. Certification isn't a requirement for physicians, but it suggests a person has successfully completed examinations designed by leaders in his or her field.*
>
> *You may also want to find out if your personal doctor is board certified.*

• *Does the health plan still use "fee-for-service" payment?* These plans typically establish fee schedules for paying primary-care physicians and specialists for services. Some plans withhold part of the fee for each service—usually 10 to 20 percent—and give it to the physician at the end of the year based on the performance of the individual physician or the plan as a whole. Fee-for-service gives physicians an incentive to provide as much treatment as necessary and potentially an incentive to overtreat you or to favor expensive, high-tech care. On the other hand, some critics believe that fee withholding may result in incentives to undertreat individuals.

• *Do physicians receive bonuses at the end of the year based on the plan's financial performance?* Some plans withhold none of the fee but award physicians a bonus if the cost of

Dissatisfied Docs?

Are many of a plan's affiliated physicians not taking new members as patients? It could mean the doctors are unhappy—and that could have serious consequences for you. Besides the obvious fact that your choice of providers is more limited than you thought, the physicians' attitude could reflect poor quality in the plan as a whole. A rapid turnover of physicians in a health plan could also indicate problems.

Domestic Partners

Domestic partners consider themselves a family but either choose not to marry or are legally prevented from doing so because they are lesbian or gay.

A few employers have begun to extend health insurance and other family benefits to domestic partners. Seattle and San Francisco are among the municipalities offering full health-insurance benefits to city employees, as do Lotus Development Corp., Ben and Jerry's, New York's Museum of Modern Art, and a growing number of other private employers. Several insurers underwrite domestic-partner policies on a case-by-case basis.

For more information, contact Gay and Lesbian Advocates and Defenders (GLAD), P.O. Box 218, Boston, MA 02112 (617)426-1350.

referrals and hospitalizations is below the plan's budget targets. Sometimes, the plan links the bonus to member satisfaction and quality.

• *If it's an HMO, does it pay a primary-care physician a fixed monthly payment for each member signed up with the doctor, regardless of how often the member sees the doctor?* HMOs may set this "capitation" to cover the expected average cost of treating a member. In some arrangements, the capitation only covers services provided directly by the primary-care physician; in other HMOs, the capitation is intended to include the cost of referrals to specialists and other services.

While capitation payments eliminate incentives to overtreat, they may create an incentive for undertreatment; your physician could discourage you from visiting the office for minor complaints. Capitation can also discourage referrals to specialists when that referral affects the primary-care physician's bonus or withhold.

While it's impossible to know the quality of a health plan based *only* on how it pays providers, this is one factor to consider when evaluating different plans. Member turnover, a common indicator of consumer satisfaction, is lowest at HMOs that pay primary-care physicians a salary. You may want to ask your current health-care providers how satisfied they are with the method and level of payment from particular health plans.

What If You Leave Your Job or Move Away?

Not all health plans are alike in the coverage they'll provide if you lose your job or move outside the plan's service area. You usually have a legal right to maintain insurance under an employer's plan for between eighteen months and three years, even if you lose your group coverage due to job loss, the death of a spouse, or a divorce. However, you may not be eligible for continued coverage in all circumstances. And if you belong to an HMO or PPO but move outside of the plan's geographic area, you generally can't continue membership. Also, retirees who spend several months a year in seasonal homes may not be eligible for some plans.

HMOs generally require you to live in the state a minimum of nine months a year.

Track Record

How long has the HMO been in business? Older HMOs tend to be larger and more stable financially. They also have a track record—for better or worse— with providers and consumers, so it's easier to get information about them.

Most health plans will give you the option of converting your group policy to an individual or non-group plan if you lose your group eligibility, but the benefits are usually lower than in most group plans. HMO policies usually provide better conversion benefits than policies offered by indemnity insurers.

If you convert from a traditional insurer, you could find yourself facing limitations or restrictions for medical conditions you already have when you enroll—even if you aren't aware you are ill. If you are thinking about moving or face some insecurity on the job front, these may be important factors to consider when comparing and picking a health plan.

PART III: THE QUALITY QUESTION

Traditional indemnity insurers do little or nothing to manage the quality of care their policyholders receive. An advantage of some managed-care plans is that they take some responsibility for assuring the quality of service and care rendered to members. In fact, quality management is a hot trend in health care, although many HMOs have engaged in some quality-assurance activities for years.

Unfortunately, it's very difficult to measure quality of care, and few health plans scientifically assess the quality of medical care that members receive. Still, many plans do engage in a variety of activities aimed at improving the quality of your care:

• *Provider Credentialing:* Health plans choose providers to join their networks through a process called "credentialing." Credentialing usually focuses on physicians. Some plans have minimal requirements, such as a state license and hospital admitting privileges. More selective plans require such qualifications as board certification, admitting

Prior Approval

Some managed-care plans require *you* to get approval before going to the hospital, except in an emergency; in others, your doctor obtains the approval for you. Learn the rules of your plan. If you don't follow them, you could be without coverage, even for necessary medical care.

Although you don't need prior approval for emergency hospital care, what does the plan call an emergency? An emergency in the eyes of a concerned parent may not meet the plan's medical standards. To avoid an unpleasant surprise, get a clear, detailed explanation of what your health plan considers an emergency.

If Your Provider Leaves the Plan

Despite your most careful research, no one can guarantee that the provider you select will stay with your health plan. Relationships between providers and plans end for a variety of reasons, often with little or no notice to you.

If you are a member of an HMO or other plan that limits your choices, and your provider drops—or is dropped by—the health plan, the only way to continue seeing your provider may be to pay the full cost yourself. You could ask the physician you want how satisfied she or he is *before* you join the plan.

If you're in the hospital in the middle of a treatment program when the provider's contract ends, many plans require doctors and hospitals to keep treating you until you're discharged and your care can be transferred safely to another affiliated provider.

privileges at particular hospitals, and evidence of cost-effective patterns of practice. A health plan with fewer physicians might have very selective criteria—or physicians may have refused to join the plan for other reasons. Ask a plan what standards it uses to credential providers and how often it updates the information.

• *Chart Reviews and Practice Guidelines:* Many managed-care plans review medical records to determine if the care rendered to members meets certain standards. Some common standards include: regular immunizations for children, compliance with periodic screening guidelines, appropriate use of consultations, and timely review and interpretation of test results. Ask the plan if it conducts chart reviews, how often, what measures it uses, and how it uses the results to improve the quality of care. You could also ask your physician what she or he thinks of the HMO's quality-improvement activities.

• *Member Satisfaction Surveys:* Many managed-care plans regularly ask members if they are satisfied with the plan as a whole or with specific aspects of care. Often the surveys are extensive enough to provide information on individual primary-care physicians, and some plans even use the results to adjust payment to the doctor. Among the common survey questions are: How easy was it to get an appointment? How long did you have to wait in the doctor's office? How satisfied were you with the care you received? Would you recommend the doctor to others? Many managed-care plans also regularly check how many members transfer away from each primary-care provider each year and seek the reasons the

 T I P **Silence Isn't Golden**
A health plan that doesn't survey its members—or refuses to disclose the results—could have something to hide.

members switched to other doctors. Ask to see a copy of the latest survey results—but keep in mind that the plan, not an independent researcher, conducts the surveys in most cases.

• *Outcome Measurement:* Monitoring "outcomes"—how medical care affects the health and well-being of patients—

is ultimately the best way to assess the quality of care that health-plan members receive. Although this discipline is in its infancy, some managed-care plans are devoting considerable resources to analyzing which types of care work best and improve health—and which don't. For example, healthier members result when plans offer prenatal care, cancer screening, and other preventive and diagnostic programs. Before you pick a health plan, ask for information on its quality-management and improvement efforts.

3

• *Accreditation:* Find out if any outside body has accredited the health plan. The two major accreditation agencies are:

• *The National Committee on Quality Assurance:* NCQA, a not-for-profit organization, performs quality-oriented reviews of HMOs and similar types of managed-care plans.

• *The Utilization Review Accreditation Commission:* URAC, also a not-for-profit organization, reviews utilization-management firms and the utilization-review departments of insurance companies and certain types of managed-care plans. It focuses on managed-indemnity plans and PPOs.

Since accreditation programs are fairly new, don't penalize a health plan that is not accredited, but rather award "bonus points" to one that is.

SHRINKING DIFFERENCES

According to a study commissioned by the Group Health Association of American (the HMO industry association), 63 percent of people in fee-for-service plans and 72 percent in PPOs aren't covered for pre-existing conditions for several months after they join the plan. HMOs typically have no such exclusions.

However, the coverage differences between HMOs and other types of plans is shrinking. The same study looked at the proportion of employees whose plans covered adult physicals, well-baby care, outpatient mental health, inpatient mental health, and substance abuse. In each area, HMO coverage declined slightly from 1988

to 1993. At the same time, the coverage for enrollees in fee-for-service and PPO plans rose in almost every case, sometimes dramatically.

The major remaining contrasts in coverage are in adult physicals and well-baby care, two services that are key to the prevention orientation of HMOs.

Report Cards

Health-plan "report cards" on both quality and cost are emerging across the nation. Many use the Health Plan Employer Data and Information Set, commonly called "HEDIS," which looks at quality, access to care, member satisfaction, financial stability, and a number of other factors. By standardizing measures of performance quality, HEDIS will eventually enable consumers and employers to better compare health plans.

However, HEDIS is in its initial stages, and, for now, consumers have few sources of data for comparing insurers scientifically. Some plans analyze their own performance and publish the results, but these report cards only assess a narrow range of issues and are not available for every health plan. Still, they are a first step in providing you with better information with which to compare plans. Study a report card if it is available for any plan you are considering. In addition, the National Committee for Quality Assurance has begun to compile report cards that it may soon make public.

Among many other measures, a typical report card might include:

• *Percentage of Children Immunized:* Higher percentages can indicate a plan's commitment to preventive care for children;

• *Percentage of Women over a Certain Age Who Regularly Receive Mammograms and Pap Smears:* Higher numbers suggest a commitment to early detection and prevention;

• *Cesarean Section Rate for Deliveries:* Lower rates can indicate a commitment to less intrusive childbirth, including vaginal deliveries for women who have had previous cesarean sections; *and*

• *Member Dropout Rate:* If the rate is high, members may be dissatisfied, although the reasons for disenrollment could also include a job change, a move, or an employer who changes the health-plan options.

PART IV: WHEN IT'S TIME TO COMPLAIN

Always remember that *you're* the customer: the health plan works for you. You are entitled to get what you pay for

---

Federally Qualified HMOs

In the late 1970s, the federal government set up standards for HMOs. A federally qualified HMO must cover: all hospital inpatient services with no limits on costs or days; certain hospital outpatient diagnostic and treatment services, including rehabilitation services; skilled nursing care and home health services; short-term detoxification for substance abuse; medical treatment and referral for alcohol and drugs; and preventive care.

This designation is less valuable today as more comprehensive forms of HMO accreditation have emerged. Fewer than half of HMOs are now federally qualified, down from about three-quarters only a few years ago.

To get a list of federally qualified HMOs in your area, contact: Department of Health and Human Services, Office of Managed Health Care, 330 Independence Ave., SW, Washington, DC 20201 (202)619-0845.

and to receive helpful, courteous service. If you have a problem with your health plan, there are a variety of ways to get help.

File a Complaint or Grievance with the Health Plan

Talking with your health plan informally can resolve a great many questions and complaints. Still, keep careful written records of all conversations with plan representatives, including the date of your talks, the names and telephone numbers of the people to whom you speak, and a summary of the conversations. Try to talk with the same person each time you call so you can attempt to develop an advocate at the health plan. Be friendly and polite—but persistent. Being assertive often pays off.

If an informal approach doesn't work, many health plans—including most HMOs—have a formal grievance mechanism. Your member contract generally describes how to go about submitting a grievance. You can use this complaint process for any type of problem—for example, if you disagree with a plan's decision to deny your request for certain medical care, if you are dissatisfied with the level of payment made by the plan, or if you have a complaint

Your Interest versus Your Employer's

Some corporate buyers of health care pay more attention to the price for their share of the insurance bill than to high quality for you. That makes it all the more important for you to take responsibility for ensuring that you and your family get the highest quality care possible.

On the other hand, corporate buyers have also developed the most sophisticated measures of quality and consumer satisfaction.

GROUP HEALTH COOPERATIVE OF PUGET SOUND

The largest HMO in the Northwest, Group Health Cooperative, resembles other health maintenance organizations—except that consumers run it. In fact, with more than 470,000 enrollees, it's the world's largest consumer-run organization. It began in 1947 when a few consumers and physicians joined together to provide what insurance companies and the traditional medical system didn't: high quality, comprehensive care at an affordable cost.

An 11-person board of trustees, elected from the membership, sets the policies of Group Health. In addition, consumers and trustees serve on a variety of committees, including the Service/Quality Committee that oversees the development of policies, standards, and plans concerning health care and health promotion. On a local level, medical-center councils, composed of elected consumers, the physician chief, the nursing director, and the manager of each center, discuss quality and budget issues.

To find out more, contact Group Health Cooperative, Governance Office, 521 Wall St., Seattle, WA 98121 (206)448-5790.

Some HMOs have consumer members on their boards or consumer advisory committees. Find out if your HMO has one and how it selects consumer participants.

The 10 Largest HMO Companies, 1993	
Name	**Members**
Kaiser Foundation Health Plans	6,586,591
CIGNA Employee Benefits Co.	2,721,638
United HealthCare Corp.	2,122,479
Prudential Health Care Plans, Inc.	1,640,198
U.S. Healthcare, Inc.	1,568,094
Humana, Inc.	1,319,112
Health Systems International	1,286,096
Health Insurance Plan of Greater NY	1,164,840
PacifiCare Health Systems	1,150,729
Aetna Health Plans	905,211

Note: Some HMO companies operate more than one HMO under different names.

Source: Group Health Association of America, 1994 National Directory of HMOs

about the quality of care you received from a plan provider.

Check with your health plan if you are unsure about how to file a complaint or grievance. The plan's rules may require it to respond to any grievance within a given time period.

Talk to Your Employer or Benefits Department

If you belong to the health plan through your employer, you can ask your benefits manager or human-resource department for assistance. Although employers want to limit their health-insurance costs, they also usually don't want unhappy employees. Employers can be very powerful allies because they generally represent more than one customer to the health plan. For example, an HMO informed one man that his wife's surgery, scheduled for the next day, wouldn't be covered. He called the president of his company, who contacted the HMO. Just in time, the plan decided it would cover the surgery.

Of course, you will have to decide if you want anyone at your job to have details of your medical problems or those of your family. And if your employer won't, or can't, give you the information you need, go directly to the plan, if you haven't done so already.

Other Options for Complaints

• *Elicit the support of your health-care providers:* Ask your doctor and other health-care providers to help you document and support your need for services and care. Remember that if the provider is in the provider network, he or she is also an important customer of the health plan.

• *File a complaint with state regulators:* Most health plans are regulated by some state agency, generally the state department of insurance, the department of health, the attorney general's office—or all of these. While the legal authority and approach of regulators varies from state to state, they may be able to investigate and resolve your complaint. If you have a complaint about the quality of care, you can report it to the appropriate state licensing board. To locate the right regulatory agencies, contact your state insurance department or the National Association of Insurance Commissioners. Some states have insurance counselors to advise consumers.

• *Consult a consumer advocacy group or a lawyer:* The National Insurance Consumer Organization has a number of publications, including *The Buyer's Guide to Insurance.* While it doesn't provide direct assistance to consumers, NICO can refer to your state insurance commissioner for help. NICO, 414 A St., SE, Washington, DC 20003. Or contact your state insurance commission directly.

• *Go Public:* Health plans hate negative publicity. If you have tried other approaches, a phone call from an elected official—or even the media in extreme cases—can persuade a health plan to pay for services that it previously denied.

RESOURCES

Organizations

National Association of Insurance Commissioners
120 W. 12th St.
Kansas City, MO 64105
(816)842-3600
The association can direct you to your state's insurance commission.

U.S. Department of Health and Human Services
Health Care Financing Administration
Medicare Information Hotline:
(800)888-1770 (recorded message);
(800)888-1988 (to request written material or ask questions)

Publications

"Checkup on Health Insurance Choices." Free from Agency for Health Care Policy and Research, P.O. Box 8542, Silver Spring, MD 20907 (800)358-9295.

Choosing the Right Health Plan, by Henry Berman and Louisa Rose (Consumer Reports Books, 1990). $14.95.

"Consumer's Guide to Health Insurance." 16-page pamphlet available free from Health Insurance Association of America, P.O. Box 41455, Washington, DC 20018.

Consumers' Guide to Health Plans (Center for the Study of Services, 1994). $12.

Fighting Back Health Insurance Denials, by Robert Peterson, with David Tenenbaum. $14.95. Order from Center for Public Representation, 121 South Pinckney St., Madison, WI 53703 (800)369-0338.

Health Care Financing: A Guide for Families, by Julie Becket. $5.50, plus $2.50 shipping and handling. Order from National Maternal and Child

Health Resource Center, Law Building, University of Iowa, Iowa City, IO 52242 (319)335-9073.

Health Insurance Made Easy . . . Finally: How to Understand Your Health Insurance So You Start Saving Money and Stop Wasting Your Time, by Sharon L. Stark. $14.95, plus $2 postage and handling. Order from Stark Publishing, P.O. Box 8693, Shawnee Mission, KS 66208.

The HMO Health Care Companion: A Consumer's Guide to Managed Care Networks, by Alan G. Raymond (Harper Collins, 1994). $10.

Primary
Care

By Harriet Tolpin

Harriet Tolpin, PhD, is Dean of the Graduate School for Health Studies and Professor of Economics at Simmons College. She also is Clinical Professor in the Department of Community Health at Tufts University School of Medicine. As a health economist, her interests are in the financing, organization, and delivery of health-care services.

Everyone needs primary care.

• You and your eight-year-old daughter Elizabeth visit your family physician for your annual exams. A discussion of Elizabeth's school problems raises the possibility of attention deficit disorder. *For further evaluation, the doctor refers her to a pediatrician who specializes in child development.* At your exam, the doctor says your weight and blood pressure are a little higher than the year before, and your family has a history of heart attacks. *You and the physician discuss ways to lower your risk. Rather than take medication, you settle on a plan of more exercise and a better diet.*

• Your father has had mild Alzheimer's disease for several years. Recently, he entered a hospital for treatment of a blood clot in his leg. A routine chest X-ray showed he probably has lung cancer, although it's most likely curable with surgery. He hasn't prepared a living will, and the hospital environment has made him more confused than ever. Do you put him through the ordeal of surgery? *His internist convenes the family and lays out alternatives, including risks and benefits. Jointly, you decide not to operate now but to provide more home care after this hospitalization.*

• At your sister's annual gynecological visit to her nurse practitioner, she complains that she's sleeping poorly and having trouble concentrating. *Your sister and the nurse practitioner review a number of possible causes, leading to a tentative diagnosis of a mild depression. They review the pros and cons of medication versus counseling. Although the NP favors counseling initially, your sister opts for medication for the time being. The NP will monitor the medication but suggests a visit to a counselor as well.*

Each of these examples of your family's health needs falls within the province of primary care. Primary care is the appropriate place for you to make your *first* contact with health-care providers. It also constitutes your regular source of care on an ongoing basis.

Primary care aims to *prevent* premature death and disability and *enhance* your ability to function well and maintain a high quality of life. Thus, it focuses on you as a whole person, not on specific diseases or illnesses, and it emphasizes keeping you healthy—through health promotion and disease prevention, as well as by diagnosing and treating illnesses and accidents that do arise. And in most cases your primary-care provider coordinates and manages all your health care, no matter which specialists, social-service agencies, and other health professionals provide specific services that also contribute to your care.

Primary care reduces your health-care bills by detecting health problems early and initiating treatment before problems become more serious and costly to manage. Your primary-care provider's familiarity with you alerts her or him to heart disease that may run in your family or to stress in your life that might affect your health. This familiarity may also lessen the need for tests at each visit and for each condition.

PART I: WHAT A GOOD PRIMARY-CARE PROVIDER DOES

Primary care is your contact point for the health-care system. As your care coordinator and care manager, a primary-care provider makes sure you receive timely and appropriate care from all the various agencies and people in the health-care system.

Primary-care providers take a comprehensive approach that includes responsibility for:
- Promoting and maintaining good health;
- Preventing disease and disability;
- Detecting and treating common health problems;
- Educating and counseling patients and their families; *and*
- Referring patients to other providers and community agencies when appropriate.

This comprehensive approach means that primary-care providers may deliver any or all of a wide range of specific services at each visit, including:
- Physical exams and health histories;
- Health screenings and immunizations;
- Assessments and evaluations of acute illnesses such as colds, infections, and asthma;

Primary Care Is . . .

- ◆ *Comprehensive:* It focuses on you as a whole person;
- ◆ *Coordinated:* It holds together your personal health-care system;
- ◆ *Continuous:* You need it from birth to death; *and*
- ◆ *Accountable:* No matter what your problem with the health-care system, a good primary-care provider is your first resort—as well as your strong advocate —in obtaining the services you need.

- Advice on managing common, acute, and chronic conditions, such as flu, ear infections, high blood pressure, and diabetes;
- Prescriptions and care instructions for common and acute conditions;
- Family planning, prenatal care, management of normal pregnancies, and delivery;
- Identification of conditions that require referral to more specialized professionals and referral to these professionals; *and*
- Counseling on health-related lifestyle factors, such as physical activity, fitness, nutrition, smoking, substance abuse, family planning, and violent or abusive relationships.

Health Promotion at Every Stage

Primary care is critical to you, whatever your age, because it emphasizes screening, immunizations, and counseling, as well as providing an ongoing relationship between you and your provider. Indeed, *Healthy People 2000,* a major federal report, sets out specific national goals for promoting health and preventing disease in each age group. Many of these goals relate to your access to—and use of—primary care:

• *Infants:* Primary care for pregnant women improves their own health and that of newborns. Comprehensive prenatal care reduces infant death and the occurrence of low-birthweight babies. It can also lessen the incidence of infant illnesses that result from the mother's health habits, such as smoking, substance abuse, and poor nutrition.

• *Children:* Primary care helps children stay healthy. It includes immunizations, early detection of developmental problems, timely treatment of infections and respiratory illnesses, and the management of asthma and other chronic conditions. It also includes educating children about the dangers of tobacco and alcohol and the importance of exercise and good eating habits. And primary-care providers, through ongoing relationships with children and their par-

One, Two, Three

The term *primary care* refers to first-level or generalist care that you get outside a hospital.

Secondary care, often provided in hospitals and facilities for long-term care, makes more use of caregivers with specialized training.

Tertiary care is highly specialized care for severe health problems, such as that given in intensive-care, coronary-care, and trauma units.

ents, are in a good position to identify possible child abuse and other threats to children's health and well being.

• *Adolescents and Young Adults:* Primary care is an important vehicle for improving attitudes and health practices that form in adolescence and continue into adulthood. In particular, education and counseling can address smoking, alcohol and drug use, high-risk sexual behaviors, and depression. Also, the relationship primary-care providers develop with their patients as children enables them to reach out to them during the years of adolescence and early adulthood. This may reduce the risk of suicide, the second leading cause of death among young white men between ages 15 and 24.

• *Adults:* The ongoing relationship between primary-care providers and adults offers opportunities to reinforce healthy behavior. For example, the five major causes of death in the United States are cancer, heart disease, stroke, injury, and chronic lung disease. Many cases of these illnesses are preventable or curable. Regular screening of women could reduce deaths from breast cancer by 30 percent; cervical cancer can be cured if detected early by Pap smears. Smoking causes more than 85 percent of all deaths from lung cancer, the most common cancer in the United States for both men and women. Smoking raises the risk of chronic lung disease, heart disease, and stroke as well. The risks of heart disease and stroke also relate to diet and exercise. A primary-care provider can encourage people to receive appropriate screenings and to stop high-risk behaviors.

Priorities

Until recently, primary care ranked low among the hierarchy of doctor specialties in the United States, but today primary-care physicians are in demand. This is partly due to the rise of managed care, which stresses the role of primary-care providers.

In California and Minnesota, where managed care is prevalent, about half of all doctors "specialize" in primary care. This is considered to be roughly the proper proportion for average communities. For the United States as a whole, however, only about one-third of doctors are in primary care.

THE LIMITS OF PRIMARY CARE

While primary care is essential, there are limits to a generalist's capabilities:

◆ It may be difficult for a generalist to know when a condition is unusual. The tendency for a provider to fit what he or she sees into familiar boxes becomes stronger when the patient is extremely familiar. Primary-care providers may recognize a problem more slowly than a specialist would.

◆ Primary-care providers may be familiar with the "whole" you, but they may also be less competent than specialists at treating a particular part of you.

◆ As the health-care system presently operates, no individual or system can coordinate all the needs of a person or family with multiple complex problems. Inevitably, some concerns fall through the cracks.

For more information on care for women, turn to Chapter **6**

For more on care for children, turn to Chapter **7**

For more on care for elders, turn to Chapter **8**

• *Older Adults:* People over age 65 need primary care to maintain their health and prevent the early onset of life-threatening diseases and conditions. For older adults, primary care includes screening for cancers, immunizations against pneumonia and influenza, control of high blood pressure, counseling to promote healthy behaviors, and management of such chronic conditions as arthritis, osteoporosis, and incontinence. Primary-care providers also monitor medications and work with patients to offset depression by recognizing early warning signs.

Elders are especially likely to benefit from the familiarity and coordination of care that primary-care providers offer. As people age, they are more likely to have multiple complex problems that require coordination.

PART II: WHO PROVIDES PRIMARY CARE?

You will receive primary care from a generalist—a practitioner who can pay attention to all of your body's systems, as well as to environmental factors that could affect your health. Most often, this person will work in your community, in a location you can get to easily.

At least three types of providers may be trained to provide primary care:
• Physicians;
• Physician assistants; *and*
• Nurse practitioners.

Physicians

About 240,000 physicians in the United States deliver primary care, including family physicians and general internists for all adults. Obstetricians/gynecologists often function as primary-care providers for women, while pediatricians can fill that role for children. In addition, some physicians have begun to specialize in women's health or geriatrics. These fields have a primary-care orientation.

• *Family practitioners* generally receive the broadest training of any primary-care provider. They bring to mind the general practitioner you may have grown up with, but their training is far more extensive. Many general practitioners received no specialist training, while family practitioners take extra training after medical school in a half dozen fields. As a result, they understand the medical, social, and psychological factors that affect health, and they look both at individuals and at families as a whole. They can manage routine pregnancies, immunizations, physical exams, and the entire range of other primary-care services.

Family practitioners have several advantages as primary-care providers. They can care for everyone in your family and can recognize problems that arise from the family system. They receive training in psychiatry and the psychological and social aspects of illness. And they can deliver continuous care, working with you from infancy to adulthood and through old age.

Family practitioners also have disadvantages as primary-care providers. Because they must know something about everything, they can't have comprehensive knowledge of all specific health problems. Any given family practitioner is less comfortable with certain conditions than with others. However, precise weaknesses and strengths of this nature relate more closely to the person than to the field of family medicine.

• *Internists* can be either generalists or subspecialists. General internists correspond more closely to the definition of primary-care providers than do subspecialists, but internists who further specialize in such fields as cardiology (the heart) and oncology (cancer) often serve as primary-care providers for their patients.

Internists have some advantages as primary-care providers. They have more training in certain types of problems, such as heart disease. They are also more likely to provide total management for adults during a hospitalization.

There are also some disadvantages of internists as primary-care providers. They tend to order more tests than family practitioners. And an internist may be less comfortable with the full gamut of health concerns and the factors that contribute to them.

It Works

Two important components of primary care are screening to detect diseases early and patient education and counseling. These are proven effective health strategies.

Primary Care Teams

Strongly consider getting primary care from an interdisciplinary team: primary-care physicians, physician assistants, and nurse practitioners. The team might also include providers appropriate to particular needs—nutritionists and social workers for elders, for example. You can find teams in many of the settings in which primary-care services are provided—in HMOs, health centers, and private practices.

The team approach enhances your opportunities for receiving integrated medical, nursing, and social services.

Specialists As Primary Care Providers

Certain specialists can perform some of the functions of primary-care providers—for example, coordinating and managing care during a major illness. However, it's still important to have a regular primary-care provider if at all possible—that is, a person who comes to know you well over the years.

Physician Assistants

Physician assistants provide diagnostic and therapeutic medical services. Most PAs have three or more years of college-level education, with additional specialized schooling and on-the-job training. PAs always practice under the direction or supervision of a physician.

Physician assistants take health histories, perform comprehensive physical exams and minor surgery, order and complete routine diagnostic tests, develop diagnostic and management plans, provide basic treatment for patients with common illnesses, counsel patients on preventive health, and facilitate referrals to local health-care and social-service agencies. In some states, they can prescribe certain medications. They also may specialize and receive certification in specific fields, such as women's health.

Advanced Practice Nurses

Advanced practice nurses can handle up to 80 percent of primary and preventive care—and at a lower cost than doctors. Currently, more than 100,000 nurses provide primary care in the United States.

• *Nurse practitioners:* NPs provide the full range of primary-care services. They are the major non-physician providers of primary care. Their practice encompasses assessing their patients' general physical condition, diagnosing and treating common acute illnesses and injuries, educating patients in ways to promote health and prevent disease, and coordinating care. NPs train as generalists but may choose to specialize in caring for particular groups: newborns, children, women, adults, employees, families, or elders.

Many studies have documented the cost-effectiveness of nurse practitioners, the high quality of services they provide, and the satisfaction of their patients. There are 25,000 to 30,000 NPs in the United States. Most practice in community settings—neighborhood health centers, worksites, and family-planning clinics, for example.

Nurse practitioners provide care independently or in collaboration with physicians. Individual states have the authority to determine whether or not NPs may practice independently. At least 36 states require NPs to be nationally certified by the American Nurses Association or a specialty nursing organization. In at least 35 states, NPs prescribe medications.

• *Certified nurse midwives:* CNMs, who provide primary care for pregnant women, have specialized education beyond nursing school. They offer prenatal and gynecological care, deliver babies in homes, hospitals, and birthing centers, and care for a mother in the months after she gives birth. CNMs refer complicated cases to physicians, consult with physicians, or work jointly with physicians. They also provide family-planning services to women and postnatal care to normal newborns and infants.

CNMs often collaborate with physicians. Individual states determine the regulations for scope of practice.

PART III: FINDING PRIMARY CARE

Primary-care services are generally offered through:
• Private practices;
• Outpatient clinics;
• HMOs;
• Neighborhood health centers; *and*
• Community sites such as workplaces and schools.

Private Practices

Traditionally, primary care takes place in the office of a physician in your community. A physician may practice alone or in conjunction with a nurse or physician assistant. More often, physicians work in group practices, with several physicians and other health professionals who offer primary care; sometimes several physician specialists are included in the practice.

Multispecialty group practices have several advantages:
• More of your needs will be met at a single location.
• Information is more easily shared, and tests are less often repeated, than when referrals occur among isolated practitioners.
• Care tends to be better coordinated.

Alternative Care

Several types of non-traditional providers offer primary care. These include naturopaths and chiropractors. *For more information on alternative primary care, turn to Chapter* ▼ **10**

4

One for All?

It's often more efficient to use one primary-care provider for your whole family. Among other things, the provider will learn about family interactions that affect the health of each member. On the other hand, family members may prefer separate providers. Children could feel less inclined to confide in a provider who might share too much information with the parents, and vice versa.

Consumers without a regular source of primary care—both people with health insurance and those without it—often go to a hospital emergency department for basic health care. This is inappropriate, costly, and generally unsatisfying. Perhaps most significantly for you, the staff lacks a primary-care provider's invaluable knowledge of you, your medical history, and your medical records.

Multispecialty group practices also have disadvantages:

- The environment can be hectic.
- Information about you as a whole can fall between the cracks.
- More people have access to your medical record, which may threaten confidentiality.

Community Health Centers

Community health centers play a major role in providing primary care, especially but not exclusively for the poor and the uninsured. Also known as neighborhood health centers, neighborhood clinics, and primary-care centers, these organizations have strong local roots and serve the needs of the surrounding community with accessible and affordable health care.

Primary care at community health centers is often provided by an interdisciplinary team—to the benefit of patients. In addition, the centers offer services that address language, cultural, financial, transportation, and other barriers that make it hard for some people to get good health care. Most centers are affiliated with hospitals in the area.

OUTPATIENT CLINICS, AMBULATORY CARE CENTERS, AND PRIMARY CARE

Hospital outpatient clinics typically provide specialty care that doesn't require admission to the hospital. Usually, the clinics are located in the hospital.

As a source of primary care, hospital outpatient clinics offer few advantages to the consumer:

◆ They focus on disease and treatment rather than on promoting wellness.

◆ A clinic has a particular set of conditions as its focus, rather than the whole person;

◆ Most facilities are designed for following up on inpatient hospital stays rather than delivering primary care.

Ambulatory-care centers, often referred to as "Doc in the Box" or "Seven-Eleven Medicine," are convenient for routine, non-emergency conditions, such as cuts, sprains, and respiratory infections. They are usually created and owned by physicians or hospitals and provide walk-in service and offer evening

and weekend hours.

Do not substitute ambulatory care centers for a primary-care provider. These centers don't take responsibility for either the continuity or coordination of care. Rather, they are equipped to handle routine conditions if you don't have a primary-care provider available. For example, you might be on a vacation or you require minor care before you have had time to select a primary-care provider in a new city.

To an even greater extent than other primary-care providers, community health centers emphasize public-health measures as they seek to improve the health status of the communities they serve. As integral members of

TIP

Care for Everyone
Community health centers provide quality care, and not just for poor people. In general, they target underserved groups, such as people who live in rural or inner-city areas. Their services are open to everyone, regardless of income or insurance, and many middle-class consumers find that health centers excel at delivering high-quality, affordable care for an entire family.

the communities in which they are located, health centers maintain ties with other neighborhood organizations, such as schools, churches, and social-service agencies. These organizations often work with the centers in projects to educate people about particular health problems and high-risk behaviors such as domestic violence and substance abuse.

Managed Care and Primary Care

"Staff model" HMOs typically have facilities that resemble large multispecialty group practices or community health centers. Because such facilities also often handle diagnostic services, such as laboratory tests and X-rays, and minor surgeries, they provide "one stop" health care for members. They also have nurse practitioners on staff who collaborate with physicians.

HMOs are built on a foundation of primary care—it's the "health maintenance" part of their name. However, there is a growing concern among primary-care providers in HMOs that pressures to control costs limit the time they can spend with patients and thus reduce the opportunity for education and counseling. Moreover, primary-care providers in some HMOs make less money if they refer patients to a specialist. This potentially puts the doctor's financial self-interest and the patient's health into conflict. As an educated consumer in an HMO, consider this potential conflict and make sure you receive the attention you deserve.

Most doctors in solo and group private practices participate in one or more managed-care networks. And the

At Work and School

More and more Americans get their basic health care at work or at school. In recent years, several large employers have developed employee health services that provide some primary-care services, including screening, counseling, and education about lifestyle behavior. Another new initiative is the introduction of health clinics into schools, particularly middle and high schools, to improve primary health care for adolescents.

For more information on primary care within managed-care organizations, turn to Chapter 3

number of physicians affiliated with managed-care organizations is rising rapidly, reaching 70 percent in 1993, up from 59 percent only four years earlier. Such organizations rely heavily on primary-care providers to manage and coordinate their patients' care.

PART IV: CHOOSING YOUR PRIMARY CARE PROVIDER

Choosing a primary-care provider is one of the most important decisions a consumer makes. The person you select will be responsible for managing all your health care—day to day and year to year. Trust and rapport, in addition to professional training and technical competence, are leading qualities for you to consider.

Getting Started

For many people, the first step in selecting a primary-care provider is examining your health insurance. HMOs, other health insurers, and public programs

T I P **Personal Preferences**
Your choice of a primary-care provider is personal. Technical proficiency and training are critical. You may also want to weigh your preferences in such matters as a provider's age, gender, or personality.

such as Medicare and Medicaid determine which providers are eligible for reimbursement and for what specific services. Does your insurer restrict your choice in any way? For example, does your plan pay for the services of nurse practitioners and certified nurse midwives?

If you belong to a managed-care plan, you choose a primary-care provider from a list of affiliated practitioners, typically generalist physicians. The member-services department will give you information on its primary-care providers to help with your choice. While this information usually includes providers' training and availability, it may not include many facts you really want to know. In any case, state your preferences, if any, on matters like age, gender, training, and "bedside manner"—and be prepared to exercise your option to change providers.

Other health-insurance plans may require you to get a

primary-care physician to authorize specialist services. Such plans may place few limits on your choice of provider—and give you little information to help with your choice.

No matter how you pay for primary care, there are many questions you should consider. Start by finding out if a provider is accepting new patients. If so, find out more. Talk to your friends, look in the library for medical directories and other reference materials, and call each provider's office. Ask your relatives and friends about their primary-care providers. Gather information from other consumers who use—or have used—particular primary-care providers.

At this stage, it is likely that one or more providers will stand out in your mind. Now proceed to get answers to all the questions that are important to you:

- Does he or she deliver *primary care?* For adults? For children? For both? Does he or she treat the whole family (if that's what you want)?
- Does he or she focus on areas of particular relevance to your health concerns and those of your family, such as women's health, adolescent health, or elder care?
- Is this a group or an individual practice?
- How likely is it that you'll see the provider you want in a

CREDENTIAL CHECK

Although quality is a major criterion in choosing a primary-care provider, judging it is extremely difficult. Two indirect and imperfect indicators are education and experience. Did a person train specifically as a primary-care provider? Check for evidence that she or he tries to stay current through continuing professional education: board certification and recertification suggests this, although these may be better indicators of knowledge than of

skill in applying it. More and more physicians are board certified these days: 66 percent in 1994, compared to 46 percent twenty years ago. Increasing numbers of advanced practice nurses are also certified by credentialing organizations.

Check for the dates of graduation and certification. Some consumers prefer a recent date, implying up-to-date training; others look for more years of experience.

For information on education and credentials, you

can use a variety of sources, including medical and nursing directories and state licensing boards. Consulting friends and calling and visiting the provider's office may also yield important information.

Also, find out whether a provider teaches in a medical school or nursing program. Teaching indicates that a provider's colleagues consider him or her knowledgeable in a particular field.

group or team practice? Can you decide who to see?

- With which hospitals is the provider affiliated?
- Is the practice easily accessible? Are evening or weekend appointments available?

> **T I P**
>
> **Yes, No, or Maybe**
> *One key item of information about a prospective primary-care provider is whether he or she takes new patients. You should realize that a "no" may not be absolute. Often, you can get on a waiting list. Calling back periodically or writing the physician explaining your reasons for wanting to see her or him can be effective.*

- Does the provider make house calls if you can't get to the office?
- Can you readily get advice on the telephone, both before scheduling an appointment and for follow-up advice?
- Does the office provide other relevant services, such as language translators, referral relationships with social-service agencies, and arrangements for watching children who accompany a parent on a visit?
- What diagnostic facilities are available on site, such as laboratory and X-rays facilities?
- What is the provider's reputation with other physicians? With her or his patients?

FINDING CANDIDATES

Despite the shortage of people trained in primary care, most communities have a number of doctors and other health professionals from whom you can choose. Don't feel compelled to accept the first one you contact.

To compile a roster of potential primary-care providers:

◆ Ask friends and colleagues who they use.

◆ If you know any medical personnel, ask them the same question.

◆ Call the local medical and nursing societies for names of certified primary-care providers in your community.

◆ Contact local hospitals, medical schools, and nursing programs, which will identify providers on their staffs or in affiliated group practices.

◆ Contact a referral service, whether a local non-profit agency listed in the yellow pages or a for-profit national group such as Prologue.

◆ Consult publications such as the *American Medical Directory* and the *Official ABMS Directory of Board Certified Medical Specialists.*

◆ Consult a local consumer's guide if one is available.

The Try-Out

When you narrow your list to one name, make an appointment. Use this visit to decide if you feel that you can establish a comfortable relationship of trust and mutual respect with this individual. Remember, you are not only looking for someone to provide medical care but for a partner and a strong advocate in the health-care system.

A visit helps you judge the atmosphere of the office, even if you don't arrange for a regular appointment or full physical. Does the office appear well-organized and efficient? Is the staff friendly on the phone and in person? Do interactions among the staff and between staff and patients seem smooth? If the answers are yes, you have a better chance of receiving quality care. And your health will benefit from good record keeping, shorter waiting times, and enough time with caregivers.

Find out who handles routine calls and matters: is it a doctor, a nurse practitioner, or someone else? It's important that whoever handles such calls has access to the information necessary to respond appropriately. It's also important that you have direct access to the person ultimately responsible for your care in non-routine and emergency situations.

If you do schedule a regular appointment, note the following: Does the primary-care provider take enough time to learn about you and your family, or does he or she act rushed and impatient? Does the initial health assessment include questions about your lifestyle and your health habits? Does the provider's philosophy toward medical care include a strong commitment to prevention? Does the primary-care provider encourage you to ask questions, and are your questions answered satisfactorily? Does the primary-care provider share information with you that is relevant to your current and future health? Does he or she explain the reasons for all tests and treatments? Are you given options? Does the provider seem to prefer to teach or to give orders? Does the provider welcome your efforts to participate in all decisions about your health care? Does the provider offer you a copy of your medical record?

Ask a potential primary-care provider:
- What is your approach to health maintenance?
- What do you routinely check for?
- How often will I need regular check ups?
- What tests do you routinely perform and why?
- Can a friend or family member be in the exam or consulting room with me?
- Who covers for you if you are unavailable? What is their training or specialty?

Ask, Ask, Ask

Once you have chosen a primary-care provider, your real responsibility as a health-care consumer

In an Emergency

Can you reach your primary-care provider in an emergency? Make sure you'll have an effective system for covering emergencies 24 hours a day.

begins. Developing and maintaining a strong working relationship with your primary-care provider is critical to your good health.

For primary care to be effective, the relationship between primary-care provider and patient must be one of trust, cooperation, and support. Primary care is a joint enterprise. You need to feel comfortable talking frankly and openly with your primary-care provider. It's up to you to disclose all relevant information, including your chief complaints, symptoms, worries, current medications, family circumstances, and any history of alcohol or drug abuse. And it's your responsibility to ask questions, follow advice, and notify the primary-care provider if problems arise. The provider's responsibilities include presenting you with your full range of options and inviting you to express your values and preferences concerning them. These are ethical and legal obligations.

Before every appointment:
- Plan your visit.
- Determine the most important issues you want the appointment to address.
- Be familiar with your own and your family's medical history.

- Assemble any written records of your health care since your last appointment.
- Write down questions as you think of them.

> **T I P**
> **Print or Type**
> *Ask your doctor to follow the AMA's recommendation to print or type prescriptions. Poor handwriting on prescriptions leads to more illnesses, longer hospital stays, and even death.*

At the appointment:

- Ask for explanations of diagnoses and treatments.
- Ask for written summaries of X-rays and other tests.
- Volunteer facts you think may have been missed.
- Be as specific as possible.
- Ask for drugs to be prescribed by generic name.

Consider bringing a friend or relative along to all appointments, not just the initial visit. He or she can help you ask questions and take notes about instructions the primary-care provider gives you.

PART V: MONEY MATTERS

Health maintenance, or preventive care, can help you feel better and enjoy your life. It is also efficient and economical. It costs far less to prevent most health conditions or to intervene early than to treat illnesses that have reached more serious stages. Prevention and early action reduce expenses associated with tests, medications, hospital stays, and sometimes even surgery and other expensive procedures that may accompany acute illnesses.

Primary Care and Insurance

When you are considering a new primary-care provider, check:

- Will the provider deal with your insurance carrier?
- How do the provider's fees compare with what your insurance will pay?

For healthy consumers who aren't at high risk for particular diseases and illnesses, coverage for physical exams, health assessments, and screenings varies from plan to plan, as does coverage for wellness programs and other health-maintenance activities. Generally, insurance plans and

Pioneers

The inclusion of health promotion and disease prevention in benefit packages is a relatively recent phenomenon. HMOs, pioneers in this area, recognize that preventing illness costs the insurer less than treating it, and they structure their benefits accordingly.

For people who must pay out-of-pocket for their health care, primary care often seems a luxury rather than a necessity. People with no regular source of care typically enter the health-care system through an emergency room when a health problem becomes acute or life-threatening. They also often forego necessary services related to managing chronic conditions.

There are options. In particular, you can find quality providers that charge less for services, such as community health centers. Moreover, most health centers charge sliding-scale fees based on income, making them affordable for people without insurance.

In addition, you can seek help from special programs that pay for health-care services for those unable to pay themselves. A call to legal-services offices or to the state department of health, public health, human services, or public welfare can help you find out about such programs.

HMOs cover those primary-care services that relate to the diagnosis and treatment of common acute and chronic conditions. Follow-up visits for the ongoing management of such conditions are also typically covered. You'll usually have to make a "copayment" for these services. The typical benefit package also includes immunizations.

Generally, HMOs offer more comprehensive primary-care benefits than do other insurers. HMOs encourage wellness and health maintenance through a variety of mechanisms that may include patient education and wellness programs, vaccinations and other screening tests, and nutrition counseling. Participation in these activities may require a small payment from you.

All HMOs and many insurance plans, especially those with managed-care features, now require a primary-care provider, generally a physician, to authorize the services of a specialist. Primary-care

T I P **Ask in Advance**
◆ *What is the cost for an initial office visit, consultation, or exam?*
◆ *What is the cost for a routine office visit?*

providers thus act as "gatekeepers" who give approval for a patient to move into other parts of the health-care system. This makes the relationship between you and your primary-care provider even more central to all of your care.

The Smart Consumer

You can take a number of steps to save money, especially if your health insurance doesn't cover primary care. Even if it does, you can often save on your portion of the bill.

Ask about the fees for certain procedures in the office of a provider you are considering. The American Medical Association recommends that doctors post fees prominently, but if the information isn't visible, don't hesitate to ask. You might try to get fee information over the phone, but you may have to go to the office.

Here are a few other steps you can take:

T I P **Use Ma Bell**
If you can, get advice over the phone from your doctor or nurse instead of scheduling a visit. Ask a potential provider if he or she gives help by phone and what the charge is, if any.

TYPICAL PHYSICIAN CHARGES FOR A COMPLETE PHYSICAL	
Boston	$170
New York	$316
Washington	$158
Phoenix	$129
National Average	$119

Source: Medirisk

• Schedule a preliminary visit just to meet the provider. Such a visit might be free, but even if there is a charge, it's probably worth the investment in your future health.

• Shop around. Prices vary from city to city as well as within any community. The national average for a complete physical is $119, while in New York City it's $316.

• Don't shop around endlessly. You could organize your search by interviewing three recommended providers in a relatively short time period. Keep a list of attributes you consider the most important and use them to compare the providers.

• Don't use a specialist for primary care. It's expensive, and most specialists aren't trained in this area.

• Contact your primary-care provider before going to an emergency room, if you can.

RESOURCES

Organizations

American Academy of Family Physicians
8880 Ward Parkway
Kansas City, MO 64114
(816)333-9700
Call or write for referrals to family physicians and a publications catalogue.

American Medical Association Physician Data Services
525 N. State St.
Chicago, IL 60610
Write for a profile of any member of the AMA. The profile will include the person's medical education, specialty, board certifications, location of internship and residency, AMA membership, and any success-ful malpractice lawsuits. Send a written request with the doctor's name, address, specialty, and other pertinent information. Include a self-addressed envelope.

American Academy of Nurse Practitioners
Capital Station
LBJ Building
Austin, TX 787111
(512) 442-4262
Call or write for publications on what nurse practitioners do, the quality of care they provide, and why the are cost effective. Also contact the AANP for referrals to local NPs.

American Academy of Physician Assistants
950 N. Washington St.
Alexandria, VA 22314
(703)836-2272
Call or write for publications and for referrals to local PAs.

American Osteopathic Association
212 E. Ohio St.
Chicago, IL 60611
For referrals: (800)621-1773, ext. 7401.

Medical Data Source
5959 W. Century Blvd.
Los Angeles, CA 90045
(310)641-3111
(800)776-4MDS

Call for an annual membership and to receive comprehensive, easy-to-use information on medical conditions, prescription drugs, and physician backgrounds, and for referrals to local health facilities, such as nursing homes, rehabilitation centers, and support groups. Subscription rates vary depending on the level of service you choose—usually not more than $48 per year.

Mediguard/Medirisk, Inc.
Two Piedmont Center
3565 Piedmont Rd.
Atlanta, GA 30305
(800)656-3337
Mediguard is a subscriber service that allows consumers to compare their local medical prices and negotiate medical fees with their physicians. Consumers in any city can get Mediguard physician fee information and coaching via a toll-free number staffed by representatives familiar with health-care procedures and costs. Mediguard representatives can tell subscribers about premium, typical, discounted, and Medicare fees for any medical procedure in their area.

National Association of Community Health Centers
1330 New Hampshire Ave., NW
Washington, DC 20036
(202)659-8008
Call or write for information on and referrals to community health centers.

National Clearinghouse for Primary Care Information
8201 Greensboro Dr.
McLean, VA 22102
(703)821-8955
The clearinghouse provides a wide variety of publications on primary care, mostly for administrators and practitioners, although a few publications on AIDS and on medicines for elders are geared to consumers. Call or write for a list of publications.

Prologue/Consumer Health Services
(800)DOCTORS
Call for free physician referrals in Chicago, Dallas/Ft. Worth, Denver, Houston, Kansas City, Miami/Ft. Lauderdale, Philadelphia, Pittsburgh, and Washington, DC. This service matches patients and doctors on over 500 variables, such as sex,

specialty, location, hospital affiliation, and age. Doctors pay to be included, with about 30 percent of doctors in each city listed.

Publications
American Medical Directory (American Medical Association, 1988).

Healthy People 2000. Published by the U.S. Department of Health and Human Services. To order send $4 for shipping and handlng to National Health Information Center, P.O. Box 1133, Washington DC 20013-1133 (301) 565-4167.

How to Choose a Doctor, edited by Michael Rooney. Order from People's Medical Society, 462 Walnut St., Allentown, PA 18102 (800)624-8773. $4.00, plus $3.00 for shipping and handling.

How to Talk to Your Doctor: The Questions to Ask, by Janet Maurer (Simon and Schuster, 1986).

Smart Patient, Good Medicine: Working with Your Doctor to Get the Best Medical Care, by Richard L. Sribnick and Wayne B. Sribnick, (Walker and Co., 1994). $8.95.

Hospitals

By Joseph Restuccia, Alan Labonte, and Jeffrey Gelb

5

Contracting Resources

About 5,300 hospitals in the United States are *community hospitals*—that is, they primarily serve their local area. However, the number of community hospitals is declining slowly due to attrition, take-overs, mergers, and, most significantly, the fact that far fewer procedures now require an overnight stay.

Joseph Restuccia, DrPH, is associate professor of health care and operations management at Boston University School of Management. He also holds faculty appointments at the university's medicine and public-health schools. His work focuses on issues pertinent to health-care quality and productivity.

Alan Labonte has 20 years of experience in hospital management. He is currently a doctoral candidate and research associate of Boston University School of Management.

Jeffrey Gelb, MD, is a physician with clinical training in general and orthopedic surgery. He works for Total Learning Concepts, Inc., developing multimedia educational materials on medicine and managed care.

The word hospital derives from the Latin word for guest. As an institution, Western hospitals date from medieval times when monks provided hospitality and care for weary and sick travelers.

How different those welcoming images are from the one most people have of the high-tech, fast-paced, and seemingly impersonal institutions of today.

Fortunately, much of the mystique and anxiety fades for health-care consumers who understand how hospitals are organized. With careful planning and knowledge, you can be a valuable—and valued—partner with your hospital and the team of caregivers you encounter there.

As with many of your health-care choices, the time to learn about hospitals is when you are well and in a position to make a careful, informed, and objective decision. Try to get a sense now of your family's potential need for hospital care, taking into account any illnesses or conditions that currently exist, your family's medical history, your insurance coverage—and your personal preferences.

PART I: THE VARIETIES OF HOSPITAL

The vast majority of the community, specialty, and rehabilitation hospitals in the United States can provide the care you need when you are sick or injured. Many hospitals also educate doctors and other health-care professionals, promote public health through such programs as prenatal education, and encourage medical research. Some hospitals emphasize one goal; most address a combination of goals.

Teaching and Non-Teaching Hospitals

A teaching hospital is affiliated with a medical school and has a teaching program for medical students, interns, and residents. Many community hospitals are also teaching hospitals.

From the consumer's point of view, the principle strength of teaching hospitals lies in their ability to provide highly sophisticated technology and medical techniques and round-the-clock in-house physician services. Interns and residents—the "house staff"—manage day-to-day care under the guidance and supervision of fully trained attending physicians who are members of the hospital and medical-school faculty.

Nevertheless, resist the temptation to automatically select a prestigious teaching hospital as the primary source of hospital care for your family. You and your physician may very well prefer a smaller hospital that is less expensive and closer to your home. The quality at smaller community hospitals often compares to that found at large teaching institutions, particularly for routine illnesses or surgeries. And the accessibility of a local hospital for family and friends is also important. Remember, the support of family and friends is integral to the healing process.

Specialty and General Hospitals

About 1,000 hospitals specialize. That is, they treat a specific category of patient or patients with a specific type of disease or condition. You can find hospitals dedicated to a number of special purposes or constituencies, such as cancer, psychiatry, rehabilitation, orthopedics, elders, and children. If someone in your family has a chronic condition that warrants ongoing, specialized medical support and access to the latest methods of treatment, talk to your current providers about establishing a relationship with a hospital specializing in that condition.

However, specialty hospitals may be far from your home and lack the facilities and staff necessary to treat an unrelated medical complication. And even if you use a specialty hospital for one or more problems, you still need to think about your family's general medical care. Select a primary-care physician and a hospital that will work together to address your family's needs.

For-Profit and Nonprofit Hospitals

For-profit hospitals are owned by corporations or, less often, by individuals, such as doctors who practice at the hospital. Hospital corporations usually own a chain of institutions located in several states, and they often own nursing homes or other types of health-care facilities as

Who Does What

You have a right to know about the doctors and other caregivers working with you, including their training. Every hospital employee wears a tag showing his or her name and title. If a person isn't wearing a tag, ask why not and make a note of his or her name.

The doctors at non-teaching hospitals are mainly attending physicians who practice outside the hospital. Each physician is fully responsible for the patients he or she admits, with other physicians acting as consultants. Non-teaching hospitals also have a small number of hospital-based physicians on their staff, mainly to provide emergency care, radiology, anesthesiology, and pathology services. They also may help manage the hospital.

In a teaching hospital, you'll receive care from attending physicians plus first-year residents (interns), advanced residents, physicians gaining advanced training in a specialty or subspecialty (fellows), and full-time teaching faculty who may also be attending physicians.

well. For example, Columbia/HCA Corporation owns or manages about 200 hospitals and other health-care facilities.

Nonprofit hospitals are owned by private nonprofit corporations, as well as by cities, states, the federal government, and church groups. Sometimes, the nonprofit "owners" hire for-profit companies like Columbia/HCA to manage the hospital.

A few studies suggest that for-profit hospitals make much of their money by "cream-skimming"—targeting patients who are fully insured and have less serious illnesses. Other studies point to a lower quality of care in for-profits as a result of lower employee-to-bed ratios than nonprofit hospitals. In response, for-profit hospitals maintain that their profits and lower staffing ratios derive from efficiency.

In fact, most studies of for-profit and nonprofit hospitals have found them to be almost indistinguishable. No overwhelming evidence indicates major differences in either the efficiency or quality of nonprofit and for-profit hospitals, especially those that are investor-owned. Both types of hospitals receive most of their revenue from insurance com-

The Hospital: A Capsule View

Most hospitals handle patients in two basic ways:

◆ *Inpatients* stay in the hospital overnight.

◆ *Outpatients* visit the hospital for a specific treatment, procedure, or test but don't stay overnight.

HOSPITALS FOR VETERANS AND THEIR FAMILIES

Millions of Americans have access to the 171 hospitals and clinics run by the federal Department of Veterans Affairs. Tailored to veterans, the hospitals are typically affiliated with medical schools and staffed by the school's faculty, residents, interns, and students.

Advantages of VA hospitals include free care or reduced rates for veterans, programs for abuse of alcohol or drugs, and access to specialty care. Among the downsides are

the bureaucracy, the increased likelihood of receiving care from physicians in training, and the possibility of having to travel far for specialty care.

For more information about these facilities and your eligibility to use them, contact the Department of Veterans Affairs, Washington, DC 20420.

The VA also has an excellent guide called *Federal Benefits for Veterans and Dependents*. This 96-page handbook describes federal benefits such as

medical care, education, and disability compensation. It explains the eligibility requirements for different benefits and provides addresses and phone numbers for all VA offices, medical centers, and other facilities. The handbook is available for $2.75 from the Superintendent of Documents, U.S. Government Printing Office, Washington, DC 20402-9325 (202)783-3238. Refer to stock number 051-000-00-198-2.

panies. And if public hospitals owned by local governments are excluded, neither nonprofits nor for-profits provide much "free care." In the absence of more definitive evidence, it's up to you to weigh the evidence about *each* hospital individually, seeking the best providers and the best care, whether it's at a nonprofit or a for-profit institution.

PART II: OUTPATIENT CARE

If you imagine a hospital in your future, you probably picture an overnight stay. However, this isn't all—or even most—of what many hospitals provide today. Outpatient care is a major part of the services provided by hospitals, even for patients needing surgery: Americans had 12.3 million outpatient surgeries in 1992, up from 4.1 million in 1982. In contrast, there were 10.7 million inpatient surgeries in 1992, down from 15.5 million in 1982. About 88 percent of community hospitals provide some form of outpatient care.

The Emergency Room

The most common outpatient service in a hospital is the emergency room. The staff there treat and manage patients who suddenly become seriously ill or injured. Emergencies include severe and uncontrollable bleeding, severe burns from heat or chemicals, severe breathing problems, bullet or stab wounds, unconsciousness, a drug overdose, a temperature over 103 degrees, eye injuries, and more.

Hospital emergency rooms are required by law to care for everyone who comes in for help. The emergency-room staff make a judgment call about how quickly you need to receive care. If needed, the staff can draw on all the hospital's resources, and they are available 24 hours a day.

Don't wait until you need urgent care to find out about the emergency resources available at your local hospital. Determine where the closest emergency room is—not every hospital has one. And know how to call an ambulance: Does your community have a 911 telephone emergency-response system? Or would you call the police

General Trend

The proportion of specialty hospitals in the United States is declining. Hospitals are finding that they need to offer wider services to survive in today's competitive health-care marketplace.

department, the fire department, or a private insurance company? If an ambulance isn't needed or is unavailable, do you know the quickest route to the emergency room?

When you reach the hospital, the chances are quite high that the emergency-department physician won't have much information about your medical history. To get the most effective care in the least amount of time, be prepared to provide accurate information about:

T I P

Bring a Friend

Bring someone to the emergency room with you to help monitor your care, explain your problem, support you emotionally, and advocate for you with hospital staff.

- Your current medical problems;
- Your medical history, especially previous hospitalizations and surgery;
- Current medications (with the name and dose of each one, along with how often you take it); *and*
- Allergies.

Don't rely on a hospital emergency room for regular medical care, however. This is expensive and time consuming. You and your family need and deserve a personal physician to manage your overall medical care on an ongoing basis. A personal physician is better able to provide quality care for non-emergency illnesses because he or she knows you as a patient.

If you're unsure about the seriousness of your condition, try to reach your primary-care provider first. He or she may help coordinate your care by providing emergency personnel with critical medical information. Your insurance may require you to do this anyway in some circumstances.

T I P

Ambulance Service

In many situations, you'll want to call an ambulance for transportation to the emergency room. For example, you may need urgent care when no one is available to drive you to the hospital. Also, some ambulance services are staffed by trained emergency medical technicians. If you need emergency care, EMTs usually can get to you much faster than you can get to the hospital.

If you have a choice among several emergency departments, you may want to inquire about their comparative

---

A Non-Emergency Alternative

For routine care, "after-hours" health-care centers are less expensive and more convenient than emergency rooms. They are a growing alternative to emergency-room treatment of non-emergency patients, and insurers encourage people to use them for this purpose. However, avoid them in life-threatening situations.

If you use an after-hours center, arrange to forward copies of the medical records for service there to your regular provider. And check with your insurer for coverage.

capabilities. The qualifications of the physicians staffing the department is an important factor in your decision. Some hospitals use only doctors who are board-certified in emergency medicine or surgery. Others rely on residents or other physicians with little training in the treatment of major traumas and other emergency conditions. Another indication of capability is volume. The more visits a department handles, the more capable it's likely to be.

Testing and Treatment: Hospital Clinics

Throughout your lifetime, health-care providers will refer you and your family to a hospital for outpatient care for specific procedures or treatments. For example, before entering the hospital for an overnight stay, you'll probably receive some routine diagnostic tests as an outpatient, particularly if your condition isn't urgent. Usually, this is done to record certain information about your blood and heart activity, reducing the length of the inpatient stay—and reducing your total cost.

5

THE OUTPATIENT EXPERIENCE

Follow the hypothetical experience of Steve Tripton as he receives high-quality medical care without the trouble and expense of spending a night in the hospital.

Tripton twisted his knee while skiing. When his knee pain didn't improve with medication and physical therapy, his family physician referred him to Dr. Joel Jameson, an orthopedic surgeon. He diagnosed torn cartilage inside the knee and recommended surgery to remove the torn portion. Tripton agreed.

On the day of the surgery, Tripton arrived at County General Hospital. Jane Crawford, a nurse, checked him in. She asked Tripton questions about his last meal, his medical history, and drug allergies. An anesthesiologist, Dr. Ralph Narcum, came in and reviewed the medical history, asked about any previous difficulties with anesthesia, and examined Tripton. A few minutes later, Dr. Jameson arrived.

Dr. Narcum and Nurse Crawford wheeled Tripton into the operating room and gave him medication to fall asleep. The next thing Tripton remembers is waking up with his leg bandaged. He spent a few hours in the recovery room, where a physical therapist came to demonstrate the use of crutches and exercises to perform at home. Dr. Jameson scheduled a follow-up appointment with Tripton and gave him a prescription for pain medicine and written instructions, including a number to call in case of an emergency.

A friend took Tripton home a few minutes later. The next day, Tripton received a check-up call from Nurse Crawford to make sure that he was doing okay.

Because inpatient hospital stays are expensive and many patients prefer not to stay overnight anyway, the trend is toward performing surgery and other treatment on an outpatient basis. Thus, most people get eye and knee surgery in an outpatient day surgical unit. Moreover, outpatient care exposes a patient to less risk than an overnight stay of acquiring an infection from the germs that are inevitably present in hospitals. Other advantages of outpatient care—ones that contribute to a faster recovery—include less disruption of your family life and reduced psychological trauma.

If you do receive outpatient surgery, it's important that you determine exactly what kind of care you'll need afterwards. Make sure that someone can provide it—a family member, a friend, or a nurse or home-health aide arranged through a hospital clinic.

PART III: SEARCHING FOR QUALITY

Hospitals are big business. About 30 million people spend a night in a hospital each year. And Americans make over 300 million visits to hospitals for outpatient services annually.

Hospitals employ a number of methods to maintain and improve the quality of care they deliver to these millions of customers. For example, most hospitals have written policies intended to help prevent the spread of infection. In addition, committees examine every unexpected death and accident, as well as cases that may have been handled improperly. And hospitals must document the reasons for all unusual occurrences in delivering care.

Unfortunately, it's beyond the ability of most health-care consumers to assess the quality-control procedures of a given hospital. Your doctor can give you some advice, and nurses are often a good source of information. Also, ask the hospital quality-assurance department to explain its efforts to ensure that you receive the best care possible. The hospital's accreditation and indirect signals such as services and staffing can also play a role in your evaluation.

Ambulatory Care Centers: A Surgery Alternative

The popularity of outpatient surgery has stimulated the growth of independent, for-profit *ambulatory treatment centers*. If you are considering a center that isn't hospital-sponsored, find out how it handles an emergency. Remember, a medical complication can arise at any time. Is a hospital emergency department nearby? Does the center have an agreement with the hospital to take patients from the center when necessary?

Ask in advance about the credentials of the physicians, nurses, and other staff who will be responsible for your care. Make sure the facility is licensed by the proper state agency and subject to regular professional standards surveys.

Accreditation and Quality

Everyone wants high quality care. But how can you know how good your local hospital is, or any hospital that your health-care providers recommend? It isn't easy. Unfortunately, the simplest potential indicator—cost— provides no reliable signal on quality either way.

Still, *accreditation* indicates that a hospital meets at least minimum standards of quality—and perhaps much more. The *Joint Commission on Accreditation of Healthcare Organizations (JCAHO)*, an independent, nonprofit organization, conducts a quality assessment of most hospitals every three years. This process is voluntary, and about 80 percent of U.S. hospitals participate.

You are entitled to know a hospital's level of accreditation. The overwhelming number of hospitals receive simple accreditation, which does little to differentiate them from one another. A few hospitals receive accreditation with commendation, conditional accreditation, or no accreditation. Conditionally accredited facilities have six months to correct deficiencies cited by the JCAHO.

The JCAHO has begun to make detailed data on hospitals available to the public. This covers a wide variety of areas, including nursing care, infection control, patient rights, and safety.

Besides accreditation, physician *board certifications* can be used as a sign of quality. Medical and surgical specialty societies certify physicians to practice a particular specialty if they receive extra training and pass advanced tests in the field. Although certification measures knowledge more than skill, a high proportion of board-certified physicians on a hospital's medical staff suggests a higher level of expertise on hand. About two-thirds of U.S. physicians are certified.

Services, Staffing, and Quality

Several indirect measures can indicate that a hospital delivers quality care. Among these indicators are the types of nurses on staff and the kinds of services offered.

• *Nurses:* Generally, nurses are the only medical person-

JCAHO Check

You are entitled to know: the JCAHO accreditation for any hospital, when the commission last surveyed a facility, and when the next survey will occur. The hospital's director of quality assurance or quality management or another manager should be able to give you the information. If no one at the hospital will tell you, call the Joint Commission on Accreditation of Healthcare Organizations Service Center at (708)916-5800.

Call that same number if you wish to order the detailed JCAHO report on a hospital. Available as reports compiled after January 1, 1994. The cost is $30 per report. A summary volume will be available in 1995.

nel available to you immediately around the clock. And they're the ones most likely to be familiar with all aspects of your hospital care.

Registered nurses (RNs) have more medical education and training than licensed practical nurses (LPNs). Registered nurses can tailor and implement the plan of care prepared by your doctor.

The national average for hospitals is about four registered nurses to every licensed practical nurse. A higher proportion of registered nurses indicates that a hospital has a higher level of nursing expertise. Unfortunately, you'll have trouble getting statistics on nursing staffs. Ask the hospital or your state's affiliate of the American Nursing Association, or consult the American Hospital Association.

It's also important to learn about a hospital's nursing practice in general. For example, what are the overall staffing levels? Generally, one nurse can care for three to six patients. If a hospital has a higher average ratio of patients per nurse, seek an explanation. If the ratio is lower, the hos-

HOSPITALS CAN MAKE YOU SICK

By their very nature, hospitals are dangerous. They are occupied by sick people, many of whom have serious and unknown infectious illnesses. They are also filled with dangerous machinery. And healthcare personnel, even the best ones, practice a necessarily imperfect and imprecise science.

It should come as no surprise that about one in twenty U.S. patients get sick *from* their stay in a hospital. Known as iatrogenic illnesses (caused by physicians) and nocosomial infections (acquired in a hospital), these result from: infections that are carried by doctors, nurses, and others; from complications of surgery and other procedures; and from a wide variety of other sources, including, ironically, many of the technologies that save lives.

Hospital-acquired illnesses are a major concern for both patients and caregivers. About one-third to one-half of hospital-acquired infections are preventable or result from carelessness.

People with illnesses affecting their immune system—such as patients undergoing cancer treatment and those who rou-tinely take several medications—have a particularly high risk of acquiring a nocosomial infection. If you feel you may be at high risk, ask the hospital for details about its program of surveillance, prevention, and control of such illnesses. Is an infection-control practitioner on staff? If not, how does the hospital coordinate infection control? And don't hesitate to ask doctors, nurses, and other caregivers if they have washed their hands before examining or treating you.

pital's overall philosophy may be based on a commitment to patient-centered care (see below).

Perhaps the clearest indicator of nursing-care quality is organizational structure. Two methods of organization are common in nursing. With functional nursing, nurses are assigned particular tasks, such as medication, dressing changes, or clinical examinations. With primary nursing, the hospital assigns a nurse to be the main caregiver for each patient. Generally, the latter model results in better patient care. In addition, case management, a method of coordinating patient care that is compatible with either primary or functional nursing, can improve the quality of care.

• *Discharge Planning Services:* In addition to medical services, quality hospitals have a comprehensive set of discharge planning services, as well as handrails, walkers, and other equipment or appliances needed to assist in daily life. Discharge planning is especially helpful to people who continue to need care after leaving the hospital—an increasing proportion of patients with today's shorter hospital stays.

If you or someone in your family requires home-health care, rehabilitative care, long-term nursing care, or hospice care, for example, trained discharge planners can help you find and select these services. Preferably, planners are full-time hospital employees—typically nurses or licensed clinical social workers—whose job is to assess patient needs and to work with patients and their families, physicians, and insurance companies.

Find out ahead of time who does discharge planning for inpatients. A good hospital will start discharge planning when you enter the facility. This makes it easier to prepare for any possible access problems or a lack of caregiver support.

Patient-Centered Care: A Quality Perspective

More and more hospitals are instituting a *patient-centered* approach to quality, and patients are the beneficiaries.

Quantity Counts

An effective means of comparing the ability of two or more hospitals to treat your illness is to determine how often each hospital encounters it. In general, hospitals that perform more of a certain procedure tend to be safer. Ask your doctor or the hospital for the data. Your doctor will help you interpret it.

For more information on home care, turn to Chapter **13**

The elements of, and level of commitment to, this idea vary from hospital to hospital. According to the Picker/Commonwealth Program for Patient-Centered Care, look for a hospital that:

• *Respects Your Values, Preferences, and Expressed Needs:* Do caregivers consider your short-term and long-term goals? Do you decide what role you will play in decision making? Do caregivers ask what you need, want, and expect?

• *Coordinates Care and Integrates Services Within the Hospital:* Is your care from various providers effectively coordinated? Do you get consistent information from all providers?

• *Encourages Communication Between Patient and Providers:* Make sure you receive accurate, timely, and appropriate information. Expect caregivers to educate you about the long-term implications of disease and illness. Ask for the information you want about your health, diagnostic tests, and treatment options. Do you and your family know what you need to know to manage your care?

• *Enhances Your Physical Comfort:* The hospital staff should alleviate your pain as much as possible and provide

DEATH RATES AND QUALITY

The federal Health Care Financing Agency compiles mortality data—death rates—for U.S. hospitals. Unfortunately, these statistics are hard to interpret, particularly given the overwhelming number of variables involved. A high number could indicate a quality problem but may also indicate an excellent hospital that accepts the most complex cases or focuses on a very sick or elderly population.

Although *adjusted rates* can correct somewhat for the fact that some hospitals treat patients who are more frail or desperately ill, death-rate statistics mainly serve to help hospitals monitor their own quality. The federal government stopped publicizing the data in 1993.

Nevertheless, *U.S. News and World Report* uses mortality rates as one criterion in compiling an annual list of "America's Best Hospi-

tals." And the rates for 5,500 hospitals are available to the public in the *Consumer's Guide to Hospitals,* which advises readers to use them as a starting point, not as a definitive mark of hospital quality.

To order the Consumer's Guide to Hospitals, *contact the Center for the Study of Services, 733 15th St., NW, Washington, DC 20005 (800)475-7283. The cost is $12.*

the help you need with such regular activities as bathing and eating. Are limits on your ability to function adequately addressed?

• *Provides for Your Emotional Support and Alleviates Fears and Anxieties:* Do caregivers consider your concerns about your illness and its effect on your ability to care for yourself or your family? Do they consider the principal stresses in your life? Do they consider your concerns about paying medical bills or about lost income due to illness? Do you have access to appropriate support networks to help with these worries?

> **TIP**
>
> **First-Hand Look**
> *Take the time to visit hospitals you are considering to get information about the medical staff and to find out about the availability of services that may be important to you, such as chaplain services or women's health services. A visit will also give you a good sense of the hospital's atmosphere.*
>
> *Call the hospital and ask for the public relations or administrative office. Ask who to talk with. Arrange a time to visit.*

• *Involves Your Family and Friends:* The hospital staff should involve family and friends in planning and providing care. Do family and friends have the support they need to perform this function?

• *Provides for a Smooth Transition from One Location for Receiving Care to Another:* When you leave the hospital, you and your family must understand the medications to take, treatment regimens to follow, activities to pursue or avoid, and the danger signals that may arise. The hospital should make sure you receive plans for continuing care and treatment.

PART IV: MAKING A CHOICE

Quality is central to your choice of a hospital; it's a universal concern. But other factors depend on your personal preferences and needs. Do you prefer a hospital closer to home? A smaller one? One with a national reputation?

Overall, you want to find a hospital that provides the right *medical care* and a *caring atmosphere*. Both are critical to the outcome of your hospital visit.

The Best Hospital

There is no such thing as the "best hospital" for everyone, but in general better hospitals will have:

◆ Coordinated care among administrators, physicians, and support staff;

◆ Communication among staff from different departments;

◆ Family-centered, patient-centered care; *and*

◆ Comprehensive discharge planning on such matters as diet, medication, danger signals, and follow-up care.

For more information on criteria to consider when selecting a hospital, turn to Chapter **9**

Check the Services: High-Quality Care

Every hospital offers a distinct mix of services. For example, 93 percent of the community hospitals in the United States have emergency departments, but only 17 percent have open-heart facilities. At 19 percent of community hospitals, you can receive radiation therapy; 11 percent of community hospitals offer organ transplants. An impressive 85 percent have physical-therapy facilities, but for occupational therapy, the figure is 52 percent. Although only 17 percent have facilities for hospice care, 73 percent have high-tech CT scanners.

If you need, expect to need, or simply prefer to have on hand a particular type of service, talk with your primary-care provider or

> **T I P**
>
> **The Patient Handbook**
> *A hospital's patient handbook can answer many of your questions about the facility. If the hospital doesn't give you a copy when you come in, ask to see it.*

the admitting physician to make sure the hospital you select can provide what you are seeking. For example, if you want to give birth in a more home-like environment, seek hospitals with an "alternative birthing center" or similar facility.

Inquire about a hospital's ability to meet your particular needs, such as care for cancer, heart disease, or kidney disease: Does it have the services and specialties you need? Does it have experience with any conditions you or your family have now or anticipate in the future? What is its success rate with specific medical procedures? Think about your family's medical history and current health status.

In addition, ask if a hospital has:
- Education programs for patients and members of the community;
- Pre-admission testing services so you can obtain as much care as an outpatient as possible;
- Referral networks if you need to transfer to a more specialized facility;
- JCAHO accreditation;
- Staff trained and designated to prepare and manage your plan of care; *and*

- Staff trained and designated to prepare and manage your discharge plan.

Check the Services: The Caring Hospital

Your recovery depends on environmental factors as well as medical services. Is your hospital a *caring* institution?

A caring atmosphere is often as difficult to identify as high-quality care. Among other factors to consider, a hospital should offer emotional support to your friends and family if you are seriously ill. Obviously, the staff is key: Are they courteous, polite, and friendly toward patients and visitors? Do they answer questions, or are they rushed and distracted when you try to talk with them? It's hard to know about these matters before you enter the hospital, but if you experience problems while using the hospital, talk to your admitting physician.

You might be able to check ahead of time to determine if a hospital:

- Accommodates special diet requests;
- Allows your visitors to bring you food if your doctor approves;

> **T I P**
> **Quality Check**
> Does the hospital you are considering admit Medicare patients? If not, consult the state health department: the hospital may have been suspended for some reason.

- Sets liberal hours for when you can receive visitors and make phone calls;
- Has hospice services available;
- Provides accommodations for parents to spend the night with their children and for other out-of-town visitors;
- Allows patients to sit outside their rooms;
- Provides full information on patient's rights;
- Keeps waiting rooms and patients' rooms clean; *and*
- Has social workers available to help you access social, clinical, physical, and financial services.

Getting Recommendations

The phone book isn't a good place to start your search for a hospital. How you *do* start your search depends on the stage you have reached in your efforts to construct a personal health-care system for yourself and your family.

If you already have a primary-care provider, begin by discussing hospital options with him or her. Most primary-care providers are affiliated with one or more hospitals. Ask how each one excels or lags in general—and what that means for someone like you. In addition, your primary-care provider, whether a physician or someone else, can give you good advice on other hospitals, why you'd use them, and how you would be admitted should the need arise.

If you belong to a managed-care plan, also talk to administrators of the plan. Just as primary-care providers are affiliated with a limited number of hospitals, many health plans will send you to certain hospitals for certain conditions. Plan administrators should be able to provide you with information about the available options.

On the other hand, your search for information on hospitals could be one aspect of your efforts to select both a primary-care provider and a health-insurance plan. In this case:

> **T I P**
>
> **Special Needs Referrals**
>
> *If you have a special need, the appropriate organization can refer you to both local facilities and, for the most complex cases, nationally recognized facilities. For example, cancer patients may wish to contact the American Cancer Society.*

• Ask your employer's or union's benefits department for recommendations of good hospitals and for information about them.

• Consult any nurses you know. Hospital nurses have direct experience about such critical factors as the coordination of the care of each patient, the caring atmosphere, and staff satisfaction. One telling question to ask a nurse—or any other health-care provider—is whether she or he would send a family member to a particular hospital.

• Talk to friends, family, and colleagues about their experiences. Use the questions throughout this chapter to guide your conversation and look for the elements of hospital care most important to you and most relevant to your health-care needs.

The Amenities

Ambiance may not seem as important in a hospital as it is in a restaurant, but it may affect what you get out of your hospital visit nonetheless. Just as in a restaurant, you should place a higher value on a hospital in which the staff is pleasant, the food is edible—if not great—and the rooms are comfortable.

For more information on managed care and your choice of hospitals, turn to Chapter **3**

PART V: BUILDING A HEALTH CARE PARTNERSHIP

No one is as interested in the health of you and your family as you are. It is your responsibility to be informed, maintain records of your medical history, evaluate and select hospitals, and question your physician, nurse, and others about medical advice. Your doctor and the hospital's staff are professionals who want to do a good job. For them to do so, you have to play an active role in the treatment process by offering your opinions and asking questions.

> **TIP**
>
> **Alternative Admissions**
>
> *If you choose a hospital where your primary-care provider doesn't practice, you might need to find another physician to coordinate hospital care. Alternatively, a primary-care provider may refer you to a specialist who admits you to the hospital. In either case, you'll still want to keep your primary-care provider closely involved in your care.*

When a doctor recommends a hospitalization, whether for an inpatient stay or an outpatient visit, make sure you need to go to a hospital. If it's for a surgery, you'll often need a second opinion from another doctor. In fact, your insurer may require a second opinion to provide coverage.

Ask your physician:

- What is the diagnosis? What are the chances it might be wrong?
- Why does your condition require hospitalization? Can it be treated adequately without a hospital visit?
- What does the recommended treatment entail?
- What is recovery like? What can you expect? How long will it take?
- What level of equipment sophistication does it require?
- What happens if you postpone the hospital visit?
- If it's for surgery, are there nonsurgical alternatives? What are the pros and cons of other ways to treat the condition?
- Can you get the surgery or other service as an outpatient?
- Why does the physician recommend *this* hospital? Is it due to the complexity of the treatment, the special

equipment or personnel available, the convenience of the location?

- What are the risks or possible complications of the procedure? What is the chance that these will occur?
- What are the benefits? What is the chance of achieving them?

Your Role in the Partnership

Mutual and shared knowledge enhances the physician-patient relationship and improves the efficiency and effectiveness of medical care. To get the most out of your hospital visit, carefully evaluate why you are going. Review your symptoms and questions in advance, and make a list of questions or comments. This way, you won't forget to mention anything, and your physician is better able to focus the discussion, eliminate unnecessary tests, and provide you with better treatment.

Discuss any medical problems you have had in the past—the more specific the better. For example, it's better to tell caregivers you have a history of high blood pressure and had a small heart attack five years ago than to say you have heart problems. Still, give whatever information you have, even if you don't know details.

List your current drugs, including the exact name, the amount of medication in each pill, and the number of pills you take daily. Limited information—such as, "I take a green pill for my stomach once or twice a day"—is rarely sufficient. It's better to say, "I take Zantac for a peptic ulcer, 150 milligrams, twice a day." Know what allergies or reactions to medications you have had, specifying the name of the medication and the nature of your reaction—a rash, nausea, difficulty breathing, etc.

Look Who's Talking

If you have concerns about your medical care, *talk to your physician, your nurse, and other caregivers about them.* A major factor in the success or failure of medical care is your compliance with recommended treatments. If you aren't clear about—or disagree with—these recommendations, you can't comply well with the treatment and you lessen your chances of getting better. Don't be afraid to ask questions because you feel ignorant or don't want to waste a doctor's time. After all, you hire the doctor and the hospital, not the other way around.

TIP

Medication Alert

Find out as soon as possible which medicines are prescribed for you, why they were chosen, and when you should take them. That way, you can monitor your care, raise a warning flag in case of an error, keep records, and check the bills. Don't immediately swallow pills that a nurse brings you. First, confirm the name, dose, and purpose. Also, be sure to reemphasize the other medications you are already taking and ask about possible interactions with your new prescriptions.

Record any previous operations, including the reasons for the surgery, what was done, any complications, the name of your surgeon, the hospital, and the date. At any time, you can get a copy of the actual report on an operation by sending a written request to the hospital. This report can be very valuable to a new physician or hospital.

> **T I P — Ask a Nurse**
> Nurses are the true coordinators of your hospital medical care. Find out which nurse is assigned to you. She or he is central to your care in the hospital.

In the hospital, keep a careful record of your medical care. Try to keep track of any tests you receive, including X-rays, lab tests, EKGs, and so on. Make sure to request a copy of the test results; at times it's worthwhile to have actual copies of the X-ray films in your possession after you are discharged.

Before leaving the hospital after either an inpatient or outpatient visit, make sure you understand your physician's treatment plan:

> **T I P — Take Charge**
> Don't let medical personnel treat you like a child. They may have more medical training, but you are in charge of your own care. It's your body.

- What medications do you need?
- When and how should you take them?
- Should you change or stop your previous medications?
- What dietary and other restrictions should you observe?
- What additional procedures or tests will you need?
- What do you need to do to prepare for these tests and procedures?

The Hospital Records

Parallel to your own written notes, the hospital will maintain an official record of the care you receive. Many states guarantee your access to this medical record, although you may have to pay a fee to get a copy. And you may have to fight the hospital bureaucracy.

Patient medical records provide a considerable amount of detailed information about your stay in the hospital. Generally, they are in chronological order, beginning with a *medical history and physical* and ending with a *discharge*

> **Dear Diary**
> Try to write down all the care you receive *as you receive it.* A friend or family member can help with this. Record the dates you are in the hospital and the dates and nature of the services you receive, including tests, prescriptions, doctor visits, and so on.

summary that highlights your hospital stay and records your condition and status the day you leave the hospital. The middle part of the record contains the *orders* your physician gives to the hospital staff, notes on your day-to-day *progress,* the daily record of your *nursing care* and nurses' observation notes, your *test results* and finally, an *operative summary* if you have surgery.

Read the nurses' notes first. They are usually neat and easy to read and provide a highly detailed story of your hospital stay.

You may be hospitalized at the same facility several times over the years, and all of these encounters should be included in your total medical record. For this reason, specify the dates of the encounters you want to review when requesting access to your record. To speed up access, include your social-security number and date of birth.

If you move to another area, request a copy of your complete hospital medical record, as well as your family's physician records. Carry them with you to your new home. These are invaluable resources in your family's continuing medical care.

Patient Advocates

Hospitals often employ patient advocates to help you understand and deal with the hospital bureaucracy. They can help you understand how the hospital works and address minor problems you encounter during your hospital stay.

HOSPITALITY HOUSES

Friends and families are integral to health care. However, many patients must use hospitals outside their communities. For example, a person in need of major surgery may travel to a hospital far from home for a long period of time.

To meet the need for affordable lodging of patients' families and friends, *hospitality houses* are located near many hospitals around the country. For the most part, these are nonprofit organizations that offer a variety of services to families— overnight lodging, kitchen and laundry facilities, transportation, and children's playrooms. They generally offer a warm and supportive alternative to the isolation and expense of hotel rooms. The minimal charge for an overnight stay varies, and in many cases the services are free.

For more information and referrals to facilities in a particular location, call the National Association of Hospital Hospitality Houses (800)542-9730.

Families of seriously ill children can ask a hospital social worker if there's a Ronald McDonald House in the area, or look in the local phone book.

If you or someone in your family doesn't speak English fluently, access to a competent translator the moment you enter the hospital, preferably at no cost, may be an important consideration in selecting a facility.

In the past, hospitals and patients used anyone available as a translator: a family member, another patient, a random employee at the hospital. All of these choices are bad. For one thing, rarely will any of these people understand medical terminology in one, let alone two, languages. More important, none of them have training in a critical part of health care: respect for every patient's right to privacy and confidentiality. For example, a parent may hesitate to speak frankly if his or her child is the translator. Or an adult translator may censor the conversation between a child and a physician. The patient has to know the doctor heard everything he or she says, and vice versa.

More and more often, hospitals are training and enlisting translators for the languages they encounter most often. The key elements are training and 24-hour-a-day availability. If the patient wakes up in pain at 3 a.m., a translator must be available.

For emergencies, many hospitals subscribe to a telephone service that provides translators for 140 languages, available 24 hours a day. However, this is an expensive service. The charge is about $5 per minute. In contrast, interpreters charge $10-$16 per hour.

5

When Problems Arise

As a patient, you have a number of rights, many of which are supported by law. Others may come with your health plan. Others simply make sense.

As a hospital patient, you have the right to confidentiality and privacy. And no one can deny you care on the basis of race, sex, or religion.

You have the right to all the information you need to make decisions about your care. If you are an adult, only you can accept or refuse a treatment.

You have the right to refuse to be examined or treated by anyone, from an intern to the head of staff, and for any reason. You might want to ask how often a particular doctor has performed a given procedure, even if it's very basic. If an intern has never done a procedure before, you can refuse to be treated by that person or insist on close supervision.

Learn your rights. The hospital should provide you with a written statement describing them. Ask for the statement if the hospital doesn't offer it to you. Talk to your physician and insurer at once if the hospital doesn't make the statement available.

For more information on patient rights, including the hospital bill of rights, turn to Chapter **2**

Don't Be Dumped

Be wary of physicians or hospitals who want to discharge you too quickly.

Speak up if you don't think you're ready for discharge. Talk to the staff. They are responsible for your well-being, and they'll be questioned if you have to return to the hospital due to a premature discharge. And ask for home services, such as a visiting nurse, if you think they're needed.

If you are a Medicare patient, you have the right to appeal the hospital's decision. During the appeal, which usually takes a day or two, you can remain in the hospital.

The appeal steps are explained in the materials you receive when you enter the hospital. If you don't receive these, ask for them. Tell your doctor you want to appeal, and contact the state Peer Review Organization. Call (800)638-6833 to get the number of your state PRO.

If you have a complaint about the care you receive in a hospital, first talk with the staff concerned. Next check with the nurse you see most often or the head of your nursing unit. And consult your attending physician. If you can't resolve a complaint through the attending physician, try talking with the patient advocate, the director of quality, the chief of service, or the chief of staff. You may also need to find a personal advocate, whether it's a friend, a family member, or your primary-care provider.

As a last resort, you may decide to talk with your doctor about a transfer to another unit or another hospital. And you have the right to leave the hospital on your own at any time, even if it's against medical advice.

PART VI: MONEY MATTERS

While insurance may pay most of your hospital bill, you're often responsible for up to 20 percent of the bottom line. Thus, you have a strong incentive to keep that cost as low as possible while getting the best care. The prices a hospital charges for a particular service generally don't relate to the quality of care it delivers.

Before you are treated at the hospital, the admitting department will ask you for information about your health insurance and require someone to guarantee payment. However, if you have no insurance and can't pay for your hospital care, you may be entitled to free care:

• Each state has a Medicaid program that covers basic medical services for some low-income people.

• Most states also have other programs to provide free care to people who can't pay their bills. Ask the hospital about possible arrangements for free care. Speak with the hospital's social-services office or the admissions office.

Price Questions

One of the best ways to avoid a future misunderstanding about billing or payment is to educate yourself, before admission, on the intricacies of your family's health insurance. As you seek cost-effective health care, your insurer will play a major role, mostly on the side of saving itself money. Your interest differs: you want to get the best care possible—and you want the insurer to foot most or all of the bill.

As in many other situations, a little pre-planning can save lots of effort, pain, and confusion later. Take the time to investigate the following:

- Does the hospital that you'll use have a contract with your insurer? For example, HMOs typically pay the full amount of insurance only if you use participating or network hospitals.
- What copayments and deductibles are your responsibility?
- How long a stay is approved?
- If your insurance doesn't cover a private room, how much would an upgrade cost you?
- What does your insurance cover—and not cover?
- What happens if the hospital charges more for your projected care than your insurance considers reasonable?

Be aware that doctors' fees for hospital services are typically billed separately. Beforehand, ask your family physician what bills you'll receive from his or her office and what other physicians will provide medical services during your hospital stay. Then check with your employer or health insurer to determine if you are responsible for paying a portion of these bills. And once you get the bills, make sure you received all the services listed.

When you enter a hospital, a variety of factors affect the cost. Among the questions you can ask your physician in advance are:

What are the room charges? What is the price for a semiprivate room? For a bed in intensive care? What do these charges include, and what is billed separately?

What is the usual charge for my anticipated procedures?

Does the hospital have a payment counselor to help me arrange such things as installment payments?

For more information on hospitals and insurance, turn to Chapter 3

Registering a Complaint

If you feel you've received poor care or unfair treatment in a hospital, you can register a written complaint with a number of organizations either while you are in the hospital or afterwards. State your case as clearly as possible. Document it with information from your own record and the hospital's official record. If you don't have a copy, get one.

You can contact:

◆ The Joint Commission on Accreditation of Healthcare Organizations, 1 Renaissance Blvd., Oakbrook, IL 60181 (708)916-5800;

◆ The American Hospital Association, 840 N. Lake Shore Dr., Chicago, IL 60611 (312)280-6000;

◆ The state Peer Review Organization, if the problem concerns medical care, or the state Department of Public Health for non-medical care; *and*

◆ The state licensing agency for health-care facilities—usually this is in the department of health or the department of public health.

TIP — Advance Notice

If possible, either you or your doctor must tell your insurance company about a hospitalization in advance. Some policies require pre-authorization or the insurer will refuse to pay the bill.

Free Care

Most nonprofit hospitals are built with federal "Hill-Burton" funds. As a condition of receiving these funds, they must provide a limited amount of care to people who can't pay. For referrals to facilities that provide free or below-cost care for low-income people, call (800)638-0742 or, in Maryland, (800)492-0359.

Price Pointers

Ask a hospital for a written list of services and fees. Even though these rarely match the actual fees patients or insurers pay, the listed prices can help you decide among options, compare rates at hospitals, and check if your insurer will cover what you require.

At least 30 states monitor hospital charges. Check with the state health department to find out what agency is responsible. If there is such an agency, it can provide you with much of the cost information you seek. Otherwise, your best bet is to call the business office of the hospital.

The Hospital Bill

After you are treated, request a *detailed* bill that itemizes all the services you received. Simply reading it is a major challenge. Hospital bills are filled with obscure codes, seemingly meaningless abbreviations, and unending jargon. Just as annoying, it's impossible to predict what a given hospital will bill you for—a toothbrush, ambulance fees, phone calls, etc.

Moreover, besides the hospital bill, patients often receive bills directly from their own physicians—and from physicians they don't even know. These fees are usually legitimate, such as bills from the person who reads your X-rays. But you'll want to check.

 Negotiate a Payment Schedule
If you can't afford to pay your hospital bill all at once, talk to the billing department about a payment schedule. Most hospitals are happy to arrange monthly payments that you can afford.

On top of that, hospital bills contain a surprising number of errors. You'll have to wade through the details carefully, separating the legitimate charges from possible errors. For example, some services may appear twice under different names. If you find a mistake—such as a service you didn't receive—ask the billing department for an explanation and, if indicated, an adjustment. Many employers reward employees if they find a hospital billing error and secure an adjustment.

You do have several potential aides, allies, and teachers in this educational experience:

• Many states *require* hospitals to provide you with an itemized bill.

• Your physician and other health-care providers can help you decipher the language and check that you received all the care that is in the bill.

• Your insurer shares your concern that the bill is accurate.

• The staff of the billing office may try to clearly explain your bill. If so, ask particularly about charges labeled "miscellaneous."

When you receive the bill, review the dates of your stay to determine if they are correct. Don't pay for the last day if you left before the check-out time. And don't be charged for a private room if you used a semi-private room. In addition, consult your memory, the hospital's medical record, and your own written records of your hospital care to test the bill's accuracy. And get your doctor's advice as soon as possible. Examine the bill carefully to spot:

> **T I P**
> **Don't Pay Twice**
> *Occasionally, hospital staff lose or misplace records or test results. Don't pay for repeating the tests.*

- Tests and room supplies you didn't receive;
- Canceled tests;
- Treatments and special services you didn't receive;
- Double billing for a single service;
- Telephone charges you didn't make; *and*
- Charges for a higher class of service than you received.

If you were given a few days of a medication while in the hospital, the bill should only reflect that amount of the drug, not a full month's worth. In other words, does the bill cover only the medications you actually took? If the bill includes take-home prescriptions, make sure you got the medicine to take home.

> **T I P**
> **No Free Lunch**
> *Don't accept supplies you don't need—you may be billed for them. Bring items like a comb, a toothbrush, razors, shampoo, and a robe and slippers from home, or have a friend bring them. Similarly, make sure you aren't billed for buying a toothbrush, thermometer, or any other item the hospital didn't let you take home.*

If the billing department doesn't answer your questions to your satisfaction, you can contact the hospital's administration. You can also contact the state agency that licenses hospitals.

RESOURCES

Organizations

American Hospital Association
840 North Lake Shore Dr.
Chicago, IL 60611
(312)280-6000
The annual *AHA Guide to the Health Care Field* is available in libraries. It contains data on accreditation, approval for special facilities, medical-school affiliations, size, and major services. Call or write for an excellent consumer guide to hospitals and other publications.

Hill-Burton Hospital Free Care
(800)638-0742
Call for information on health facilities that participate in the Hill-Burton Hospital Free Care Program.

Joint Commission on Accreditation of Healthcare Organizations
1 Renaissance Blvd.
Oakbrook Terrace, IL 60181
To find out if a hospital is accredited, call the commission's service center at (708)916-5800. You can also ask for the hospital's accreditation history and the date of its most recent survey and the next one scheduled.

Shriner's Hospital Referral Line
(800)237-5055, (800)361-7256
Call for free referrals to Shriner's Hospitals for children under the age of 18 with orthopedic problems or burns.

Publications

The Best Hospitals in America, by Linda Sunshine and John Wright (Avon, 1987). $9.95.

The Best in Medicine: How and Where to Find the Best Health Care Available (Harmony Books, 1990).

Consumer's Guide to Hospitals, $12. Order from the Center for the Study of Services, 733 15th St., NW, Washington, DC 20005 (800)475-7283.

Take This Book To The Hospital With You, by Charles B. Inlander and Ed Weiner (Rodale Press/People's Medical Society, 1993). $14.95 ($12.95 to members of People's Medical Society).

6

Women As Health Care Consumers

By Martha Taggart

As women, we have reached a crossroads in our quest for good health care. At the start of the twentieth century, women were lucky to live through their childbearing years. Now many women live well into their ninth decade, thanks in part to antibiotics, birth control, and sterile medical procedures. We have also learned to speak up about the kind of health care we want—and good providers are listening.

Today, the health care you seek is consumer-oriented, women-centered, and based on a "wellness model" of staying healthy. You can reasonably expect health-care providers to view you as a whole person, not a sum of body parts or medical conditions.

PART I: THE HEALTH CARE RELATIONSHIP

Trust and mutual respect characterize good relationships with health-care providers. You want to be able to trust your providers to be open-minded, knowledgeable, competent, and responsible. And you want providers to respect *your* knowledge, welcoming the challenge an informed patient represents.

In general, strive to engage your providers in two very different modes:

• For *wellness counseling*, the ideal is a "health mentorship" with providers who educate you about your body, emphasize ways to prevent illness, and help you set independent health goals.

• *When your health is threatened*, you want a wise, reassuring presence. A good provider will believe what you say about your symptoms and investigate the causes by taking a medical history, conducting a physical exam, and drawing on his or her prior experience in treating you. He or she will present you with options for treatment and help *you* reach a decision based on the best information available.

Healthy or ill, exercise your right to ask questions, however complicated or prosaic, and insist on earnest and straightforward responses. And as you travel through the health-care system, demand respect for the time and knowledge *you* devote to your own health and to caring for others.

A good basis for judging your relationship with your provider comes from the steady contact required to stay in good health—things like physical exams and yearly Pap smears to screen for cervical cancer. Arrive at these tests with written notes on questions you'd like to ask, and listen carefully to the answers. Ideally, the physician or nurse will invite you to ask questions. If not, take the initiative and bring them up yourself.

Don't expect unlimited time, but insist that providers give you their complete attention. If someone cuts you off, gets impatient, or listens poorly, you can't form a real alliance or partnership. Nor will you be comfortable with a person who condescends to you or takes an oversimplified approach to your questions, opinions, and feelings. Your provider should take your concerns seriously and offer sympathy and support, as well as referrals to specialists when you ask for help with such problems as depression, substance abuse, and domestic abuse.

If you have trouble communicating with your current provider, you might want to consider these options:

> **TIP**
>
> **Trust Yourself**
> Avoid providers who try to intimidate you. Providers have medical knowledge and training on their side, but you know yourself.
>   You have the final say on any proposed treatment. Trust your instincts and be assertive about receiving the care you need.
>   On the other hand, don't let a good alliance with a provider lull you into complacency. If you're unsure of a particular recommendation or treatment, ask questions, research the topic yourself, and feel free to seek another opinion. You have a right to have questions, fears, and concerns about your health and your health care.

- Switch providers.
- Try to improve the relationship by becoming more outspoken and assertive about your health care. Perhaps take a list of your questions to your next appointment or bring someone along who can ask those questions for you.
- Redirect the relationship. If the provider's reputation or expertise impress you, you may want to see someone else in the practice or clinic with whom you can talk more directly, perhaps a nurse practitioner or a physician's assis-

Less Care?

Health-care providers often treat women much less aggressively than men. A study published in the *Annals of Internal Medicine* found that a man with an abnormal initial heart test is much more likely to get further treatment than is a woman: 62 percent of men had additional tests; only 38 percent of women received them. (Of course, *more* isn't always the same as *better*, even with health care.)

Women—and their health-care providers —must be committed to the concept of wellness.

First and foremost, schedule and keep regular appointments. Don't put off medical visits until you become ill.

Second, take responsibility. Do everything you can to maintain and improve your health. Wellness care focuses on what the patient does, not the clinician. Stop smoking, exercise regularly, lose weight if you need to, and deal with stress and emotional problems before they contribute to physical illness.

Finally, recognize that staying in good health doesn't mean no medical bills. If you can, spend the money that's necessary on things like routine physicals, Pap smears, and mammograms. Try to obtain health insurance that covers primary-preventive services or wellness care, but even if you pay the bills, prevention is the best value in health care.

tant. That way, the expert is available for consultation, yet you can form the partnership you want.

Continuity of Care

As consumers, you want health care that is ongoing and long term. Such "continuity of care" allows you and your providers to build a foundation of communication, familiarity, and trust.

Look for continuity of care in a number of ways. For example, do you get reminders for a follow-up Pap smear at a particular date? If you need a specialist, does your record from the primary-care provider reflect all necessary information, including your medical history and risk factors, test results, and prenatal courses? Many doctors complete a preprinted form that centralizes this vital information.

Office and computer systems that link information about you, your providers, and all your medical visits contribute to continuity of care. HMOs, women's clinics, and even hospitals and other acute-care settings can enhance continuity of care in a number of other ways as well—for example by using case managers, taking a team approach to caregiving, and encouraging frequent staff communication.

Counseling and Prevention

Avoiding health risks—smoking, poor nutrition, physical inactivity, other substance abuse, injuries, and so on— holds the greatest promise of improving your overall well-being. Even though it's important for doctors and other health-care providers to examine you regularly and screen for early disease, such conventional medical activities ultimately may prove of less value to you than counseling and education on what *you* can do for yourself.

You can gauge health-care providers on this measure. Does your doctor or nurse:

• Strive to develop a "therapeutic alliance" with you— that is, act as an expert consultant while recognizing that *you* control your own health-care choices?

• Counsel you in ways appropriate to your age, race, sex, income, and personality?

• Connect behavior and health by explaining the health risks of smoking, lack of exercise, poor nutrition, and other lifestyle factors?

• Work with you to develop and act on plans to foster healthy behavior?

PART II: HEALTH CARE PROVIDERS FOR WOMEN

Your options for a primary medical provider depend partly on your state of health and your age. For example, if you have a special health condition, such as diabetes, you may get regular care from a physician who can treat it and also take care of your routine health-care needs. That would probably be an internist. Or if you are nearing menopause, you may want to talk to your current primary-care provider about changing to or adding a gynecologist with specialized knowledge of reproductive hormones.

Women with relatively basic health-care needs can choose among several types of providers. Each has its own strengths and weaknesses. Bear in mind that any individual may be an exception to the rule.

6

CHECK YOUR INSURANCE PLAN

Your provider options relate closely to your health insurance. More and more plans rely on primary-care providers as gate-keepers and may or may not allow you to see an ob-gyn or other specialist for such routine care.

Also, don't take it on faith that your insurance policy offers "comprehensive" coverage. Read the fine print and consult your agent. Such benefits as maternity coverage may be available, but only for a surcharge.

You may also want coverage for:

◆ *Infertility Treatment:* In vitro fertilization, which usually requires two or more tries, can cost $4,000 to $11,000 per attempt;

◆ *Routine Pregnancy and Labor:* The cost is on the order of $5,000 for a normal delivery and $8,000 for a cesarean delivery;

◆ *Prenatal Diagnostic Testing:* If you're over 35, amniocentesis or another prenatal diagnostic test is recommended—these can run nearly $1,000;

◆ *Preventive Health Benefits:* Mammograms and Pap tests, for example, can be used for screening rather than diagnostic purposes;

◆ *Newborn Care;*

◆ *Well Baby Care:* Healthy babies require about six medical check-ups in the first year—with immunizations and testing, these can run over $100 apiece; *and*

◆ *Outpatient Mental Health Benefits.*

For more information on health plans, turn to Chapter 3.

Family Physicians

Family physicians train in several different fields that prepare them to deliver general medical and surgical care to people of all ages: internal medicine, pediatrics, ob/gyn, surgery, psychiatry and neurology, and public-health medicine. As such, family physicians are among the rare doctors with specific training in preventive medicine.

Their comprehensive training predisposes family physicians to treat the whole person, not just conditions and symptoms that relate to a narrow specialty. Another advantage for you is that taking care of the routine health needs of an entire family gives family physicians insight into individual and cumulative health problems, enhancing continuity of care.

Using one person for a wide range of services can be very convenient, lessening the time and expense of referral care. For example, it's hard to think of an obstetrician checking your hearing, even though these specialists are sometimes considered primary-care physicians. On the other hand, only about one-third of all family physicians perform obstetric care, and those that do may only be able to help you with routine needs. If your needs are more extensive, consider seeing an obstetrician or gynecologist in addition to a family physician. Or look for a family practitioner with special experience in women's health concerns. Particularly in smaller communities, family physicians provide a great deal of obstetric care: over two-thirds of the prenatal care providers in rural areas are family physicians.

Specialists in family medicine often profess that women are people first, and that much of medical care is asexual. Many women disagree and feel that medical care must take their gender and special needs into account. For example, the medical profession presumes standard treatments for substance abuse and heart disease to be effective in women because they work in men. This isn't necessarily true. Of course, this drawback isn't the fault of family physicians. And the growing numbers of women in the specialty (nearly 40 percent of all family physicians in training are women) could translate into more specialization in

Women's Health Specialty

The American Board of Medical Specialties doesn't recognize women's health as an "official" specialty in which physicians can acquire certification. Advocates for such a medical specialty argue that it would benefit women by creating a pool of experts who can treat most of women's health needs, emphasizing the whole person, not just the reproductive system. Training would cover internal medicine, gynecology, psychiatry, endocrinology, nutrition, orthopedics, and sports medicine, with obstetrics as an option.

Opponents of a women's health specialty argue that it would marginalize the care of women and maintain the mainstream focus on men. They propose that women's health be an integral part of the medical training for all physicians.

women's health in the future. Women now comprise 15 to 20 percent of practicing family physicians.

Obstetricians and Gynecologists ("Ob-Gyns")

Obstetricians and gynecologists treat only women. Physicians usually practice these closely related specialties together. The typical gynecologist has in-depth knowledge of the female reproductive system, urinary system, and endocrine system (which involves reproductive hormones), and a background in screening and treating cancers particular to women. Delivering babies is the province of obstetricians.

Ob-gyns are evolving from doctors who mainly deliver babies to providing lifelong care for women. Many in the specialty have even dropped obstetrics altogether in favor of general gynecology, some emphasizing adolescent gynecology, others treating primarily older women. Both are reasonable choices as primary-care providers for women in those age groups.

Of all physicians discussed here, ob-gyns most consistently ensure that women receive regular Pap smears and screening mammograms. And obstetricians *at their best* take to heart many of the

> **T I P**
> **Keep Track**
> *If you receive your regular medical care from an ob-gyn, keep track of whether he or she screens you for hypertension and cholesterol, asks about your moods, and broaches topics like diet, exercise, smoking, and alcohol use. If the ob-gyn doesn't, you may need to clarify your relationship or seek a provider trained in primary care.*

premises of primary-care practice, including an emphasis on wellness over disease and a low-tech, holistic approach that favors counseling and prevention over procedures.

However, the ambivalence and relative inexperience of many ob-gyns in treating other parts of the person—the heart and the emotions, for example—are probably their greatest drawback as primary-care providers. Even if you dutifully see an ob-gyn for a yearly Pap smear and pelvic and breast exams, don't assume you're getting primary care.

Collaborative Care

Many ob-gyns work collaboratively with nurse-midwives, nurse practitioners, physician assistants, or other non-physician providers. They often employ these caregivers in their private practices. As a result, you may benefit from more time with a provider and from the collective skills and experiences of more than one person.

Internists

Internists, or internal medicine specialists, are known as expert diagnosticians—the "Sherlock Holmeses" of medicine. They draw on training in microbiology, pharmacology, and chemistry and have studied all the body's organs. In situations in which other doctors might conduct tests or exploratory surgery to find out what's going on inside you, internists pride themselves on doing more thinking and less cutting or testing.

Because internists like to employ deductive reasoning, they often excel at cases that frustrate and puzzle other doctors by weighing a number of symptoms that might suggest different medical conditions—and determining their cause. They are also good at treating several health problems simultaneously, taking into account such factors as potential interactions among medications. Prescribing and adjusting drugs is another strength of internists and represents their primary means of treating patients. All this makes internists an excellent choice for women with complicated and chronic health problems, particularly ones that don't involve the reproductive tract.

> **T I P**
>
> **Internists and Tests**
> *If you are under the care of an internist for specific health problems, make sure you also get regular screening tests, including Pap tests, breast exams, and referrals for mammograms. These tests are especially important for older women.*

For women—and men—the internist's "high-powered" reasoning can be reassuring, as is their ability to integrate the diagnosis and management of different systems of the body. Within the field, your best choice is a general internist with a stated interest in health maintenance, preventive care, and women's health, unless you already have a serious health problem requiring a subspecialist.

Advanced Practice Nurses

Advanced practice nurses are gaining favor as an alternative to physician-centered health care for women. They have completed graduate-level education or are certified in a specialty. Their technical skills tend to equal those of physicians for the services they offer, and their fees are significantly lower.

Some advanced practice nurses practice independently or in conjunction with individual physicians. Most work in clinics, hospitals, and HMOs.

Three types of advanced practice nurse are of particular interest to women:

• *Nurse practitioners* (NPs) typically do almost everything physicians do: examine patients (including conducting gynecological and breast exams), take medical histories, diagnose and treat minor illnesses and injuries, order and interpret lab tests and X-rays, and counsel patients. They refer patients to physicians if more expert medical attention is required. Many states allow NPs to prescribe medications.

Nearly 50,000 NPs practice in the United States, many in such specialties as adult health, family health, gerontology, ob/gyn, and community health. The congressional Office of Technology Assessment has found that the quality of NP care is as good or better than physician primary health care—and that NPs may have better communication, counseling, and interviewing skills.

• *Clinical nurse specialists* (CNSs) are registered nurses with master's or doctoral degrees in specialized areas, such as mental health, maternal and child health, gerontology, cancer, diabetes, and cardiac care. About 58,000 are in practice—traditionally in hospitals but increasingly in HMOs and clinics, where they often provide mental-health services. A CNS can provide primary care and psychotherapy, conduct health assessments, and diagnose and treat illnesses.

• *Certified nurse-midwives* (CNMs) supervise labor, perform routine deliveries, and provide gynecological exams and prenatal and postpartum care. They deliver about 4 percent of babies in the United States.

If you prefer a natural birth, a CNM is an excellent choice. They are more apt to allow labor and delivery to progress naturally, with less use of electronic fetal monitoring and fewer procedures. CNMs attend births in all set-

Birth Centers

Birth centers provide maternity care for women at low risk for complications. According to a 1989 study published in the *New England Journal of Medicine*, they offer a safe and acceptable alternative to hospital confinement for most women. This is particularly true for centers that have links with high-tech facilities, such as hospitals, in the event of a complication.

Most states regulate birth centers, and most health insurance plans cover their services. Certified nurse midwives provide most of the delivery services, with on-call back-up from affiliated obstetricians and nearby hospitals.

tings—primarily in hospitals, with 11 percent in birth centers and 4 percent in homes. They usually collaborate with obstetricians to whom they refer patients with complications, but ask about this. And if you plan to deliver outside a hospital, find out how you will be transferred if an emergency arises.

CNMs are trained and practice according to guidelines set by the American College of Nurse-Midwives. They can practice legally in all 50 states. Lay midwifery, on the other hand, is illegal in most states. Insurance usually doesn't cover the services of lay midwives, although many plans now cover CNMs who are affiliated with an obstetrician.

PART III: SEARCHING FOR A PROVIDER

The successful health-care relationship depends largely on three factors: the qualifications of the provider, the quality of your personal interaction, and convenience. These will guide your search for a person who can respond to your health-care needs as a woman.

Of course, no selection process is foolproof in predicting your relationship with a particular provider. Still, you can proceed methodically:

DOUBLE COVERAGE

Does your doctor or nurse follow a standard set of guidelines for preventive screening and counseling? Keep track of whether you're getting the screening tests and counseling you need according to the established schedule. If you aren't, you're probably better off finding another provider.

Another possibility is to split your care between two providers—say a family physician and an ob-gyn. In a survey conducted by the Gallup Organization, three out of four women saw a gynecologist plus a second provider for non-gynecological health problems and routine checkups.

If you use two providers, clarify who is responsible for what. If something seems to be slipping through the cracks, bring it to the attention of both providers. And be sure they share all relevant information. You may have to facilitate this by getting copies of your records and taking them to each provider. Also, ask your insurance company which doctor needs to make referrals for specialist services.

1. List your needs and requirements in order of importance.
2. Begin your search.
3. Interview candidates.
4. Decide.

Step 1: List Your Needs and Requirements

What type of provider and what setting is best for you? List the factors that matter to you in order of importance: you undoubtedly will have to compromise on some items.

For many women, the top considerations are the provider's training, specialties, licenses and certification, and hospital privileges. Beyond that, a good match will probably be determined by whether your personalities are compatible.

Convenience factors are also important: Where is the practice located? Does it offer evening and weekend hours? Is free parking available? Do you want a female physician or nurse? Do you prefer an individual practice, a group, or a clinic? Do you want to see specialists who focus on women for all your health needs? Do you want a health-care provider who focuses on people of your age? Does your health plan allow you the option of seeing an ob-gyn as a primary-care provider?

Step 2: Begin Your Search

Create a list of providers who meet your criteria. To do this, you can:

- Seek referrals from pediatricians, nurses, and other health-care providers you know;
- Talk to friends and acquaintances about their care and their providers;
- Ask your last provider to recommend a person near your new home, if you recently moved;
- Contact local women's organizations and speak with a person involved in health-care issues;
- Ask women's health centers and Planned Parenthood clinics for referrals;

Women's Health Centers

The "women's health center" has joined the health-care scene, with more than 300 facilities across the country. A center may be a clinic or a group of programs for women. Most are attached to or affiliated with hospitals, but some are freestanding. Examples of the latter include family-planning clinics.

The focus of women's health centers varies from obstetrics and reproductive health care to a full range of primary-care and mental-health services. Advantages include convenience and continuity of care, with services from many different providers coordinated under one roof.

At their best, women's health centers empower women to become partners in their own care by offering educational programs and resource libraries in addition to counseling, screening, and diagnostic and treatment services. At their worst, they amount to a marketing ploy by some hospitals and other providers to attract more business.

In other words, apply the same standards, and ask the same questions, you would for any health-care provider.

- Check local newspapers and magazines for recent features on women's health care;
- Seek referrals from medical societies and other provider organizations;
- Consult the county medical society; *and*
- Contact other referral agencies.

Your choice of provider may seem unlimited at this point: keep your criteria in mind to narrow the field.

Next, pick up the phone. Introduce yourself and state that you're searching for a personal caregiver. At this point, a member of the office staff can probably answer some of your initial questions. Is the practice taking new patients? Mention your health insurance to get some indication of what it might cover for this doctor or nurse.

If you've gotten a green light so far, ask more questions. If the person at the other end of the line acts harried, ask if there's a better time to call or if someone from the practice can call you back. With luck, you'll soon speak to a nurse or office manager.

Start with open-ended questions. These encourage the person at the other end to give a full description rather than one-word answers. In general, seek:

• *Information About the Provider:* Ask the same questions you would of any prospective health-care provider. For example, what is the person's training and certification? Does he or she have any special interests in practice? Does his or her general philosophy about medical care include a strong role for you as a partner in your own health care?

If you are considering surgery, what types is the doctor qualified to perform? Has she or he had any special training, such as for infertility procedures? Does the doctor routinely counsel patients about diet, exercise, alcohol and drug use, and smoking? Does he or she deliver babies? Does the doctor perform abortions or sterilizations? Is the doctor willing to refer you to another provider if you wish an abortion or sterilization? How does her or his hysterectomy rate compare to the national average of about 6 per 1,000 women? How would he or she manage a problem such as abnormal uterine bleeding or uterine fibroids, two common reasons for performing hysterectomies?

• *Information About the Practice:* How many providers are in the practice? What are their specialties? If your own doctor were unavailable, would someone else in the practice see you? Does the practice offer educational materials for patients? Does the practice focus on patients like you with respect to such factors as age and sex?

What is the practice's philosophy regarding cesarean delivery, and does it have any policy for breech births or the delivery of twins? Are infertility patients treated or referred elsewhere? Do appointments tend to run on time, making working-day visits more feasible? Are test results delivered by phone? Are guidelines followed for preventive health screening—mammograms, Pap smears, and so on—and are reminders issued to patients?

T I P Dig a Little Deeper
Some practices will mail you an information brochure after you call. While this will help you narrow the field, it won't answer all your questions. Review it and call back.

For more information on what to ask primary-care providers, turn to Chapter 4

For information on what to ask medical specialists, turn to Chapter 9

Step 3: Interview Candidates

Say Doctor or Nurse X has the qualifications you seek, and the practice seems to offer the right features. It's time to meet. Ask whether the practice has a special way of handling the first appointment. Some doctors will set aside time to meet with prospective patients at no charge. If not, and if you're fairly confident this provider is for you, perhaps schedule a routine physical examination. This allows you and the provider to get to know one another while you're healthy. As an added benefit, you'll have time for the provider to take a thorough medical history, which is critical for establishing the relationship and forming a foundation for your ongoing care.

At this first meeting, determine the level of care the provider can offer. Will this be a primary-care provider? Will he or she handle your childbirth needs? Will he or she follow you beyond your reproductive years and into menopause?

Pursue any questions left unanswered in your initial

Hysterectomies

Hysterectomies are second only to cesarean sections as the most frequently performed major surgery in the United States. At least one in three American women eventually has the operation, usually in their 30s or 40s.

Hysterectomy rates across the country, and around the world, vary greatly, reflecting the inconsistency among doctors in recommending the procedure. Differences are due in part to practice styles and the way doctors are paid. Payment per surgery leads to higher rates compared to payment in a prepaid health plan.

Although some life-threatening diseases, including uterine and ovarian cancer, call for a hysterectomy, it's usually only one of the options for relieving pain, heavy bleeding, or certain other types of chronic discomfort. Ask your doctor about alternatives to the surgery, and gather as much information from an independent source as you can. And get a second opinion.

phone calls, and zero in on aspects of care that are important to you. If you're interested in stopping smoking, for example, ask if the provider has helped patients to do that successfully. Has he or she routinely cared for women with your needs? Had experience with treatments you're considering?

In general, get a sense of this person's practice style and experience. For example, you may want to know about his or her attitude toward cesarean sections and how often he or she delivers babies this way. And, if you've given birth by c-section previously, you may still want to explore the possibility of a vaginal birth for your next child. Ask if he or she believes in giving this a try. Be aware, however, that many providers resent such questions: you may decide to step carefully, while focusing on your need for information.

Similarly, discuss your concerns about both current and future needs, such as problems surrounding birth control and menstruation. You might also seek this

> **T I P**
>
> **Levels of Care**
> Women's health care, as provided by conventional medical specialties, is too often fragmented among a variety of caregivers, and some problems slip through the cracks. To keep that from happening, start by letting a provider know if you are interested in seeing her or him in a primary-care capacity, not just as a specialist. That is, will he or she take care of all your health needs? You want to be confident that he or she will comfortably assume this role.

person's views on a hysterectomy. Usually, practitioners who are overeager to perform this surgery will assure you it makes no difference—or even stands to improve your quality of life. Be wary if they don't also explain the drawbacks.

Ask about "on-call" schedules. This is particularly important if you're interviewing a physician or nurse midwife for childbirth. Are you apt to be delivered by someone else in the practice? At what point in your labor will the provider appear?

After this first meeting, you'll form an overall impression of the provider and the practice. Certain considerations will be more important to some individuals than to others. Consider the following as suggestions to guide your thinking:

• If your appointment included a physical exam, did you get a chance to meet the doctor or nurse before an assistant ushered you into an examining room and asked you to remove your clothes?

• If you declined to undress before meeting the doctor or nurse, was this request accepted and treated as normal?

• Did the doctor or nurse make eye contact? Did he or she ask permission before calling you by your first name?

• Did the doctor or nurse seem comfortable and take the time to answer your questions? If not, did he or she offer any explanation, such as a crisis with another patient?

• Did he or she volunteer information about his or her practice style or beliefs?

• Did he or she seem genuinely interested in you?

C-SECTIONS

What's the fuss about cesarean sections? Why does Public Citizen's Health Research Group term it "a national epidemic?" It's mainly because c-sections are the most frequently performed unnecessary surgery in the United States, exposing women to many health risks, often without any benefit. National rates rose from 5.5 percent of all births in 1974 to 24.7 percent in 1988. After much media attention and many research studies, rates have begun to fall slightly, although c-sections continue to be the most commonly performed major surgery in the United States.

The increased rates were due to advances in technology that enabled doctors to detect fetal problems more easily. In addition, fear of malpractice claims led obstetricians to perform c-sections when normal vaginal deliveries appeared difficult. The thinking—"once a c-section, always a c-section"—also added to the numbers, but that assumption has proven incorrect.

When looking for an obstetrician, the Health Research Group suggests you ask:

◆ Under what conditions would the doctor perform a c-section?

◆ Will you have a choice?

◆ What is the doctor's c-section rate? Ideally, doctors dealing with high-risk pregnancies should conduct c-sections in less than 17 percent of their cases, and doctors with low-risk practices should have rates under 10 percent. Try to avoid doctors with unexplained rates above the national average, about 23 percent.

◆ If you already had a baby delivered by c-section, would the doctor deliver one vaginally now? The answer may depend on the type of incision from the previous birth.

For more information, including the overall c-section rates for most states, see Unnecessary Cesarean Sections: Halting a National Epidemic, *by Ingrid Van Tuinen and Sidney M. Wolfe. To order a copy, contact the Health Research Group, Publications Department, 2000 P St., NW, Washington, DC 20036 (202)833-3000.*

Step 4: Make a Decision

You know the type of health-care relationship you seek. Is it possible with this individual? Trust your instincts to tell you yes or no.

If your answer is yes, nurture the relationship. Assert yourself and become an active partner in your care. If your instincts tell you no, continue the selection process with another candidate on your list.

A third option is to delay your decision, particularly if extenuating circumstances at the first appointment may have made it impossible to judge. You can wait and see how you feel after your *next* appointment. In the meantime, however, you risk continuing in the care of someone who may be unsuitable.

PART IV: ADDRESSING WOMEN'S HEALTH CONCERNS

Most women are cared for by several providers—simultaneously or sequentially—over the course of their lives. Rarely will any one of them see that a woman gets *all* the counseling, tests, and procedures she needs at any given moment, let alone throughout her life. As a result, many vital aspects of preventive care—referral for mammograms, for example—tend to slip through the cracks.

These gaps in continuity of care are narrowing. Within the past five years, all the specialty groups representing physicians who traditionally have provided women's health care have issued lifelong health-screening guidelines for women. These include the American College of Obstetricians and Gynecologists, the American College of Physicians (representing internists), and the American Academy of Family Physicians.

It takes time for recommendations to filter down from professional organizations to individual practices, however. This makes the partnership approach to care all the more essential. Women must actively question their providers to ensure that nothing is overlooked.

Start by learning about your own health. Don't be put off by thinking that the task is too difficult or the informa-

The Difference

In a 1993 Commonwealth Fund study, dissatisfaction led two in five women to change physicians at some point. One in four men did so. A third of the women cited communication problems as the leading reason.

Health-care providers are more apt to condescend to women than to men. One in four women—versus one in eight men—said the physician talked down to her or treated her like a child. The physicians told 17 percent of women that a medical condition was "all in their head." Only 7 percent of men were insulted in this way.

tion too complicated. A foray through your local library or the health section of any bookstore can fill your arms with excellent books, some of which are listed at the end of this chapter. Once you begin your research, you will realize how satisfying and empowering it is to have direct access to such information.

The pages ahead will introduce you to a few of the major health challenges facing women at different stages in their lives. These are the concerns you and your health-care providers will address and keep in mind.

Young Womanhood: The Teen Years

Parents should steer teenage daughters toward lasting, one-on-one relationships with providers. As a parent, encourage your daughter to speak openly about her health concerns, and even to rehearse or write down questions. And it's best if the mother and father aren't always in the examining room.

Puberty, which in adolescent girls usually arrives between 10 and 14 years, is an especially critical time for individualized health counseling. Early maturing girls are

BATTERING AND ABUSE

Women are frequently the target of physical violence, often within the home. An estimated one-fourth of all American women have suffered physical abuse from an intimate partner at some time.

A doctor's office or clinic represents one of the few safe havens an abused woman can turn to when she is cut off from the rest of the world. All health-care providers should respect your confidentiality and do nothing to jeopardize your safety. For example, make sure they hold all discussions about abuse

out of earshot of your partner.

Good caregivers are alert to bruises and other signs of unexplained injury and emotional distress. While not apt to intervene directly, they may gently question you about the nature of the abuse, refer you to sources of help in the community, and assist you in formulating a plan to leave the abusive relationship.

The consequences can be devastating if you don't seek help. Abuse travels through generations. An abused child is much more

likely to be part of a violent family in the future, in part due to impaired self-esteem and difficulty in managing anger and forming intimate relationships. Treatment involves the whole family, working for at least 18 months with teams of professionals—psychologists, social workers, nurses, school officials, law-enforcement officials, and community agencies.

Health-care providers may be legally required to report cases of child abuse to authorities. Women are the perpetrators of child abuse just as often as men.

most at risk for a number of problems, including the early onset of sexual activity, poor body image, and depression.

Health-care providers can help parents discuss menarche and puberty in advance to prepare a girl for the physical and emotional changes that are in store for her. If you think your daughter may become sexually active soon, explain her contraceptive options and provide information about how she can protect herself from sexually transmitted diseases. Even if her health-care provider handles this topic, it's essential for her parents to be involved and supportive.

Too few youngsters get the mental-health counseling they need. You want your daughter's health-care providers to address risk-taking behaviors related to the major causes of death and injury among young women—motor-vehicle accidents, homicide, and suicide. Risk taking and impulsiveness may be linked to depression or a lack of self esteem, and alcohol or drug use makes such behaviors even deadlier.

Preventive health care can yield lifelong benefits in many areas. It can help keep young women from smoking, which they are more likely to do than their male peers—or any other sex/age group. Also, the link between sexually transmitted diseases and subsequent infertility, as well as a possible link with gynecological cancers, should be explained, as should the importance of avoiding sun exposure because of the link between ultraviolet radiation and skin cancer.

During adolescence, many young women begin to feel that they have outgrown the "baby doctors" of their childhood, and it's time for their first visit with a gynecologist. The proper time is age 18 at the latest, and earlier if a young woman is or expects to become sexually active.

One of the most significant goals of this first visit is to serve as an "ice breaker" between a young woman and the gynecologist who could meet many of her health needs for years to come. Parents and health-care providers should encourage the young woman to speak candidly, be it about her sexuality, body image, eating habits, health fears, or complexion.

Teenagers and Privacy

Adolescent patients deserve the same confidentiality that protects the adult physician-patient relationship. Anything less is unacceptable. The earlier a young woman can discuss her health concerns and learn responsible behavior, the better she can protect her health and well-being in the years to come.

Early Adulthood

A woman's 20s and 30s are her reproductive years. Not every woman gives birth, but the ebb and flow of reproductive hormones, particularly estrogen, have a great impact on health at this time.

While the leading cause of death in early adulthood is still motor-vehicle accidents, by this age you and your health-care providers will watch for signs of heart disease, AIDS, stroke, and breast and uterine cancer, all of which are among the top ten mortality risks for women.

Now is the time to take steps to prevent many diseases that can appear later in life. Osteoporosis, a weakening of the bones that makes a person more prone to fractures and other ailments, afflicts 50 percent of women over age 45 and 90 percent of women over the age of 75. A good health-care provider will recommend simple preventive health strategies for these conditions: exercise, diet, and screening for risk factors.

Another issue at this time of life is control of fertility. Women who desire children later can combine contraception with barrier methods to protect their fertility from the onslaught of sexually transmitted diseases. These increase the risk of gynecological cancers and worsen opportunistic

Stop Smoking

Perhaps the single most important thing you can do to protect your health now and in the future is to stop smoking. This reduces cardiovascular and cancer risks—not just for lung cancer, but also for cervical and breast cancer—and helps prevent pregnancy complications. Your provider should counsel you and help you to quit, referring you for treatment again and again, if necessary.

IF YOU THINK YOU'RE INFERTILE

Perhaps 15 percent of couples don't conceive after 12 months of trying, which is considered the signpost for when it's time to seek help.

Help begins with a basic work-up for both the man and the woman. It determines such things as whether the woman is ovulating and whether she might be producing antibodies to her partner's sperm, as well as whether

the man's sperm count is high enough. The woman may then be checked to find out if her fallopian tubes are scarred or blocked. Depending on the cause of the problem, solutions may consist of artificial insemination, drugs to induce ovulation, or altering the technique, timing, or position of intercourse.

In vitro fertilization is also a possible solution, but it's expensive—at least

$4,000 per attempt—and succeeds only about 14 percent of the time. Usually a couple must be committed to several tries. Be sure you're in the hands of a qualified clinic or provider.

For more information, contact Resolve or the American Society for Reproductive Medicine, both listed at the end of this chapter.

For more information on childbirth, turn to Chapter **7**

infections associated with AIDS. Infertility can also be caused by endometriosis, a disorder in which uterine-like tissue grows outside the uterus. Particularly because women today are attempting to have babies at a later age, when they are less fertile, infertility is sometimes called the disease of the modern age.

Middle Age

Middle age is said to begin in the years surrounding menopause, which for most women occurs around age 50. These years are a window through which you can view the last third of your life. If you take the right steps, you can enjoy those years in relative health and vitality.

During middle age, the risk of most gynecological cancers, as well as colorectal and breast cancer, grows. Once women's ovaries cease to function and estrogen levels in the blood fall, women begin to develop heart disease in proportions equal to men, albeit somewhat delayed. Heart disease is by far the leading cause of death for women in their mid-60s and upward, and even premenopausal women have the same chance of dying from heart disease as they do from breast cancer. The loss of estrogen also leads to the threat of osteoporosis.

Women at heightened risk of either heart disease or osteoporosis may face a decision about hormone replacement therapy (HRT). Estrogen circulating in the systems of reproductive-aged women appears to protect against the development of heart disease until some time after menopause. Women who undergo HRT after menopause have half the rate of fatal heart attacks as those not undergoing HRT. Estrogen also protects against osteo-

THE COST OF SERVICES: TYPICAL CHARGES		
	Mammogram	Gynecological Exam and Pap Smear
National Average	$123	$110
Boston	$131	$157
New York	$150	$264
Washington	$146	$268
Phoenix	$126	$114
Source: Medirisk, Inc.		

porosis and alleviates unpleasant symptoms of menopause—which is most often why women opt for HRT in the first place.

Despite these advantages, only about 15 percent of postmenopausal women take estrogen in the United States. This is due to fears about a slightly increased risk of breast cancer and a six-fold increase in the risk of endometrial cancer. To protect against cancer, progestin is added routinely to estrogen preparations for HRT, but the therapy remains a source of controversy.

If you are a postmenopausal woman, particularly if you have highly elevated cholesterol or a family history of heart disease, the benefits of estrogen use may outweigh the risks. If you elect to undergo HRT, make sure you're in the care of a physician who has extensive experience managing this therapy.

Old Age

Optimistically, you will be in good shape when old age arrives, but no one can postpone health problems forever. Anticipate your health needs before they arise.

A very real threat facing older women is widowhood. The loss of a spouse, partners, relatives, and friends can cause loneliness and isolation. Physicians caring for older women should be alert for normal and abnormal grieving.

The loss of friends and family members may also lead older people to place more trust in health-care providers. They could be reluctant to second guess them because they

High Consumption

At all ages, women make one-quarter more visits to physicians than men. Women 65 years and older see physicians the most, averaging 8.8 visits per year, versus 6.1 visits for reproductive-aged women.

Ironically, more visits don't necessarily mean better care. Older women are most apt to go without preventive services.

HORMONE DEBATE

Health professionals disagree about the use of combined hormone replacement therapy for relieving menopause symptoms. Some people object to the use of drugs to manage a natural occurrence in women's lives. Also, HRT isn't for everyone, and it may be 25 years before researchers know the long-term effects of the combined therapy.

There are alternatives that also help reduce the risk of heart disease and bone fractures for postmenopausal women, such as moderate exercise and quitting smoking. Explore the risks, benefits, and alternatives to HRT. *For more information, call the National Women's Health Network Clearinghouse at (202)628-7814.*

fear rocking the boat or severing that tie. As a good health-care consumer, you'll do just the opposite. Ask many questions. Older women are underscreened and undertreated for cancer and other major health problems, including urinary incontinence, osteoporosis, and heart disease.

Urinary incontinence is too often tolerated in old age, despite the fact that health-care providers can treat it. More older women might talk to their doctors about this condition if they knew that incontinence makes it more likely a nursing home will appear necessary. An estimated half of individuals experiencing urinary incontinence don't get

THE IMPORTANCE OF MAMMOGRAMS

The Jacobs Institute of Women's Health asked American women why they get screening mammograms less often than they should. The most frequent reason: their doctors had never recommended it! Second was the erroneous assumption that if no breast cancer existed in their family, they were not at risk.

All women run the risk of breast cancer as they grow older. One out of every nine U.S. women will develop it. In four out of five cases, age is the only known risk factor.

Most breast cancer can be treated successfully if discovered early enough. Mammograms detect breast lumps when they are mere specks on film—up to two years before they can be felt by hand.

Soon, minimum federal standards will apply to all mammography facilities. It will take some time for

them to become accredited, however. Until then, the local American Cancer Society branch can refer you to an accredited facility and give you information about average costs. Also, check if a facility has accreditation from the American College of Radiology. This is voluntary: a high-quality facility may not seek it, but it's a sign of quality for those that choose to be accredited.

When choosing a mammography facility, consider quality and cost. The cost of a screening mammogram ranges from $50 to $200. Facilities doing the highest volume usually offer the best quality at the lowest price.

Get referrals for mammograms from your physician or call a local hospital. And check under what conditions your insurance policy will cover mammograms.

When you call around

for an appointment, ask:

◆ *Is the X-ray equipment designed specifically for mammography?* "Dedicated" mammography machines provide higher quality.

◆ *Are the technicians trained in mammography and certified by the American Board of Radiology?*

◆ *How many mammograms does the radiologist read in a week?* They should read at least 10 a week to be skilled enough to identify the signs of a cancerous tumor.

◆ *How often is the mammography machine calibrated?* It should be tested for correct measurements and radiation doses at least once a year.

If a facility can't answer these questions to your satisfaction, go elsewhere.

If possible, ask that two radiologists from the same center look at your X-ray. They are more likely to spot a cancer.

REMEMBER THE GUIDELINES

Older women should stick to cancer screening guidelines and have regular Pap smears and mammograms. Unfortunately, about half of women over 65 don't do so. As a result, a disproportionate amount of cancer is detected at advanced stages in older women. As one example, women over 65 years comprise 20 percent of all U.S. women but 41 percent of the mortality from invasive cervical cancer.

Along with insufficient screening for early detection, some health-care providers are reluctant to treat even early cancers aggressively in older women because of fears of age-related complications. These fears are probably unwarranted. When older women receive hysterectomies for early cervical cancer, their survival rate is comparable to that of younger women.

Medicare pays for women over 65 to have one mammogram every two years. Unfortunately, few women know this. Just as dangerous, many women believe that their risk of getting breast cancer decreases as they get older. In fact, cases peak up to about age 75.

---

appropriate care. The actual treatment approach depends upon the cause of the problem and varies from surgery to drug therapy to biofeedback.

At any time in your life, make sure that your providers justify the trust you place in them—that you base your trust on good care and not merely on familiarity. As you age, your health-care needs grow. Keep a sharp eye on your health-care providers—and find new ones if your current providers seem indifferent or reluctant to treat you.

For more information on biofeedback, turn to Chapter **9**

For more information on the health concerns of elders, turn to Chapter **8**

RESOURCES

Organizations

American College of Nurse-Midwives
818 Connecticut Ave., NW
Washington, DC 20006
(202)728-9860
Call for their directory of nurse-midwife practices and to get help locating a certified nurse midwife in your community.

American College of Obstetricians and Gynecologists
409 12th St., SW
Washington, DC 20024-2188
(800)673-8444
(202)638-5577
Call or write for information and literature on women's health.

American Society for Reproductive Medicine
1209 Montgomery Highway
Birmingham, AL 35216-2809
(205)978-5000
Call or write for information on a variety of reproductive health matters, including in vitro fertilization and other reproductive technologies.

Boston Women's Health Book Collective
240A Elm St.
Somerville, MA 02144
(617)625-0271
Fax questions to: (617)625-0294
Contact the Women's Health Information Line with questions. Ask for a literature list of useful health

books, packets of information, and referrals to local self-help groups.

FDA Breast Implant Information Line
(800)638-6725; (301)881-0256 in Maryland
Call to report problems or to get updated information about breast implants.

HERS Foundation (Hysterectomy Educational Resources and Services)
422 Bryn Mawr Ave.
Bala Cynwyd, PA 19004
(215)667-7757
Call or write for free telephone counseling, referrals, and a list of publications. A quarterly newsletter

is available for $20 per year, and a free lending library of books, audio tapes, and video tapes circulates by mail.

Susan G. Komen Breast Cancer Foundation
(800)IM-AWARE
Call for information on breast health and breast cancer.

National Abortion Federation Hotline
(800)772-9100
Call for facts about abortion and referrals to member clinics.

National CDC/STD Hotline (Sexually Transmitted Diseases)
(800)227-8922
Call for information on sexually transmitted diseases, as well as for local and national referrals.

National Women's Health Network
514 10th St., NW
Washington, DC 20004
(202)347-1140
This national public-interest membership organization provides free or low-cost information on a wide variety of topics in women's health. Call or write for information and a publications list.

National Women's Health Resource Center
2440 M St., NW
Washington, DC 20037
(202)293-6045
Call or write for a publications list and referrals to physicians and self-help groups. A one-year subscription to the "National Women's Health Report" is $25.

Planned Parenthood Federation of America
810 7th Ave.
New York, NY 10019
(800)829-7732
(212)541-7800
Call or write for information on family-planning issues and referrals to local Planned Parenthood clinics.

Resolve, Inc.
1310 Broadway
Somerville, MA 02144-1731
Helpline: (617)623-0744
Call for information on infertility and referrals to physicians, IVF clinics, local chapters, and support groups.

Women's Cancer Resource Center
3023 Shattuck Ave.
Berkeley, CA 94705
(510)548-9272
A hotline offers information and referrals on specific types of cancer, support groups, and mainstream and alternative treatments. Volunteer lawyers offer workshops, free consultations, and referrals. Also, call or write for information on receiving a newsletter and a wide variety of educational resources.

WMM—Women: Midlife and Menopause
7337 Morrison Dr.
Greenbelt, MD 20770
This mutual-help group offers information, referrals, and help in starting local groups. Send $5 for a materials packet.

Y-Me National Association for Breast Cancer
(800)221-2141 or (708)799-8228
Call for information, support, counseling, and advocacy.

Publications

The Black Women's Health Book: Speaking for Ourselves, edited by Evelyn C. White (Seal Press, 1994). $14.95.

Dr. Susan Love's Breast Book, by Susan M. Love, with Karen Lindsey (Addison-Wesley, 1990). $13.95.

Harvard Women's Health Watch. Monthly newsletter from Harvard Medical School, $24 for an annual subscription. Call (800)829-5921 or write to P.O. Box 420235, Palm Coast, FL 32142.

Men, Women, and Infertility: Intervention and Treatment Strategies, by Aline P. Zoldbrod (Lexington Books, 1993). $29.95.

The Menopause Self Help Book: A Woman's Guide to Feeling Wonderful for the Second Half of Her Life, by Susan M. Lark. (Celestial Arts, 1990, P.O. Box 7327, Berkeley, CA 94707).

The New Our Bodies, Ourselves, by the Boston Women's Health Book Collective (Simon & Schuster, 1992). $20.00.

The New Ourselves, Growing Older: Women Aging with Knowledge and Power, by Paula B. Doress-Worters and Diana Laskin Siegal with the Boston Women's Health Book Collective (Touchstone Books, 1994). $18.00.

Planning for Pregnancy, Birth, and Beyond, by Harrison C. Visscher and Rebecca D. Rinehart. (American College of Obstetricians and Gynecologists, 1990).

Take This Book to the Gynecologist With You, by Gale Maleskey and Charles B. Inlander (Addison-Wesley, 1991) and *Take This Book to the Obstetrician With You,* by Karla Morales and Charles B. Inlander (Addison-Wesley, 1991). Each book is $9.95 and can be ordered from People's Medical Society, 462 Walnut St., Allentown, PA 18102 (800)624-8773.

Trusting Ourselves: The Complete Guide to Emotional Well-Being for Women, by Karen Johnson (Atlantic Monthly Press, 1991). Mental self-help from a feminist and historical perspective.

Women and Doctors, by John M. Smith (Atlantic Monthly Press, 1992). $20.95

Women's Health Alert, by Sidney M. Wolfe (Addison-Wesley, 1991). $7.95. Send check or money order to Public Citizen Books, 2000 P St., NW, Washington, DC 20036.

Parents As Health Care Consumers

By Nora Wells

What Matters

The potential to build a lasting relationship with your child's health-care provider may be more important to you if you plan to see the provider often, over a long period of time. This is the case with a primary-care provider or with a specialist for a chronic problem. This issue may be less significant if you plan to see the provider only once or a few times.

Of course, high quality and mutual respect are always critical.

As a parent, you make many major decisions in the life of your child. No choices you make matter more than those surrounding his or her health care. You are responsible for deciding when to seek medical care, and you choose the people who are best qualified to provide it.

As you take these steps, you also serve as a role model for your daughters and sons. With your help—and that of their health-care providers—your children will prepare to take over their own care and decision-making responsibilities as they reach adolescence.

PART I: PRIMARY CARE

The first important decision you must make is the choice of a primary-care provider for your child. This is the all-important person who will:

- Provide "well-child" care—that is, the preventive measures you, your child, and health-care professionals take to keep your child healthy;
- Maintain basic medical records on your child;
- Treat your child when he or she is sick;
- Refer your child to specialists if needed;
- Give you medical advice on caring for your child; *and*
- Work with you to monitor your child's growth and development.

Guidelines for Parents

For a free copy of the pamphlet "You and Your Pediatrician: Guidelines for Parents," send a stamped, self-addressed envelope to the American Academy of Pediatrics, Department C, P.O. Box 927, Elk Grove Village, IL 60009.

Providers of Primary Care for Children

Every child needs a primary-care provider from the day he or she is born. Parents can get this basic, ongoing care for their children from many kinds of providers. Depending on where you live, certain types may be more plentiful than others:

Pediatricians are medical doctors who specialize in the care of children.

Nora Wells is the parent of sons ages 22, 18, and 12, one of whom has cerebral palsy. She has been active in parent advocacy activities for the past 20 years at both the state and national levels. She is one of the authors of Paying the Bills: Tips for Families on Financing Health Care for Children with Special Needs.

Family practitioners are medical doctors with special training to care for all members of a family, including children.

Nurse practitioners are nurses who are trained to assist doctors; they can also perform a number of well-child and other routine procedures.

Choosing a Provider for Primary Care

In many cases, a pivotal factor in the choice of a child's primary-care provider is your family's medical payment plan. Traditional indemnity insurance, if it covers primary care, usually allows you to choose any board-certified physician. However, more and more families now participate in managed-care plans, such as HMOs. Managed-care plans almost always include primary care, but you usually must choose from plan-affiliated providers. Sometimes you have many choices of providers; sometimes you're limited to the physicians at a center near your home. In either case, it's up to you whether everyone in your family will share the same primary-care provider, or whether you will each see a different person.

Tap into a variety of sources of information to find the primary-care provider who suits your needs.

Word of mouth is one excellent source: Talk to your family and friends. Who do their children use? What do your friends like—or dislike—about these providers? Ask your own doctor for a recommendation. Seek referrals from local child agencies, such as day-care centers, pre-schools, schools, and early-intervention programs.

If your child has special needs, ask specific questions about a potential provider's experience with your child's condition. For example, if your child has respiratory problems, you might want to know how much of the responsibility for chronic care the primary-care provider feels comfortable taking on. Are there other children in the practice with similar special needs? What specialists, agencies, and hospitals does the provider work with on a regular basis? How will you decide together to handle emergencies?

School Based Adolescent Care

More and more adolescents can now get health services through their schools. The schools help health-care providers reach this group, which is often medically underserved.

School-based centers make use of multidisciplinary teams—nurse practitioners, physicians, social workers, nurses, and health educators—to provide comprehensive care to adolescents, including on-site appointments, referrals, and follow-up.

Primary Dental Care for Children

Just as several types of professionals handle medical care for your children, there are a variety of choices when it comes to their routine dental care as well:

◆ *Pediatric dentists* specialize in the care of children;

◆ *General dentists* treat both children and adults; *and*

◆ *Orthodontists* specialize in straightening teeth for both children and adults.

For more information on dental care, turn to Chapter ▼**14**

For more information on choosing a primary-care provider and questions to ask, turn to Chapter ▼**4**

The Factors to Consider

When you meet potential providers, weigh all of the criteria that are important to you. Remember, no one provider is perfect in every way. Only you can evaluate the importance of each factor.

Think about personality and style. Do you approve of the way the provider interacts with children and parents? Do you think his or her style fits the needs of you and your child? Does she or he support the right of families to be with their child for procedures and treatments? Does he or she believe in sharing all information with patients?

Keep in mind a number of other points as well:

• How important is location? Can you get to the office or health center quickly if your child has an emergency? Is there a beeper number you can call? An answering service? How quickly does the doctor respond when a parent calls about a sick child? Is there a phone number you can call for routine questions?

• How do you get an appointment if your child is sick? Is this a group practice, with providers covering one another's patients when they aren't available themselves?

• Are the office hours convenient for your child's regular appointments? If you work days or your child is school-age, can you readily arrange evening or weekend appointments?

• Do you find it easy to communicate with the provider and to ask questions? Just as important, does your child?

Priority One: Immunizations

To keep your children healthy, make sure they receive all of their immunizations at the recommended times.

It's remarkable how many families don't take this simple step in primary care. A study published in the *New England Journal of Medicine* looked at the vaccination records of the children of 1,500 adults

T I P Cheap Shots

Your medical insurance may not cover all your child's immunizations, or you may not have insurance. In most cases, you can get immunizations free or at a low cost through your local health department. If you do, keep a written report of the shots as part of your child's complete health-care record.

with health insurance. Only 55.3 percent of the children had received all recommended vaccines by the age of 6. The biggest obstacle: the parents couldn't take time away from work to get to a physician.

The American Academy of Pediatrics suggests this immunization schedule:

Age	Routine Vaccine
Birth	Hepatitis B
1 to 2 months	Hepatitis B
2 months	Diphtheria/tetanus/pertussis Polio Hemophilus influenza B
4 months	Diphtheria/tetanus/pertussis Polio Hemophilus influenza B
6 months	Diphtheria/tetanus/pertussis
6 to 18 months	Hemophilus influenza B Polio Hepatitis B
12 to 15 months	Hemophilus influenza B Measles/mumps/rubella
15 to 18 months	Diphtheria/tetanus/pertussis
4 to 6 years	Diphtheria/tetanus/pertussis Polio
11 to 12 years	Measles/mumps/rubella
14 to 16 years	Diphtheria/tetanus

PART II: SPECIALISTS FOR CHILDREN

At times, your child may require a specialist to diagnose or treat a specific problem or condition. Your primary-care provider will refer you to specialists. His or her office may either make appointments for you or give you the names and numbers of the specialists. Many primary-care providers work regularly with certain specialists to whom they refer patients when necessary.

Large hospitals and specialized children's hospitals have pediatric specialists in many departments. In some managed-care plans, such as HMOs, a wide variety of pediatric specialists are on staff or closely affiliated; other plans have few or no established relationships with these specialists. If the specialists your child needs aren't in the plan, it may be harder to get a referral to them. However, even under such plans, parents can often get the referrals they need—if they know enough to ask for them specifically. In any case, review your health-plan materials or call member services to make sure the referral is covered.

If you are referred to a specialist, ask about his or her experience treating people with your child's condition. You'll also want to know about insurance coverage and access to any needed facilities, such as specialty hospitals. If a local specialist doesn't have extensive experience with your child's specific problem, you may decide to travel elsewhere in the country for help.

The Specialists

People with pediatric training practice within almost every medical specialty. Their training is likely—though not guaranteed—to make them particularly sensitive to and knowledgeable about children's care. Specialists may have a private practice, either alone or with a group, or work in a community health center, HMO, or hospital.

Be sure all the specialists you work with report to your primary-care provider as well as to you. And arrange to discuss these reports with the primary-care provider either over the phone or in person.

The following list describes many—but far from all—of the pediatric specialties:

Pediatric cardiologists evaluate and treat patients with congenital or acquired heart disease and symptoms related to heart disease or rhythm irregularities.

Pediatric hematologists specialize in blood disorders such as anemia, sickle cell disease, and hemophilia.

Pediatric oncologists treat cancer. Major pediatric cancer-treatment centers will have subspecialists in many fields.

Specialists in *adolescent and young-adult medicine* provide care for patients 12 to 23 years old, often including med-

For more information on "going out of plan," turn to Chapter **3**

For more information on choosing and using specialists, turn to Chapter **9**

Timely Questions

Some questions about providers and treatment are much easier to consider fully when you have time to plan ahead. But if your child needs emergency care, the situation may be so pressing or emotionally charged that you'll unavoidably postpone many important tasks. In these situations, get the best care you can immediately, then go back and tackle the rest of your questions when you have more time and feel more in control.

ical, gynecological, and psychological care.

Pediatric endocrinologists treat glandular disorders that might affect a child's height, weight, and development.

Specialists in *genetics* diagnose and manage inherited diseases, such as congenital malformations and chromosomal disorders. Genetic counselors discuss with families the chance of future children being affected and methods of diagnosis.

> **T**
> **I**
> **P**
>
> **Before Birth**
> *Select a primary-care provider for your child before an emergency arises—ideally, before or during the pregnancy. If you move to a new area, make identifying a primary-care provider for your child a high priority.*
> *After completing the selection process, don't throw away other recommendations. You may need a second opinion or a new provider in the future.*

Specialists in *pediatric allergy and immunology* evaluate and treat children with diseases such as asthma, drug allergies, insect-sting hypersensitivity, and immunodeficiency disorders.

Specialists in *pulmonary medicine* evaluate and care for children with cystic fibrosis, recurrent respiratory tract infections, chronic coughs, and other pulmonary diseases.

Pediatric neurologists evaluate and treat such problems as seizures, headaches, developmental problems, hyperactivity, neuromuscular disorders, and learning disabilities.

Pediatric orthopedic surgeons diagnose and treat congenital and acquired orthopedic conditions, such as bone fractures, cerebral palsy, and dislocated joints.

Psychopharmacologists specialize in using medicine to treat psychiatric disorders, including mood and anxiety disorders.

Child psychiatrists, trained as MDs, specialize in children's emotional problems.

Child psychologists, trained as PhDs, evaluate and treat children with emotional and behavioral issues.

Specialists and Hospitalization

An important factor in choosing a specialist (as well as a primary-care provider) is the hospitals to which he or she could send your child. If you live in an area with only one local hospital, this isn't an issue. On the other hand, ask your providers where they have admitting privileges if you live in a large city or a rural area equidistant from several medical centers, especially if you have reason to prefer a particular facility.

Hospitals differ in their attitudes about involving the family of a hospitalized child. Nevertheless, children and families weather hospitalizations best when they can interact as much as possible in their usual ways. Find out if a hospital allows parents to stay with their children during procedures and overnight, keeps parents fully informed about the plan of care, and helps parents take part in that care as much as they wish. Siblings and extended family members who visit can also help maintain a more normal life during these stressful times.

Discuss these issues with your health-care providers before a hospitalization. Ideally, they'll support your views and rights—and advocate for them with hospital personnel.

For more information on choosing and using hospitals, turn to Chapter 5

For more information on health care for women, turn to Chapter 6

Birthing Options

The most common class of specialist consulted by many families provides services related to having a child. The prospective mother's primary-care provider also plays a central role in this event.

Couples have many decisions to make in the months leading up to a childbirth. As you locate a primary-care provider for your new child, prepare your home, and choose a name, you might also want to check on these services and options:

• *Childbirth Education:* Also called birthing classes, these teach parents what to expect during labor and delivery. Parents who attend these classes gain more control over the birth and undergo fewer cesarean deliveries and interventions to relieve pain.

• *Birth Arrangements:* Does your hospital offer birthing rooms? Must your insurer certify admission in advance? Can siblings be present?

• *Obstetric Anesthesia:* Does the mother want to have an epidural block to relieve the pain of childbirth? Clearly state your wishes.

• *Breastfeeding:* Will the hospital respect your instructions about feedings and bring the newborn to you for feeding at your request? Does it offer breastfeeding classes or instruction? If the mother wants to breast feed, don't go home without learning how to express milk with a hand-held pump.

• *Circumcision:* Once routine, this custom has joined the list of medical procedures whose necessity is being questioned. Read up on it, keep an open mind, and try to reach an informed decision.

PART III: YOUR ROLE IN THE PARTNERSHIP

Once you identify a health-care provider for your son or daughter, build a partnership in which you each clearly identify your needs. From the point of view of a quality provider, you're an essential source of information about your child's development. To effectively communicate your questions and concerns to your child's provider, write them down before you call or visit. *All of your questions and opinions are legitimate and important.* Your perspective on your child is unique.

Some of your questions may not be easy to answer— many medical questions have no certain answers. This makes it extremely important that you share all your concerns and questions openly with providers and listen carefully to their replies. *If you don't understand a reply, don't hesitate to ask again—and again.* Because many medical situations are emotionally charged, it can help if you articulate your concerns and worries clearly and ask when you need more information. If you think of an additional question when you return home after an appointment, never hesitate to call the provider's office and ask.

You can also learn a great deal, and gain a great deal of support, from other adults. Talk with other parents and your children's teachers, day-care providers, and baby-sitters about your health concerns. These people can be important sources of information about your child. Likewise, advocacy and mutual-help organizations provide

You, Your Child, and Hospitals

To make a hospital more responsive to your desires, question your doctor and hospital personnel about hospital policy on parental rights before your child is admitted. Select the health-care providers and hospitals best able to make the arrangements you seek.

For example, you may want to be present while your child is receiving a treatment. If so, be prepared to negotiate directly with a person in authority, such as the chief of pediatrics or the chief of anesthesia.

For more information, contact Children in Hospitals, the Federation for Children with Special Needs, or another advocacy group with experience in dealing with health-care institutions and securing the rights of parents. The addresses and phone numbers are listed at the end of this chapter.

7

For information on
mutual-help groups, turn
to Chapter **19**

information, support, and other forms of assistance to parents of children with a variety of specific health conditions.

The most important aspect of your relationship with your child's medical providers is the quality of trust and communication you establish. At the most basic level, medical treatments probably won't succeed if you and your child can't follow the instructions carefully. And providers can't give reasonable care to your child if you don't openly report your concerns. Your child's providers will rely on you to follow the treatment plan and to report any changes you see in your child during treatment. If the plan isn't working or causes you or your child concern, check back with your provider. The plan may need to be adjusted.

Families need to completely understand:

- Prescribed treatments;
- The reasons for the treatments;
- The expected results;
- What might happen during treatment; *and*
- What to do in any given eventuality.

Make sure you understand what might happen if you refuse the treatment. What are your options? Particularly if you are considering a complicated procedure such as surgery, ask for materials to read and for the names of other families in similar situations.

Whenever your child receives care, give

> **T I P**
>
> **Two Appointments**
> Sometimes you have so many questions about your child's health that you can't cover them all during a single exam or treatment. If need be, schedule a separate time to discuss your questions with your child's providers, whether in person or on the phone.

providers feedback. Discuss those aspects you particularly liked as well as those that worried or displeased you. Providers usually listen carefully to this kind of input and find it very helpful. It could also significantly improve the care your child receives in the future.

Keep Records

Build and maintain a complete record of every contact with all your child's health-care providers, both in person and over the phone, and write down what providers report

Time to Change Providers?

If you are genuinely unhappy with your child's care, be willing to change providers. However, remember that continuity is important for good health care, as is the relationship you and a particular health-care provider build over the years. In other words, try to select your providers carefully from the first and always communicate with them fully. Invest the time and effort required to build a strong relationship.

and recommend. Include in this record a log of all immunizations, medications, and other treatments prescribed for your son or daughter. For immunizations, note the type of shot, the date, the location, and the provider. For medications, write down the dosages and the times when the child takes each medicine. Keep note of any special considerations:

- Could a drug interact dangerously with any foods or other medications?
- What possible side effects should you look for?
- What should you do in case of a reaction to the medication?

These records will improve the health of your children in several ways. First, even if you think you'll remember instructions after a visit, it's easy to forget critical details a few days later—or even a few hours later. Second, your written record helps if you need to follow up with another provider about the same problem. Third, if your child has an emergency, the records may be critical to a nurse or doctor who doesn't know your child's medical history. Fourth, they are critical when you move and enter into a partnership with a new provider.

Always read your child's medical records yourself and ask about anything you don't understand. If your child is referred to a specialist, ask the specialist to send a report to the primary-care provider so that your child's record is always complete.

Keep your records handy at *home,* and bring them with you to all health visits. One good idea is to assemble all the records you keep into a "passport." Such booklets contain a range of information, from your child's height, weight, and immunization record to a complete set of health records. The passport not only keeps information in one place but helps to empower you as a parent to actively participate in your child's care, both in sickness and health.

There are many types of parent-held child health records. Perhaps the most thorough is the Denver Child Health Passport, maintained jointly by parents and their children's health-care providers. A notebook with tear-out sheets designed to fit into a diaper bag or a large purse, the passport covers the first six years of life and includes the family's social and medical histories, health evaluations from the neonatal examination through the six-year health visit, a summary chart documenting the dates of each preventive service, and much more.

The Denver Child Health Passports are being distributed through physicians. For more information,

Pages from the Denver Child Health Passport

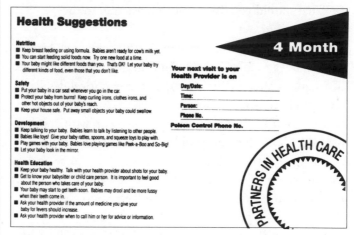

A health-care provider fills in the information at the right before the parent leaves the office after the child's four-month visit.

At the child's four-month visit, the parent fills in the information on the top of the form, and the health-care provider fills in the information on the bottom half.

write to Community Child Development, Children's Hospital, 1056 E. 19th Ave., Box B215, Denver, CO 80218.

Children and Rights

In most cases, parents make health-care decisions for their daughters and sons. However, they don't have unlimited rights regarding their children's medical care. And parents usually want to involve their children as much as possible in making health-care choices.

In most states, children can consent to medical care on their own for certain conditions, such as treatments associated with drug dependency, pregnancy, and sexually transmitted diseases. In addition, an "emancipated minor"— a member of the armed forces, for example—can make medical decisions without parental permission. While the laws vary from state to state, an emancipated minor must generally live apart from his or her parents and be self-supporting.

In most cases, any mature minor can consent to care as long as he or she can understand the nature, extent, and consequences of the medical treatment. In fact, a child can sometimes agree to treatment over the objections of parents, usually for simple procedures. By the same token, a child who is legally allowed to say yes to medical care can also say no.

Hospitals have certain rights with regard to the care of children. In a life-threatening emergency, they'll give treatment immediately—parental consent isn't needed. And if parents object to some types of treatment, a hospital can turn to a court for permission to treat a child whose life is in danger. If the court sides with the hospital, it will appoint a guardian to make decisions about whether or not to proceed with a treatment.

On the other hand, hospitals can't restrict parents' right to visit hospitalized children—*at any time of day*—if the law requires them to give informed consent. Hospitals can only restrict parents' access when it would interfere with the care of other patients.

Second Opinions

Don't hesitate to seek a second opinion if you're unhappy about your child's care—or if you simply want reassurance about a diagnosis or recommended treatment. Medical providers often differ widely on the best course of treatment. Even if they do agree, a second opinion will sometimes help you understand a situation better or feel more at ease. Still, always let your primary provider know what you are doing and why you are doing it.

For more information on second opinions and specialists, turn to Chapter **9**

PART IV: MONEY MATTERS

Long-standing, strong relationships in which providers work in concert with one another are crucial to both primary and specialty care. However, continuity of care is hard to maintain these days. For one thing, a rapidly changing health-care marketplace makes it difficult for many families to stay with the same providers. Moreover, families sometimes want to take advantage of an opportunity to choose a new health plan, such as when they begin a new job with better benefits or during "open-enrollment" periods that some employers offer yearly. At these times, look carefully at the providers and benefits offered by different health plans.

Picking a Plan

Parents are making more decisions than ever before about health-insurance coverage for their children. As a mother or father, you probably need health insurance that covers all your children until they are 21 years old, perhaps longer if they're still in school. Along with the questions you ask of insurers you consider for your own care, the American Academy of Pediatrics recommends you check each plan's coverage for:

- Family-planning services;
- Well care, including immunizations;
- Pregnancy services, including prenatal care, prenatal consultation with a pediatrician, and care for the pregnancy of a single dependent daughter;
- Care of newborn infants, including a pediatric specialist to attend high-risk pregnancies, exams and health checks from the time of birth, and treatment of birth defects and other illnesses and injuries;
- Services to help a child recover from an illness or injury, including physical therapy, speech therapy, and occupational therapy;
- Long-term care; *and*
- Hospice care for a terminally ill child.

Talk with your pediatrician about your children's health-care needs for the coming year. Are his or her services covered by the insurance plan you're considering? If not, do you want to change pediatricians, pay for your pediatrician's care out of pocket, or change plans? How many preventive visits can the family foresee in the coming year and what will they cost? The American Academy of Pediatrics recommends six well-child visits in the first year, three visits the next year, one yearly visit for ages three to six, and one every other year for ages seven and up. And don't forget other charges, such as lab tests, prescription drugs, and immunizations.

No matter what health-insurance plan you choose, learn how it works for children. When comparing plans and deciding on options, find out:

- What are the basic costs associated with the plan?
- Is your choice of providers limited?
- Are affiliated pediatricians board certified?
- How many pediatricians are available to you? Who are they?
- Can your child see the same pediatrician for most visits?
- What limits are placed on referrals to subspecialists, such as pediatric cardiologists or pediatric allergists?
- Can your child go to a special hospital that treats children, if need be?

Also consider coverage for children's mental health when buying insurance:

- Does your health plan pay for the mental-health services your family may need, such as outpatient therapy, day-treatment programs, hospital treatment, and treatment programs for alcohol and other types of drug abuse?
- Will it allow you to choose an expert: a qualified child and adolescent mental-health professional to provide and direct your child's treatment?
- Does the plan provide broad enough coverage to permit an adequate period of treatment in a setting appropriate to the disorder?

Your Teenagers and Health Insurance

When planning your family's health-care coverage, keep in mind the special needs of your teenage children. Many

---

Respect Your Child's Privacy

Children have a right to privacy about medical care. Confidentiality is critical to any patient-doctor relationship, even if the parent is the person who gives consent.

If a child doesn't want certain information to reach his or her parents, doctors and other medical personnel should only tell parents what they need to know to give or withhold informed consent for treatment. If you need to discuss some topics with your child's provider in private, ask to be allowed to do so.

Privacy is especially important to teenagers. A physician with training in adolescent medicine will almost invariably keep the content of your teen's visits in confidence. On the other hand, some pediatricians are used to telling Mom and Dad everything—to the detriment of everyone concerned.

For more information on choosing a health plan, turn to Chapter **3**

SOME TYPICAL FEES		
	Well-Baby Checkup	Normal Delivery of a Baby
Boston	$72	$3,714
New York City	$117	$5,130
Washington, DC	$68	$3,160
Phoenix	$45	$2,472
National Average	$45	$2,254

Source: Medirisk, Inc.

Two Plans?

Many health-insurance plans have special payment methods if both parents are insured. Find out in advance which plan will be the one with the main responsibility for your children's coverage and how the two plans coordinate payments.

teens aren't covered after a specific age—typically 18 or 21, or 25 if your son or daughter is a full-time student. If your teen is in college and isn't covered under your plan, a school policy may cover his or her health care. If so, check the extent of coverage.

Even if your family policy covers your teenage son or daughter, he or she may want and need confidential services. A few insurance companies will make arrangements for your teenager, not you, to receive the bill.

Choosing an HMO as your insurer results in significant benefits for teenagers, particularly in terms of coverage for preventive services. However, HMOs also have shortcom-

CHILDREN WITH SPECIAL NEEDS

Even as health-care costs soar, 39 million people have no health insurance, and an additional 59 million find their coverage inadequate to meet family needs. Families whose children have serious ongoing health needs are disproportionately represented in both groups.

Children with special health needs or chronic health conditions are heavy users of health care, and their families spend a great deal of effort trying to work out how to pay for it. Solutions often require a complicated mix of private health insurers and public programs. Families need help assembling this package of payers.

Paying the Bills: Tips for Families on Financing Health Care for Children with Special Needs is a booklet written by parents who have children with special needs. To order a free copy, send a self-addressed 9"x12" envelope with $1.05 in postage affixed to New England SERVE, 101 Tremont St., Boston, MA 02108 (617)574-9493.

ings. They typically exclude or provide poor coverage for specific teen illnesses, such as anorexia nervosa. In addition, an HMO might steer you away from particular options you'd prefer. For example, an HMO could save money by prescribing birth-control pills that you'd pay for rather than Norplant or another long-acting birth control that would be fully covered.

RESOURCES

Organizations
American Academy of Child and Adolescent Psychiatry
3615 Wisconsin Ave., NW
Washington, DC 20016
(202)966-7300
Call or write for a list of publications and resources, including a series of pamphlets called "Facts for Families" with information on topics such as children and grief, bed-wetting, day care, children and divorce, lead exposure, discipline, and conduct disorders. Also available is a free brochure with recommended insurance coverage for children's mental-health services. For free copies of individual pamphlets, send a self-addressed stamped envelope to AACAP Public Information, P.O. Box 96106, Washington, DC 20090.

American Academy of Husband-Coached Childbirth
P.O. Box 5224
Sherman Oaks, CA 91413
(800)423-2397
Write for information on preparing for natural childbirth.

American Academy of Pediatric Dentistry
211 E. Chicago Ave.
Chicago, IL 60611
(312)337-2169
Call or write for referrals and for pamphlets on safety, sealants, regular dental visits, dental care for babies, care for teens, and other topics.

American Academy of Pediatrics
Department C
P.O. Box 927
Elk Grove Village, IL 60009
(800)433-9016

Free brochures are available on allergies in children, child sexual abuse, day care, diaper rash, family health insurance, immunization schedules, managed care for families, temper tantrums, tobacco abuse, and many other topics. Send a stamped, self-addressed envelope for any of these brochures or a publications list.

American College of Nurse-Midwives
818 Connecticut Ave., NW
Washington, DC 20006
(202)782-9860
Send $6.95 for the *Directory of Nurse-Midwifery in the United States.*

American Society for Psychoprophylaxis in Obstetrics (ASPO/Lamaze)
(800)368-4404
Call for information about prepared childbirth and referrals to ASPO/Lamaze childbirth educators.

Association for the Care of Children's Health
7910 Woodmont Ave.
Bethesda, MD 20814
(301)654-6549
This organization has a number of educational booklets available at a small charge on such topics as "Caring for Your Child in the Emergency Room" and "For Teenagers: Your Stay in the Hospital." Call or write for a resource catalogue. The association also operates the National Information Clearinghouse for Infants with Disabilities and Life-Threatening Conditions, serving family members and health-care

providers. For a list of services and fact sheets, call (800)922-9234, extension 201.

Association of Maternal and Child Health Programs
1350 Connecticut Ave., NW
Washington, DC 20036
(202)775-0436
Call to get the phone number of your state's program for children with special health-care needs.

Cesarean/Support, Education and Concern
22 Forest Rd.
Framingham, MA 01701
(508)877-8266
Parents and professionals can write or call for information and support on cesarean birth, prevention, and vaginal birth after a cesarean (VBAC).

Children in Hospitals
31 Wilshire Park
Needham, MA 02192
(617)482-2915
This national consumer organization is dedicated to helping parents stay with and support their children during hospitalization. Call or write for referrals to local organizations.

Federation for Children with Special Needs
95 Berkeley St.
Boston, MA 02116
(617)482-2915
Call for referrals to local organizations that advocate on behalf of children and families with special needs.

Informed Birth and Parenting
P.O. Box 3675
Ann Arbor, MI 48106
(313)662-6857
Call or write for a publications list and information and referrals on childbirth education training.

International Cesarean Awareness Network
P.O. Box 152
Syracuse, NY 13210
(315)424-1942
This national organization provides counseling for women seeking a vaginal birth after a cesarean (VBAC) and referrals for labor support.

International Childbirth Education Association
P.O. Box 20048
Minneapolis, MN 55420
Write for information on family-centered maternity care and freedom of choice based on knowing your alternatives.

Le Leche League International
P.O. Box 1209
Franklin Park, IL 60131-8209
(800)525-3243
Call or write for information and support on breastfeeding, as well as referrals to local groups.

March of Dimes Birth Defects Foundation
1275 Mamaroneck Ave.
White Plains, NY 10605
(914)997-4701
Write or call to get the number of your local chapter as well as information on prenatal care and healthy pregnancies.

National Maternal and Child Health Clearinghouse
8201 Greensboro Dr.
McLean, VA 22102
(703)821-8955
Call or write for information and a publications catalogue.

Parents Choice Book Center
57 Stevens St.
Stoneham, MA 02180
(800)722-2939 or
(617)438-8791
Call or write for a mail-order catalog of childbirth and parenting books.

Publications

Caring for Your Baby and Child: Birth to Age 5 (American Academy of Pediatrics, 1991). $15.95; *Caring for Your Adolescent: Ages 12 to 21* (American Academy of Pediatrics, 1991). $19.95. To order either book, call (800)433-9016. (A book on ages 5 to 12 is scheduled for late 1995.)

Fighting Back Health Insurance Denials, by Robert Peterson, with David Tenenbaum. Order from the Center for Public Representation, 121 South Pinckney St., Madison, WI 53703 (800)369-0338. $14.95.

Home Care for the Chronically Ill or Disabled Child: A Manual and Services Book for Parents and Professionals, by Monica Loose Jones (Harper and Row, 1985). $12.95.

Ourselves and Our Children, by the Boston Women's Health Book Collective (Random House, 1978). Out of print but available in many libraries.

Special Needs/Special Solutions: How to Get Quality Care for a Child with Special Health Needs, by Georgianna Larson and Judith A. Kahn (1990). Order from Life Line Press, 2500 University Ave., St. Paul, MN 55141. $7.95.

"SSI: New Opportunities for Children with Disabilities," pamphlet by Joseph Manes and Lee Carty. Order from Mental Health Law Project, 1101 15th St., NW, Washington, DC 20005 (202)467-5730. $3.

Take This Book to the Pediatrician with You, by Charles B. Inlander and J. Lynee Dodson. Order from People's Medical Society, 462 Walnut St., Allentown, PA 18102 (800)624-8773. $14.95, plus $3 shipping and handling.

Elders As Health Care Consumers

By Lou Glasse and Mal Schechter

This chapter summarizes the health-care needs of elder consumers. But elders share many concerns —and services— with people of all ages, so you'll find important information throughout this book. In particular, refer to Chapter 3 on rights, Chapter 12 on home care, Chapter 13 on long-term care, and Chapter 18 on death with dignity.

Lou Glasse is a consultant on aging policies and services. She is President of the Older Women's League and former Director of the New York State Office for the Aging.

Mal Schechter is Associate Director of the International Leadership Center on Longevity and Security and Assistant Professor of Geriatrics and Adult Development at the Mount Sinai School of Medicine in New York City.

P*eople are living longer.* Since the beginning of the twentieth century, life expectancy in the United States has improved from 47 years to 75 years. Better public health and advanced medical technology have brought about this extraordinary advance.

More people survive into their 70s and 80s. Americans who reach the age of 65 will live, on average, another 17 years. People over the age of 85 comprise one of the fastest growing age groups. And the number of centenarians quadrupled from 15,000 in 1980 to 61,000 in 1989. By the turn of the century, 100,000 Americans will live to reach their hundredth birthday.

Said another way, many more elders than ever are making short-term and long-term consumer decisions about health care. Some of the challenges they face mirror those that other consumers face: choosing the right services, forming partnerships with health-care providers, investing limited financial resources wisely.

At the same time, elders also have special concerns and needs. It's important for you, your health-care providers, and your family to recognize that:

• The U.S. health-care system tends to deny or misinterpret—or it simply isn't geared to handle—the many needs of older people.

• Older people respond in distinctive ways to drugs, foods, stress, infections, and wounds.

• Elders are far more likely to need long-term care.

• Elders are more likely to be a victim of a wide variety of both single and combined health problems.

• A federal insurance system (Medicare) pays for a significant part of the health care of almost all elders; on the other hand, elders more often live on tight, fixed incomes and devote far more of their income to health care than do younger adults.

PART I: AGING, HEALTH, AND WELL-BEING

For you as an elder, the most disturbing aspect of the health-care system may well be the lack of providers with training specific and appropriate to your circumstances. Older people aren't middle-aged adults, just as children aren't small adults. Organs and tissues change, as does your ability to move and think. You respond to diseases differently from the way you did as a young adult, and diseases may appear differently and take different courses. You may have a heart attack without experiencing any chest pain. Infection may not be accompanied by much fever. Moreover, very old patients tend to have more than one disease or chronic condition at a time, complicating care significantly.

Elder Women

Advances in child and maternal health have benefited women enormously. Women comprise a majority of Americans over 65. To speak of elders and their problems often means to speak of women. This is especially true after age 75 or 80. Women are the major givers, recipients, and advocates of care for elders.

> **TIP**
>
> **Gold Stars**
>
> *With far too few people fully trained in geriatrics, you can't use the lack of such training to eliminate a candidate for providing your care. But look more favorably on providers who have a certificate for completing a geriatrics course, participate in a group practice with access to a geriatrician, or belong to a relevant professional group, such as the American Geriatrics Society or the Gerontological Society of America.*

Unfortunately, health-care providers trained to work with older Americans are in critically short supply. Geriatrics is an unpopular field for doctors, in part due to society's unwillingness to confront age and death, but also because geriatrics offers physicians lower average incomes than do many other specialties. A severe shortage of teachers and teaching programs in geriatrics means that consumers can expect this state of affairs to last for the foreseeable future.

This makes it all the more important for you to educate yourself and take an active role in fostering your own well-being.

Habits and Health

Your chances of living a long life depend on a number of variables, of which the supply of trained medical personnel is only one. Perhaps even more so than for younger people, you can reap rewards by paying attention to your health. Although you can't determine how long you'll live, you can live in ways likely to improve your health and lengthen your life:

- Don't smoke or abuse alcohol or drugs.
- Wear seat belts.

For information on occupational health and safety, turn to Chapter **16**

Avoiding the Inheritance

Gladys, a 50-year-old woman, knew that both her mother and grandmother had suffered from osteoporosis, a painful and disabling disease. She realized that she was at risk of suffering the same disease in the future.

In consultation with her physician, Gladys has changed her diet to one rich in calcium and developed a regimen of proper exercise to lessen the risk. Just as important, she and her physician will monitor her condition so they can identify the disease early if it occurs and begin treatment.

• Eat a diet rich in fruits, vegetables, and grains. Avoid a diet based on convenience and fast foods.

• Exercise regularly. Don't be a couch potato.

• If you are employed, check your workplace for environmental hazards such as dangerous chemicals.

Your mental and social health can affect not only the length but the quality of your life as well:

• Socialize regularly with friends and family.

• Participate in stimulating activities such as hobbies, public affairs, and education.

In addition to these "lifestyle" factors, you and your primary-care provider and other health-care personnel should pay attention to your family's medical history for clues to your own future health. The genes you inherit may predispose you to certain maladies, such as cancer. Although you can't select your genes, knowing your family medical history can help you avoid particular kinds of behavior that increase your risk.

The Health Care Spectrum

At any age, but particularly late in life, your health-care needs span a spectrum that includes several components:

• *Health promotion and disease and accident prevention,* including good nutrition, vaccinations, and a sound lifestyle that includes not smoking;

• *Acute care* for immediate threats to life and limb;

• *Rehabilitation* to restore your ability to do as much for yourself as possible;

• *Custodial or long-term care* to meet your needs for bathing, eating, moving from bed to chair, grooming, and going to the toilet; *and*

• *Social support services.*

This list may help you find your way to the care you need, whether it's simple and requires a single service or is complex and requires an organized system of providers. It can be difficult to find the right single provider, and it can be even harder to find the right system. You may have to put a service plan together yourself or with help from your doctor or a care coordinator.

Because people with chronic illnesses and disabilities may experience sudden acute illnesses, both acute and long-term care require close coordination. Some authorities call this "chronic care" or "integrated acute and long-term care." Ask your doctor, hospital, HMO, nursing home, and home-health agency about preparing for these possible needs.

Chronic Illness

You can't be sure how long you'll live, what chronic diseases may arise, how much they'll interfere with your activities, and how much you'll be able to compensate for any losses of function. Even if you avoid major diseases and trauma, you can't be sure of the exact extent to which your physical and mental functioning will change. Keep in mind that half of 85-year olds lead independent lives.

In general, people become more prone to a chronic illness or disability as they age. The list of conditions they face includes arthritis, osteoporosis, diabetes, and incontinence, as well as heart disease, stroke, cancer, and dementia. As a health-care consumer, be aware that chronic illnesses are likely to curtail your ability to carry out your normal activities of life. The self-sufficiency you now take for granted may be reduced. In 1993, one American in seven faced major limitations on their activities due to chronic illness, including about two-fifths of all elders.

You can take steps throughout your life to improve your chances of avoiding or minimizing these spoilers and killers. Keep in mind two opposing forces. Physical aging means that the peak performance of your body's organs and tissues will gradually decline, even without disease or trauma or any noticeable effect on your ordinary activities. On the other hand, you have good resources to adjust or to compensate for losses. These resources are both internal and external: You can learn how to use an impaired arm or leg. You can rely on people as well as mechanical and other aids to help you do things. And you and your friends can watch out for and avoid problems.

People age differently, and good care for elders recognizes this fact. Many people remain vigorous and healthy throughout a long life. Others suffer debilitating illnesses decades before age 65. Alzheimer's and other diseases can impair the mental and physical abilities of some people in their 40s and 50s.

To prepare for—or respond to—any declining abilities, you, your relatives and friends, and your primary-care physician and other health-care providers should consider some basic questions:

- Can family members and good friends assist you if you can't care for yourself? Do these people live nearby?
- Will you need help in your home? What community services could help you remain in your own home? If you can't climb stairs or walk to the bathroom in your home, can you modify it, or should you move to a new living environment?
- How will you decide if you need a nursing home? How will you select one? How much will it cost? Do you have the financial resources to pay for nursing-home care?
- Do you have access to health-care providers who can help you define and meet your evolving needs as you age?
- Do you have insurance or other financial resources to cover the health-care services you may need?
- Have you made personal and legal arrangements in case you become mentally or physically incapable of making health-care decisions and handling financial affairs?

PART II: CAREGIVING/CAREGIVERS

Nine out of ten disabled elders not in nursing homes depend on their families and friends for help. This assistance may be for a few weeks, or it may extend for many years. The need may vary from handling financial matters and running errands to around-the-clock care, seven days a week. Most families willingly aid aging relatives and adjust their other commitments to do so.

Depending upon the complexity of the care and the duration of your infirmity, family and friends may not be able to provide all the needed assistance in your home or the home of a relative. To prepare for this possibility, you and your family may need to consider two general types of alternative arrangements for long-term care:

- Paying for services in your home and community; *and*
- Moving to another living arrangement where services are provided.

For information on nursing homes, read "long-term care" in Chapter **12**

For information on planning for future incapacity, turn to Chapter **17**

Planning the Transition

It's not easy to prepare yourself for major changes in the way you live. Few people can imagine depending on others to eat, move from a bed to a chair, or go to the toilet. To minimize this loss of independence—while securing the assistance that you need—take steps early. Just as you plan in your younger years for your child's education or for buying a house, think and plan for the transitions you may face as you grow older.

Long Term Care and the Consumer

Long-term care means services that help you with activities you must do every day. Though they relate to health, these services don't necessarily require a physician or a skilled nurse. Services are provided in the home, in the community, or in a variety of residential settings.

As the U.S. population ages and the need for services in both homes and institutions expand, more organizations are providing long-term care. Both for-profit and nonprofit agencies are responding to the growing demand. Fortunately, government regulation of nursing homes has been strengthened over the years with Medicare or Medicaid. If you're paying the bill yourself, nursing-home and home-care charges may be higher than under the government programs. You may need professional help in judging these prices and evaluating the quality of the services offered. Official standards for quality of home care, in particular, are in their infancy, and their connection to your health is still unclear.

Given the choice, most people choose to live at home even if they require ongoing, around-the-clock services and can no longer care for themselves. About one-third of older Americans—mostly women—live alone. If no family

Use It or Lose It

Lying in a bed without exercise may be damaging. If you need long-term care after a hospital stay for an acute illness, professional help, particularly from your primary-care provider and consulting specialists, is often essential as you prepare to leave a hospital.

ELDER ABUSE

One to two million elders are victims of abuse every year, and millions more fear it.

Abuse takes two basic forms: physical or emotional injury and financial exploitation. According to the National Center on Elder Abuse, neglect by caregivers accounts for 37 percent of cases; 26 percent are cases of physical abuse; 20 percent result from financial exploitation; 11 percent are psychologi-cal abuse; and 6 percent result from other causes.

Situations that could make you vulnerable to abuse include:
◆ Lack of family support;
◆ The reluctance of caregivers to provide care;
◆ Frustrations in giving care;
◆ A lack of knowledge and professional guidance for caregivers;
◆ Disharmony among caregivers who share responsibility;
◆ Overcrowding;
◆ Isolation;
◆ Marital conflict; and
◆ Financial, job, and family pressures.

Most elder-abuse victims are women. Most abusers within the family are spouses or children, usually male.

For more information, contact the National Center on Elder Abuse, 810 1st St., NE, Washington, DC 20002 (202)682-2470.

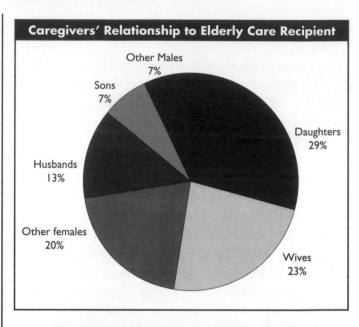

Caregivers' Relationship to Elderly Care Recipient

Other Males 7%

Sons 7%

Daughters 29%

Husbands 13%

Other females 20%

Wives 23%

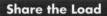

Share the Load

In almost three out of four families, the role of caregiver falls to women: wives—often elders themselves—daughters, and daughters-in-law. Husbands are also important caregivers if their wives become chronically ill. If families share this responsibility among sons as well as daughters, grandchildren, and other relatives, the burden of care is spread. That reduces the likelihood of overburdening one person.

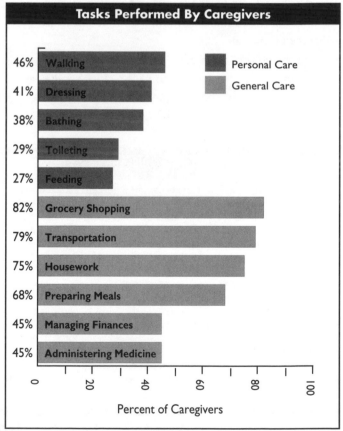

Tasks Performed By Caregivers

■ Personal Care
■ General Care

46%	Walking
41%	Dressing
38%	Bathing
29%	Toileting
27%	Feeding
82%	Grocery Shopping
79%	Transportation
75%	Housework
68%	Preparing Meals
45%	Managing Finances
45%	Administering Medicine

Percent of Caregivers

member is immediately available to provide care, affordable and qualified home-care providers are available in many communities

Still, it can be difficult and expensive to arrange a complete set of home-care services. As a result, people who live alone and have major care needs are more likely to move into assisted-living facilities or a nursing home. Most facilities for assisted living only admit residents who are ambulatory. Thus, advanced planning is usually essential.

For information on home care, turn to Chapter ▼**13**

Much of long-term care is frequently called custodial care: it doesn't include rehabilitation, and a cure is seldom expected. Because older people more frequently suffer chronic illnesses than do younger people, they are the primary clients for long-term care. The goal is to provide you with the necessary supports to be as independent as possible. Many people live for decades with some limits on their activity while still participating in and enjoying daily life. The elder consumer plays an important role in long-term-care services. Even when you must draw heavily on the expertise of

> **T I P**
> **Mix and Match**
> *Specialists trained to help you develop a plan for long-term care may be hard to find, especially in rural areas and inner cities. Check with your local Area Agency on Aging and senior advocacy organizations such as the American Association of Retired Persons and the Older Women's League.*

physicians, long-term care should center on *your* concerns and *your* resources. A wide variety of options may be available in your community. It's important that you and your advocates clearly understand your needs, especially because you (or a family caregiver) may actually employ and manage several providers to obtain all the long-term services you require.

PART III: THE ELEMENTS OF GERIATRIC CARE

For more information on long-term care, assisted living, and nursing homes, turn to Chapter ▼**12**

Geriatrics encompasses the special knowledge and skills applied through medicine, nursing, social work, and other areas to help elders stay independent, despite impairments.

As you enter the last phase of your life, you and your family will encounter a new set of critical issues.

First of all, both you and your caregivers must always remember that dying is a part of life. Even more than death, most people in their last few months fear isolation and pain. Communication with family and friends is essential. You may also want to consider hospices, which are committed to helping people die at home or in a home-like facility, free from pain and without the use of extreme medical interventions.

Second, you retain all the rights of an adult. Exercise these rights. For example, you decide what medical treatment is best for you, and you can refuse any treatment for any reason.

Third, when you can't understand the information needed to make an informed decision about health care, your guardian or next-of-kin can act for you. If you haven't expressed your wishes beforehand, the next of kin or guardian should have your authority act in your best interest. If you can, decide now on a health advocate or provide a durable power of attorney to someone you trust and with whom you have discussed your wishes.

For more information on dying with dignity, turn to Chapter 17.

Geriatric care isn't confined to long-term care. It covers care for acute and chronic illnesses in a hospital, your own home, your community, or a nursing home.

Geriatrics is concerned principally with:

- Your ability to function as independently as possible;
- You as a whole person, including your emotions, values, interests, and physical, mental, and social functioning;
- Your capacity for rehabilitation and emotional growth;
- Helping you compensate for limitations;
- Involving you and your family in planning care;
- Adjusting your physical and social environment to make it easier for you to function; *and*
- Using the appropriate team of professionals and paraprofessionals to address the multiple needs of you and your family.

With far too few health-care practitioners specializing in geriatrics, your knowledge of what constitutes a comprehensive approach can help you—and the caregivers available to you—assemble a better plan for care.

The basic components of organized geriatric care are:

- *Diagnosing* (or assessing) your social, nursing, and medical problems;
- *Developing* a care plan;

- *Implementing* the plan; *and*
- *Adjusting* it periodically as problems and conditions change.

The Geriatric Assessment

You, your family, and professionals collaborate in developing a plan of care. Together, you'll develop a sense of your potential, resources, and limitations as they relate to possible courses of treatment.

The process rests on a geriatric assessment. Ideally, this looks at your:
- Functional and mental status;
- Socioeconomic status;
- Environment; *and*
- Physical status.

A geriatric assessment will differ from a younger person's assessment. First of all, it takes longer. Simply recording your medical history takes longer. Some older people are lonely and stretch the encounter, requiring patience on the part of providers and family members. Also, hearing often weakens with age. And elders tend to leave out things when reporting symptoms, in part because they may not be clear about facts and problems. Despite these hurdles, the interviewer must still take all your symptoms seriously because they may be clues to a problem. Your social, sexual, and medication histories as well as a physical examination are all important in establishing a diagnosis.

To answer your needs, geriatricians are versed in understanding the unusual ways illnesses manifest themselves in elders, especially when other factors mask the main symptoms or when symptoms occur in confusing combinations. For example, diseases may have different signs and symptoms in older and younger adults. And elders are especially likely to suffer medical, physical, and functional problems at the same time, while differing disorders may produce similar disabilities. Certain diseases may be heralded by general symptoms, such as fatigue, low sodium concentrations in the blood, and depression.

Geriatricians are sensitive to these and many other con-

Individual Treatment

The comprehensive approach of geriatrics requires practitioners to have a thorough understanding of you and your background. Your doctor, nurse, and social worker can take little for granted, and they can't rely on stereotypes. The older population is very diverse, and as people grow older, treatments must become more individualized.

ditions that occur more frequently among elders. For example, a frequent cause of an older person's declining ability to function is malnutrition, in part because enjoyment of food may decline along with age-associated decreases in smell and taste perception. Malnutrition may slow recovery from an illness, and it can contribute to pressure sores, infections, muscle wasting, and ambulatory weakness.

> **T I P**
>
> **Autonomy Is Healthy**
> *The more autonomous and self-reliant you are, the more likely you will be to survive a disease and regain your health.* A wise practitioner knows when to push you to do more. A wise patient knows when to take it easy.

Geriatric Discharge Planning

If you are completing a stay in a hospital or nursing home, you should receive help in preparing for the move home. This "discharge planning" aims to:

- Prevent a readmission to the hospital or nursing home;
- Lessen your need for visits to the emergency room; *and*
- Make it less likely that you'll require a nursing home, home-care programs, and other services in the future.

Like geriatric-care assessments in general, part of discharge planning is a *nursing and social-work assessment* to determine the supports available to you and your family in the community and at home. This means finding out who you live with, what medications you take, and how well you can move around and feed yourself. The assessment covers family and other supports, as well as the availability of insurance and income to cover health care and other basic needs. The nurse determines what follow-up examinations may be needed to check on your response to therapy.

A *physical therapy evaluation* may also be part of your discharge planning in some cases. The physical therapist identifies physical problems that make living at home difficult for you, and he or she assesses your strength, flexibility, and sensation in relation to general movement, particularly walking, climbing, and rising. Physical therapy begins in the hospital or nursing home and continues at home.

A *nutritional evaluation* may be included in discharge

Your Plan

Together with professionals, you'll assemble an individualized plan of care that:

◆ *Integrates* acute care and long-term care;

◆ *Provides* services for mental health, rehabilitation, and prevention;

◆ *Integrates* medical care with other services—for example, assisted housing with physician and nurse services;

◆ *Coordinates* paid and unpaid—and formal and informal—caregivers; *and*

◆ *Assures* the quality of the system and of direct services.

planning. Nutritionists find out about problems that might interfere with eating, swallowing, chewing, and denture fit.

PART IV: MONEY MATTERS

Despite federal health insurance for most older Americans, the average elder family pays about $3,000 a year for health care; the average person over 85 pays over $5,000. Moreover, elders spend six times as much of their income on health as do younger people.

Medicare

Medicare and supplemental insurance pay a significant portion of the bills for acute medical care for 95 percent of older Americans. Medicare is the federal health-insurance program for older Americans, as well as for certain younger adults who are disabled. If you are eligible for Social Security or Railroad Retirement benefits and are 65 or older, you qualify for Medicare, as does your spouse when he or she reaches 65.

For more information on health-care insurance, turn to Chapter 3

DRUG USE AND ABUSE

Side effects from drugs account for a substantial proportion of elders' problems with memory, attention, and mood, as well as constipation, incontinence, depression, male impotence, appetite changes, dizziness, and many other conditions. Doctors who aren't trained to work with elders may not realize that many side effects are common in older people even if they're rare in younger people taking the same drugs. Make sure that your caregivers consider these issues.

The use of prescribed or over-the-counter drugs may be hazardous and can complicate treatment of an illness or disability. Elders are two to seven times more likely than younger adults to react badly to drugs. Moreover, the consequences of improper drugs and improper use are much more severe in elders. The misuse of drugs includes forgetting or omitting a dose, intentionally changing the dosage, taking a medicine for an unintended purpose, using outdated prescriptions, or using prescribed drugs in improper combinations with over-the-counter medicines.

For all these reasons, *pharmacists* often play a central role in developing and implementing a geriatric plan. The pharmacist takes account of physiologic changes that influence drug metabolism, ability to swallow pills of given sizes, sensitivities to drugs, drug interactions, and the possibility of combining pills to make taking medications easier at home. Geriatric caregivers discourage self-medication and hasty resort to prescribed drugs: 90 percent of elders take at least one medication; most take two or more.

Health and Income

Good health relates to income, but as people age, income tends to decline. The older people are, the lower their income tends to be. The median income for people over the age of 85 is substantially below that for people in their 60s and early 70s.

This puts the very old more at risk of poor care—just when they're likely to need health services more. Few pension plans include cost-of-living adjustments, and out-of-pocket health care expenditures eat up more of elders' savings each year. Some older people can't afford the high cost of prescription drugs or long-term-care services.

For more information on home health care, turn to Chapter **13**

Medicare applications are handled through your local Social Security office. If you are eligible, you should receive Medicare automatically, effective the month you turn 65. Still, to ensure that your enrollment goes smoothly, contact your local Social Security office during the three months before you turn 65. Medicare only covers one individual, not dependents. Many younger spouses lose their health insurance as dependents when the working spouse turns 65 and switches to Medicare. This is especially important to consider as more companies cut back or eliminate coverage for retirees and their families. Still, a spouse covered through your former employer usually has the right to buy the group insurance for three years.

Medicare has two parts:

• *Medicare Part A,* hospital insurance, applies to hospital costs, skilled nursing facilities, psychiatric hospitals, and hospice care. Part A is free if you qualify for Medicare. (You've paid for it in payroll taxes.) If you don't automatically qualify for Medicare, you can buy Part A: in 1994 the cost ranged from $184 to $245 per month.

• *Medicare Part B,* medical insurance, is automatically yours unless you decline it. It covers certain doctor's fees, laboratory tests, X-rays, many outpatient services, some ambulance facilities, home health care, and in-home use of durable medical equipment. For Part B coverage in 1994, the government deducted $41.40 from your monthly Social Security check.

For a summary of Medicare-covered services, turn to the charts on pages 152 and 153.

As you choose health-care providers, one major question concerns "Medicare assignment." This is an agreement between a doctor and Medicare that he or she can collect only the amount Medicare approves for Medicare-covered services. Assignment limits the amount you must pay.

Ask providers:

• Do you accept Medicare?
• Do you accept Medicare assignment?

In addition, always present your Medicare card to your health-care provider at the time of service. Be sure to ask if

Medicare covers the service you plan to receive.

Medicare will pay for many of your health-care expenses—but not all of them. In particular, *Medicare doesn't cover most nursing-home care, long-term care in the home, or prescription drugs outside a hospital.* Even though disability, frailty, and memory loss may heighten your need for services, such chronic conditions don't normally require a hospital stay or the daily attention of a doctor or skilled nurse. If a medical problem isn't acute, Medicare probably won't pay for it.

Unfortunately, Medicare also doesn't cover:

- Custodial care that could be given safely and reasonably by a person who is not medically skilled and mainly helps you with daily living;
- Most care outside the United States;
- Dental care and dentures, except when related to acute care;
- Routine checkups and related tests (except for some screening tests, Pap smears, and mammograms);
- Most immunization shots (flu shots are covered);
- Most prescription drugs, except those you receive while hospitalized;
- Routine foot care;
- Tests for, and the cost of, eyeglasses and hearing aids; *or*
- Personal comfort items, such as a phone or TV in your hospital room.

> **T I P** **Getting Help**
> For information about Medicare, Medigap insurance, benefits for low-income people, and flu shots, you can call a hotline operated by the Department of Health and Human Services at (800)638-6833. You can also call this number to report suspected fraud or abuse on the part of insurers or providers.

Beyond Medicare: Medigap and Other Options

A variety of private insurance policies can help you pay for medical expenses, services, and supplies that Medicare covers only partly or not at all. There are several basic types of policies:

- Medicare supplement policies—*Medigap insurance—*

For Low Income Seniors

Medicare offers two programs for low-income people over age 65 and for the disabled.

Under the *Qualified Medicare Beneficiaries Program,* people with incomes at or below the federal poverty level don't have to pay the standard Medicare premiums, deductibles, and coinsurance. The state picks up those costs.

The *Specified Low-Income Medicare Beneficiary Program* assists people with incomes at or near the poverty level. The state pays only the Part B premium.

For more information on these programs, contact your local Department of Social Services or Area Agency on Aging or call the Medicare hotline at (800)638-6833.

—*Excerpted from* Consumer Reports, *September 1994*

Medicare Part A: Hospital Insurance Coverage for 1994			
Services	Benefit	Medicare Pays	You Pay
Hospitalization: semiprivate room and board, general nursing and hospital services and supplies	First 60 days 61st to 90th day 91st to 150th day Beyond 150 days	All but $696 All but $174 a day All but $348 a day Nothing	$696 $174 a day $348 a day All costs
Skilled Nursing Facility Care: semiprivate room and board, general nursing, skilled nursing and rehabilitative services, and other services and supplies	First 20 days Additional 80 days Beyond 100 days	All of approved amount All but $87 a day Nothing	Nothing Up to $87 a day All costs
Home Health Care: part-time or intermittent skilled care, home health aide services, durable medical equipment and supplies, and other services	For as long as you meet Medicare requirements for home health benefits	All of approved amount, 80 percent of approved amount for durable medical equipment	Nothing for services; 20 percent of approved amount for durable medical equipment
Hospice Care: pain relief, symptom management, and support services for the terminally ill	For as long as doctor certifies need	All but limited costs for outpatient drugs and inpatient respite care	Limited costs for outpatient drugs and inpatient respite care
Blood	Unlimited if medically necessary	All but 3 pints per calendar year	For first 3 pints unless you replace them or arrange for another person to do so

Rising Costs

A 1994 study by the American Association of Retired Persons and the Urban Institute projected that retirees would spend an average of $2,803 in out-of-pocket health costs during that year, more than twice as much as in 1987.

pay some of the amounts that Medicare doesn't pay for covered services.

• *Coordinated care plans,* including HMOs, provide health-care services directly for a fixed monthly premium.

• Some employers allow retirees to continue *employer-provided policies,* although sometimes the consumer has to pay more—or all—of the monthly premium.

• *Policies for nursing-home care or long-term care* pay fixed amounts for each day of covered services.

• *Hospital indemnity policies* pay fixed amounts for each day of inpatient hospital services.

• Some policies provide *coverage for specified diseases.*

By far the most important option is Medigap insurance. Some Medigap policies cover Medicare's deductibles; most

Medicare Part B:
Medical Insurance Coverage for 1994

Services	Benefit	Medicare Pays	You Pay
Medical Expenses: doctors' services, inpatient and outpatient medical and surgical supplies, physical and speech therapy, diagnostic tests, durable medical equipment, mental health, and other services	Unlimited if medically necessary	80 percent of approved amount after $100 deductible; 50 percent of approved charges for most outpatient mental-health services	$100 deductible, 20 percent of approved amount and limited charges above approved amount
Clinical Laboratory Services: blood tests, urinalyses, and more	Unlimited if medically necessary	Generally 100 percent of approved amount	Nothing for services
Home Health Care: part-time or intermittent skilled care, home-health-aide services, durable medical equipment and supplies, and other services	For as long as you meet Medicare requirements for home-health benefits	100 percent of approved amount; 80 percent of approved amount for durable medical equipment	Nothing for services; 20 percent of approved amount for durable medical equipment
Outpatient Hospital Treatment services for the diagnosis or treatment of illness or injury	Unlimited if medically necessary	Medicare payment to hospital based on hospital cost	20 percent of billed amount, after $100 deductible
Blood	Unlimited if medically necessary	80 percent of approved amount, after $100 deductible and starting with 4th pint	First 3 pints, plus 20 percent of approved amount for additional pints, after $100 deductible

pay the coinsurance amount. Some also pay for health services not covered by Medicare at all. Consider buying Medigap insurance if you need and can afford private insurance to meet health-care costs that Medicare doesn't cover and you aren't covered by a former employer's health-insurance plan. People with serious health problems who are approaching 65 should definitely take advantage of the open enrollment period for Medigap policies, which ends six months after you first enroll in Medicare Part B. During this period, insurance companies can't deny coverage to you based on your medical history.

In most states, you can choose among 10 standard Medigap plans, labeled "A" through "J." (Some states have fewer than 10, and the federal government has granted

How Medicare Patients are Bilked

To extract more money from Medicare patients, some physicians engage in questionable, if not illegal, practices that make patients pay more than they should. Three to watch out for are overcharges, retainers, and waivers.

Overcharges: In 1993, doctors overcharged nearly 1.5 million Medicare beneficiaries a total of some $101 million. It's illegal under federal law for a doctor who accepts Medicare assignment to collect more than the Medicare-approved charge for a service.

Retainers: Some doctors may require new Medicare patients to sign a retainer agreement obligating them to pay hundreds of dollars for a package of services, implying that Medicare doesn't cover these items. These retainers may be illegal. They also duplicate provisions in Medigap policies.

Waivers: Many doctors ask patients to waive the right to have the doctor bill Medicare directly for his or her services. Doctors may also ask patients to pay separately for telephone calls, medical conferences, and prescription refills—all services Medicare considers part of the fees it pays physicians. The only legal waiver is one that lists a specific uncovered procedure, such as cosmetic surgery.
—*Excerpted from* Consumer Reports, *August 1994*

Medigap Ratings

Consumer Reports has ranked over 70 Medigap policies nationally by price and also lists the best policies in 64 cities. To receive a reprint of the article containing this data, send a check or money order for $3 to Consumer Reports Reprints, P.O. Box 53016, Boulder, CO 80322. Ask for Reprint RO138.

Massachusetts, Minnesota, and Wisconsin waivers to allow slightly different plans.) This makes it easier for consumers to compare coverage and premiums. But *don't* purchase more than one Medigap policy. It's illegal for insurance agents to sell consumers duplicate policies or to use scare tactics to frighten them into dropping existing policies or purchasing policies they don't need or can't afford.

Shop carefully before deciding on the best policy to fit your needs. Except in Massachusetts, Minnesota, and Wisconsin, all new Medigap policies conform to one of the standard benefit plans—*although not at the same price.* In fact, the costs vary significantly. Compare benefits and premiums and satisfy yourself that the insurer is reputable before buying. And in selecting Medigap benefits to meet your needs, remember that Medicare pays only for services it determines to be medically necessary and only the amount it determines to be reasonable. If Medicare won't pay for a particular service, Medigap usually won't either.

Special Medicare reimbursement rules apply if you have health insurance through your job or your spouse's job. If you accept the employer plan *and* join Medicare, Medicare supplements your insurance if the employer plan pays less than Medicare would have paid as primary payer. If you reject the employer plan, Medicare is the only payer, and the employer can't offer you a Medicare Supplemental Policy (Medigap insurance).

> **T I P**
> **If It's Not Medigap**
> *Federal and state laws regulate Medigap policies, which must be clearly identified as Medicare supplemental insurance. Medigap regulations don't necessarily apply to other insurance that might complement Medicare.*

Ask the PROs

The federal government contracts with a Peer Review Organization (PRO) in each state to ensure that Medicare beneficiaries receive care that is reasonable, medically necessary, provided in the most appropriate setting, and meets professionally accepted standards of quality. Directed by physicians, PROs review all written complaints from beneficiaries and their representatives concerning quality of care. They also review bills and records to determine when Medicare shouldn't pay. You can appeal these decisions.

If you're admitted to a hospital, you'll receive a notice explaining your rights under Medicare and how to contact

THE 10 MEDIGAP PLANS

All 10 plans include the basic benefit: Coverage for the Medicare Part A coinsurance for days 61-90 in a hospital, the Medicare coinsurance for a lifetime-reserve days 91-150, 100 percent of the cost of 365 additional lifetime hospital days after all Medicare hospital benefits are exhausted, the reasonable costs under Part A and B for the first three pints of blood, and the Part B coinsurance. These benefits together constitute Plan A.

ADDITIONAL BENEFITS	Plan A	Plan B	Plan C	Plan D	Plan E	Plan F	Plan G	Plan H	Plan I	Plan J
Skilled nursing home coinsurance (days 21-100)			Yes	Yes	Yes	Yes	Yes	Yes	Yes	Yes
Part A hospital deductible		Yes	Yes	Yes	Yes	Yes	Yes	Yes	Yes	Yes
Part B physician deductible			Yes			Yes				Yes
Part B excess physician charges						100%	80%		100%	100%
Foreign travel emergency			Yes	Yes	Yes	Yes	Yes	Yes	Yes	Yes
At-home recovery				Yes			Yes		Yes	Yes
Prescription drugs								*	*	**
Preventive screening					Yes					Yes

* Basic drug benefit with a $250 annual deductible, 50 percent coinsurance, and a $1,250 maximum annual benefit
** Extended drug benefit containing a $250 annual deductible, 50 percent coinsurance, and a $3,000 maximum annual benefit.

Medicare Medigap Frauds

Many insurance companies and agents have thwarted the best intentions of Congress when it mandated uniform Medigap policies. They may:

◆ Steer you to only one or two plans and strongly disparage the others, instead of offering you a choice of the full range of available policies;

◆ Fail to give you price information as required by law;

◆ Urge you to buy benefits you don't need, using misleading sales pitches; and

◆ Play pricing games that will mean nasty surprises for you later on. Different insurance companies charge premiums that vary by hundreds of dollars for the same set of benefits in the same city.

If you suspect fraud or abuse of the Medicare or Medigap programs, call your state Medicare carrier, your state department of insurance, or either of two federal government hot-lines: (800)638-6833 and (800)368-5779.

—Excerpted from
CONSUMER REPORTS,
August 1994

the PRO if the need arises. In some states, the PRO has a toll-free phone number for Medicare beneficiaries to call with questions or complaints. For the phone number of the PRO in your state, call (800)638-6833.

Medicare and HMOs

Medicare usually operates on a fee-for-service basis: you are billed for each visit to a health-care provider. In some locations, HMOs and similar forms of prepaid health-care are available to Medicare enrollees.

HMOs can offer significant benefits to Medicare beneficiaries. Many people find the coverage more comprehensive—and thus preferable to—fee-for-service arrangements. However, most HMOs lock enrollees to providers affiliated with the plan. A member who goes "outside the plan" to a different provider may have to pay more out of pocket.

Medicare coverage can apply to three types of HMOs:

• *Risk contract HMOs* are most common. Medicare pays the HMO a monthly sum to provide your Medicare-covered health care. Depending on the plan, you may have to pay a monthly premium, deductibles, and copayments or coinsurance for certain services. The name "risk contract" comes from the fact that the plan assumes the financial risk for providing your health care.

If you join a risk-contract HMO, follow the plan's rules. If you don't use plan-affiliated providers, you—not Medicare—pay the bills, except in the case of an emergency or urgent care away from the plan's service area.

Risk-contract HMOs must take all applicants who are Medicare beneficiaries, except people with end-stage kidney disease and those already in a Medicare hospice program. These HMOs are especially valuable to people with "pre-existing" serious medical problems.

• If you join a *cost-contract HMO,* Medicare pays the plan a fee to provide all Medicare-covered services. You may have to pay the usual Medicare copayments, deductibles, and extra physicians' charges. You may also pay the HMO a monthly premium to cover Medicare deductibles and copayments. Because cost-contract HMOs also must take all Medicare enrollees who apply, they are another good option for people with a serious medical condition.

• With *health-care prepayment plans,* Medicare pays the plan to provide physician visits, X-rays, lab tests, and other diagnostic tests. Other medical services may be included. You can go outside the plan and still have Medicare benefits. The HMO can deny enrollment to applicants, such as those with serious medical conditions.

Medicare risk-contract HMOs, promoted by the federal government, are growing rapidly in many places. In California, enrollment accounts for about 15 percent of the Medicare population—over half a million enrollees. One-fourth of all southern California Medicare beneficiaries are in risk-contrast HMOs.

The Center for Health Care Rights, a nonprofit organization that provides free education, counseling, and legal assistance to Medicare beneficiaries in Los Angeles County, conducted a study of risk-contract HMOs and found them to be "a cost-effective, high-quality provider of medical services to Medicare beneficiaries." However, the center points out, Medicare HMOs, like fee-for-service medicine, have both advantages and disadvantages for elder health-care consumers.

On the plus side:

• HMOs cost members less. For example, enrollees don't pay the Part B deductible or 20 percent coinsurance. Thus, HMO enrollees don't need a Medicare supplemental health insurance policy (Medigap Insurance), which saves them $700 to $2,000 a year in premiums.

• HMOs often provide additional benefits such as out-patient prescription drugs, optometry, and preventive care at little or no added cost.

• Primary-care physicians coordinate care.

• HMOs have no financial incentive to provide unnecessary—and potentially harmful—medical care.

Pre-Medicare: Younger Elders

The least-insured group of older Americans are people out of work, whether due to job loss or early retirement, but too young for Medicare. According to the American Association of Retired Persons, "50-64 year-olds are more critical of the U.S. health care-system than any other age group." About 55 percent of men and 50 percent of women of this age rate it as poor, compared to about one-third of men and women ages 18 to 49 and over 65. More than 40 percent of 50-64 year olds believe that the quality of their health coverage will decline in the future or that they will lose coverage entirely.

About 2.7 million Americans aged 55 to 64 have no health insurance, and about 60 percent of these uninsured have been without coverage for at least five years.

The SHMO

A new type of Medicare HMO, the Social HMO, is being tested in Boston, Brooklyn, Minneapolis, Portland, Oreg., and Long Beach. The benefits of a SHMO include coverage for a modest amount of long-term care and care management.

For more information on HMOs and Medicaid, turn to Chapter **3**

• Enrollees don't have to complete any paperwork for Medicare-covered services except in emergencies.

On the down side:

• Enrollees in risk-contract and cost-contract HMOs must use plan-affiliated health-care facilities and physicians except in emergencies.

• Enrollees must obtain approval in advance to see a specialist, have non-emergency surgery, or obtain durable medical equipment or other medical services.

• HMOs may have an incentive to cut down on services.

• You can usually receive care only within the HMO's service region except in emergencies. This is especially an issue for people who might winter outside this area.

• It can take up to 30 days to quit the plan.

A Medicaid recipient who is also eligible for Medicare can join an HMO that contracts with Medicare. If you are

WHICH MEDIGAP POLICY IS FOR YOU?

For most people, the important Medigap options to consider are coverage for Medicare's hospital deductible, the coinsurance required for a stay in a skilled nursing facility, and coverage for at-home recovery services, a potentially useful although limited benefit.

Plans B, C, and D cover most basics with few frills. Unless you live in a state where you face a high risk of running into claims from providers who don't accept Medicare assignment, you'll save money if you skip Plan F and its higher-priced cousins, Plans G, I, and J. The plans with drug coverage (H, I, and J) don't appear to be worth the added cost.

Plan B, if you can find it, is a better choice than Plan C. It covers most of the important gaps and is about 16 percent cheaper on average than Plan C.

Plan D is also a better value than Plan C but unfortunately just as hard to find as Plan B. Unlike Plan C, it doesn't cover the $100 deductible for Medicare physicians and outpatient services—a benefit that sometimes adds more than $100 to the premium. Instead, Plan D covers some at-home recovery services that could be useful.

Plans C and F, the darlings of the insurance industry, are nearly identical, but Plan F is particularly attractive to *insurers*. It covers excess physicians'

charges—the amounts doctors can bill patients above Medicare's approved charge. Until recently, doctors had carte blanche to sock patients with high excess charges, a practice known as "balance billing." Horror stories about balance billing have made Plan F an easy sell to consumers. Excess charges are increasingly a thing of the past, however, and insurers seldom have to pay off on that benefit. The average premium for Plan F runs about $160 more than Plan C—in some cases $500 more—yet the estimated average value of the extra benefit is only $53.

—Excerpted from CONSUMER REPORTS, *August 1994*

HMO Misinformation

Consumer Reports has detailed significant abuses by some HMOs that seek elder members whose bills are paid by Medicare:

◆ Sales representatives mislead customers about their plans and even Medicare itself. Sales people often fail to explain that Medicare won't pay for service outside the plan. This lack of knowledge could be financially devastating.

◆ Sales people employ high-pressure tactics.

Despite the sales abuses, *Consumer Reports* concludes that, for many people, obtaining Medicare benefits from an HMO may be an appealing alternative to Medicare coverage and a traditional Medigap policy.

At their best, HMOs offer special programs for Medicare members, screening them for illnesses after they join, directing them to preventive services, keeping track of the drugs they take, and mak-

ing ombudspeople available to resolve complaints and answer questions. At their worst, some HMOs make the elderly fight for benefits, especially those for costly skilled nursing or home care that plans must provide as part of the customary Medicare package.
—*Excerpted from* Consumer Reports, *August 1992*

eligible for Medicare *and* currently receive Medicaid benefits, the state Medicaid program may pay the Medicare Part B premium and, where necessary, the Medicare Part A premium. Contact your local Medicaid office.

RESOURCES

For resources on long-term care, turn to Chapter 12. For resources on home care, turn to Chapter 13. For resources on death with dignity, turn to Chapter 17. For general issues, turn to Chapter 19.

Organizations

American Association of Retired Persons
601 E St., NW
Washington, DC 20049
(202)434-2277
AARP is the largest organization for Americans age 50 and over. It offers a wide range of benefits, including *Modern Maturity* magazine and the monthly "Bulletin." Call or write for membership information and a catalogue of publications and audio-visual materials. For legal assistance, contact AARP's Legal Council for the Elderly at (202)434-2120.

Center for Health Care Rights
520 S. Lafayette Park Pl.
Los Angeles, CA 90057
(213)383-4519
Send $1.00 per pamphlet and a self-addressed stamped envelope for fact sheets on Medicare assignment, how Medicare works, Medicare HMOs, Medigap insurance, long-term-care insurance, and Medicare nursing-home benefits. Send $3.00 for "Your Rights to Medicare Skilled Nursing Home Care: An Advocate's Guide."

Children of Aging Parents, Inc.
Woodbourne Office Campus
1609 Woodbourne Rd.
Levittown, PA 19057
(215)945-6900
Call or write for information, referrals, and publications for caregivers.

Health Insurance Association of America
P.O. Box 41455
Washington, DC 20018
(202)223-7780
Write for free pamphlets: "A Consumer's Guide to Medicare Supplement Insurance," "A Consumer's Guide to Disability Insurance," and "A Consumer's Guide to Long-Term Care Insurance."

National Academy of Elder Law Attorneys
655 North Alvernon Way
Tucson, AZ 85711
(602)881-4005
Call for referrals to attorneys who serve elders or to order a directory .

National Association of Area Agencies on Aging
1112 16th St., NW
Washington, DC 20036
(202)296-8130
The association runs the Eldercare Locator for identifying information and referral services provided by state and local Agencies on Aging. Call (800)677-1116 to get free referrals to elder services and to order *The National Directory for Eldercare Information and Referral.*

National Association of Private Geriatric Care Managers
655 N. Alvernon Way
Tucson, AZ 85711
(602)881-8008
Call or write for referrals to geriatric care managers. You can also order a national directory for $35.

National Council of Senior Citizens
1331 F St., NW
Washington, DC 20004
(202)347-8800
Call or write for general information and assistance in finding a nursing home and solving Social Security and Medicare problems.

National Council on the Aging
409 Third St., SW
Washington, DC 20024
(202)479-1200
Call or write for publications and information on elder services, independent living, and other forms of long-term care.

National Senior Citizens Law Center
1815 H St., NW
Washington, DC 20006
(202)887-5280
Call or write for information about Medigap insurance and referrals to legal services in your area.

Older Women's League
666 11th St., NW
Washington, DC 20001
(202)783-6686
This membership organization advocates for the rights of mid-life and older women. Call or write for low-cost information on caregiving.

United Seniors Health Cooperative
1331 H St., NW
Washington, DC 20005
(202)393-6222
USHC works to improve the quality and reduce the cost of services for elders. Call or write for membership information and a list of publications and other services. *United Seniors Health Report* ($15 for five issues per year) keeps subscribers informed about health care, financial issues, and USHC activities.

**U.S. Department of Health and Human Services
Health Care Financing Administration**
6325 Security Blvd.
Baltimore, MD 21207
(410)966-3000
Write HCFA or contact any Social Security office for many free publications related to Medicare, including "Medicare Q & A: 85 Commonly Asked Questions," "The Medicare Handbook," "Guide to Health Insurance for People with Medicare," "Medicare and Coordinated Care Plans," "Medicare Hospice Benefits," "Medicare Coverage for Second Surgical Opinions," and "Medicare and Your Physician's Bill."

**U.S. Department of Health and Human Services
Social Security Administration**
Baltimore, Maryland 21235
(800)772-1213
Call or write for free copies of many publications in English and Spanish on Social Security benefits, including "Medicare," "Understanding Social Security," "Retirement," "Disability," and other topics. For the most up-to-date figures on deductibles and coinsurance payments, ask for *Social Security Update.*

RESOURCES

Publications

Beyond Medicare: Achieving Long-Term Care Security, by Malvin Schechter (Jossey-Bass, 1993). $34.95.

The Caregiver's Guide: Helping Elderly Relatives Cope with Health and Safety Problems, by Caroline Rob (Houghton Mifflin, 1991). $14.45.

The Columbia University School of Public Health 40+ Guide to Good Health, by Robert Weiss and Gesell Subak-Sharpe (Consumer Reports Books, 1992). $27.95.

Elders Assert Their Rights: A Guide for Residents, Family Members, and Advocates to the Legal Rights of Elderly People with Mental Disabilities in Nursing Homes. $6.95. Order from Elders Project of the Bazelon Center, 1101 15th St., NW, Washington, DC 20005 (202)467-5730.

How to Care for Your Parents: A Handbook for Adult Children, by Nora Jean Levin (Storm King Press, 1992). $6.95.

The Johns Hopkins Medical Handbook: The 100 Major Medical Disorders of People Over the Age of 50 (Rebus, 1992). $39.95.

Looking Forward: The Complete Medical Guide to Successful Aging, by Isadore Rossman (Dutton, 1989). $22.95.

Medicare Made Easy: Everything You Need to Know to Make Medicare Work for You, by Charles Inlander and Charles Mackay (People's Medical Society, 1989). $13.95 ($12.95 for members).

Medicare/Medigap, by Carl Oshiro and Harry Snyder (Consumer Reports Books, 1994). $13.95.

Parentcare Survival Guide: Helping Your Folks Through the Not-So-Golden Years, by Enid Pritikin and Trudy Reece (Barron's, 1993). $8.95.

The 36-Hour Day: A Family Guide to Caring for Persons with Alzheimer's, by Nancy Mace and Peter V. Rabins (Johns Hopkins University Press, 1981). $7.95.

When Parents Age: What Children Can Do, by Tom Adams and Kathryn Armstrong (Berkley Books, 1993). $7.95.

Physician Specialists

By June Mendelson

S ome of the most difficult medical decisions for consumers center on advanced care: When should you see a specialist? What kind of specialist is best for you? What can the specialist do for you?

Fortunately, the person you visit for primary care—the family physician, your child's pediatrician, a gynecologist, a nurse practitioner—will be your key to answering these questions. Most people visit a specialist on the advice of a primary-care provider, so this chapter will help you be an informed partner in making the best possible choices.

Indeed, the questions surrounding your use of a specialist highlight the importance of forming a

> **T I P**
>
> **Your Best Ally**
> *Always work closely with your primary-care provider in seeking a specialist. Indicate to him or her the qualities you desire.* The primary-care provider typically knows the backgrounds of specialists he or she recommends and can provide you with important information

strong partnership with your primary-care provider. He or she will be your first—though not exclusive—source of information both about specialists and about other options. And if the two of you decide that you should consult a specialist, your primary-care provider can continue to help monitor the adequacy of your care.

PART I: CHOOSING A SPECIALIST

Unfortunately, the distinctions among the multitude of medical specialties often make little sense from the patient's perspective. For example, three types of specialists focus on the age of the patient—pediatricians for children, adolescent-medicine physicians for teenagers, and gerontologists for older people—while obstetricians and gynecologists treat only women. Many more specialties focus on parts of the body, such as the heart or the lungs. Surgeons constitute a particularly large and broad group; most specialize even further, dealing with only one organ or area of the body. Psychiatrists treat behavior but share their domain with non-physician psychologists, social workers, and others in the field of mental health. Moreover, the list of "official" medical specialties is in flux, and the realms of

June Ellen Mendelson is a health policy analyst. She has a doctorate in social welfare from Brandeis University.

9

various specialists overlap, making your choice even more complicated.

As a result of this illogical system, a person with a pain of unknown origin faces a seemingly overwhelming challenge. Do you choose a provider appropriate to your age or sex? Or one who specializes in the part of your body where it hurts? How do you find proper treatment? And how do you get the right amount of treatment—neither too much nor too little?

As you face these and other dilemmas, your primary-care provider is an invaluable asset. For one thing, most people lack the training to fully diagnose their own medical needs. Second, some specialists will make an appointment with you only if you have a referral from a primary-care provider. There is also some degree of danger inherent in specialization: specialists focus on a narrower field of knowledge than do primary-care physicians. The many parts of your body all relate to one another, and an illness in one part often affects the rest of you.

The Referral

If you agree with your primary-care provider on the need to see a specialist, he or she will refer you to an appropriate provider. At this point, make sure you understand why you need to see a specialist, why that type of specialist, why that person, and what the specialist will look for. Ask your primary-care provider about dangers, cost, time, options— and what happens if you say no. You might also ask if your primary-care provider has ties to this specialist. Such ties may exist if your primary-care provider belongs to a group practice of which the specialist is also a member.

Ties certainly exist if you belong to a health maintenance organization or other form of managed-care health plan, where the primary-care provider acts as a gatekeeper and makes referrals to a selected panel of specialists within the plan. These managed-care plans are more likely than traditional health insurers to monitor the physician's recommendations and your choice of procedures and treatments. And only rarely will a physician in a managed-care

What to Look for in a Specialist

Good specialists—like good primary-care providers—willingly devote the time it takes to respond to all your concerns about health care, explaining diagnoses and the choices inherent in treatment plans.

plan refer you to a specialist outside the plan's network, although he or she may do so if you require highly specialized care not offered at plan facilities. Certainly, you can expect your primary-care provider to be your ally in convincing the plan of your need for specialized care.

For more information on managed care, turn to Chapter 3

Few people have a problem getting a referral to a specialist when the primary-care provider considers it *medically* necessary. But physicians and patients don't always agree on what constitutes necessary. If you disagree with your primary-care provider, you can:

• *Call* your insurance company or, in a managed-care plan, the medical director or the member-services department. Explain your concern. Explain that you have requested a referral and that your doctor has refused to make one. You'll have to present a strong case.

> **T I P**
>
> **Know Your Insurance**
> Find out what types of specialty care your insurance covers, including restrictions on who provides it. Glossy brochures advertising the benefits of health insurance seldom include a frank discussion of referrals to out-of-plan specialists. Ask before joining a new plan.

• *Persist* with your primary-care provider. Evidence from your own library research might convince him or her that a specialist's care is warranted.

• *Find* a specialist on your own and foot the bill yourself, at least until the specialist provides the evidence you need to convince your primary-care provider or insurer of your need for such care.

Getting a Referral for Complex Care

If you need highly complex care, either your primary-care provider or a specialist may refer you to a subspecialist. Subspecialists are usually associated with academic health centers or teaching hospitals.

More and more consumers are enrolled in managed-care systems that may have few subspecialists in their networks. Some managed-care plans also restrict your choice of medical facilities, perhaps excluding the teaching hospitals where more subspecialists and the most advanced technology are usually found. For example, if a specialist recom-

If you or someone in your family has a very rare problem, chances are a hospital affiliated with a medical school will be the best place to receive treatment. These tend to be the most up-to-date and best-equipped institutions, with relevant specialists and subspecialists on staff.

If a specialist refers you to a hospital for complex care, ask him or her many probing questions, such as:

◆ How often does this hospital treat patients with a problem like yours?

◆ What are the most common complications resulting from treating this condition? What are they in this hospital?

◆ Who is on call at night? Is a senior physician available?

◆ Will a case manager coordinate all aspects of your care? Is this person available by phone? What kind of training does the case manager have?

◆ What type of care can the hospital deliver to your home?

For more questions to ask about a hospital, turn to Chapter 5 ▼

mends cardiac bypass surgery for you, your managed-care plan may restrict you to specific surgeons and facilities. This may satisfy you—or it may not.

Managed-care plans occasionally refer patients out-of-plan. An educated consumer can enter into a discussion with plan providers and perhaps convince them to authorize a controversial treatment. Managed-care plans do have an interest in your health, and they certainly want to avoid malpractice lawsuits, so consumers have some leverage to obtain the care that they need.

Evaluating a Specialist

If your primary-care provider suggests you see a specialist, you'll decide together which person is best qualified to perform the proposed diagnostic procedure or treatment. This decision will make a significant difference in the care you receive. So express your preferences, regardless of whether you have traditional indemnity insurance, participate in a managed-care plan, or lack insurance coverage altogether.

As you decide on a specialist, look for many of the same qualities you seek in anyone from whom you receive health care. First, the specialist must be *competent* to treat your illness. Second, the specialist should inspire *trust* and *respect*. Look for a specialist who treats you as an individual, *listens* to you, and *explains* your problems and options in language you can understand, without condescension.

You can make up your mind about personal characteristics by interviewing a specialist. However, judging competency is a challenge. As a start, your state's Board of Registration in Medicine can provide some information about licensing and credentials. These boards keep public records on all physicians in the state, including:

• Medical school and date of graduation;

• Board certification; *and*

• Hospital privileges.

State medical boards also keep records of formal disciplinary actions—for example in cases concerning mental illness, drug abuse, and alcohol addiction that limit a physician's ability to practice. Most keep track of malpractice and related lawsuits as well, but not out-of-court settlements. If your state has a Freedom of Information Act, you can request information from the state board; some state boards release the information as a matter of course.

Although state governments license physicians, the medical profession itself controls specialist certification. The professional societies set requirements for training and offer specialty examinations and certification. Board certification does offer some confirmation of a physician's competence in a particular field. Conversely, physicians practicing outside their specialty may be less experienced and thus more prone to error.

A physician can specialize—that is, limit his or her practice to an area of interest—without any board certification. However, it's increasingly important for physicians to become board certified in a particular specialty in order to get a job at a hospital and health plan, maintain a private practice and get referrals, or obtain insurance compensation for the care they deliver.

If you are contemplating major surgery, the hospital may tell you if your physician is in good standing. Hospitals don't generally share this information with the consumer, but they may at least let you know if the hospital approved the doctor for the procedure in question. Hospitals also keep licensing, performance, and quality-assurance records about their staff physicians, and the trend is toward making more information available to the public.

Bad Docs?

Physician disciplinary actions hit an all-time high in 1993, with 3,078 doctors disciplined by state medical boards. In 1,176 cases, the board revoked or suspended the doctor's license, imposing milder sanctions on the others. To obtain a list of physicians with disciplinary actions, contact your state board of registration in medicine.

The National Practitioner Databank keeps selected information on malpractice cases and formal disciplinary actions against physicians across the country. The information is available to health-care organizations and to the state medical boards that monitor licensing. Unfortunately, it isn't available directly to you, although Congress may change this soon.

You can also consult *Questionable Doctors,* available from Public Citizen's Health Research Group. It names 10,289 doctors disciplined by the states

> **T I P**
>
> **Disciplinary Record**
> *To order a copy of* Questionable Doctors, *contact the* Public Citizen Health Research Group, 2000 P St., NW, Washington, DC 20036 (202)833-3000. *$200 for complete U.S. listing; $15 for a single state.*

and the federal government since 1986. About 70 percent of these doctors were allowed to keep practicing. The total cases includes 1,346 criminal convictions, 1,130 instances of over-prescribing drugs or prescribing the wrong ones, 817 instances of alcohol or drug abuse, and 173 instances of sexual misconduct with a patient.

PART II: GETTING GOOD SPECIALIST CARE

Specialists deal with two general facets of medical care: diagnosis and treatment. To find the right specialist, seek satisfactory answers to questions about both areas of care. If a specialist doesn't have the time to answer all your questions immediately, set up another appointment to talk further. Insist that the specialist take all the time you require to understand what's going on with your body. A frank discussion and probing questions will aid you in making the best decisions in collaboration with your doctors. Also, feel free to seek the help of your primary-care provider in evaluating what the specialist tells you.

If a specialist proposes a particular test, ask:
- Will this test tell you if you are all right?
- What are the chances the test will be wrong?
- How will you find out about the results?
- How often will you need another test?
- What additional tests will you need?

If the specialist says you have a serious medical problem

When a Credential Isn't a Credential

According to *Money* magazine, more than 100 self-styled medical boards offer membership with few or no requirements. "Be sure the certification a doctor claims reflects membership in one of the...boards recognized by the American Board of Medical Specialties." *Contact the ABMS for information.*

and recommends a particular treatment, ask:

- What is wrong with you? What is your illness or condition?
- What are the immediate and long-term risks and side effects of the recommended treatment?
- What are the benefits of the recommended treatment?
- Will you be better in one year due to the treatment? In five years?
- What is the specialist's experience with cases like yours?
- What complications might arise?
- Can you see your medical record and keep a copy?

Before Agreeing to Surgery

Specialists, more often than generalists, appear to rely on surgical interventions and technology to diagnose and treat patients. Because any surgery is dangerous, and because you only want to receive surgery that is absolutely necessary, find out:

- What will happen during the surgery?
- What will happen if you refuse surgery?
- Who will perform the surgery? How often has he or she done it in the past? What's his or her success rate? How

VIDEO ASSIST

Some specialists use interactive video programs to educate patients about treatment options and involve them more deeply in making decisions. Developed by the Foundation for Informed Medical Decision Making, these videos provide the patient—and the doctor—with the information and options needed to make smart decisions about treatment.

The video on breast cancer, for example, includes interviews with several women regarding their surgical experiences. It provides clear and simple explanations of the risks and benefits of the various options for treatment after surgery, such as chemotherapy and hormone treatment.

The foundation's programs present unbiased information about the potential harms and benefits of surgical and nonsurgical treatments. In one study, conducted at Group Health Cooperative, an HMO in Washington State, surgery rates were cut in half among men who watched the video on prostate disease, with many viewers opting instead for watchful waiting. Yet the video contains no apparent bias against surgery. No wonder both patients *and* insurers have positive comments about this tool for strengthening the partnership between you and your health-care providers.

For more information, contact the Foundation for Informed Medical Decision Making, P.O. Box 5457, Hanover, NH 03755-5457.

9

often has he or she seen a condition like yours?

- Who will choose the anesthesiologist? What is his or her experience?
- What is the general success rate for this kind of procedure?
- What alternative treatments are available? What are the risks and benefits of each?
- How much will the surgery cost?
- What are the most common complications?
- Will you be able to resume your former activities?
- When will you be able to return to work?
- What's the best you can expect?
- What's most likely to occur?
- What if you wait until next year, or until you have insurance coverage?

Second Opinions

If you disagree with a specialist on what constitutes the best care for you, try again to work things out. That physician already knows a great deal about you and your problem. Moreover, your care is essentially under way, and it's possible that you misunderstood the initial explanations. If you can't resolve the problem in this way, consult your primary-care provider for advice about your options.

One of those options is getting a "second opinion" from another specialist. Remember, medicine is an inexact science. Uncertainties about treatments and diagnoses arise because doctors differ in their practice styles, education, and training—sometimes in controversial ways. Indeed, the list of conditions for which the treatment plans are controversial is long, and it changes constantly as evidence accumulates in favor of or against long-accepted practices. A few examples of maladies and procedures for which doctors differ significantly are: breast cancer, prostate cancer, other cancers, back pain, recurrent colds in children, tonsillectomies, high blood pressure, and cardiac bypass surgery.

This list is far from comprehensive; rather, it illustrates what physicians and patients confront when there is no definitive solution. This is a major reason patients seek—with the support of insurance companies—second opinions before accepting a specialist's diagnosis or recommended treatment.

Two doctors rarely offer greatly divergent diagnoses. More likely, they'll differ on the alternatives they propose and on your chances of getting better. If the outcome is especially uncertain, you might find almost as many opinions as there are doctors; you must then pay special attention to working with healthcare professionals to make a wise decision.

> **Shopping Around**
> *Second opinions can be invaluable, but don't seek one just to shop for the diagnosis you'd like to hear. There is a chance you could needlessly damage your relationship with the first specialist or your primary-care providers.*

A second opinion is especially critical for surgery and other "invasive" procedures. In fact, many insurers, and even some states, require second opinions before many types of surgery. A second opinion helps you and the doctor decide if such a drastic step is really needed. It can also help you discover alternatives that could be safer, cheaper, less painful, and even more effective.

Usually, you'll want a board-certified doctor for the second opinion. And try to get the second opinion from someone independent of the person who gave the first opinion. Don't let your specialist refer you to a friend of his or hers or to someone with essentially the same training.

> **Copy Your Records**
> *Your insurance company might pay for a second opinion but not for a repeat test. Get copies of your test records or X-rays and bring them to the person providing the second opinion.*

Of course, finding a truly independent physician can be more difficult in an HMO, where you normally consult only doctors within the plan. Check with the HMO's member-services department about going outside the plan for a second opinion.

Fortunately, it's not as hard as you might expect to tell a specialist you want a second opinion. Because it's such a common practice, even a requirement in many instances, few doctors will treat you as uppity for suggesting it. To find the best person to give you a second opinion:

• Ask your primary-care provider;
• Check with local medical societies; *and*
• Call the Second Surgical Opinion Hot Line, operated by the U.S. Department of Health and Human Services: (800)638-6833; in Maryland only, call (800)492-5603.

PART III: MONEY MATTERS

Specialists cost more. How much that fact matters to you is a very personal issue that rests in part on one point: do you have medical insurance?

If you do, find out what your policy covers. Will the insurance pay for the kind, quality, and quantity of specialized care you and your physician decide is warranted? After all, that's one purpose of insurance: to ensure that your personal finances don't force you to go without care you need. On the other hand, your insurance status doesn't affect your need for a particular procedure, only your ability to pay for it.

The insurance company may encourage you to use less-expensive providers or seek less expensive forms of care— *both of which may make sense for you as well.* If you have insurance through your employer, he or she may share the interest of the insurer in limiting the medical bill, perhaps leading him or her to pay less attention to quality than you would yourself.

If you don't have insurance, or if your insurance doesn't cover the recommended care, you'll have to add a strong concern for cost-effectiveness to your demand for quality. Seek out the same data that cost-conscious insurers use, comparing the specialist's fees to standard rates for the procedures he or she is recommending. To get this data, you can look in major libraries for *Medical Economics* magazine, which regularly publishes price information. You can also ask in the library's business section for insurance publications that include the data you need.

Alternatively, private companies sell information on fees. For example, Medirisk, based in Atlanta, offers a subscriber

---

Third Opinions!

A third opinion may be in order if two specialists differ significantly in their reports. Also consider a third voice if you feel you have good cause to be dissatisfied with the first two opinions. Medicare often covers third opinions, as do other insurers. Check your policy.

Convincing insurers to pay for a third opinion is usually simple if two specialists disagree. It will be hardest to convince insurers of your need for a third opinion if the first two say treatment isn't warranted. You may have to become a sleuth and conduct research in medical libraries. And you may decide to consult a lawyer.

If you are a member of an HMO, you might choose to pay for a visit to an out-of-plan physician. It may be worth it, both in terms of your financial health and your medical care.

service through which you can find out pricing information.

Some Specialist Fees					
Procedure	Boston	New York	Washington	Phoenix	National Average
Radial Keratotomy	$1,782	$3,627	$1,964	$1,438	$1,405
Open Heart Surgery	$8,728	$10,075	$8,051	$7,015	$7,855
Tonsillectomy	$836	$1,547	$990	$816	$774

Source: Medirisk, Inc.

Primary Means First

If at all possible, see a primary-care provider before consulting a specialist. This saves money, plus you'll benefit from the doctor's more general knowledge.

Primary-care providers can handle about 70 percent of physician office visits effectively. However, in the United States, specialists provide most medical care, and most practicing physicians limit their work to a specialty. One-third of all primary care is delivered by specialists, often at higher specialist rates. This contrasts with the situation in Western Europe and Canada and yet one more reason why U.S. medical bills are sky high.

The predominance of specialists in the United States contributes to rising costs and compromises quality by contributing to a piecework, procedure-oriented medical system. Specialists tend to use more health-care resources than primary-care providers because they depend more on technology, tests, and procedures. One indicator of the impact this has on cost and quality comes from studies by Dr. John Wennberg revealing the incidence of back surgery "epidemics" upon the arrival of a neurosurgeon to an area.

Judgment Calls

For certain types of specialty care, you may have to fight to get your insurer to foot the bill, especially if the treatment could be considered experimental or optional. For example, according to a study published in the *New England Journal of Medicine*, insurers are "arbitrary and

Bargaining

"While most of us might feel uncomfortable haggling with our doctors, and while most doctors would rather not have to justify their fees, there are times when medical bills could and should be discussed." That's the advice of *Boston Globe* health-care writer Madeline Drexler.

Most health insurers bargain with providers in some way, and you can too—if you lack insurance or if you decide to get care that your insurance doesn't cover.

"If you can't pay up," notes Drexler, "your physician or hospital billing department might offer to discount the charge, arrange payment over time, or, in rare cases, throw out the bill."

capricious" about paying for experimental bone-marrow transplants and high-dose chemotherapy for breast cancer.

Conducted by Duke University physicians William Peters and Mark Rogers, the study found that insurers refused to pay for the procedures for 121 out of a group of 533 patients. The major reason given for the denial: the treatments are experimental and unproved. Of course, insurers also resist paying for these procedures because of the price tag: $100,000 or more for a bone-marrow transplant.

On the other hand, the study illustrates the pay-off for consumer persistence. Of the 121 people the insurers initially told no deal, 62 ultimately received payment after hiring attorneys.

Physician Self-Referral and Unnecessary Tests

If you have insurance, your health plan will scrutinize a specialist's bill for unwarranted tests and other procedures and may even insist that you get authorization for tests in advance. If you are paying the bills yourself, it's up to you to watch out for unnecessary tests and padded bills.

Consider the results of a 1994 investigation by the federal General Accounting Office. The study analyzed 2.4 million records involving seven types of diagnostic tests and found strong patterns of abuse. Physicians who belonged to a practice owning the equipment for special imaging tests, such as MRIs and X-rays, were far more likely to recommend such tests than were physicians who sent patients to unaffiliated providers. "The in-practice rates were about 3 times higher for MRI scans, about 2 times higher for CT scans, 4.5 to 5 times higher for ultrasound, echocardiology, and diagnostic nuclear medicine imaging, and about 2 times higher for complex and simple X-rays." An MRI costs $400 to $1,000.

This problem goes by the name of "self-referral," where physicians benefit financially from sending you to certain providers for care. About 10 percent of physicians have ownership interests that raise issues of self-referral. "By trading on their patients' trust," writes Steven Sternberg in *Mother Jones,* "doctors . . . use what's known as 'self-referral' to enhance their annual incomes—they send their patients to companies in which they have a financial interest, companies which may be more expensive or less qualified to perform the services needed."

Only New York, Florida, Illinois, and New Jersey restrict self-referral in any way, and these restrictions don't apply to many situations.

PART IV: WHO DOES WHAT

No introduction to physician specialists would be complete without some explanation of the many types of specialists you might encounter. The American Board of Medical Specialties recognizes 24 medical specialty boards and 73 subspecialties. Subspecialists must be certified in one of the specialties before completing their subspecialty training.

The categories of specialists and subspecialists have steadily grown in number over the past decade, as have the requirements for training. The ABMS publishes a book listing board-certified physicians. You can find it in many libraries.

Primary-care providers can help you choose among the many specialties. As you can see from the list of specialties, the areas of expertise overlap significantly from the point of view of patients. For example, a cardiologist and thoracic surgeon both treat heart disease, but their approaches to treatment reflect their differing training. Similarly, for back pain, you might consult a neurologist, orthopedic surgeon, neurosurgeon, or a sports-medicine doctor.

Medical and Surgical Specialties

For each of the following specialties, a member board of the American Board of Medical Specialties certifies physicians in that field. For example, there is an American Board of Allergy/Immunology, an American Board of Anesthesiology, and an American Board of Colon and Rectal Surgery.

AMA on Physician Self-Referrals

The Council on Ethical and Judicial Affairs of the American Medical Association suggests that physicians not refer patients to an outside health-care facility in which they have an investment, unless they also directly provide care or services at the facility.

The council also says that physicians should disclose their investment interest to patients when making a referral. Patients should get a list of alternative facilities.

Sports Medicine

Sports medicine is a rapidly growing focus for physicians, who specialize in enhancing health and fitness and also in preventing injury and illness. Many are trained in orthopedic surgery and add training in such diverse areas as exercise physiology, nutrition, and psychology.

For information on alternative specialists and specialties, turn to Chapter **10**

Medical or Surgical

Specialists and sub-specialists fall into two major categories: medical and surgical. Among the surgical specialists and sub-specialists are *colon and rectal surgeons, neurosurgeons, ophthalmologists, orthopedic surgeons, plastic surgeons, thoracic surgeons,* and *urologists.* Medical specialists and subspecialists include *cardiologists, endocrinologists, gastroenterologists, hematologists, pediatricians,* and *rheumatologists.*

For more information on primary care, turn to Chapter ▼ **4**

Allergists and immunologists diagnose and manage disorders of the immune system, such as asthma, eczema and other adverse allergic reactions.

Anesthesiologists administer medications during or after surgery. They work with surgeons in operations, and some work independently to treat chronic pain and relax patients.

Colon and rectal surgeons deal with disorders affecting the lower digestive tract.

Dermatologists deal with diseases of the skin, mouth, external genitalia, hair, and nails, and with related sexually transmitted diseases.

Emergency medicine deals with care in a hospital emergency ward, including recognizing and treating a wide spectrum of physical and mental conditions.

> **T I P** **Surgery Advice**
>
> The American College of Surgeons publishes a series of free pamphlets, "When You Need an Operation." For copies, write to the ACS, Office of Public Information, 55 E. Erie St., Chicago, IL 60611 (312)664-4050.
>
> The American Society of Anesthesiologists and the American Association of Nurse Anesthetists both have free booklets on what you should know about anesthesia. For copies, write to ASA, 520 Northwest Highway, Park Ridge, IL 60068 (708)825-5586 or AANA, 222 S. Prospect Ave., Park Ridge, IL 60068 (708)692-7050.

Family practice deals with preventing, diagnosing, and treating a wide variety of ailments in patients of all ages.

Internists focus on managing common and acute illnesses, including long-term follow up. They provide primary care, but over half of all internists also train in a subspecialty. For example, a growing subspecialty in gerontology focuses on aging.

Medical geneticists diagnose and advise patients with diseases that are inherited.

Nephrologists treat diseases of the kidney.

Neurologists deal with the diagnosis and treatment of diseases and impaired functions of the brain, spinal cord, and autonomic nervous system.

Neurological surgeons perform surgery on the nervous system. This includes the diagnosis and surgical treatment of disease or impaired function of the brain, spinal cord, peripheral nerves, muscles, and autonomic nervous system.

Nuclear medicine makes use of radioactive isotopes for diagnosis, therapy, and research.

Obstetricians and gynecologists specialize in female reproductive system and associated disorders.

Ophthalmologists provide comprehensive vision and eye care, including surgery.

Orthopedic surgeons use surgery to restore function to damaged joints, backs, feet, and other extremities.

Otolaryngologists are surgeons who diagnose and treat disorders of the head and neck. The specialty focuses on hearing and speech pathology and disorders of the esophagus, nose, throat, face, and jaw.

Pathologists examine clinical samples for the purpose of diagnosing and understanding disease. Pathology has many subspecialties, including forensic pathology, which contributes to criminal investigations.

Pediatricians care for children. The many subspecialties of pediatrics include adolescent medicine, pediatric emergency medicine, and pediatric infectious disease.

Physical medicine focuses on diagnosing and treating patients with disabilities that impair their ability to complete the activities of daily living.

Plastic surgeons repair and reconstruct all areas of the body. They reduce scars, reconstruct breasts for cancer patients, and correct undesirable structures.

Preventive medicine aims to promote and maintain the health of groups of people. Screening programs for tuberculosis, cholesterol, and AIDS are the province of this specialty.

For more information on health care providers for women, turn to Chapter **6**

For more information on eye care, turn to Chapter **15**

For more information on care for children, turn to Chapter **7**

A Welcome Reversal

Several recently established medical specialties and subspecialties each cover a broad range of diseases, reflecting a trend toward more generalized care:

Family medicine resembles general medical practice as a field. Family medicine practitioners fulfill an obvious need, and consumers seek them out.

Occupational medicine focuses on the myriad diseases associated with the workplace. For more on occupational illnesses and hazards, turn to Chapter 16.

Preventive medicine focuses on ways to prevent disease. These physicians study internal medicine and public health.

Psychiatrists diagnose and treat disorders of the mind and brain, including mental, emotional, and addictive disorders.

Pulmonary specialists treat diseases of the lung and respiratory system.

Radiologists use X-rays to diagnose and treat diseases, especially malignant tumors.

General surgeons receive training to manage a broad range of surgical conditions affecting almost any area of the body. Most continue their training with education in a subspecialty.

Thoracic surgeons operate on the chest.

Urologists manage medical and surgical problems of the genitourinary system. Their expertise encompasses disorders of the kidney, bladder, adrenal gland, and the male reproductive system.

RESOURCES

For more resources on primary care, turn to the resources section in Chapter 4. For general resources, turn to Chapter 19.

Organizations

American Board of Medical Specialties
1007 Church St.
Evanston, IL 60201
(708)491-9091
Send $1.50 for a copy of the ABMS's 30-page pamphlet, "Which Medical Specialist Is for You?" The ABMS can also provide you with the names and addresses of the various boards of specialization it recognizes. *The Directory of Medical Specialists,* published by the ABMS, lists all board-certified specialists throughout the United States; copies are available in major libraries.

Mediguard/Medirisk, Inc.
Two Piedmont Center
3565 Piedmont Rd.
Atlanta, GA 30305
(800)656-3337
Mediguard is a subscriber service that allows consumers to compare local medical prices and negotiate medical fees with their physicians. Consumers in any city can get Mediguard physician fee information and coaching via a toll-free number staffed by representatives familiar with health-care procedures and costs. Mediguard representatives can tell subscribers about premium, typical, discounted, and Medicare fees for any medical procedure in their area.

Publications

Good Operations, Bad Operations, by Charles Inlander and the staff of the People's Medical Society. Order from People's Medical Society, 462 Walnut St., Allentown, PA 18102 (800)624-8773. $27.50 ($22.50 for members).

"Medicare Coverage for Second Surgical Opinions: Your Choice Facing Elective Surgery." Free. Write to the Health Care Financing Administration, Office of Public Affairs, Room 403B, 200 Independence Ave., SW, Washington, DC 20201. Ask for Publication No. HCFA 02173.

The Patient's Guide to Surgery, by Edward L. Bradley (Consumer Reports, 1994). $16.95.

Alternative Health Care

By Nicolás P. Carballeira

A growing number of people in the United States are seeking alternative ways to address their health concerns. The prestigious *New England Journal of Medicine* reports that as many as one-third of all American health-care consumers try alternative healing practices in a given year—sometimes exclusively, although more often at the same time as they seek conventional care. Moreover, under a mandate from Congress, the National Institutes of Health has grudgingly begun to study alternative medicines. And many Americans continue to utilize the Asian, African, Native American, and Middle Eastern traditional medicines that are part of their own culture's history, even as these same approaches to health and healing attract other Americans as well.

In fact, if you hesitate to depend totally on conventional medicine, you'll find a bewildering abundance of choices, and they'll have names as exotic as those in mainstream health-care practice: ayurveda, naturopathy, chiropractic, osteopathy, Tibb Unani.... How can you make informed decisions amid this veritable jumble of probably unfamiliar healing practices? And just as important, why should you explore them at all?

PART I: A SHORT HISTORY

Despite the growing popularity of alternatives in health care, many Americans still approach the terrain with ambivalence, confusion, or fear. Thus, it's well to begin at the beginning, with a capsule history of the divergence of conventional and alternative health care.

Conventional medicine's dominance over health care in the United States is actually a fairly recent phenomenon. Into the early twentieth century, U.S. medicine was quite pluralistic. Conventional medical doctors—also known as allopaths—outnumbered other types of trained medical providers, yet homeopaths, herbalists, and others comprised about 20 percent of all practitioners.

It was the 1910 *Flexner Report*, commissioned by the Carnegie Foundation and backed by the Rockefeller Institute for Medical Research, that transformed U.S. medicine

Nicolás P. Carballeira, ND, MPH, directs the Latino Health Institute of Massachusetts. He is a doctor of naturopathy.

into a research-oriented, hospital-based science practiced almost exclusively by those who had the means to undertake eight years of university study. Upon publishing his report, Abraham

> **T**
> **I**
> **P**
>
> **Time to Walk**
> *When it comes to health care, no one—neither conventional nor alternative providers—can guarantee the result you seek. If anyone does, start walking. You want practitioners who recognize the limitations, as well as the strengths, of their respective systems.*

Flexner visited 155 medical schools, recommending funding for those which agreed to pattern themselves on German laboratory-based medical education. By 1922, more than a third of the medical schools in existence in 1900 had closed—including over 70 percent of the schools primarily training minorities and 100 percent of those primarily training women.

While some aspects of the quality of conventional medical education undoubtedly improved as a result of the Flexner report, such training became virtually out of reach for anyone other than upper-middle-class white men. This fed the shortage of conventional medical care for the poor, women, and minorities. Moreover, mainstream funding bypassed alternative medical systems, making training and credentialing of these approaches less reliable. In short, alternative healing retreated from the public eye into the status of marginal knowledge.

Today, many Americans regard alternative healers with suspicion even as they have learned to doubt the infallibility of conventional medicine and its practitioners. And their suspicion is probably often justified, given the fragmentation and minimal opportunities for clinical training in alternative healing. As a result, the consumer's task of finding trustworthy, well-trained practitioners is especially important—and challenging.

A Question of Balance

Even as conventional and alternative medicine have followed separate paths, they have continued to influence one another. Indeed, along with alternative practitioners, some conventional providers today understand health as a proper

Consumer Reports on Alternative Health Care Providers

"Anyone venturing into the world of alternative medicine . . . is likely to find it as frustrating to explore as it is enticing. This is a field that encompasses vastly different treatments. It's a field whose practitioners range from sober academic physicians to entrepreneurial faith healers. And it's a field where there are still too few careful scientific studies, and where investigators haven't even agreed on what rules of evidence should apply."

10

What Is Holistic Medicine?

Holistic medicine, a broad term, encompasses a range of healing philosophies that view a patient as a whole person, not just as a disease or a collection of symptoms. Holistic practitioners often address their clients' emotional and spiritual dimensions, as well as nutritional, environmental, and lifestyle factors that may contribute to illness. Many holistic practitioners combine natural or alternative techniques with conventional ones like medication and surgery.

balance, specific to each individual, that changes with the seasons and time of life. Health isn't just the absence of symptoms of disease. Rather, it's the normal, natural state that enables a person to thrive in, or adapt to, a wide range of environments and stresses. Illness is an imbalance or disharmony arising from stresses that inordinately tax the organism's vital force.

The predominant alternative practitioner's view on healthy behavior is best summarized in Hippocrates' dictum *primum, non nocere*—first, do no harm. When illness arises, the therapist's task is to determine how and why the patient is out of balance and then prescribe dietary and gentle intervention measures to help the whole person return to the natural state of health. This moves the emphasis away from treatments that encourage long-term dependence on strong external measures and medications and toward prevention and mild corrective measures in opposition to the cause of the disease.

TIP

Mix and Match?
You might benefit from specific alternative or conventional treatments without accepting an entire system or endorsing your practitioner's total medical philosophy.

ENTERING THE MAINSTREAM

A 1993 *New England Journal of Medicine* article woke up the mainstream medical profession to the widespread use of alternative practices in the United States—and to the need to recognize this fact. Entitled "Unconventional Medicine in the United States," the article was based on a survey of 1,539 adults: 34 percent had used at least one unconventional therapy in the past year.

According to the arti-cle, American consumers spent $10.3 billion out of their pockets on unconventional treatments in 1990, compared to $12.8 billion for out-of-pocket hospitalization costs and $23.5 billion out of pocket for all physician services.

The average person seeking unconventional therapy spent $27.60 for each of 19 visits over the year. The people most likely to use unconventional care had relatively more educa-tion and higher income than the average American—as is true of health care in general.

People tended to seek alternative care and an allopathic physician for the same condition. However, most consumers didn't tell their allopathic doctor about the unconventional treatment. Thus, the article suggests that medical doctors routinely ask patients about their use of unconventional therapy.

Central to the strength of alternative practices is that they relate health and healing to a person's whole social environment, including his or her spiritual or religious beliefs. A common critique of conventional medicine is that it ignores connections between the individual and the surrounding environment. In contrast, most systems of alternative medicine claim to treat the body and mind as indivisible.

PART II: WHO DOES WHAT?

In a single chapter, it's impossible to do justice to every system of alternative medicine, or even to any one approach. Both the depth and the variety of the field are tremendous. Some techniques are geared to the long term and others to a few office visits. Some might form your primary medical care; others you'd consider if you had a specific need, such as a chronic headache. Some people seek all their health care from alternative providers, but, just as often, conventional and alternative practices can complement one another beneficially.

Start by reviewing the following capsule descriptions of a few major systems and techniques that are considered alternative. Then consult a number of publications on those that appeal to you the most. You can also contact the organizations listed at the end of this chapter. Most of them can supply more information on their approach to health care, as well as the names of practitioners in your area.

Naturopathy

Naturopathic physicians provide primary care, including handling natural childbirth. They treat disease and restore health using nutrition, herbal medicine, homeopathy, physical medicine, exercise therapy, lifestyle counseling, acupuncture, and psychotherapy. Naturopathic physicians cooperate with all branches of medical science, referring patients to other practitioners for diagnosis or treatment when appropriate. A major component of naturopathic medicine is a detailed patient history that provides a comprehensive background. In addition, when appropriate,

---

Hippocrates on Diseases and Cures

"Diseases caused by overeating are cured by fasting; those caused by starvation are cured by feeding up. Diseases caused by exertion are cured by rest; those caused by indolence are cured by exertion. To put it briefly, the physician should treat disease by the principle of opposition to the cause of the disease according to its form, its seasonal and age incidence, countering tenseness by relaxation and vice versa. This will bring the patient most relief and seems to me to be the principle of healing."

—*Hippocrates, credited with originating all Western medicine*

naturopathic physicians use diagnostic tests, such as blood tests, X-rays, and examining by touch.

Alaska, Arizona, Connecticut, Florida, Hawaii, Montana, Oregon, Rhode Island, Utah, and Washington license naturopathic physicians. The District of Columbia registers naturopathic doctors.

Naturopathic physicians study conventional medical sciences, although they don't receive a degree as allopathic medical doctors (MD). To become a naturopathic physician (ND), a person must complete at least four years of graduate study, with courses in traditional naturopathic philosophy, medical science, and natural therapeutics.

Osteopathy

Osteopathic medicine rests on the theory that the entire body must be considered when treating disease. An osteopathic physician (DO) provides comprehensive medical care, including preventive medicine, diagnosis, surgery, hospital referrals, prescriptions, and other medications.

In diagnosis and treatment, osteopathic physicians pay particular attention to the joints, bones, muscles, and nerves. They are specially trained in osteopathic manipulative treat-

Naturopathy Training

The only three recognized colleges of naturopathic medicine in the United States are Bastyr College in Seattle, Washington, National University in Portland, Oregon, and South West College in Scottsdale, Arizona. The Council on Naturopathic Medical Education accredits these schools.

OFFICIAL RECOGNITION?

In 1991, the National Institutes of Health, the federal agency funding medical research, established the Office of Alternative Medicine. The office is an information clearinghouse on alternative medicine, and it awards grants for evaluating alternative approaches to medical care.

With a $2 million budget to start, the office is the government's first institutional foray into alternative medicine. While the office doesn't advocate particular treatments, its existence has added to the credibility of alternatives. And its congressional support reflects in part the public's frustration with rising medical costs and the growing awareness that conventional medicine is itself far from a precise science.

However, the Office of Alternative Medicine has had a troubled beginning. In mid-1994, Dr. Joseph Jacobs resigned after 20 months as director. According to the New York Times, he complained of a "ridiculously small" budget and political interference. One source of ongoing controversy is that mainstream scientists want the office to rely on clinical trials to determine the safety and effectiveness of medicines, while advocates of alternatives seek more reliance on long-term field investigations in which researchers examine a practice on site.

ment—using their hands to diagnose, treat, and prevent illness. Some rely on the manipulation of the cervical vertebrae to treat headaches. All 50 states license osteopathic physicians to perform surgery and prescribe medication.

Osteopathy shares much the same scientific foundation as conventional medicine. For example, osteopaths apply the standard methods of diagnosis and treatment. The major distinction is manipulative therapy.

Like conventional medical doctors, osteopaths can specialize, and in essentially the same fields. These specialists are board certified. Some hospitals grant privileges to both MDs and DOs.

Chinese Medicine and Acupuncture

Encompassing a variety of practices, Chinese medicine rests on understanding the relationships between *yin* and *yang* and the five elements. Illness results when these forces don't balance. Chinese medical practitioners treat a broad range of both chronic and acute illnesses with a variety of ancient and modern therapeutic methods—including herbal medicine, massage and manipulation, heat therapy, and counseling on nutrition and lifestyle. They rely heavily on basic diagnostic methods: looking, listening, smelling, asking, and touching.

Acupuncture is perhaps the best known and most popular Chinese healing technique. Acupuncturists insert very thin needles into the patient's skin. Often recognized in the United States as a way to relieve pain, acupuncture is also used to improve their patients' overall well-being and to treat acute, chronic, and degenerative conditions.

> **T I P**
>
> **Warning Sign**
> *Be wary if an acupuncturist tells you to leave your current doctor or stop taking prescribed medications. Consult your doctor or another primary-care provider first.*

Acupressure involves the same concepts as acupuncture but replaces the needles with finger pressure.

Twenty-two states restrict the practice of acupuncture to physicians or people operating under the strict supervision of a physician. In general, there are no restrictions on acu-

10

Acupuncture Credentials

All states allow physicians to practice acupuncture; 14 require them to have formal training. Physician acupuncturists often belong to the American Academy of Medical Acupuncture. The National Commission for the Certification of Acupuncturists certifies nonphysician acupuncturists. Twenty-four states and the District of Columbia license nonphysicians to practice acupuncture.

pressure, but some states require a massage license.

Consumer Reports recommends a list of points to consider if you are thinking about acupuncture:

• Consult your doctor before you visit an acupuncturist. Your primary-care physician should know about, and cooperate with, all your health-care providers.

• Insist that an acupuncturist use sterile, disposable needles to lessen the risk of infection.

• Discuss fees and any possibility of insurance coverage before treatment.

• Discuss your expectations with the practitioner.

• Evaluate your progress. If six to eight treatments don't produce some benefit, either the treatment or the practitioner isn't right for you.

Homeopathy

Homeopaths address illness by administering infinitesimal amounts of natural substances that in larger amounts would cause the same illness to occur in a healthy person. They commonly treat infant and childhood diseases, infections, fatigue, allergies, arthritis, and other chronic illnesses.

Homeopaths claim to enhance a body's natural defense mechanisms and stimulate a person's own healing process while avoiding harmful side effects. The remedies are available from homeopaths, health-food stores, and drugstores, as well as by mail. Homeopathic remedies appeal to some people who are afraid of more potent drugs.

Homeopathic remedies often contain *no detectable amount of any active ingredient.* As a result, federal regulations don't apply to these remedies. However, they are also exempt from FDA requirements for scientific proof that a drug is effective against disease.

Homeopathic remedies, because they are so diluted, are safe in themselves. The danger lies in the possibility that you might forego other necessary treatments or fall victim to excessive claims or insufficient warnings on labels.

Chiropractic

Chiropractic rests on the premise that the spine is a fundamental conduit and support: misaligned vertebrae press on the spinal cord and lead to illness or otherwise diminish a person's ability to function. A chiropractic doctor (DC) seeks to analyze and correct these misalignments. Most people consult chiropractors for pain. Spinal manipulation is generally recognized to help some people with lower back pain. Chiropractors also prescribe diet modification and exercise to promote wellness. Some chiropractors incorporate other alternative therapies into their practice as well.

All 50 states and the District of Columbia license chiropractors, and the Council on Chiropractic Education accredits schools that teach chiropractic.

Chiropractors don't provide primary care. As with all specialists, consult the person from whom you get your primary care before working with a chiropractor. And make sure the chiropractor you select will work with your primary-care provider and keep that person informed about your care.

Biofeedback

Biofeedback is a painless method with which people learn to improve their health and to control such involuntary functions as respiration, heart beat, and body temperature by using signals from their own bodies.

Biofeedback is a technique rather than a system of medicine. Both conventional and alternative practitioners—psychologists, medical doctors, physical therapists, counselors, nurses, and others—use or prescribe biofeedback. According to the National Institute of Mental Health, biofeedback can be used to address an ever-lengthening list of conditions, including:
- Migraine headaches and tension headaches;
- Many other types of pain;
- Digestive disorders;
- High and low blood pressure;
- Abnormal heartbeat rhythms;
- Raynaud's disease, a circulatory disorder that causes uncomfortably cold hands;
- Epilepsy; *and*

• Paralysis and other movement disorders.

Your primary-care provider can help you decide if biofeedback might help you. If the answer is yes, work only with a professional biofeedback trainer. You might want to talk with several trainers before choosing one with whom you feel comfortable.

PART III: MAKING A CHOICE

Given the array of techniques and systems that fall under the rubric of "alternative health care," how do you select one?

You might start by looking into practices that are more familiar to you. For example, if you find it difficult to deal

A FEW MORE ALTERNATIVE MEDICAL APPROACHES

• *Ayurvedic medicine,* practiced in India for over 5,000 years, holds that health is a state of balance among the physical, emotional, and spiritual components of the person. Illness, a state of imbalance, is detected through such diagnostic procedures as reading the pulse, palpation, auscultation, observation, and inquiry. Practitioners use nutrition counseling, massage, natural medications, meditation, and other methods to address a broad spectrum of ailments, from allergies to AIDS.

• *Clinical hypnotherapy* induces a relaxed or altered state of awareness, consciousness, or perception to focus the mind and make it receptive to therapeutic suggestion. Hypnotherapy is used for both physical and psychological problems. There is no formal licensing for hypnotists,

but you might check about membership in the American Society for Clinical Hypnosis or the Society for Clinical and Experimental Hypnosis. And seek therapy from a hypnotist who is also licensed in another field as a health-care practitioner.

• *Herbal medicine* uses natural herbs and plants to prevent and cure illnesses. Herbalists claim that their remedies avoid the harmful side effects so common in modern medicines

• *Massage therapy* is an art in which hand manipulation of the body and its muscles eases muscle tension, produces relaxation, alleviates aches and pains, and aids in blood circulation. There are several types of massage therapy, including Swedish, shiatsu, rolfing, polarity, and bioenergetics.

• *Metabolic therapy*

emphasizes ways to strengthen the body's immune system and ward off illness by ridding the body of toxic substances, adjusting diet and nutrition, prescribing vitamins and supplements, and changing the person's lifestyle.

• *Orthomolecular therapy* emphasizes the use of very large doses of vitamins to treat illness. It also emphasizes dietary changes to improve the body's nutrient intake.

• *Tibb Unani,* another name for Greek-Arabic medicine, is a system of healing that relies on reestablishing balance among the body's qualities, such as heat and cold, dryness and moisture. Tibb is the base on which European medicine rested for centuries. It is practiced today in Arabic countries and by many Muslims in the United States.

with terms and concepts from other cultures, you might feel more comfortable with naturopathy or another broad-based, eclectic Western approach. If you have an affinity for Indian, Chinese, or Arabic culture, you could explore, respectively, Ayurveda, Chinese medicine, or Tibb Unani.

You can also ask relatives, friends, and your current health-care providers about their experiences and recommendations. Study each system that appeals to you in more depth to narrow down the field; then concentrate your research and ask more questions.

Your choice will be influenced by the scope of care you are seeking. For example, if you want an alternative practitioner who is licensed in primary care, look into osteopathy or naturopathy. For specialized needs, other licensed health-care practitioners include chiropractors and acupuncturists. In addition, a growing number of conventional medical doctors, registered nurses, and dentists practice forms of holistic medicine and dentistry.

The Rules of the Game

Finding alternative health care requires research, probably in more depth than for conventional types of health care. As the term "alternative" implies, many of these approaches lie outside the medical mainstream. As a result, getting solid information about proper care—and related dangers—is less straightforward than researching the conventional medical literature.

Fortunately, the more you examine alternative healing practices, the more you'll find that nothing is particularly strange or mysterious about many of the most popular options. Indeed, as with any practice that potentially affects your health, you'll find good practitioners—and some to avoid. Some will treat you with respect—and others will use jargon instead of plain English to explain what they're doing to your body. In other words, approach alternative healing respectfully and cautiously, just as you would in the case of all your health care:

• Remember the old adage: *if it sounds too good to be true, it probably is.* No system provides a cure in every case.

• Do your research thoroughly. Libraries and reputable organizations can provide you with information on different approaches to health care, including those listed at the end of this chapter. Keep in mind, however, that alternative approaches don't easily lend themselves to clinical trials because they encompass a wide variety of treatments that tend to differ for each individual based on his or her circumstances.

• Give the practitioner and the system you choose a fair try. Stick to a system if you respond well on any level: physical, spiritual, or mental. But discontinue care if you have reason to believe that a treatment is hurting you and the explanations you receive aren't satisfactory.

Before you begin treatment, make sure you understand what the practitioner says will happen. Learn your treatment plan. Discuss what to expect in terms of best-case and worst-case scenarios.

Once you locate a practitioner, ask specific questions. Investigate credentials. And don't be surprised that most of the questions match those you'd ask a "regular" doctor:

- What did your training entail?
- What clinical experience did your training include?
- If applicable, what board certifications and licenses do you have?

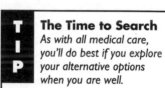

The Time to Search
As with all medical care, you'll do best if you explore your alternative options when you are well.

- What did you have to do to receive your certifications and licenses?
- What does your training qualify you to treat?
- What clinical studies support your diagnosis and recommended treatments?

If you think you are seriously ill, consult your primary-care provider first if at all possible. No matter who you go to for treatment, someone with a thorough clinical training should diagnose your symptoms.

And always remember that you are in charge of your medical care. At any time in the process, you have the right to stop any treatment for any reason. And no treatment can be done without your *informed consent.*

Finding Local Alternative Providers

The best way to locate providers of alternative health services is through the recommendation of relatives, friends, and neighbors who may have relationships with serious, qualified practitioners.

T I P

The Rules Apply. . . and Then Some

The questions to ask and the rules to follow as you seek care from alternative providers are essentially the same as for any health-care practitioner. For more on these guidelines, see Chapter 5 on primary care and Chapter 10 on physician specialists.

However, given the wide variation in the background and training of alternative practitioners, take your research task especially seriously. Licensing regulations outside the medical mainstream vary in effectiveness and scope from state to state and field to field—if they exist at all.

However, should you not have access to this source of information, call a reputable national organization. Ask for the names of two or three local practitioners.

If you are looking for alternative primary care, call the American Association of Naturopathic Physicians, the American Holistic Medical Association, or the American Osteopathic Association. They can refer you to qualified primary-care naturopaths, holistic allopaths, or osteopaths in your vicinity.

There are also some excellent guides that may be available at health-food stores and at comprehensive bookstores that carry alternative-health publications.

PART IV: MONEY MATTERS

Alternative medicine, with its relatively low reliance on high technology and pharmaceutical drugs, could prove less expensive than allopathic care in many cases. One limited study compares the cost-effectiveness of naturopathic and allopathic conventional care and clearly shows the medical and economic advantages of naturopathic care. Contact the American Association of Naturopathic Physicians for a copy of this study. In addition, government-sponsored research in this country and Canada demonstrates that chiropractic care is less expensive and more effective in alleviating back pain than conventional

Get Answers

Honest health-care practitioners don't hesitate to provide clear, direct answers to questions about their training and your needs. If answers don't make sense to you, or if you are still doubtful, ask a practitioner to give you references from other clients and health-care providers—or move on.

medical treatment.

Depending on where you reside and the licensing laws of your state, however, your insurance may or may not cover particular alternative health ser-

> **TIP**
>
> **Insurance Source**
> *Call or write the American Asso-ciation of Naturopathic Physi-cians for a brochure that assists patients who wish to obtain insurance coverage for alternative providers. AANP, 2366 Eastlake Ave. East, Suite 322, Seattle, WA 98102 (206)323-7610.*

vices. Be sure to ask providers and your insurers before making an appointment. If the alternative care you seek isn't covered, you'll have to pay out of your own pocket.

Work with your alternative provider to reduce your out-of-pocket costs by exploring all options for reimbursement. A responsible alternative practitioner should be able to guide you in this matter. A cooperative conventional doctor may increase the likelihood of reimbursement by making appropriate referrals.

Some health plans cover both conventional and alternative medicine, but usually not through group plans. However, you may be able to get coverage for alternative treatment if your insurance doesn't restrict you to a list of providers and your state licenses alternative practitioners. Because the laws of each state and the various health insurance plans differ so widely,

Selected Typical Fees		
	Initial Visit	**Follow Ups**
Acupuncture	$65-$100	$40-$75
Biofeedback	$90-$125	$60-$90
Chiropractic	$65-$135	$40-$90
(Add $25-$85 if X-rays are needed.)		
Naturopathy	$50-$170	$30-$75
Homeopathic MD	$125-$150	$48-$60
Osteopathy	$70-$185	$45-$90
Source: Health Awareness Resource Center		

make sure to research the exact situation in your locality before incurring alternative-medicine expenses. Alternative practitioners usually aren't included in state-sponsored free-care pools. On the other hand, at least 80 private insurers and Medicaid programs in some states cover acupuncture for certain conditions.

RESOURCES

Organizations

American Association of Acupuncture and Oriental Medicine
433 Front St.
Catasauqua, PA 18032-2506
(610)433-2448
Call or write for referrals and general information.

American Association of Naturopathic Physicians
2366 Eastlake Ave. East, Suite 322
Seattle, WA 98102
(206)323-7610
Send a stamped, self-addressed envelope for general information and a listing of naturopathic physicians in your area. Call or write for referrals to primary-care naturopaths in your area and for information on insurance.

American Chiropractic Association
1701 Clarendon Blvd.
Arlington, VA 22209
(703)276-8800
Call or write for general information about chiropractic.

American Foundation of Traditional Chinese Medicine
505 Beach St.
San Francisco, CA 94133
(415)776-0502
Call or write for information.

American Herbalists Guild
P.O. Box 1683
Suquel, CA 95073
(408)464-2441
Send $3 for a recommended-reading list; send $4 for a directory of schools and resources.

American Holistic Medical Association
4101 Lake Boone Trail
Raleigh, NC 27607
(919)787-5146
Call or write for general information, including referrals to conventional medical doctors who take a holistic approach. Send $8 for a directory listing association members.

American Massage Therapy Association
820 Davis St.
Evanston, IL 60201
(708)864-0123
Call or write for references and referrals.

American Oriental Bodywork Therapy Association
6801 Jericho Turnpike
Syosset, NY 11791
(516)364-5533
Call or write for referrals and membership information.

American Osteopathic Association
142 East Ontario St.
Chicago, IL 60611
(312)280-5800
Call or write for referrals.

American Society of Clinical Hypnosis
22000 East Deven Ave.
Des Plaines, IL 60018-4534
(708)297-3317
Send a self-addressed stamped envelope for listings of local providers.

Association for Applied Psychophysiology and Biofeedback
10200 W. 44th Ave.
Wheat Ridge, CO 80033
(303)422-8436
Send a self-addressed envelope to receive listings of local providers. Send $30 for a national directory.

Ayurvedic Institute
P.O. Box 23445
Albuquerque, NM 87192
(505)291-9698
Call or write for information on traditional Indian medicine.

Commonweal
P.O. Box 316
Bolinas, CA 94924
(415)868-0970
Call for information about alternative cancer therapies

Health Awareness, Inc.
18 Old Padonia Rd.
Cockeysville, MD 21030
(410)560-6864
This nonprofit service organization provides educational resources on many holistic practices including naturopathy, osteopathy, acupressure and food additives. No charge for services, but donations are suggested. Publishes "Awareness Update" quarterly; $20 per year.

Health Information Network International
4213 Montgomery Dr.
Santa Rosa, CA 95405

(800)743-6996
(707)539-3967
Call or write for information and research on natural health substances and treatment alternatives.

Holistic Dental Association
P.O. Box 5007
Durango, CO 81301
(303)259-1091
Send a self-addressed stamped envelope for a listing of local holistic dental practitioners.

National Center for Homeopathy
801 North Fairfax St.
Alexandria, VA 22314
(703)548-7790
Send $5 for a directory of homeopathic doctors, pharmacists, and other resources.

Office of Alternative Medicine
National Institutes of Health
Executive Plaza South, Suite 450
6120 Executive Blvd.
Rockville, MD 20892-9904
(301)402-2467
(301)402-2466 to receive information by computer.

Society for Clinical and Experimental Hypnosis
6728 Old McLean Village Dr.
McLean, VA 22101-3906
(703)556-9222
Call or write for general information and referrals to local organizations.

Publications

Alternative Medicine Yellow Pages: The Comprehensive Guide to the New World of Health ($13) and *Alternative Medicine: The Definitive Guide* ($48, plus $5.50 for shipping and handling). Both available Health Awareness, Inc., 18 Old Padonia Rd., Cockeysville, MD 21030 (410)560-6864.

Consumer Reports. A series of three in-depth articles covering acupuncture, homeopathy, and chiropractic. January, March, and June 1994.

Family Guide to Natural Medicine How to Stay Healthy the Natural Way. (Reader's Digest Association, 1993). $30.

RESOURCES

Full Catastrophe Living: Using the Wisdom of Your Body and Mind to Face Stress, Pain, and Illness, by Jon Kabat-Zinn (Delta/Dell, 1990). $12.

"Holistic Health Directory." Order from *New Age Journal,* 42 Pleasant St., Watertown, MA 02172 (617)926-0200. $5.95. Lists 7,000 alternative providers in the United States and Canada.

Mind/Body Medicine: How to Use Your Mind for Better Health, edited by Daniel Goleman and Joel Gurin (Consumer Reports Books, 1993). $24.95.

The Natural Family Doctor: The Comprehensive Self-Help Guide to Health and Natural Medicine, by Andrew Stanway and Richard Grossman. (Simon and Schuster, 1987). $12.95.

Natural Health, Natural Medicine: A Comprehensive Manual for Wellness and Self-Care, by Andrew Weil (Houghton Mifflin, 1990). $19.45.

"Options in Health Care: Understanding Traditional and Alternative Methods." Order from People's Medical Society, 14 East Minor St., Emmaus, PA 18049 (800)624-8773. $4.00 ($3.00 for members).

Mental Health

by Cindy Brach and Gail K. Robinson

Cindy Brach is policy associate for policy and research at the Mental Health Policy Resource Center in Washington, DC. She has a masters of public policy from the University of California at Berkeley, where she is a doctoral candidate, and has been a human services consultant, a state-level public administrator, and a municipal policy analyst.

Dr. Gail K. Robinson is associate director of the Mental Health Policy Resource Center. She has been director for the Bureau of Demonstration Projects and associate director of strategic plan-ning and project develop-ment for the New York State Office of Mental Health. She also directed the Office of Planning and Analysis for Mental Health, Addictions and Developmental Disabilities for the State of Maryland.

In any given year, mental disorders affect 22 percent of the adults in the United States. From 5 to 22 percent of children and adolescents suffer from mental disorders. Suicide is the third leading cause of death among teenagers.

Mental illness encompasses a variety of disorders that range in severity. That is, they result in greater and lesser degrees of mental well-being. Furthermore, mental well-being is dynamic: some people experience severe short-term problems, while others have long-term conditions with symptoms that occur only intermittently.

Today, you can get effective treatment for many mental health problems—whether your condition is mild or severe, short-term or long-lasting. You should seek profes-sional help if you are distressed and your efforts—such as exercising, meditating, or talking to friends—haven't helped you overcome your problem. As you travel the road to better mental health, a wide variety of professionals can provide you with many forms of assistance and treatment.

Step One: Educate Yourself. The start of any treatment is learning where your distress comes from and studying the options for getting help. Education is the key to consumer empowerment. Read this chapter, contact the organizations listed at the end, and then move on to the library and the self-help aisle of your local bookstore.

Step Two: Create a Partnership with a Provider. Responsi-ble mental health providers actively contribute to their patients' knowledge and insight about distress. Good rela-tionships with providers are characterized by trust and equality. Join with your provider to figure out what is wrong, why it's wrong—and what to do about it.

Recognize, however, that providers take many different perspectives on mental health and therapy. Don't assume that the first person you consult makes a good match for you and your needs. Take time to discover the right provider with the right approach for you.

Step Three: Continually Assess and Reassess Your Treatment. Caregivers, friends, and family may offer valuable advice, but you are ultimately responsible for yourself. You say when to continue or stop a treatment. Can you manage your distress without professional support? If the answer is yes, you can stop treatment for the time being.

You can measure the mental health care you receive by how well it helps you meet four primary goals:

- Does it reduce or eliminate the symptoms of your disorder?
- Does it restore or improve your ability to socialize and work?
- Does it maximize your sense of well-being and that of your family? *and*
- Does it help to prevent injury to yourself and to others?

If you now receive mental health care yet feel unable to manage on a day-to-day basis, consider two possible explanations. One, you need to allow yourself more time, working with your current providers. Two, the services don't fit you: it's probably time to investigate new providers.

PART I: CHOOSING A PROVIDER

Psychiatrists, psychologists, clinical social workers, psychiatric nurses, marriage and family therapists, and professional counselors all provide mental health services. These practitioners vary in their level of education, their orientation, the amount of regulation to which they are subject,

Substance Abuse

One out of six adults abuses alcohol or drugs at some point in his or her lifetime. Although mental health and substance-abuse services overlap to some extent, the two systems are largely distinct.

For more information on substance abuse, contact:

The National Clearing-house for Alcohol and Drug Information (800)SAY-NO-TO;

Alcoholics Anonymous (212)870-3400; or

Narcotics Anonymous (818)780-3951.

SOME COMMON MENTAL DISORDERS

Phobias: Obsessive, unrealistic, persistent fears of particular objects or situations. For example, people with claustrophobia fear enclosed spaces.

Panic: Discrete periods of sudden, overwhelming anxiety that produce terror and actual physical effects on your body, such as hyperventilation.

Obsessive-Compulsive Behavior: Persistent intrusion of unwanted and uncontrollable thoughts or actions. Repeated hand washing is an example.

Depression: Feeling sad or desperate for no apparent reason.

Manic-Depression: Depressed feelings alternating with manic periods characterized by euphoria, an expansive or irritable mood, hyperactivity, less need for sleep, distractibility, and impaired judgment.

Dysthymia: A mild but chronic despondency lasting for months, often years. This is probably the most common form of clinical

depression. The person can work and maintain relationships, but everything is flat and colorless. Brief breaks in mood don't last.

Schizophrenia: A group of psychotic disorders characterized by a disintegrated personality. People with schizophrenia can misinterpret reality; for example, they may suffer delusions and hallucinations, mood changes, and withdrawn, regressive and bizarre behavior.

and whether insurance will cover their bills.

Your selection of the right professional is critical. As in so many other areas of health care, research mental health providers carefully. For recommendations, you can look to a variety of sources:

- Your physician;
- Family and friends;
- Professional societies of mental health providers;
- Psychiatric or psychology departments at universities;
- Government social-services agencies;
- Religious organizations;
- Your priest, rabbi, or minister; *and*
- Community-based agencies.

Ask every contact to recommend two or three individuals, institutions, or organizations. Interview potential providers. And don't be afraid to "comparison shop"—to make appointments with more than one provider and choose among them. You can also get a diagnostic assessment, which may take several sessions, before you commit yourself to treatment. Expect to be billed for each session.

Consider the kinds of services you want from among those described in Part II of this chapter. If you think you may need medication, seek a provider with the authority to write a prescription—for example, a psychologist who works in collaboration with a physician.

If you have a personal concern—regarding your health, marriage, family, stress, financial matters, alcohol or drug abuse, or emotional issues—you may be able to get help from an Employee Assistance Program (EAP). Many employers sponsor workplace-based EAPs that provide confidential assessment and referral services, including follow-up services in many cases. Frequently, employees can reach EAPs by phone 24 hours a day. Ask your personnel department for information.

Your Choice of Provider

Choosing a mental health provider can be even more difficult than choosing a primary-care provider, in part because you can select from among a variety of types and specialties. And the decision-making process can resemble picking out a new car: your choice depends on the size and nature of your need, the extra features you value, and what you can afford. Like different makes of cars, different types of providers may give essentially identical care, despite appearances. And you need to think about more than the "brand" name: each type of provider can come in different models, one of which may suit your needs.

Cost is almost always a factor. Some health insurance (including Medicaid and Medicare) covers only certain care from certain types of providers; other policies may limit the number of covered visits. Find out how much your insurer will pay. And check for copayments and for gaps between the reimbursement level and what providers charge.

The specialties presented here are listed roughly in order of cost, beginning with the most expensive.

Psychiatrists are physicians who specialize in diagnosing and treating mental and emotional disorders. As medical doctors, they may be more likely than other mental health practitioners to see physical roots to mental illness, although they also practice psychotherapy and may have psychoanalytic training. Like other medical doctors, psychiatrists can write prescriptions. The American Board of Psychiatry and Neurology certifies psychiatrists.

Of all mental health providers, psychiatrists receive the highest fees. On the other hand, all insurance policies that cover mental health treatment accept psychiatrists as providers.

Clinical psychologists have master's or doctoral degrees in psychology and training in psychotherapy. Like psychiatrists, some psychologists receive psychoanalytic training. However, with the exception of some psychologists within the Indian Health Service and the Department of Veterans Affairs, psychologists can't prescribe drugs. The American Psychological Association and the American Board of Professional Psychology both credential clinical psychologists. Many states only license psychologists with a doctorate and two years of clinical experience. Virtually all insurance policies that cover mental health accept PhD psychologists as providers.

Clinical social workers have a degree in social work— usually a master's degree—and special training in counseling. Clinical social work is an increasingly popular credential for providers and clients. For the providers, the training doesn't require getting a doctoral degree. For clients, social workers are usually cheaper, more are available, and they are frequently oriented toward problem solving and advocacy. All but three states certify or license social workers. Health insurance covers social workers more now than in the past but still less frequently than psychiatrists and psychologists. Thirty-two states require insurers to reimburse clinical social workers for people who have mental health coverage.

Professional counselors have completed a master's degree, received clinical training, and passed an exam. Some counselors specialize, such as in gerontology. Forty-two states credential professional counselors. In the past, insurers didn't pay for professional counseling, but a growing number of states (currently 10) require reimbursement of professional counselors for people who have mental health coverage.

Marriage and family therapists consider the family as a whole, whether the problem relates to marital and family relationships or a specific mental or emotional disorder. Most marriage and family therapists have a graduate degree in the field. The remainder are psychiatrists, psychologists, psychiatric nurses, clinical social workers, and pastoral counselors. Most states license or certify marriage and family therapists. Most insurance policies exclude marriage and family therapy from coverage, although this is changing. Six states require insurers to reimburse marriage and family therapists for people

---

Pastoral Counselors

In pastoral counseling, the counselor, as a representative of a religious tradition or community, uses the insights and principles of religion, theology, and modern behavioral sciences in helping individuals, couples, families, groups, and institutions work toward wholeness and health. Many pastoral counselors also receive training and mental health credentials in other fields, such as social work.

T I P | **Getting the Right Information**
For in-depth information about specific mental disorders, you can contact a host of organizations, such as the Anxiety Disorders Association of America. For information on some of these organizations, turn to the resources at the end of this chapter.

who have mental health coverage.

Psychiatric nurse specialists are registered nurses who specialize in treating mental disorders. They often assist with drug therapy and electroconvulsive therapy and act as psychotherapists under the direction of a psychiatrist. Psychiatric nursing services are often dispensed in conjunction

DEPRESSION

Genette is 68 years old, married, and retired. Recently, she has found herself inexplicably fatigued. She has lost energy, stopped eating, and wakes at night feeling down. Although she would like to organize the house, she has difficulty concentrating and can't seem to accomplish anything. Even the art classes she loves have fallen by the wayside. She feels worthless.

Like Genette, one in four women and one in ten men will suffer from depression in their lifetime. Two out of three depressed people don't get appropriate treatment because their symptoms are:
- Not recognized;
- Blamed on personal weakness;
- So disabling that they can't reach out for help; or
- Misdiagnosed and wrongly treated.

Some people experience a few symptoms; others experience many. The severity of the symptoms also varies. Seek professional advice if you experience several of the following symptoms for more than two weeks or if they interfere with work or family life:

- Persistent sad or "empty" mood;
- Loss of interest or pleasure in activities you used to enjoy, including sex;
- Decreased energy, constant fatigue, feeling "slowed down;"
- Feelings of hopelessness, guilt, worthlessness, or helplessness;
- Trouble sleeping or sleeping too much;
- Increase or decrease in appetite or weight;
- Difficulty concentrating, thinking, remembering, or making decisions;
- Thoughts of death or suicide;
- Excessive crying or irritability;
- Chronic aches and pains that don't respond to treatment.

Treatment can help about four out of five severely depressed people, often in a matter of weeks. However, severely depressed people may need encouragement from family and friends to seek treatment. For information, contact your family physician, your Employee Assistance Program, the local health department or mental health center, or one of the national groups listed at the end of this chapter.

Also, many university medical centers have special programs for treating depression.

While you are waiting for treatment to take effect:
- Don't set yourself difficult goals or take on a great deal of responsibility.
- Break large tasks into small ones, set some priorities, and do what you can as you can.
- Try to be with other people—it's usually better than being alone.
- Participate in activities that may make you feel better, such as mild exercise, going to a movie, or participating in religious activities.
- Don't expect to snap out of your depression. People rarely do.
- Postpone important decisions, such as changing jobs or getting a divorce, until your depression has lifted or you can at least consult others who know you well.
- Remember that your symptoms are part of the depression and will disappear as your depression responds to treatment.

with physician services or to patients who stay overnight in a hospital or other institution. As a result, they usually aren't billed separately.

Interviewing the Candidates

It's very important to select a mental health provider in whom you can place confidence and trust. You will probably have to spend some time with a provider before deciding whether you feel comfortable, but there may be some characteristics that you look for at the outset. To shorten your search process, think about which criteria are most important to you. For example, if you are gay you might feel strongly that your provider have experience with gay patients.

Ask a potential provider the following questions to help you decide if he or she is the right person for you:

• *What is your education and what are your certifications and licenses?* Make sure the provider has the minimum qualifications to practice. Some certifications signal advanced achievement but are not prerequisites to being a mental health provider.

• *With which hospitals are you affiliated?* You may prefer a particular facility should you need hospital services.

• *What teaching or staff appointments do you have?* Associations with universities or treatment facilities can give you insight into the provider's orientation.

• *How many years of clinical experience do you have?* If a provider is relatively inexperienced, be sure to ask if he or she is receiving supervision.

> **T I P**
>
> **Check It Out**
> *If you want to know if a provider is certified and whether any complaints have been filed against him or her,* contact the relevant professional association. For example, call or write the American Psychological Association for information about psychologists. If the person is also a medical doctor, as are all psychiatrists, you can also check with the state board that examines and certifies physicians.

• *In what settings have you practiced?* Some clinicians have primarily private practices, and others see clients at a clinic or a hospital.

• *How old are you?* Age can affect your level of comfort

with a provider. For example, an older client might feel more comfortable with a person close to her or his age—or one who is much younger!

• *What type of clientele do you generally serve?* You may want to choose a provider who has experience with clients who are culturally similar to you or have similar mental health problems.

• *How long is an average appointment and how frequently do you usually see clients?* You may want more or less intensive services.

• *What is your therapeutic style and what techniques do you use? For example, do you tend to prescribe drugs (or have them prescribed)? Are you active in your questioning? Do you use behavioral techniques like assigning homework or teaching relaxation exercises?* Finding out about the style and techniques can help you determine if there's a good match between you and the provider.

• *Do you have any specialties, such as treating drug addiction?*

PART II: THE VARIETY OF MENTAL HEALTH SERVICES

If you decide to seek professional help for yourself or someone in your family, you will not only encounter diverse providers but also a broad, perhaps bewildering, array of services. Indeed, your choice of a mental health provider can depend on the service you feel is right for you.

The first step in mental health treatment is a psychiatric examination—a systematic look at your current emotional state and mental functions. Based on this exam and your history, the examiner will make a provisional diagnosis and recommend certain services and treatments. You might receive the following services as an outpatient or as part of an inpatient or residential program:

• *Individual Psychotherapy:* Treatment of mental and emotional disorders based primarily on communication between a client and a provider.

• *Group Psychotherapy:* Application of psychotherapy to a group, usually six to eight people. The interactions of the

Psychoanalysis

Based on the theory that repressing painful or undesirable experiences influences one's mental health, psychoanalysis attempts to elicit past emotional experiences using such methods as dream interpretation and evaluating resistance to treatment. Psychoanalysis is an intensive treatment that strives to resolve patients' conflicts. It's often used by patients who don't suffer from mental illness to gain insight into their personality and behavior.

Psychoanalysis differs from psychoanalytic psychotherapy, which uses some of the same principles to reduce symptoms and improve functioning. Psychoanalytic psychotherapy undertakes less profound personality changes and emphasizes the patient's life situation rather than the analyst-patient relationship.

members of the group provide some of the material for the therapy.

• *Family Therapy:* Treatment of two or more family members in the same session. This approach assumes that a mental disorder in one person may relate to a disorder in other members of the family and affect how they all interact and function.

• *Self-Help and Peer Groups:* Troubled people with a common problem helping one another through personal and group support. Self-help groups exist for many common mental disorders and in many communities.

> **T I P**
> **Putting It Together**
> *Your options for mental health services aren't necessarily mutually exclusive. Many people combine two or more, either concurrently or sequentially, to create a personalized treatment package.*

For more information on self-help groups, turn to Chapter 19

DRUGS AND MENTAL HEALTH

Medications have gained widespread acceptance in treating people with severe mental illness as well as those with milder impairments. Proven agents combat some psychoses, depression, and anxiety. Frequently, several classes of drugs can be used for any given disorder.

No hard and fast rules determine which drugs and what dosages will be most successful with a particular patient. Moreover, sometimes patients try more than one drug before finding one or a combination of drugs that is satisfactory. If you have an unusually hard time finding an appropriate medication, enlist the services of a pharmacologist—a physician who specializes in prescribing drugs.

Most drugs have potential side effects, some more serious than others. In fact, some drugs—Prozac (fluoxetine) is an example—are popular because they have fewer negative side effects rather than because they succeed more often. Make sure your mental health provider explains the most common side effects before you start any medication. If you experience side effects, discuss them with your provider immediately and before you stop taking your medication—some drugs have to be stopped gradually to give your body time to adjust.

Drugs aren't necessarily an alternative to psychotherapy—and some people believe that combining both treatments is superior to either one alone. This is especially true for people who don't respond to either psychotherapy or drugs alone. Furthermore,

psychotherapy plays a role during the weeks it takes patients receiving drugs to respond to medication and helps patients deal with emotional turmoil and reluctance to take long-term medication.

Two types of mental health service focus on helping patients with medications as part of their therapy:

◆ *Management of Psychotropic Medication:* Monitoring and evaluating a person's use of medicines administered as part of mental health care to determine when and if to continue using them or to adjust the doses.

◆ *Medication Management Training:* Instruction on how to administer your own medication, evaluate its impact, and identify side effects.

• *Psychoeducation:* Education to promote behavioral changes, such as educational counseling to prevent AIDS.

Services for People with Severe Mental Illnesses

Many mental health services focus on severely ill people. Some services are offered on a short-term basis, while others last indefinitely to help the person continue to live in the community rather than in an institution. These services are generally available through the state or local department of mental health, as part of follow-up care after a person leaves a hospital, or from a local mental health organization.

• *In-Home Mental Health Services:* Assistance in such areas as activities of daily living, budgeting, managing behavior, respite services, and responding to a crisis.

• *Drop-In Programs:* Members discuss mutual concerns without feeling stigmatized. They also socialize and enjoy refreshments. Professional staff counsel members, provide information and referrals, and conduct educational and recreational activities on a scheduled or ad-hoc basis.

• *Crisis Stabilization:* Non-residential professionals are on call in the event of a crisis. Programs may offer hotlines—for suicide prevention, for example—and staff who provide in-home services

• *Adult Protective Services:* Government-sponsored services available to people with mental health or physical dysfunctions who can't manage their own affairs or protect themselves from exploitation and have no guardian, relative, or other person available to assist them.

• *Case Management:* An assessment of a person's need for services, plus coordination, planning, and follow-through on the provision of those services.

Many programs for people with severe mental illnesses help them learn critical skills. These programs focus on such topics as:

• *Independent Living:* One-on-one or group instruction in cooking, the use of leisure time, money management, meal planning, house cleaning, obtaining needed services from the community, and so on.

Family Aids

Some services for people with severe mental illness target families and other caregivers:

Respite Care: Temporary relief for the caregiver from some tasks. For a short time, the person with mental illness gets assistance at home or in a residential facility.

Behavioral Family Management: Education for the families of people with mental illness about mental disorders and treatment, communication skills, and problem-solving. The goals are to meet the needs of families and involve them in treatment and rehabilitation.

Partial Hospitalization

Partial-hospitalization programs provide a set of coordinated clinical services for people with a significant psychiatric, emotional, or behavioral disorder. Although also known as day treatment, partial hospitalization offers three or more hours a day of programming during the day, evening, night, or weekend.

Treatment includes such services as individual and group psychotherapy, medication evaluation, family and expressive therapies, and psycho-educational therapy groups as well as other therapeutic activities, including cooking, budgeting, personal hygiene, and recreation.

• *Health and Hygiene:* Instruction in nutrition, relaxation, physical fitness, grooming, clothing, sexuality, self-care, and the use of medication.

• *Problem Solving and Alternative Coping:* Instruction on how to identify a problem, devise a set of options, and then decide what to do.

• *Job-Related Skills:* Instruction to help trainees understand the meaning, value, and demands of work; training in identifying sources of job leads, writing a resume, and interviewing; and actual job placement using leads provided by counselors who identify the best options and help clients develop realistic expectations and deal with stress.

• *Transitional Employment:* Entry-level, part-time, or full-time jobs, with clients and program staff cooperating until both feel the client can handle the job successfully.

• *Supported Employment:* Part-time or full-time jobs in the community that receive less staff backup than transitional employment.

PART III: WHERE DO I GO? FINDING APPROPRIATE CARE

Most people receiving mental health care live at home and visit providers for appointments. In the private sector, people generally receive care in practitioners' offices. In addition, many public outpatient mental health clinics and organizations provide services. Community mental health centers, in particular, are prime providers of mental health care, although not every city or town has one. Also, some psychiatric clinics operate under the auspices of general hospitals, mental hospitals, Veterans Affairs medical centers, and family-service agencies, and hospitals provide psychiatric or psychological treatment in emergency rooms.

If Your Need Is Great

People with more severe mental illnesses and those who need intensive, long-term treatment might receive inpatient care—24-hour care in an institution. Sites for such care include state or county mental hospitals, private psychiatric hospitals, and psychiatric wards or scattered beds in general hospitals or Veterans Affairs medical centers.

However, hospital care is generally a last resort, and used on a short-term basis, to stabilize a person's condition so that he or she can return to a less restrictive environment. Nursing homes provide long-term residential care for those who either have a physical condition requiring 24-hour nursing care or whose mental condition (specified by law, including Alzheimer's and dementia), while not requiring continuous active mental health treatment, requires a specialized setting and services.

For more information on nursing homes, turn to Chapter ▼**12**

The following types of residential care represent differing levels of patient independence and professional oversight:

Community residences, including halfway houses, group homes, and boarding houses all are non-medical facilities with three or more beds and overnight or round-the-clock staffing. Clients receive room, board, supervision, and some supportive or rehabilitative services. The most com-

CHILDREN AND ADOLESCENTS

Children and adolescents receive many of the same mental health services as adults, and their systems of care are largely parallel. For example, specialized psychiatric hospitals treat children and adolescents, community residences for children and adolescents provide therapeutic residential care for small groups, and therapeutic foster care places emotionally disturbed children with trained foster parents.

Some services have been developed especially for children and adolescents:

◆ *Family-Based Treatment:* Surrogate families ("professional parents") who main-tain and treat severely emotionally disturbed youths in their homes.

◆ *Family Support:* Support for families to care for their own emotionally disturbed child through parent education, support groups, advocacy training, respite care, and after-school care.

◆ *Home Care:* Support in the homes of emotionally disturbed children and adolescents, such as help supervising the child and education in parenting and administering medications.

◆ *Risk-Factor-Specific Programs:* Programs to assist youths in coping with a specific risk, such as parental divorce, school transition, or gang violence.

In addition, schools often have counselors and health clinics that assist students with mental health problems. Some before-school and after-school programs are also connected to school systems. The child-welfare system and the juvenile-justice system may provide services—such as respite care and psychiatric evaluations—for children and adolescents with mental or emotional problems. And some suicide-prevention programs are based in schools.

For more information, turn to Chapter 7, Parents As Health Care Consumers.

To find out about mental health services in your community, contact:

◆ The state or local department of mental health;

◆ The state or local department of social services;

◆ The state or local department of health;

◆ Religious social-services agencies;

◆ Your priest, rabbi, or minister;

◆ Neighborhood service centers; *and*

◆ Local hospitals and health clinics.

mon forms of in-house mental health care are individual therapy, group counseling, group meetings, and recreational services. Other services may include remedial and basic education, training in the skills of daily living, prevocational and vocational training, social services, medication monitoring, nursing services, and case management.

Fairweather lodges are long-term, unstaffed living arrangements that are affiliated with a business that provides jobs and job training for residents.

Supportive community living ranges from supervised apartments with 24-hour live-in staff and semi-supervised apartments with part-time live-in staff to cluster apartments in which clients live close to one another and cooperatives in which clients share an apartment with staff available on-call. The supports can range from service planning and intervening when a person behaves inappropriately to providing meals and transportation.

Foster care families are licensed and paid to provide room, board, and minimal services to one or more individuals in the family's home. Sometimes mental health professionals supervise and back up the foster-care family. Family foster care is also known as, or available as part of, substitute family care, alternate homes, home care, family care, alternate families, community living, community residential care, supportive living, and cooperative living.

PART IV: MONEY MATTERS

As with other forms of medical care, there are a variety of ways to pay the bills, control expenses, and get financial assistance. And even if you don't have private insurance or qualify for public assistance, you can often obtain public mental health services at little or no cost. Many of the organizations listed in this chapter can provide information about such options. Private practitioners may offer a sliding-scale fee: they will consider your ability to pay when setting the fee.

Insurance and Mental Health

If you are shopping for health insurance or choosing among plans offered by your employer, always check the mental health coverage of the available policies. Some plans don't cover mental health, and those that do may deny some or even most benefits or make them prohibitively expensive to actually use.

When assessing the mental health coverage of an insurance plan, ask:

• *What criteria does the plan use to exclude people from mental health benefits?* Some policies don't cover conditions you have before you join the plan; other policies won't provide mental health benefits to anyone who has ever used mental health services. Still other policies restrict or exclude benefits for specific disorders, such as attention deficit disorder for children and chronic schizophrenia for adults.

• *What is the extra premium for mental health coverage?* Whether it's assessed separately or not, insurance plans with mental health coverage generally cost more.

• *What services does the plan cover?* Does it include a broad range of treatments, such as partial hospitalization and residential services?

• *What are the annual or lifetime limits on the quantity of treatment that will be covered?* For example, a plan may allow a maximum of 20 outpatient psychotherapy visits each year or 120 days lifetime maximum of inpatient treatment. Are your needs likely to exceed those limits? Treatment for difficult life events, such as divorce or work stress, tends to be short. But treatment for severe mental disorders, such as depression, can be prolonged and expensive.

• *What types of providers does the plan cover?* For example, would the policy cover a visit to a clinical social worker? Are there different limits for different providers?

• *How do you get care?* Does a physician need to give you authorization before you receive mental health treatment? Will care be subject to review during treatment to obtain approval for its continuation?

If you belong to an HMO, PPO, or other managed-care plan, find out how you'll get mental health care. For example, you may receive care from a primary-care physician or have to see a primary-care physician first for a referral to a

Emergencies and Hospitals

In case of a crisis— when a person is violent or suicidal, for example—the emergency room of a hospital can be the appropriate place to go.

Some hospitals are better equipped to deal with mental health emergencies than others. If you help care for someone who might require such services in the future, investigate now which hospitals can best handle the person's problem. Also keep handy the phone numbers of whoever has been providing mental health treatment and call them in case of an emergency.

mental health specialist.

Learn about the quality of mental health services a managed-care plan offers:

How quickly can mental health care be accessed? Does the health plan offer a toll-free access number 24 hours a day? Does it require its providers to offer acute care for a crisis, such as a paralyzing depression, within six hours? Subacute care, such as for a major marital dispute, within 24 hours? Routine care within 72 hours? Policy may differ from reality: find out how long the actual wait is for a mental health appointment.

How large is the provider network? Can you receive care within 30 minutes of home or work?

How specialized is the provider network? Do members have access to enough specialists to ensure high-quality care for special needs, from schizophrenia to anorexia nervosa?

Is there any coverage for providers who aren't part of the network?

Does the plan have providers who meet your language and cultural needs?

Does the plan regularly monitor and strengthen its mental health services using:

- Consumer satisfaction surveys: A sample of patients should receive a survey after they receive treatment. Check whether the plan compensates providers partially based on consumer satisfaction.
- Questionnaires to determine what treatment is provided for specific conditions: This practice helps members know that the treatment they receive is accepted and valid.
- Measures of the outcome of care: Investigate whether the health plan can tell consumers its record on the results of treatment.
- Educational tools: Ask if the health plan continually educates its staff. Plans that participate in the Consortium for Clinical Excellence have access to a national program to help clinicians stay abreast of treatments for specific conditions.

Insurance Copayments

Check the copayments on policies you are considering. Policies may subject mental health treatment to a different copayment than other health services. You should also be aware that copayments typically increase with the length of treatment. Are copayments for mental health services applied to your overall annual deductible and the ceiling on out-of-pocket payments?

If Your Insurance Doesn't Cover Mental Health

Federal and state programs can pay for some mental health treatment for some people. If you are receiving cash assistance from the government, such as Aid to Families with Dependent Children or Supplemental Security Income, you are automatically eligible for Medicaid if you have no health insurance, and most states offer some Medicaid coverage to low-income, medically needy persons.

Medicaid covers outpatient and inpatient general hospital services, physician services, and Early and Periodic Screening, Diagnosis, and Treatment (EPSDT). In many states, it also includes rehabilitative and clinic services, prescriptions, services by practitioners other than physicians, inpatient psychiatric hospital services for children, and services in institutions for mental diseases for children and the elderly.

> **T**
> **I**
> **P**
>
> **Reimbursement**
> *If you qualify for Medicaid or Medicare, ask your provider if she or he accepts Medicaid and Medicare reimbursement as payment in full.*

Most people over 65 participate in Medicare, available to those eligible for Social Security and others with specified conditions. Medicare Part A provides coverage for hospital inpatient care, with lifetime limits, deductibles, and copayments. Part B includes coverage for some outpatient mental health services, with a copayment of 50 percent.

PART VI: THE RIGHTS OF MENTAL PATIENTS

If you have a mental illness, you don't give up your rights. Some legal rights apply specifically to people receiving mental health care, while most belong to every patient—and every citizen. Remember, however, that laws vary among the states, and the courts are constantly refining the interpretation and breadth of your rights.

Your rights include:

The Right to Refuse Treatment: Except in limited circumstances, adults can refuse any mental health treatment.

What Can You Pay?

If you don't have insurance, ask yourself how much you're prepared to pay. Bear in mind that you can get some mental health care in many communities at little or no cost from public or non-profit agencies.

For more on Medicare and Medicaid, see Chapters **3** and **8**

For information on long-term care, turn to Chapter **12**

For more information on patient rights, turn to Chapter **2**

Leaving Can Be Difficult

Legally, people who voluntarily enter inpatient facilities can discharge themselves at any time. However, getting out can be hard. Inpatients who express an intention to leave can be threatened with civil commitment as a way of deterring them from exercising this right.

If Someone Is Mistreated in the Mental Health System...

The federal government funds Protection and Advocacy for Individuals with Mental Illness (PAIMI) programs in every state. Contact your state's PAIMI for assistance or to complain about abuse, neglect, or rights violations. *To locate your state's PAIMI program, call the National Association of Protection and Advocacy Systems at (202)408-9514.*

This includes the right to refuse medication or painful techniques to change behavior, such as electroshock therapy. This is based on the principle that your informed consent is necessary before any medical treatment can begin.

There are two exceptions to bars on forced medication: to prevent serious harm to the patient or to others in an emergency situation in an institution and to treat a patient who has been declared legally incompetent by a court.

Inpatient psychiatric treatment can be required for a person who is dangerous to himself or herself or to others. However, procedural due process is required before an adult can be hospitalized without his or her consent. A person can be detained in an emergency, but most states require a commitment hearing within two to four days. As at any civil hearing, a person is entitled to an attorney and must be allowed to cross-examine witnesses, get an independent evaluation, and see relevant information such as medical records.

If you are receiving mental health services, you also have:

The Right to Treatment: Institutionalized mental patients have a right to treatment. In many states, this includes the right to an individualized treatment plan and treatment that meets professionally accepted standards in the least restrictive setting possible.

The Right to Protection from intrusive and hazardous procedures, such as forced sterilization, and from harm, such as from corporal punishment or unsanitary conditions.

The Right to Communicate with Relatives, Friends, and Counsel.

The Right to Confidentiality and Access to Records: Just like other medical records, psychiatric records are confidential. Without a court order, they can't be disclosed to people not involved in your treatment without the informed consent of you or your guardian. Conversely, you are entitled to know the content of your records.

The Right to Control Your Own Assets: Mental patients are presumed to be capable of handling their own funds.

Discrimination

The Americans with Disabilities Act (ADA) prohibits discrimination against disabled people, including those with mental disabilities. The act also requires employers to make reasonable accommodations for people with disabilities.

A number of organizations can help you learn about, and protect, your rights under the ADA:

• *The Job Accommodation Network* specializes in responding to employment discrimination at (800)526-7234.

• *The Disability Rights Education and Defense Fund* specializes in combating discrimination in public accommodations and by state and local governments. It operates an ADA Hotline: (800)466-4232.

• *The ADA Information Center* of the Disability and Business Technical Assistance Centers provides general information about rights under the ADA. Call (800)949-4232.

RESOURCES

Organizations

American Association for Marriage and Family Therapy
1100 17th St., NW
Washington, DC 20036
(202)452-0109
For referrals: (800)374-2638
Call or write for a list of marriage and family counselors in your area, as well as for a copy of the pamphlet "Consumer's Guide to Marriage and Family Therapy."

American Psychiatric Association
Division of Public Affairs
1400 K St., NW
Washington, DC 20005
(202)682-6220
Call or write for information and referrals to local societies. Write for a list of publications. Their 18-pamphlet series, "Let's Talk Facts About Mental Illness," includes "How to Choose a Psychiatrist."

American Psychological Association
Public Affairs
750 First St., NE
Washington, DC 20002
(202)336-5700
Call or write for referrals to local associations. Contact the public affairs office for a list of brochures on topics such as controlling anger, anxiety disorders, and choosing a psychotherapist.

Anxiety Disorders Association of America
6000 Executive Blvd.
Rockville, MD 20852
(301)231-9350
Call or write for information, literature recommendations, and referrals to professional treatment providers.

National Alliance for the Mentally Ill
2101 Wilson Boulevard
Suite 302
Arlington, VA 22201
(703)524-7600
Toll free help-line: (800)950-6264

This national grassroots family support and advocacy organization is dedicated to improving the lives of people with severe mental illnesses. It has 1,000 affiliate groups in all 50 states and operates networks that focus on children and adolescents, forensics, religious outreach, and veterans. Write or call for a list of publications.

National Association of Social Workers
750 First St., NE
Washington, DC 20002
(202)408-8600
(800)638-8799
Call or write for referrals. Chapters in every state can also provide referrals, and the national registry is available in major libraries.

National Depressive and Manic Depressive Association
730 N. Franklin St.
Chicago, IL 60610
(312)642-0049
(800)82-NDMDA (826-3632)

RESOURCES

Call or write for information, a catalog of books, videos, and pamphlets, and referrals to their network of 275 local chapters and support groups.

National Foundation for Depressive Illness
P.O. Box 2257
New York, NY 10116
(800)248-4344 for a recorded message about depression.
Write for referrals and information.

National Institute of Mental Health
Information Resources and Inquiries Branch
5600 Fishers Lane, Room 7C-02
Rockville, MD 20857
(301)443-4513.
This federal agency supports research on mental illness and mental health. The Information Resources and Inquiries Branch responds to requests from the lay public, clinicians, and the scientific community with a variety of publications on such topics as Alzheimer's disease, depression, eating disorders, panic, schizophrenia, and stress. Call or write for a list of publications, including several in Spanish.

National Mental Health Association
1021 Prince St.
Alexandria, VA 22314
(703)684-7722
This national organization performs education and advocacy through state and local affiliates. Write or call for free pamphlets, fact sheets, and referrals.

Publications

Consumer's Guide to Psychotherapy, by Jack Engler and Daniel Goleman (Simon & Schuster, 1992). $17.

"Depression Is a Treatable Illness: A Patient's Guide," free pamphlet available from U.S. Department of Health and Human Services, Agency for Health Care Policy and Research. Call (800)358-9295.

The Essential Guide to Psychiatric Drugs, by Jack M. Gorman (St. Martin's Press, 1990). $22.95.

Mental Disability Law: A Primer, by Deborah Zuckerman and Marc Charmatz (Commission on Mental and Physical Disability Law and the American Bar Association, 1992).

Mental Health Consumers in the Workplace: How the Americans with Disabilities Act Protects You Against Employer Discrimination (Mental Health Law Project, 1992). $6.95.

"Principles of Good Mental Health," pamphlet available free from United Seniors Health Cooperative, 1334 G St., NW, Washington, DC 20005.

The Self-Help Sourcebook: Finding and Forming Mutual Aid Self-Help Groups, by Barbara J. White and Edward J. Madera (American Self-Help Clearinghouse and Saint Clares-Riverside Medical Center, 1992). $10.

Long Term Care

By Peggy Denker

Be a Better Consumer

The available services for long-term care vary tremendously across the country, as do their costs and insurance coverage. By learning now what is available—and what kinds of help you or your family might need—you can make yourself a wiser consumer of long-term care.

Long Term Care: A Family Concern

Families caring for a loved one indefinitely are both consumers and providers of care. They struggle to assemble an assortment of services, often despite limited resources and funds. They care for loved ones, sometimes to the detriment of their own physical and financial well-being. And they turn to "respite programs," where available, to give themselves a breather from caregiving responsibilities.

Peggy Denker researches and writes on long-term care and other issues for Families USA. She directs a.s.a.p., Families USA's grassroots advocacy network.

Joan Evans has had a stroke, and her prospects for full recovery are uncertain. Until the stroke, Joan had enjoyed a full and independent life in the town where she and her late husband had raised their children. Her children no longer live nearby.

Saul Miller was recently diagnosed with Alzheimer's disease. He had been living with his daughter's family—partly to save money but mostly to be a part of his grandchildren's lives. In fact, Saul often cared for the grandchildren while his daughter worked. Physically, Saul is robust, and his other children support their sister's determination to care for their father. But the mystery and tragedy of Alzheimer's confuses and frightens them.

Claudia Taylor takes care of her husband Oscar, who has Parkinson's, but her heart condition has worsened, and she requires surgery. Claudia will need to recuperate in a skilled nursing facility after leaving the hospital, so she confronts two decisions. What kind of care can she arrange for her husband during her hospitalization and recovery? What arrangements can she make for both of them in the longer term?

What options do these families have as their lives change? How much control can they keep?

Because every family's situation is different, this chapter can't cover all issues in depth. Instead, the needs of these three families will introduce you to issues and services to help you develop your own plan for long-term care, a challenge most of us will face, whether for ourselves or someone in our family. Their situations can help you understand long-term care *before* you or someone you love needs it. Or, if like most people, you have an immediate need for information, this chapter can help you find assistance now. In either case, it will guide your way through a complicated and emotionally challenging landscape.

What Is Long Term Care and Who Might Need It?

Long-term care is just that: care provided over a long period of time to people who can't take care of themselves

without assistance. The kind and amount of care depend on the nature and severity of the disability. Care can be as simple as providing occasional help with meals and running errands for an older person. Or it can be as complex as around-the-clock medical attention for someone with a serious illness.

Nursing homes provide long-term care, but they are neither the only source, nor even the major one. In fact, most long-term care takes place at home, provided free of charge by family members who run errands, prepare meals, help with medications, and otherwise attend to the needs of a relative who has difficulty functioning independently.

PART I: GETTING STARTED

Whether looking ahead or dealing with a crisis, you'll answer five basic questions as you develop a plan of action:

1. What kind of care is needed?
2. Who will provide care?
3. Where will care be provided?
4. What will care cost?
5. Who will pay for care?

How Severe Is the Disability?

Professionals measure the need for long-term care by looking at how well a person can manage certain tasks. Bathing, dressing, eating, going to the toilet, or getting in or out of a bed are called "Activities of Daily Living," or ADLs. Other important functions necessary to independence —cooking, cleaning, shopping, taking medicine, paying bills—are "Instrumental Activities of Daily Living," or IADLs. The severity of a person's disability—and often his or her eligibility for assistance—is generally expressed in terms of the number of ADL or IADL limitations.

Over 10 million Americans can't perform one or more of these activities. Although people of all ages are affected, two-thirds of those with ADL or IADL limitations are 65 and over, and the likelihood of limitation increases dramatically with age. Fewer than one in ten people age 65 to 69 have difficulty with even one ADL or IADL, but nearly six in ten people over age 85 do.

While ADL and IADL limitations are common measures of dependency, these aren't always appropriate yardsticks. For example, people with Alzheimer's disease may be *able* to eat or go to the toilet but forget to do so.

People are usually considered "severely disabled" if they need help with three ADLs. Many people who need help with two also require some form of long-term care.

Plan Ahead

Arranging long-term care, whether for yourself or a relative, is much easier if you plan ahead. If possible, start looking into facilities before you need them. The more time you take to thoroughly research and think through the issues you will confront, the more confident you will be about the decisions you make.

As you conduct your research, you'll find some facilities and services that aren't immediately available. Ask about placing a name on waiting lists, particularly if you anticipate a need for a nursing home. If your circumstances change or you decide on other arrangements, you can always withdraw the name.

Self-Determination

If you're planning care for another person, consider his or her wishes and feelings. If possible, consult your loved ones as you plan. And leave him or her free to make choices you might not like. Everyone dreads losing independence, and we're all entitled to as much control over our lives as is reasonable.

Question 1:
What Kind of Care Is Needed?

The first step is to get a clear idea of what help is needed. Very ill people may require around-the-clock, highly skilled nursing care. But many older people are basically in good health and can get by with someone who looks in on them occasionally and perhaps runs errands from time to time. To address this range of needs, begin by arranging for a comprehensive assessment of the health and self-sufficiency of the person who will use long-term care.

> ### T I P Be Organized
> Keep track of the information you gather by putting it all in one place—a notebook, for example. Note the date and the name of the people with whom you speak, and take a moment to write down the most important points of each conversation. Use these notes to keep track of information and refresh your memory as you go along.

A person disabled by a serious illness or injury may need *medical care* or *skilled nursing care*. Make an appointment with the attending or family physician. He or she can tell you what kind of medical care is needed and how often.

Still, keep in mind that medical professionals don't always consider non-medical issues and options when proposing a plan of care. And many of the medical services your doctor may propose can be provided in your home, a hospital outpatient wing, a health-care center, or other facility. Medical needs are important, but address them as part of an overall plan of care and family needs and resources.

In fact, most of the care adults need doesn't require special medical training. Assistance in getting to the toilet and preparing meals are typical aspects of caring. This kind of help is often called *custodial care.*

The plan you develop won't be static—you'll modify it as circumstances change. For example, rehabilitation can improve functioning, and that could lessen or eliminate the need for care. Or the caregiver may become ill and need to make alternative arrangements. It may be possible to manage Alzheimer's or Parkinson's at home in the early stages, but an alternative living situation may become necessary as the condition worsens.

Question 2:
Who Will Provide the Care?

Once you thoroughly assess needs, match them to the resources available. Start by deciding how much care your family can realistically provide: 70 percent of the severely disabled not in nursing homes receive all their care from family and friends, without the assistance of any paid services.

However, care is sometimes needed at unpredictable times of the day—such as help going to the toilet. Someone must be available. In those cases, the primary caregiver would have to work at home.

Both the cost and availability of services affect decisions about the family's role in caregiving. As you search for affordable, high-quality care, research alternatives thoroughly. This will give you the tools to construct the best possible plan, one that meets the needs of both the person getting care and the family. Careful research can also save you money.

Question 3:
Where Will Care Be Provided?

Many people automatically assume that only nursing homes provide long-term care, but that isn't the case. Long-term care can also be provided in the home, in the community at facilities that people visit during the day, or in other family-like housing arrangements. Most people who are chronically ill, disabled, or infirm live at home. Most seniors in need of long-term care—5.6 million people—live outside nursing homes.

Sometimes a family supplements the care they can handle themselves by hiring a person to come into the home and help out or by taking advantage of services in the community—senior centers or adult day-care centers, for example. Many communities have volunteer and nonprofit long-term-care programs, and for-profit businesses have identified long-term care as a market niche to fill.

In any case, the time may come when care in your home no longer makes sense. You'll need to make alternative arrangements if the disability is no longer manageable at home, if no family members can realistically provide the

Be Realistic: What Care Can You Give?

For the sake of the person needing care, as well as for the rest of your family, be honest about how much each person can do. Don't underestimate the difficulties of caregiving. It may make considerable physical demands and will certainly make substantial emotional demands.

care, or if the family can no longer cope, even with help from community services.

You may find a solution from the growing array of housing alternatives: retirement communities, congregate housing, assisted living units, adult foster care. These facilities often provide some limited assistance to residents, such as meals or cleaning. But at times a nursing home is the most responsible choice.

Question 4: What Will Care Cost?

Even unpaid family care involves costs. When family members make a commitment to care for someone, they may give up some income or even jeopardize their careers. Other costs can result from remodeling a home to compensate for a disability: for example, your disabled parent might be able to stay in your home if you add a handrail in the bathroom and augment stairs with ramps.

Still, family care, even if supplemented with paid services, usually costs less than a nursing home. On the other hand, if someone is severely disabled and requires around-the-clock medical care, a nursing home may actual-

Respite Care

If family members provide most of the care, investigate *respite care*. Family members may find a temporary break from caregiving through government or private programs.

STAY INVOLVED

Family members often hesitate to place a parent or spouse in a nursing home. You fear that the nursing home won't ensure high-quality care. You may also feel guilty, believing you'll no longer play a role in your loved one's life.

In fact, families do stay involved, managing the selection of a home, dealing with the admissions process, and monitoring the care continually. You also consult with nursing-home staff and often retain financial responsibility. In fact, you're needed now as

much as before: you provide the personal contact that helps transform a facility into your relative's new home.

The members of your family might arrange their schedules to visit on different days to bring news of the family and listen to your relative talk. Whenever possible, take your relative home for holidays and weekend visits or even for a few hours. Remind other family members to telephone regularly, especially on birthdays, anniversaries, and other

important dates.

Some facilities suggest that family members not call or visit for the first few weeks, to give the residents time to adjust. *This is bad advice.* Just the opposite: visit as often as possible. Residents are happier when family and friends visit regularly.

Nurses and aides may pay more attention to residents whose families visit regularly. And an occasional word of thanks and encouragement to the staff helps, too.

ly cost less. With these considerations in mind, you can begin to estimate the cost for a plan of care.

The total cost for paid services provided in the home or the community ranges from just a few dollars a week for someone to come in occasionally to lend a hand, to $200 a week for an adult day-care center, to $5 to $20 an hour for a paid aide, to $50,000 or $60,000 a year for intensive home care. For a nursing home, the cost may be less than $20,000 a year in rural areas—or more than $60,000 in major cities. The average is around $35,000 a year.

Question 5: Who Will Pay for Care?

As you flesh out a plan of care, considerations of cost and reimbursement will influence your choices. What financial contribution, if any, can the family make toward buying needed services? Even if care is desirable, you may not be able to afford it unless you are reimbursed by private insurance or covered by a program such as Medicaid.

Medicaid is a federal-state program for the very poor. It is reserved for people meeting very strict income and asset levels, but the high cost of health care could consume an individual's income and assets so that he or she might become eligible for Medicaid.

Medicare, also a federal program, covers skilled nursing care and rehabilitation therapy in the home if it is provided by a Medicare-certified agency and a physician stipulates that the patient's condition is expected to improve. Medicare is the largest payer for home health, despite severe limitations on what it covers.

PART II: FINDING SERVICES

The array of long-term-care services is neither well-coordinated nor fully funded, and not all services are available everywhere. Finding a full set of services is particularly challenging in rural communities.

In many cases, you can start with the Eldercare Locator. Operated by the National Association of Area Agencies on Aging, it can direct you to information and referral services in your community. The Locator can also direct you to

For more information on paying for care, turn to Part III of this chapter and Chapters ▼3▼ and ▼8▼

Who Are the Caregivers?

Thousands of Americans work all day, then go home to feed and bathe and otherwise care for their aging parents. Three-quarters of these family caregivers are women. Many wives, daughters, and daughters-in-law tend disabled husbands or parents around the clock.

Younger members of a family also may help out. Children may help look after a grandparent with Alzheimer's disease, for instance.

Most family caregivers spend at least four hours a day, seven days a week, providing care, despite the fact that one in three caregivers is also in relatively poor health.

TIP

Check the License
If you locate a suitable program or agency, find out if it has the licenses and certifications to qualify for reimbursement from the relevant sources—Medicare, Medicaid, the Department of Veterans Affairs, or your private insurance.

High Cost Care

Overall, nursing-home care is the costliest long-term care, and sources of financial help are woefully inadequate. In 1992, the total cost of nursing-home care amounted to nearly $65 billion, and families paid nearly half that amount out of their own pockets. The Department of Veterans Affairs, Medicare, and private insurance paid only about 8 percent of the total, around $5 billion.

Medicaid paid the balance. In part, Medicaid's large share results from a sad irony: nursing homes cost so much that the bills impoverish people who then qualify for Medicaid.

your local Area Agency on Aging. Established under the Older Americans Act, these agencies provide information and referral services either directly or by subcontracting with another local group.

The Department of Veterans Affairs is a good source of information for veterans who need long-term services. For your local VA office, look in the federal government section of the telephone directory.

Senior centers can also help you locate services. Religious service organizations, visiting nurses associations, and other volunteer service groups may have suggestions. And many associations (the Alzheimer's Association, for example) operate information and referral services for families that have a member with the disease. If an illness has led to hospitalization, you might consult the hospital's social worker or discharge planner.

Finally, ask everyone you know about services for long-term care. In all likelihood, many of your neighbors and co-workers have been through a similar experience. Clergy may also be able to help. Any of these people may know of unique local services—grocery stores or pharmacies that provide home delivery, for example. What is more, they may give you information about the quality and affordability of various options.

Assessment Services

Assessment or *care-management* services can help you develop a plan of care, find services to carry it out, and monitor the care provided. The Eldercare Locator, your local Area Agency on Aging, and the National Association of Professional Geriatric Care Managers can direct you to care-management services in your community.

Your local department or office on aging, as well as nonprofit or charitable agencies, may also offer free or low-cost assessment services. Look under *Social Services* in the phone

book. The local chapter
of the National Associa-
tion of Social Workers
may be able to refer you
to social workers who
can manage and coordi-
nate care. Hospitals run
geriatric screening pro-

12

> **T
> I
> P** **Eldercare Locator**
> *Call the Eldercare Locator at
> (800)677-1116 for free infor-
> mation on services in your com-
> munity. When you call, you'll be
> asked for the name and address of
> the older person for whom you seek
> information and a brief description of
> the problem.*

grams that can be especially helpful if the diagnosis is
Alzheimer's disease. Independent social workers or *care
managers* employed by local home-health agencies are also
skilled in conducting assessments.

If there are no free or low-cost care-assessment services
near you, or you don't qualify for them, expect to pay from
$50 to $150 an hour or a flat fee of $75 to $300. The cost

> **T
> I
> P** **Care Managers**
> *If possible, consult a care
> manager who is indepen-
> dent of the services he or
> she recommends. Care
> managers who work for agencies
> have an incentive to recommend
> the services their employers offer.*

will depend on where you
live as well as the scope
and depth of the assess-
ment. Be sure to ask for a
fee schedule and for written information detailing
what the fee includes.

Home Care Services

Volunteers and paid professionals offer a wide scope of
services that can be provided in your home.

Skilled medical care, such as that offered by a nurse or a
physical therapist, can be arranged in consultation with
your doctor or hospital. It is referred to as *home health care*.
However, many people who don't need medical care still
need some assistance with daily activities. These services are
referred to as *home care* or *custodial care*.

Personal-care services, such as help with grooming or
dressing, may be available through volunteer programs or
home-care agencies.

Homemaker or *chore services,* including household
repairs, cleaning, laundry, cooking, yard work, and shopping, are available from many volunteer and paid sources.

Friendly-visitor services provide volunteers from church-

*For more information on
home care and home-
health services, turn to
Chapter* **13**

es, synagogues, service groups, and other organizations to look in on and lend a hand to people who live alone.

Home-delivered meals—"Meals on Wheels"—can help homebound elders get nutritious meals even if they can't cook for themselves.

Loan closets are free, informal "lending libraries" of equipment such as walkers, bedside toilets, bath seats, and even wheelchairs.

Telephone-reassurance services are volunteer programs that periodically phone those who live alone to make sure they are doing well.

Respite care gives family members a breather from caregiving responsibilities while ensuring them their loved one remains in good hands.

Support groups give families a chance to share their caregiving concerns and express their feelings.

Emergency-response systems link seniors to hospitals, other health facilities, the fire department, or social-service agencies through buzzers installed in the home or through a small push-button control worn around the neck like jewelry.

Home improvements, such as ramps in place of stairs, can help those who use wheelchairs or walkers to get around.

Community Based Care Services

Most communities, even small towns, provide a variety of programs to serve senior citizens at locations outside the home. Many programs offer services to people in need of care and to their families—services such as meals, counseling, and referrals.

Adult day care covers a variety of health, social, and related support services for adults who have functional impairments and need supervision. Adult day care can provide a chance for a person to interact with others, lessening the sense of isolation. Adult day-care centers often employ staff skilled in responding to the special needs of people with Alzheimer's. Be sure to inquire. These centers may provide transportation to and from the facility. In cities, the usual fee for adult day care is about $30 or $40 dollars a day.

12

Adult day health centers offer skilled health services, generally rehabilitation therapy or other services specifically related to health care. These centers may also help with specific tasks that are especially hard for a family to manage, such as bathing. Medicaid may cover adult day health care. Your Area Agency on Aging can direct you to local services.

Congregate meal programs provide nutritious hot meals to older people in senior centers, schools, churches, and other community settings. A meal program may request a modest donation for each meal served. Congregate meal programs provide at least one-third of the recommended daily diet, as do Meals on Wheels programs. Contact your local Area Agency on Aging.

Senior centers, sometimes called multipurpose senior centers, are community or neighborhood facilities offering older people social and recreational opportunities and a broad spectrum of supportive services. Senior centers may provide health, educational, counseling, and legal services along with congregate meals. Many senior centers offer transportation to and from the facility. Senior centers may ask for a modest donation for some of their services.

Transportation and *escort services* take people to and from medical appointments, senior centers, shopping, and other local services. Some of these services, funded by the Older Americans Act, charge no fee (although they may suggest a

YOUNG PEOPLE AND NURSING HOMES

A small number of nursing-home patients are between 25 and 55 years old. Some are disabled from birth; others are victims of strokes or accidents. If you seek a nursing home for someone under 55, ask facilities about their special pro-grams for young adults.

Too often, younger residents have no one their own age to talk to. Traditional programs do little to meet the emotional needs of young adults, who must struggle in an environment designed for the elderly. Try to choose a facility geared to young adults or one that has young adult residents already.

For more information, call the National Head Injury Foundation at (800)242-0030. Many young adults in need of long-term care are head injury victims.

contribution). Many local and state governments operate van services or dial-a-ride programs for seniors or offer other forms of transportation

> **T I P** **Transportation Help**
> To find out what assistance is available in your community, call the National Transit Hotline, operated by Community Transportation Association of America, at (800)527-8279.

assistance. For example, some counties sell vouchers that seniors can use toward taxi fare. Associations such as the Multiple Sclerosis Society provide transportation or offer financial assistance for transportation services.

Hospice programs assist people with terminal illnesses by offering comfort and controlling pain. Often sponsored by religious organizations, services may be provided in your home, in a hospital, or in a nursing home. To be accepted for hospice care, a person generally expects to live less than six months. Medicare pays for hospice care, and a few private insurance policies cover it as well.

For more information on hospices, turn to Chapter 17

Legal-assistance programs can help with a variety of matters. The local bar association can direct you to estate-planning attorneys who specialize in drawing up wills and trusts, planning for inheritance taxes, and dealing with guardianship for mentally incapacitated people. Elder-law attorneys handle legal matters such as reverse mortgages, Medicaid planning, and nursing-home insurance.

For more information on legal services, turn to Chapter 8

Housing Options in the Community

> **T I P** **Senior Center Search**
> There are more than 12,000 senior centers across the United States. To locate those in your community, call your local Area Agency on Aging or the Eldercare Locator.

A person needing long-term care has many more options than staying in the family home, selling it and moving in with a relative, or entering a nursing home.

Senior housing or *retirement communities* feature apartments or townhouses that are suitable for people who can care for themselves with little assistance. Some are rental units, and some are condominiums. Many of these communities include such features as bathroom handrails and electrical outlets at a convenient height. They may also offer meals, transportation, planned social activities, and other supportive services.

Assisted-living units serve those who need daily assistance but not constant nursing care. These are also called *board-and-care homes, sheltered housing, domiciliary care,* or *adult foster care.* Assisted living accommodations vary from single or double rooms to suites or apartments. Typical services include reminders about or physical assistance with meals, bathing, dressing, eating, medication, transportation, shopping, housekeeping, laundry, and other activities. Some assisted living arrangements are strictly regulated; others aren't. Be sure to ask questions and get references because the appropriateness of facilities varies. Make sure that a home that claims to offer personal care or supervision actually does so.

TIP

Assisted Living Resource
Consult the Assisted Living Facilities Association of America, 9401 Lee Highway, Fairfax, VA 22031 (703)691-8100. The association can send you a checklist of 50 questions to ask providers.

A *continuing care retirement community* is an attractive option for those who can afford it. These communities are unique because they provide a continuum of care, offering residents a long-term contract covering housing, nursing care, and other services. Typical offerings include nursing and other health services, meals and special diets, housekeeping, transportation, emergency help, personal assistance, and recreational activities. Whether operated as for-profit or nonprofit enterprises, continuing-care communities have substantial entrance fees and monthly fees.

Nursing Home Services

Contrary to popular belief, not all stays in a nursing home are long. Nursing homes are often used for short periods to recuperate from an illness or injury: 45 percent of people who enter nursing homes leave within three months. A long-term stay in a nursing home is more often appropriate for a person with a degenerative disease such as

Congregate Housing

For many seniors who don't require constant supervision, congregate housing offers a long-term alternative to "institutional" life in a nursing home. These residences integrate a cooperative living environment with supportive services on site or nearby. In part becuse people share certain facilities—kitchens, for example—congregate housing encourages residents to socialize and support one another.

Alzheimer's or Parkinson's.

Public programs and private insurance often classify nursing homes according to the kinds of care offered—skilled care or custodial care.

Skilled nursing care is 24-hour specialized medical care for people convalescing from serious illness or injury. A registered nurse or other medical specialist provides the care. Medicare, Medicaid, and private insurance all cover skilled care under certain conditions:

- The patient needs *daily* skilled care;
- The facility is certified for reimbursement by Medicare; *and*
- The care is provided under the orders of a doctor who stipulates that improvement is expected.

Medicare covers the full cost of the first 20 days of care and a small portion of the cost for the next 80 days.

Custodial care refers to assistance with non-medical activities: bathing, grooming, getting in and out of bed, going to the toilet. Most long-term care is custodial and requires no medical training.

To find a suitable nursing home, begin with a list of the facilities in your area—you may have to compile it yourself. Your doctor or care manager will have suggestions. And seek recommendations from the local Area Agency on Aging. Friends and neighbors may also have ideas.

Once you have a list of nursing homes, telephone to get basic information about location, costs, and services. Follow up with a visit to each facility that sounds promising.

As you tour a nursing home, ask questions. Speak to the appropriate staff person for specific information. For example, speak to the director of nursing to find out how the facility would manage requirements for specific care. Talk with the activities director for information on the activities program. Keep in mind that quality is the most important issue in choosing a facility.

Federal law requires states to inspect nursing homes peri-

How Old?
When looking into alternative housing, consider the ages of the residents. Some older people may be happy in a home with a wide age range; others may feel more comfortable with their peers.

The Transition

A person's transition to a nursing or rest home can be eased by:

◆ Frequent visits by family and friends;

◆ Family outings as often as possible;

◆ Providing comfortable, washable clothing with name tags sewn in;

◆ Providing a supply of writing paper and stamps;

◆ Arranging for subscriptions to newspapers and magazines;

◆ Encouraging the resident to participate in activities; *and*

◆ Providing personal items to make the room as home-like as possible.

odically as part of the certification process for Medicare and Medicaid. The inspection results are on file at the facility, and you are entitled to see them. Ask a staff member to show you the survey report. You can also get a copy from your state's nursing-home inspection office for a small charge.

> **TIP**
> **Shop Around**
> *If you can, visit more than one nursing home and visit each one that looks promising. And also visit the ones that appear best at different times of the day.*

If you want to find out about health and safety violations at a particular nursing home, you can read the deficiency lists. These provide a detailed history of a nursing home's problems and the state's efforts to correct them. Keep in mind that some of the lists contain hundreds of pages. It takes patience and determination to fully understand these materials.

Some deficiencies are more serious than others. A facility with a lot of deficiencies may actually provide better care than one with fewer but more serious violations. When touring a nursing home, see if you notice any of the same problems that appear on the deficiency lists.

Inquire about the nursing home's policy on physical and

ASK THE OMBUDSMAN

Your state's long-term-care ombudsman, who is responsible for investigating and seeking to resolve consumer complaints, can advise you about your legal rights and suggest questions to ask when you contact nursing homes. These ombudsmen visit nursing homes on a regular basis and often know about facilities in their communities.

In addition, ombudsmen receive and investigate complaints made by or on behalf of nursing home residents and work to resolve the problems. If they can't resolve problems or if they find serious violations of standards, ombudsmen refer complaints to state health departments for action.

Ask the local ombudsman about:
◆ The latest survey report on facilities;
◆ Complaints against nursing homes you plan to visit;
◆ The number and nature of complaints for the past year against a facility;
◆ The results of investigations into these complaints; *and*
◆ Tell-tale signs of good care in facilities.

There is no charge for ombudsman services. To locate the long-term-care ombudsman in your community, call the Eldercare Locator or your Area Agency on Aging.

chemical (drug) restraints. Who decides when restraints are appropriate? How closely monitored are residents who are restrained? Federal law prohibits nursing homes from using physical and chemical restraints on residents for discipline or for the convenience of nursing-home personnel. Restraints are only in order when necessary to treat medical symptoms or to ensure the safety of the person being restrained or other residents. Except in emergencies, physical and chemical restraints require written orders of physicians.

NURSING HOME RESIDENTS HAVE RIGHTS

If you live in a nursing home, you have many rights under federal and state law. The facility must provide you with a written statement of these rights when you sign a contract.

Services and Fees: The nursing home must inform you about its services and fees in writing before you enter the home and periodically during your stay.

Managing Your Money: You have the right to manage your money or to designate someone you trust to do so. If you allow a nursing home to manage your funds, you must sign a written agreement and receive regular account statements.

Privacy: You have the right to privacy in all aspects of your medical care, as well as privacy in your room. The home must provide safe and secure storage for your possessions.

Respect: You don't have to tolerate mental or phys-ical abuse. You have the right to be treated with consideration, respect, and courtesy.

Visitors: You have the right to associate privately with anyone you choose at any reasonable hour. You have the right to send and receive mail without having it opened and to use a telephone for private conversations at reasonable hours. The home must give you immediate access to family, friends, and any agency or individual who provides you with health, social, or legal services.

Moving Out: Living in a nursing home is voluntary. You are free to move to another nursing home—or to any other place. You can call a taxi or your family or friends to take you home. If a court has declared you to be incompetent, your guardian can authorize your leaving.

Medical Care: The nursing home's doctor or your private physician must keep you informed about your medical treatments and your physical condition. You have the right to see all your medical records, to participate in planning your medical care, and to refuse any medications or treatments. You also have the right to use your own doctor.

Going to the Hospital: If you must go to the hospital and you are paying for the nursing home, the facility must hold your place as long as you continue to pay for it. If you are on Medicaid, the law requires the facility to hold your bed for up to 15 days.

Durable Power of Attorney: You have the same rights in a nursing home that you have elsewhere. You can make all your own decisions, or you can choose someone you trust to make them for you by signing a Durable Power of Attorney.

For more information on rights, turn to Chapter 3.

CHOOSING A NURSING HOME: A CHECKLIST

- The first question to ask is, "Do you have an opening?" Many nursing homes have waiting lists. If you are not facing a crisis, get on the waiting list.
- Is the facility clean, friendly, and attractive? Be wary of unpleasant odors.
- Check the food service. Visit at meal time.
- Are the nursing home and its administrator licensed by the state?
- If you seek coverage under Medicare or Medicaid, is the facility certified by Medicare and/or Medicaid?
- Is the location convenient for family visits and visits by the family doctor? If your doctor won't travel to nursing homes —and many won't— what doctors visit patients in the facility?
- How many registered nurses, licensed practical nurses, and nurse's aides does the facility have? What are their qualifications? What is the ratio of these staff to residents? How does staffing change from the day shift to the night shift? There are no "right answers" to these questions, but they will help you compare one facility to another.
- How long have staff members worked at the facility? Rapid turnover often signals problems.
- What are the visiting hours? Is the family welcome at all times?
- What activities are provided for residents? Are activities challenging and tailored to the interests of the residents? Does the nursing home have special activities that engage residents with a particular disease such as Alzheimer's.
- Does the nursing home allow residents to keep some of their own furniture and to decorate their rooms?
- Does the nursing home require residents to sign over personal property or real estate in exchange for care?
- Is care coordinated with a health plan or an HMO?
- What is the "typical profile" of residents? For example, if you require temporary rehabilitation services and the home specializes in caring for people with Alzheimer's, it's probably not a good match.

If you see residents with restraints, carefully question the staff about the nursing home's philosophy on the use of restraints. Ask what kind of activities and rehabilitation are used to keep residents restraint-free.

PART III: MONEY MATTERS

Americans spend some $65 billion a year on nursing-home care and additional amounts for supplemental care in the home or the community. In most states, public programs (Medicaid, Medicare, the Department of Veterans Affairs, etc.) or private insurance pay a small portion of this bill—leaving the disabled and their families to pay the major part themselves.

While no one knows the full out-of-pocket costs for

For more information on Medicare, turn to Chapter **8**

long-term care, the overwhelming bulk of the money goes to nursing homes. With annual costs for a nursing home averaging over $35,000 a year, many older people face bills upwards of $150,000. Unless you plan ahead, you could find your life savings wiped out. Nearly one-half of the total cost of nursing homes comes directly from the pockets of American families, a burden that is increasing steadily.

And the remaining half of the bill?

The Supplemental Security Income program covers six weeks of care in a skilled nursing facility for the elderly poor. This program, plus small ones operated by the states and private long-term-care insurance, account for a few percent of the total payments for nursing-home care.

Medicare, the government health-insurance program for elders, pays about 4 percent of the total. Aimed chiefly at insuring against major illnesses, Medicare only pays for nursing-home care under very narrow circumstances. Medicare only covers nursing-home care when needed to recuperate from an acute illness or injury. It *doesn't* cover non-medical, or custodial, care.

Medicare pays for up to 100 days in a skilled nursing facility for those who require daily skilled nursing care or rehabilitation services. The facility must be Medicare-certified. Medicare pays the full cost of the first 20 days in a skilled nursing facility and, in 1994, all but $87 a day for the next 80 days. After 100 days, the patient or his or her insurance policy must pick up the whole tab.

If your doctor discharges you from a hospital to a skilled nursing facility, be sure to find out which services Medicare will cover. Ask your doctor and your hospital discharge planner. If you have questions, contact the group that administers Medicare in your area.

The Department of Veterans Affairs operates 128 nursing homes; they served nearly 30,000 veterans in 1991. In addition, the VA paid for care in private nursing homes or state homes for another 44,000 veterans.

Veterans suffering from service-connected disabilities, former prisoners of war, and World War II veterans eligible for Medicaid are all eligible for VA care. For most other

12

veterans, a complicated "eligibility assessment" determines if you qualify for care. If the assessment finds that your income is above a specified level, you must pay part of the bills for your care. Nursing-home care may be provided to any qualifying veterans *if space and resources are available.*

If you think you may qualify for VA nursing-home care, contact the nearest VA office or medical facility. They are listed in the federal government section of the telephone directory under "Department of Veterans Affairs."

The major public program paying for long-term care is Medicaid, which pays nearly half the total cost. The Medicaid program, established in 1965 to provide health care to the nation's poor, covers care for those with limited income and assets. It's now the primary government program covering long-term care.

The federal government and the states administer and finance Medicaid jointly. The federal government pays half or more of the states' costs and sets guidelines on who must be covered and what services must be provided. Within those broad guidelines, states have great leeway in determining eligibility and coverage, and specific features of the Medicaid program vary substantially from state to state. All

NURSING HOME CONTRACTS: BEFORE YOU SIGN...

Obtain a copy of the contract and review it ahead of time in the privacy of your own home. If the home won't give you a copy, ask why not. And get a lawyer's advice.

Ask the nursing facility about any part of the contract you find confusing or unfair. If you make changes in the contract, both you and the institution's representative must initial them. If the nursing home is uncooperative, take an advocate with you to help negotiate.

Make sure the contract has no blank spaces and that it's fully completed and correct at the time you sign it.

A comprehensive contract:
◆ States your rights and obligations as a resident, including safeguards and grievance procedures;
◆ Specifies how much you must pay each day or month to live in the nursing home;
◆ Details the prices for items not included in the basic monthly or daily charge;
◆ States the facility's policy on holding a bed if you temporarily leave the home for hospitalization, vacation, or other reason; *and*
◆ States whether the facility is Medicaid or Medicare certified.

states *must* cover care in a skilled nursing facility for those who qualify for Medicaid under the "categorically needy" definition. These services, for people who need daily skilled nursing or rehabilitation services, must be ordered by a doctor and be directly under her or his supervision.

For those who don't need daily skilled nursing care, all states cover care in a state-licensed intermediate care facility or nursing home, either through the categorically needy or the "medically needy" programs. Medicaid will cover room and board, nursing care, and custodial care. Although the amount Medicaid pays for these services is less than the going rate for the facility, the nursing home *can't* charge the patient or family extra for these items. The nursing home may charge patients for materials and services not covered by Medicaid, such as a visit by a hairdresser or a dental hygienist.

Medicaid is a mixed blessing. For many seniors, it provides much-needed financial support for the staggering burden of nursing-home costs. Unlike Medicare, Medicaid pays for the less-specialized care most often needed—and does so indefinitely. Unlike private insurance, Medicaid doesn't require you to pay very high premiums for many years before you can collect limited benefits.

It has been estimated that about one-third of those going into nursing homes are already enrolled in Medicaid. Sixty-five percent of all nursing-home residents receive Medicaid at some time while they are in an institution. Medicaid is the only major safety net against the catastrophe of nursing-home bills.

And now the bad news. Medicaid is, in essence, a welfare program: you must use up your income and assets—to impoverish yourself—before you receive benefits. If your spouse is not institutionalized, he or she is left with very little in assets or income.

Insurance for Long Term Care: Buyer Beware!

The insurance industry has developed special types of policies in response to public alarm over skyrocketing costs

Planning Ahead for Medicaid

If you think that you or someone in your family might qualify for Medicaid assistance to help pay for nursing-home care, get specific information on your state's Medicaid program. Do your homework early. What are the eligibility criteria? What is counted as income? As assets?

If you are not eligible now, are there steps you can take to receive Medicaid benefits later? Call the Eldercare Locator for a referral to help in your state.

for long-term care. Private insurance today pays less than 2 percent of the total national bill for nursing homes.

A strong word of caution is necessary regarding long-term-care insurance. Most financial experts advise against purchasing these policies unless you have substantial assets. The United Seniors Health Cooperative, a consumer group, advises seniors to skip long-term-care insurance unless they have at least $40,000 in savings for individuals or $100,000 for couples.

Many policies offer very little coverage for the services described in this chapter. Policies may also have exceptions for pre-existing conditions or stringent medical requirements. Before purchasing any long-term-care policy, examine it carefully and get a second opinion—including the advice of a lawyer familiar with the needs of seniors.

Criticism of these policies revolves primarily around high costs and stingy benefits. What's worse, so many insurance agents have been guilty of outright fraud and abuse in the sale of these policies that Congress has taken up legislation to clean up the long-term-care market.

If you are interested in a long-term-care insurance policy, look for:

- Guaranteed renewability for life;
- A "waiver of premiums" provision that continues your coverage at no further cost while you're collecting benefits;
- Coverage of any level of care, from custodial care to skilled care, without any requirement that hospitalization or skilled care precede the care;
- Coverage of Alzheimer's and other mental impairments;
- A deductible (also called a "waiting period" or "elimination period") of no less than 20 days, no more than 100;
- A grace period for late payments to guard against cancellations;
- No limitations on pre-existing conditions; *and*
- "Non-forfeiture provisions" that give you a partial refund if you cancel your policy.

Medicaid and the "Snapshot Date"

Under the Spousal Impoverishment Law, Medicaid must permit the at-home spouse to retain a share of the couple's combined assets. Unless you plan ahead, Medicaid will determine how much the at-home spouse can keep based on an accounting of total assets at the time of application.

Protect against this unnecessary loss of assets by asking the state to establish the total value of your assets *on the first day of institutionalization.* This is sometimes called the "snapshot date." Medicaid will use this higher amount as the basis for determining how much the community spouse

PART IV: WHAT NOW? ASSEMBLING A PLAN

Now that you've read about the possibilities, let's revisit the three families who introduced this chapter and see how they meet their needs for long-term care.

Joan Evans had a stroke. She probably won't fully recover, but a needs assessment determined that, with physical

MEDICAID DISCRIMINATION

Medicaid pays nursing homes less than do individuals who aren't on Medicaid. As a result, some nursing homes accept only "private-pay" patients. But even Medicaid-certified nursing homes often try to limit the number of lower-paying Medicaid patients by limiting the number of beds available for Medicaid patients.

When you apply to a nursing home, the staff will ask about your financial resources and your plans for paying for care. Some homes will demand that you prove you have the resources to pay for your own care at the private-pay rate for one or even two years, delaying the time when they might have to accept the lower Medicaid rate for you. This is illegal in many states and of questionable legality under federal law. Contact your long-term-care ombudsman to find out your state's laws.

In addition, some nursing homes insist that Med-

icaid recipients or their families "supplement" the Medicaid payment with contributions, gifts, or donations. Whether required as a condition of admission or continued stay, *this is expressly prohibited under federal law.*

If you enter a nursing home as a private-pay patient but then deplete your resources and qualify for Medicaid, a private-pay facility can transfer you to another nursing home, if one is available. Medicaid-certified nursing homes must continue to serve patients, but many people encounter discrimination once their status changes. They may be transferred to less desirable rooms or denied services they once received. In some instances, Medicaid patients sit in separate areas of the dining room, receive different food selections, or aren't allowed to participate in the same activities. *Federal law prohibits discrimination in the services provided on the basis of the source*

of payment.

If you or a family member encounter Medicaid discrimination, voice your concerns to the administrator of the nursing home. Make it clear that you are monitoring the care provided and that you know your legal rights. State your concerns clearly and forcefully, without unnecessary rancor.

If you don't get satisfactory answers, contact your state's long-term-care ombudsman. In addition, the Office of the Inspector General at the U.S. Department of Health and Human Services maintains a toll-free Hot Line for complaints about Medicaid discrimination. The number is (800)368-5779; in Maryland, call (800)638-3986. Or write to: HHS, Office of the Inspector General, Hot Line, P.O. Box 17303, Baltimore, MD 21203-7303. Or contact the National Senior Law Center, 2025 M St., NW, Washington, DC 20036 (202)887-5280.

therapy, she'll be able to move on her own from her wheelchair to a chair or bed. Since Joan's doctor diagnosed that
therapy will improve her condition, Medicare covers part
of those costs. Her Medigap insurance covers a significant
portion of the remainder.

*For more on Medigap
insurance, turn to
Chapter* **8**

Although her speech is slow, Joan can make herself
understood, and she retains all her mental faculties. Joan
has begun therapy and regained considerable stability and
strength. She'll receive home-delivered meals until she feels
more competent in her own kitchen. Through personal-
care services, Joan gets help with bathing every other day.

A borrowed walker from a loan closet lessens the expense
of equipment. Through her local Area Agency on Aging,
Joan learned about a volunteer group that provides some
housekeeping. At present she relies on neighbors to pick up
her groceries, but she is exploring alternatives, being reluctant to become a burden on their good will.

In short, Joan faces much uncertainty, but her stroke
hasn't devastated her life. Although she doesn't expect to
remain in her home permanently, the changes she faces are
far less frightening now.

Saul Miller, diagnosed with Alzheimer's disease, is fine
physically, but he wanders from home at all hours and can
be alternately combative and withdrawn. His behavior
threatens his own well-being, and his family can't supervise
him 24-hours a day indefinitely.

An adult day-care center with a special component for
people with Alzheimer's offers Saul a program well-suited
for his needs. The center costs $200 a week, and Saul's
children split the bill. His daughter's family can carry on
with their daily lives. Saul returns to his daughter's home
each evening, and family members share responsibility for
ensuring his safety during the night.

Recognizing the progressive deterioration of Saul's condition, his family is exploring nursing homes, reserving a
decision while they investigate more intensive home care.
The family is reluctant to place Saul in a nursing home,
but they have put his name on a waiting list in case this
option becomes necessary in the future.

THE SPECIAL NEEDS OF ALZHEIMER'S PATIENTS IN NURSING FACILITIES

If you plan on placing a family member in a nursing home, keep in mind that most homes integrate Alzheimer's patients onto existing, non-specialized floors. As many as 40 to 60 percent of patients in most nursing homes have Alzheimer's disease.

Only a few specialized units for people with Alzheimer's are available. Because these facilities are in very short supply and have admissions priorities, don't apply only to special-care units.

In examining a nursing home without a special-care unit for a person with Alzheimer's, interview admissions personnel about the facility and its programs. Trust your instincts as you seek answers to the following questions:

Does the facility acknowledge that it has other Alzheimer's patients? Ask to speak with family members who have Alzheimer patients there.

Is the environment simple? Simple design and lower levels of auditory and visual stimulation are more appropriate for patients with cognitive impairments.

Is the environment safe? Doors and windows should be secure, especially if the patient is a wanderer. Is there a security system to prevent wandering outside? An uncluttered space for the patient to walk?

What is the staff-to-patient ratio on all shifts, including weekends? The generally accepted optimal ratio is one to six; the minimum is one to nine.

Do activities include the Alzheimer's patient? Talk to the activities director and look at the weekly schedule of activities. Do activities meet the needs of cognitively impaired patients? Some facilities conduct parallel activities that benefit patients for whom standard activities are difficult. Is a staff person available to supervise activities on at least two shifts?

Claudia Taylor had to cope with the impact of her own heart surgery *and* the effect of her absence and poor health on her husband Oscar, who had Parkinson's. Because Oscar's health was failing and she herself would have to convalesce for two months after surgery, Claudia placed her husband in a nursing home, knowing that his placement was permanent. After her surgery, Claudia recuperated in the same nursing home. After 30 days, she returned home. Medicare paid in full for her nursing-home care, but Claudia uses savings to pay for Oscar's care.

As the savings have been drawn down, Claudia has sought the advice of an elder-law attorney about getting Medicaid coverage for Oscar. The attorney has reviewed Claudia's financial situation, explained how Medicaid coverage of her husband would affect *her,* and advised her of her options.

THE SPECIAL NEEDS OF ALZHEIMER'S PATIENTS CONTINUED

12

Does the staff address patients with respect or with condescension and scolding?

Is there assistance at meals, and are special diets available to patients?

How does the facility deal with unruly or inappropriate behavior?

Do staff members talk with the family and let the family's experience help guide the care of the patient?

As a patient's condition declines, is he or she moved to another area of the facility? Moves should be kept to a minimum and are most appropriate when the patient reaches a severe stage of the disease.

What is the policy on the use of physical and chemical restraints?

What is the procedure for care of a terminal patient? For example, will the facility allow families to refuse feeding tubes or extraordinary measures for later-stage patients?

How and by whom has the staff been trained in the care of Alzheimer patients?

Who provides primary medical care for the facility? You may want to interview these providers.

Who provides psychiatric services for Alzheimer's patients?

What is the policy on visiting?

Does the facility sponsor an Alzheimer family-support group?

Does the facility or its staff belong to the Alzheimer's Association?

Does the facility have a written waiting list? Will you receive notice when your turn comes?

Does the facility accept Medicaid after the patient's private funds are exhausted?

Are there any additional costs (now or later) because the patient has Alzheimer's disease?

—adapted from *Guide to Nursing and Rest Homes in Massachusetts,* edited by Diane K. Goldman (Women's Education and Industrial Union, 1994)

RESOURCES

For additional resources on long-term care, turn to Chapter 2 on consumer rights, Chapter 8 on elders, Chapter 13 on home care, and Chapter 19 for general resources.

Organizations

Alzheimer's Association
919 Michigan Ave.
Chicago, IL 60611
(800)272-3900
(312)335-8700
Call or write for a free brochure.

American Association of Homes for the Aging
901 E St., NW
Washington, DC 20004
(202)783-2242
Call or write for publications for caregivers and elders.

American Association of Retired Persons
601 E St., NW
Washington, DC 20049
Consumer Affairs: (202)434-6030
Social Outreach and Support: (202)434-2262
Call or write for a free catalogue of AARP publications, many of which are free. Among the titles are "Care Management: Arranging for Long Term Care," "A Checklist of Concern: Resources for Caregivers," "Coping and Caring: Living with Alzheimer's Disease," "Making Wise Decisions for Long-Term Care," "Nursing Home Life: A Guide for Residents and their Families," and "Selecting Retirement Housing." AARP also maintains a database of retirement communities, with information on fees, services, amenities, sponsorship, and other factors. To obtain a list of communities in one or two metropolitan areas, write the Retirement Communities Database, Correspondence Unit at AARP.

Assisted Living Facilities Association of America
9401 Lee Highway
Fairfax, VA 22031
(703)691-8100
Call or write for brochures, including a consumer checklist of services and information on assisted living.

B'nai B'rith International
1640 Rhode Island Ave., NW
Washington, DC 20036
(202)857-6600
For a small fee, the Caring Network Program will give you referrals to organizations that provide assistance and information.

RESOURCES

**National Association
of Meal Programs**
101 N. Alfred
Alexandria, VA 22314
(703)548-5558
Call for information on meal programs in your area.

**National Association of Professional
Geriatric Care Managers**
655 N. Alvernon Way
Tucson, AZ 85711
(602)881-8008
An association of private professionals who help caregivers identify needs and resources in the community. Call for referrals to local providers.

**National Citizens' Coalition for
Nursing Home Reform**
1224 M St., NW
Washington, DC 20005-5183
(202)393-4122
Call or write for a catalogue of publications on nursing homes, physical and chemical restraints, and other long-term-care topics.

**National Senior Citizens
Law Center**
2025 M St., NW
Washington, DC 20036
(202)887-5280

Publications

Beating the Nursing Home Trap: A Consumer's Guide to Choosing/Financing Long-Term Care, by Joseph Matthews (Nolo Press, 1993). $19.95.

The Complete Nursing Home Guide: Finding Quality Care for Your Loved Ones, by Mary B. Forrest, Christopher B. Forrest, and Richard Forrest (Taylor Publishing, 1993). $14.95.

"A Consumer Guide to Home Health Care," $4.00, and "A Consumer Guide to Life Care Communities," $3.00. Both are published by the National Consumer's League, 815 15th St., NW, Washington, DC 20005.

A Family's Guide to Selecting, Financing, and Asserting Rights in a Nursing Home. Published by the Center for Public Representation, 520 University Ave., Madison, WI 53703. $15.00.

"Guide to Choosing a Nursing Home." Published by the U.S. Department of Health and Human Services, Health Care Financing Agency. Pub. No. HCFA-02174.

How to Evaluate and Select a Nursing Home, by R. Barker Bausell, Michael A. Rooney, and Charles B. Inlander (People's Medical Society, 1988). $7.95.

"How to Pay for Nursing Home Care: Here's Help." For a free copy, contact the American Health Care Association, 1201 L St., NW, Washington, DC 20005-4014 (202)842-8444.

Long Term Living: How to Live Independently as Long as You Can and Plan for the Time When You Can't, by Susan Polniaszek (Acropolis Books, 1990). $9.95.

National Directory for Eldercare Information and Referral. Published by the National Association of Area Agencies on Aging, 1112 16th St., NW, Washington, DC 20036. $40 ($30 for members).

"Nursing Home Insurance: Who Can Afford It?" (Families USA, 1993). $5.

"Nursing Home Patients Bill of Rights: An Illustrated Guide for Consumers and Providers." Published by the National Senior Citizens Education and Research Center, Nursing Home Information Service, 925 15th St., NW, Washington, DC 20005. Free.

"Nursing Homes: What You Need to Know." Maryland Attorney General's Office, Consumer Protection Division. Free.

The 36-Hour Day: A Family Guide to Caring for Persons with Alzheimer's, by Nancy Mace and Peter V. Rabins, MD (Johns Hopkins University Press, 1981). $7.95

You, Your Parent, and the Nursing Home, by Nancy Fox. Available from Prometheus Books, 700 E. Amherst, Buffalo, NY 14215. $11.95.

Home Care

By Anne P. Werner and James P. Firman

Your Choice

You do have choices. If you need care at home, you don't need to surrender control over your life and let others tell you what you must do.

Supplemental Care

Home care often supplements care that a spouse or other family member provides. A woman may not be strong enough to help her husband bathe, even though she can manage most of his care. Or the many tasks of caring for his disabled wife may be too much for a husband who has arthritis. In both cases, an aide can preserve the mental and physical health of the caregiver.

Anne P. Werner is Director of Community Services and James P. Firman is President and Executive Director of the United Seniors Health Cooperative. This chapter is excerpted and adapted from Home Care for Older People: A Consumer's Guide, *published by USHC.*

chapter copyright © USHC 1994

"Home care." These two simple words encompass a wide and complex range of services. Home care can mean anything from help with the everyday tasks of living to advanced medical care. Regardless, the many kinds of home care all share one thing in common. They take place where most people prefer to be: in their own homes.

Whether you live in an apartment, a house, a room in your child's house, or a retirement residence, home care can benefit you when you are frail, ill, or disabled. The goal is to maintain or restore your ability to function well enough to continue living at home.

PART I: GETTING STARTED

As many as seven million elders, plus millions of disabled people of all ages, need help with at least one of the five "activities of daily living"—bathing, dressing, walking, eating, or using the toilet. Even more people need occasional assistance with other routine tasks, such as grocery shopping, getting to the doctor, managing chores, and paying bills.

Home care varies to fit these and other situations. For example, after surgery, a physical therapist may visit you at home for a few weeks. As you recover, you may progress to much simpler needs that a home-health aide might provide.

Who Provides Home Care?

Family members—mainly women—provide nearly 80 percent of home care. When your family can't handle the amount of assistance you need, or lacks the required technical training, you can choose from two types of outside home care: *home health care* and *home support services.* Sometimes these categories are distinct; on other occasions, they can blend into one another.

Home health care is administered by professional practitioners. A doctor orders the care, and a registered nurse, licensed practical nurse, or trained rehabilitation therapist provides it. Sometimes, a medical social worker or nutritionist joins a home-health-care team.

Home-health aides, trained professionals or semi-professionals, are also members of home-care teams. Sometimes called home-care aides, they assist nurses or therapists with such tasks as taking your temperature, helping you with prescribed exercises, and doing household tasks—shopping, cooking, and laundry.

Homemaker's duties overlap with those of home-health aides when it comes to managing a household. The homemaker normally does more extensive house cleaning, including dusting, vacuuming, and cleaning the kitchen and bathroom. However, homemakers aren't trained to check a pulse or assist with exercise routines.

Home support services include all the other non-technical services a person may need to continue living at home. You can get these from an agency or from an individual working independently. Sometimes volunteers help with certain tasks, such as transportation to a medical appointment or the grocery store. The various people providing home support services include:

- Homemakers and home-health aides;
- The person who comes to do heavy chores and yard work; *and*
- The aide or volunteer who handles paperwork, such as filing Medicare claims or balancing checkbooks.

Assessing Your Needs

If you have been in a hospital, your doctor and hospital personnel will help you plan for home care. If you haven't been hospitalized, a variety of local organizations can help you assess your needs and figure out how to meet them. And if your requirements are relatively simple, this chapter may be all you need to get started.

As you prepare to leave the hospital and get skilled home care, your doctor should write a *plan of care* for you. Even if the doctor doesn't give you a formal plan, ask for written information about what you'll need—and need to do—at home. You'll have too much on your mind to remember everything, and written instructions will also help others

Living Alone

Women usually outlive men, so they are more likely to need home care at some time during their lives. Regardless of gender, people who live alone and lack a network of friends, neighbors, and other helpers most often take advantage of home-care services.

"HOME SERVICES" OUTSIDE THE HOME

In many communities, a wealth of services enrich the lives of people needing home care, as well as those of the family caregivers. Here are a few:

◆ *Adult day care or day health centers* offer a safe, pleasant environment for people who can't safely remain at home alone or who can benefit from spending more time with others of similar age and interests. Day health centers also offer preventive care, health screenings, and therapy programs. Adult day-care programs are a real health-care bargain.

◆ *Respite care,* either at home or in a nursing home, provides a tempo-rary "vacation" for the family members providing care. This refreshes care-givers and can greatly reduce burnout. Respite care may be given by some-one who comes into the home or by staff in a nurs-ing home or assisted-living facility during a short admission.

◆ *Home-delivered meals,* often called Meals on Wheels, are available in many communities at a modest cost. Hot and cold meals are delivered to a person's home, three to five days a week.

◆ *Personal emergency response systems* are often called Medical Alert Pro-grams. A person wears an electronic device around the neck or wrist. When activated, the device signals a hospital or central dis-patcher to summon assis-tance.

◆ *Adult protective services* protect older and disabled adults from physical or mental abuse, neglect, and exploitation. Your Area Agency on Aging can tell you how to contact the local protective service. All health-care workers must report suspected abuse, neglect, or exploitation. Whether you file a report yourself or on behalf of someone else, your identity will be confidential.

The Family Plan

Discharge planners and other home-care advisors can do a lot, but they can't do their job alone. Your input is vital to devising a plan that meets your needs and considers your preferences on timing, frequency, and manner of care. A good plan gives you, the client, the responsibility you wish to assume. And family members should take part in the discussion with the discharge planner or advisor, if possible.

who assist you.

Ask the doctor or nursing supervisor to arrange for a *discharge planner* to talk with you about arranging your home care. All hospitals have a social-services department to help you plan your discharge. In addition, about one-third of the nation's hospitals offer home-health services, either through their own staff or through an affiliated agency.

Alternatively, the discharge planner may call on an outside agency to provide services for you at home. In many cases, the agency will write your plan of care and present it to your doctor to sign. When your home health care requires a doctor's oversight and a nurse's supervision, the plan will describe exactly what care you'll need, who'll provide it, and how often. It will also specify treatments, medical equipment and supplies, medications, and any special diet.

If the plan is complex, involving providers outside the agency, it should include a clear, written statement of who is in charge, and who will do what, how often, and at what cost to you. One key question your plan should answer: Who assumes responsibility for coordinating all the care providers? Find out who to call if there are any problems with an outside provider?

If you don't have access to discharge services through a hospital, you can determine your home-care needs with a *geriatric assessment.* In addition to identifying your medical, nursing, and rehabilitation needs, this assessment will consider your family circumstances and lifestyle. How much care can you or your family provide? How safe is your home? How well does it suit your current needs?

A home-health agency can conduct this assessment. Normally agencies don't charge for the service if you are likely to become a client. If your case is complicated and your budget permits, consider hiring a private geriatric-care manager. Some long-term-care insurance will pay for or provide an assessment. As a less-expensive alternative, ask a nurse or social worker to advise you. The local Area Agency on Aging may direct you to these professionals.

PART II: CHOOSING THE RIGHT PROVIDERS

After surgery, you may need skilled nursing care. In this case, you'll look for a Medicare-certified home-health agency. On the other hand, if you are living at home and simply finding daily tasks difficult to manage, you'll probably look for a homemaker or a companion. If your requirements fall somewhere between skilled and basic care, three main sources of help are available: a home-health agency, a registry of nurses or aides, and independent workers.

Should you decide to use an agency, you'll receive more support than you will if you decide to hire help on your own. The care provided through home-health agencies often qualifies as *skilled care,* the type of home care that health insurance is most likely to cover. However, if you don't need skilled services, *homemaker* or *home-health-aide agencies* may fulfill your needs. These frequently aren't Medicare-certified but tend to cost less because they don't have to satisfy many regulations or hire highly trained

For more information on health-care needs of elders, turn to Chapter **8**

When Home Care Is Not Enough

Family unity, health, and finances are all part of an equation that must be measured against the desires and needs of the person receiving care at home. While older people may fear going into a nursing home, they usually don't want to burden others either.

One way to deal with this issue is by convening a family council. It may also help to consult a member of the clergy, a trusted friend, or an attorney. And learn about the growing number of alternatives to nursing homes, such as assisted-living facilities. You may be pleasantly surprised when you investigate the variety of living arrangements offered in your community.

For more on long-term care, turn to Chapter **12**

personnel.

If you decide to use a registry or a private source instead of an agency, you'll be the direct employer, which gives you more control over the situation as well as lower costs.

> **T I P**
>
> **Simple Needs**
> *If a caring person with modest training would meet your needs, a less-regulated agency will suffice. Thirty-eight states require such agencies to maintain a state license, although standards tend to be less exacting than those of Medicare.*

Assembling Information

As you address the following considerations, suggested by the National Association for Home Care, seek answers from the home-care agencies themselves as well as from other sources, such as local organizations that advocate for elders. Base your ultimate decision on the balance of factors that suits your situation.

- How long has the agency served the community?
- Is the agency accredited?
- Is the plan of care written out?
- Does the plan make clear the purpose and amount of care deemed practical for the conditions being treated or served?
- What are the arrangements for emergencies?

SELECTING A HOME CARE PROVIDER—WHO AND WHAT TO ASK

What to Find Out:	Home Health Agency	Homemaker/ Aide Service	Registry	Independent Worker
Is the agency Medicare-certified?	✓	✓		
Is it state-licensed?	✓	✓		
What is its reputation?	✓	✓	✓	✓
Is home assessment available?	✓	✓		
How are workers supervised?	✓	✓	✓	
How are workers trained?	✓	✓	✓	
Is there an established complaint process?	✓	✓	✓	
Is there client input in the plan of care?	✓	✓		
Who handles paperwork?	✓	✓	✓	
Will the agency refer you to another source if necessary?	✓	✓		

246

- How does the agency protect the confidentiality of its clients?
- Does the agency describe its services, eligibility requirements, fees, and funding sources in writing?
- What are the financial arrangements?
- What arrangements will the agency make for you if you exhaust your reimbursement sources?

The Job Offer

Whether you hire an aide directly or through a registry, prepare yourself to become a "home care manager."

The Job Description: As the first step in hiring your own aide, write down exactly what you want the person to do for you. List all the steps that each task entails. If the aide will help you bathe, you'll want the tub cleaned afterwards. Make the job description specific. How often will each task be done? How long should it take to do the tasks right? Outline a typical daily routine. Include the salary or hourly rate in the job description. If you don't know how much to pay, ask your Area Agency on Aging to suggest a fair wage.

The Interview: Ask a prospective homemaker or aide:

- *Where have you worked before?* Get the names and phone numbers of three previous employers and contact them.
- *What were your duties?* Look for an aide who has had direct experience with the duties and conditions your situation entails.
- *How long were you employed in previous jobs?*
- *How long can you work on this job?*
- *Do you smoke?* If you don't smoke, a non-smoker is your obvious choice. If your best candidate smokes, consider how you might work this out.
- *Are there any duties in this job that you feel you can't do?* A caring person may be willing to learn new tasks; an inflexible attitude indicates possible problems ahead.
- *Would anything in your situation keep you from arriving on time?* You might prepare a back-up plan if the aide cannot come due to illness or a family problem.

Making the Decision: If you have several good

13

candidates, you may base your final decision largely on personality: how do you feel about inviting this person into your home? Trust your instincts. After all, you must feel comfortable with the person who will spend time with you in your home.

The Contract: After an applicant accepts your job offer, prepare an employment agreement that you both sign. If you hire the worker through an agency, sign the contract with the agency rather than the individual. This document should spell out what the agency will—and won't—do. It should specify the duties of the worker, and how often he or she will perform them.

In some situations, you and an agency may share responsibility for selecting and supervising a worker. For example, a registry may do some screening and provide an orientation. As the employer, you may choose to use either a formal contract or a simpler agreement clarifying the expectations and responsibilities of both parties.

PART III: MANAGING YOUR HOME CARE

A home-care worker who comes to you through an agency will be trained by that agency and instructed to contact his or her supervisor about any health-related concerns or changes to the plan of care. Even so, this person works in your home, where you are the daily supervisor. And "employer" may be a difficult role for you when you are not feeling your best, especially if you have never employed anyone in your home before.

To understand the challenge of care management, picture a symphony orchestra. The conductor leads the orchestra through a piece of music, cueing in the strings, woodwinds, brass, and perhaps a soloist in a precise, synchronized fashion. Like the orchestra, a person recovering from a serious illness or accident may need a "conductor"

Home Care as a Vocation

Some people choose to work in home care because they like helping people. Part of their reward is knowing they are helping you live independently, recover from an illness or accident, or simply find some comfort each day. Others like the flexibility of working only a few days a week or a few hours a day.

That said, most home-care aides take jobs in this field because it is the best work available given their education, training, or language skills. The typical home-care worker earns less than $6.00 an hour and comes from a family whose total income averages about $20,000 a year. Home care offers low pay, few fringe benefits, irregular hours, and limited opportunities for advancement.

TIP

Care Manager Source
Your local Area Agency or Office on Aging is the place to start gathering information on care managers. If the agency doesn't manage care, the staff can direct you to an appropriate source. If you can afford to pay for a care manager, the agency may ask you to do so.

WRITING AN EMPLOYMENT CONTRACT

This is a sample agreement between a person needing home care and a provider. It's based on a form developed by IONA Senior Services of Washington, DC:

Employment contract between:

Employer _____ and Employee _____

Salary $_____ per hour   Fringe benefits _____

Terms of payment: when _____   how _____

Hours of work: from _____to_____on _____
Changes in scheduled hours are negotiable

Employee's Social Security Number_____

HOUSEHOLD TASKS:

☐ light housekeeping   ☐ bedmaking   ☐ cooking
☐ laundry   ☐ escort on short trips ☐ taking out garbage
☐ errands & shopping   ☐ washing dishes   ☐ companionship & support

PERSONAL CARE TASKS:

☐ bathing & grooming   ☐ dressing   ☐ getting out of bed
☐ getting around   ☐ feeding   ☐ diet planning & cooking
☐ exercise   ☐ medication reminders

SCHEDULE FOR DUTIES TO BE PERFORMED:

Household tasks: dust and vacuum once a week, mop kitchen once a week, change sheets once a week, wash laundry once a week, shop for food once a week, wash dishes after each meal

Personal-care tasks: assist with bath and shampoo once a week, transport to doctor's appointment once a month, provide some conversation, cook lunch

Non-acceptable behavior: smoking at work, using foul language, evidence of intoxication, coming to work late

TERMINATION

Each party will give two weeks' notice before terminating this contract.

Reasons for termination without notice include theft, failure to carry out duties, evidence of non-acceptable behavior, and endangering employer's health or safety.

For unsatisfactory work, the employer will give two warnings. If the work continues to be unsatisfactory, a termination date will be set.

Signed: _____   _____
                  (employer)   (employee)

Date: _____   _____

Homes Rules

Attach a list of "home rules" to the contract you sign with an individual or an agency. Give the rules to each person who comes to work in your home and post them where they can be easily read.

One man listed these rules:

◆ No smoking in my house, please. It hurts my eyes.

◆ Be kind to my dog and he will be your friend for life.

◆ Foul language offends me. Please spare my feelings.

◆ Please respect my belongings. They may not seem like much to you, but they are very precious to me.

with training to synchronize and coordinate a large array of home-care providers. Fortunately, specialists are available to help in this situation.

You and Your Home Care Workers

Managing home-care workers requires sensitivity. Tell aides what you like about their work. Let them know that you appreciate the small, extra things they do. Aides often make efforts above and beyond their assigned duties; recognize and appreciate this.

Be equally clear about problems. For example, if a worker arrives late often, ask if a particular situation is causing the tardiness. Would it be better for the aide to come later in the morning and stay later in the afternoon? Many people have a tendency to slide a bit in their work if they feel it won't be noticed, so speak up in a constructive way to deal with such issues early in the relationship.

If your aide comes from an agency, a supervisor should call periodically to ask you about the aide's performance. If this doesn't happen after a few weeks, call the supervisor yourself and volunteer your objective appraisal of the person's work. Use this time to work out any problems *and* to register praise.

PAPERWORK, PAPERWORK, PAPERWORK

For some people, the prospect of filing reports, keeping records, and handling tax payments is reason enough to use an agency for home-care workers. Others find the paperwork required of employers manageable once the initial forms are filed, and they appreciate the flexibility and control associated with doing their own hiring and supervision. In fact, people who are actively involved in their own care may recover more quickly and completely.

As an employer, you are responsible for making certain payments on behalf of each person you hire directly to work in your home, be it a nurse, an aide, or a person to help with chores. For example, you must report the wages and deduct Social Security taxes if you pay a worker more than $50 during a quarter. Also, you and your workers must agree on whether you will withhold federal and state income taxes from their wages. And your state may require you to pay into its unemployment fund.

How to Complain About Quality

If home-care workers or health-care personnel come to you through an agency, you have several options should you need to register a complaint:

• Large agencies have a grievance process generally. Ask for the chief operating officer or the person who handles "quality of care."

• Call the Better Business Bureau if the agency's practices are unethical or if you think some type of fraud may be taking place.

• If you receive care under Medicare Part A and feel that the care is inferior, you may ask the state "Peer Review Organization" to investigate. PROs monitor the appropriateness and quality of care. To locate your state's PRO, call the Social Security Administration.

• Contact the state long-term-care ombudsman.

PART IV: MONEY MATTERS

For most people, the biggest challenge of home care is paying the bills. An aide for four hours a day, five days a week can cost from $8,000 to $14,000 annually. And you'll confront a hodgepodge of government programs that, even when pieced together, often leave big gaps in coverage.

Medicare

Most Americans over the age of 65 qualify for Medicare. In addition, some three million Americans under age 65 qualify because they have severe long-term disabilities.

If you are enrolled in Medicare and require skilled care, this is the preferred way to finance your home care. Medicare will pay all of the *Medicare-approved amount* for skilled health services delivered at home under certain circumstances. You must be homebound, under the care of a physician who signs a plan of care, *and* in need of only part-time or intermittent home-health services. You must also receive the care from a Medicare-certified agency. Consult your local Area Agency on Aging.

For information on ombudsman, turn to Chapter **12**

Empowerment and Dependency

13

In an earnest effort to do everything possible for a spouse, parent, or other relative, families can do too much, robbing the patient of independence.

If the patient's mental faculties are not impaired, families should present alternatives, discuss the advantages and disadvantages of each, and let the patient decide. Because so many natural losses can come with aging, it's important to preserve the patient's decision-making to the fullest degree possible. And take time to listen as well as to talk to the person for whom you are caring.

Even patients with the most debilitating physical problems can give something of themselves to others. A man who worked as an accountant may be able to keep his own books and help someone else as well.

For more information on Medicare and Medicaid, turn to Chapter **8**

Consumers, Medicare, and Home Care

◆ Medicare reimbursement doesn't depend on hospitalization. Your need for skilled services is the key.

◆ Get your doctor to document your need for skilled services.

◆ If you think your care is being terminated too soon, contact the local Medicare fiscal intermediary. Call (800)772-1213 to find the appropriate organization.

◆ Don't be afraid to appeal decisions made by the certified home-health agency.

Veterans Home Care

Veteran Affairs Hospital-Based Home Care is available in a few communities. Veterans who are at least 50 percent disabled due to a condition connected with their military service are eligible. A team consisting of a doctor, nurse, dietitian, social worker, and physical therapist teaches a veteran's relatives or friends to care for him or her.

An excellent source of information on home care for veterans is the Veterans' Benefits Department of the Paralyzed Veterans of America. Call them at (800)424-8200.

Medicaid

Medicaid, a federal/state insurance program for low-income people, can be a viable option to help pay for home care. However, people must meet strict income and asset requirements to qualify for coverage. These amounts vary from state to state, but in 1993 the typical maximum annual income was $4,800 for a single person and $6,500 for a couple. Typical limits on assets (excluding your home and a $1,500 burial fund) were $2,000 for an individual and $3,000 for a couple.

In many states, people with higher incomes can qualify for Medicaid if they have high medical expenses. Under these "spend down" provisions, your medical expenses are deducted from your income. This is how most people qualify for Medicaid's long-term-care benefits.

Medicaid potentially covers five types of home care:

T I P   Applying for Medicaid
To find out if you qualify for Medicaid or to apply for benefits, contact your local welfare office. In some states, you can also apply at senior-citizen centers and other locations.

1. *Home-Health Services Covered by Medicare:* If a person qualifies for both Medicaid and Medicare, Medicaid will pay the 20 percent co-payment required for some Medicare home-health services, such as durable medical equipment.

2. *Home-Health Services Covered by Medicaid Only:* All states offer home-health services to people eligible for Medicaid. These services include skilled nursing, home-health-aide services, and medical equipment and supplies.

3. *Private Nursing:* In 28 states, Medicaid pays for extended hours of home nursing care.

4. *Personal-Care Services:* In about 30 states, Medicaid also pays for personal-care services under certain circumstances.

5. *Home and Community-Based Waiver Services:* States can apply to the federal government for permission to offer additional non-medical services. Some 49 states offer services under this program but often make it difficult to qualify.

The Older Americans Act

Your local Area Agency on Aging receives funds under the Older Americans Act to enable older people with frailties or disabilities to remain independent. Anyone 60 or over can receive services, which are directed particularly to people with the greatest social and financial need who could otherwise not remain in their homes.

Each area agency has a degree of flexibility in how it will meet the needs of its community's residents. Services fall into three major categories: home, community, and access.

• *Services in the home* include homemakers, chore service, and meal delivery. You apply to the Area Agency on Aging, which may provide the service directly or through another agency.

• *Services in the community* include senior centers, day health-care programs, protective services, and legal counseling.

• *Access services* include transportation to help older people travel to senior centers, medical appointments, Social Security offices, and shopping areas.

PRIVATE PAYMENT OPTIONS FOR HOME CARE

If government programs don't suit your situation, you have several potential private options for paying for home care. Two important options are Medigap insurance and insurance for long-term care.

◆ While you receive Medicare-covered home health care, you may be eligible for additional payments if you've bought a Medicare Supplemental Insurance Policy (*Medigap insurance*). If you purchase plans D, G, I, or J of the ten standard Medigap polices, an At-Home Recovery Benefit will include some payment for personal-care services. This benefit could allow you more time for healing or rehabilitation. *For more information, turn to Chapter 8, Elders As Health Care Consumers.*

Private long-term-care insurance, a relatively new type of policy, is intended to protect people from the catastrophic expense of a lengthy stay in a nursing home. However, the home-care coverage of most policies is relatively weak, and the policies themselves are the subject of intense criticism. *For more information, turn to Chapter 12 on long-term care.*

RESOURCES

Organizations

**American Association
of Retired Persons**
601 E St., NW
Washington, DC 20049
(202)434-6030
Call or write for a catalogue of publications, including the free pamphlets "A Handbook About Care in
the Home," "A Consumer's Guide to
Homesharing," "The Doable
Renewable Home: Making Your
Home Fit Your Needs," and "Your
Home, Your Choice."

**National Association for
Home Care**
519 C St., NE
Washington, DC 20002
(202)547-9559
Call or write for information,
including a free copy of "How to
Choose a Home Care Agency."

**National Association of
Area Agencies on Aging**
1112 16th St., NW
Washington, DC 20036
(202)296-8130
Eldercare Locator: (800)677-1116
Call the Eldercare Locator for assistance in finding the most appropriate information source for home care
anywhere in the country.

**National Association of Professional
Geriatric Care Managers**
655 N. Alvernon Way
Tucson, AZ 85711
(602)881-8008
This is an association of private
professionals who help caregivers
identify needs and resources in the
community. Call for referrals to local
providers.

United Seniors Health Cooperative
1331 H St., NW
Washington, DC 20005
(202)393-6222
USHC is a nonprofit membership
organization working to promote
good health, independence and
financial security for older people in
the Washington, DC, area. Call or
write for information about programs or to receive a publications
list. Also call or write to order a copy
of *Home Care for Older People* by
Anne P. Werner and James P. Firman, $12.00; *Long-Term Care: A
Dollar and Sense Guide* by Susan
Polniaszek, $10; or *Managing Your
Health Care Finances: Getting the
Most Out of Medicare and Medigap
Insurance* by Susan Polniaszek, $10.

Publications

*The Caregiver's Guide: Helping Elder-
ly Relatives Cope with Health and
Safety Problems* (Houghton Mifflin,
1991). $14.45.

"A Consumers Guide to Home
Health Care." 36-page discussion of
home health care, including a consumer checklist. Order from National Consumers League, 815 15th St.,
NW, Washington, DC 20005. $4.

*Golden Opportunities: Hundreds of
Money-Making, Money-Saving Gems
for Anyone Over Fifty,* by Amy Bud-
ish and Armond Budish, $27.50;
*Home Safety Guide for Older People:
Check It Out/Fix It Up,* by John
Pynoos and Evelyn Cohen, $13.95;
and *Retirement Income on the House:
Cashing in on Your Mortgage with a
Reverse Mortgage,* by Ken Scholen,
$29.95. Order any of these books
from Serif Press, 1331 H St., NW,
Washington, DC 20005 (800)221-
4272.

Home Health Care, by Jo-Ann Friedman (W.W. Norton, 1986). $25.

"The Medicare Handbook." Available free from U.S. Department of
Health and Human Services, Health
Care Financing Administration. Call
(800)772-1213.

"Safety for Older Consumers: Home
Safety Checklist." Available from
Consumer Product Safety Commis-
sion, Washington, DC 20207.

Caring for Your Teeth

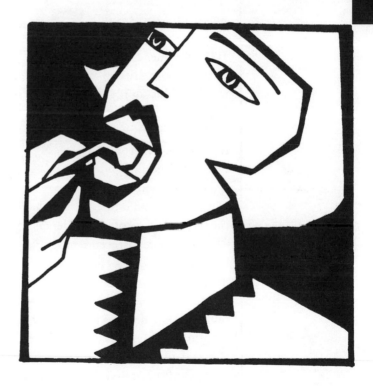

By Robert Krughoff

Smile. Flash the good news. Teeth and gums are healthier. Decay is down. About half the school children in the United States have no decay in their permanent teeth, almost twice as good a record as two decades ago. There's a little less gum disease also, and far fewer toothless working adults.

Mouths look better as well. Advanced techniques and materials make it possible to model attractive, natural-looking teeth on top of stained, chipped, or irregular ones. And more and more adults are having their teeth straightened, encouraged by new, barely visible orthodontic appliances.

Improved dental health, particularly in the area of preventing tooth decay has held back demand for dental care. At the same time, the supply of dentists is up, from 47 dentists per 100,000 Americans in 1970 to more than 60 in 1990. This supply-demand relationship may have slightly restrained prices for dental care (although the ratio of dentists to consumers could return to 1970 levels in ten years due to the recent closure of several dental schools).

Prevention $$

Preventive dental care saved close to $100 billion during the 1980s.

> **T I P**
> **Where to Complain**
> *If you have a complaint, first discuss it with your dentist. If you can't resolve the issue, contact the state board of dental examiners.*
> *Another good consumer resource is your state dental director, who usually operates out of the state Department of Health. In many large cities, you can also contact the dental director of the local health department.*

Unfortunately, the current ample supply of dentists may serve to increase risks for consumers. Although the vast majority of dentists rely on their best judgment, other less professional considerations might influence a few practitioners. Some dentists might lean toward procedures they'd avoid if they were busier. And there's a chance that a general-care dentist will perform procedures—such as complicated types of root-canal therapy, implants, or orthodontics—that specialists might do better.

In any case, the high price of establishing a dental practice will push consumer costs up. The average dentist now starts out with a school debt of over $50,000 and invests about $100,000 to open an office.

Robert Krughoff directs the Center for the Study of Services, based in Washington, DC, and San Francisco. The center publishes Checkbook *magazine, from which this chapter is adapted.*

Just as important, despite rapid progress in prevention, most Americans' mouths still bear witness to the ravages of dental caries (cavities) and gum disease. In fact, the continuing prevalence of oral diseases in the United States has been called a "neglected epidemic." About 30,000 oral cancers are diagnosed each year—about 4 percent of all cancers in this country—killing about 8,000 people. The average child has one cavity by age 9, four by age 14, and eight by age 17. Over half of working adults and 95 percent of people over 65 are missing more than one tooth; 10 percent of Americans wear full dentures. Over half of homebound elders haven't seen a dentist in 10 years, and 41 percent of people over 65 have no teeth.

Keep all this in mind as you begin your search for a dentist or talk to your current dentist about your routine and specialized care.

PART I: WHAT A GOOD DENTIST DOES

More important than anything a dentist can do for you is what you do for yourself. Thus, you want a dentist or dental hygienist who thoroughly explains proper brushing and flossing and advises you on selecting the best types of brush, floss, fluoride toothpaste, and other supplies. Equal-

FLUORIDE: THE MAGIC INGREDIENT

Throughout recorded history, tooth decay has probably caused more pain than any other infectious disease. It still leads to the loss of more teeth, at all ages, than any other cause.

Fluoride is the magic ingredient in preventing caries. Even for people who benefit from a fluoridated water supply, fluoride toothpastes and mouth rinses, used daily or weekly, reduce caries. Also, a topical fluoride treatment—in which a dentist applies fluoride to teeth—performed twice annually can reduce caries significantly, particularly for people without a fluoridated water supply. It will likely benefit those who drink fluoridated water as well.

Your best defense against dental decay is to live in a community with fluoridated water. However, more than 100 million people in the United States don't enjoy this benefit.

Eight of the fifty largest cities lack community water fluoridation. The three and half million residents of Los Angeles, the million residents of San Diego, and almost one million people in San Antonio don't get fluoridated water from the city. Other major cities lacking community water fluoridation include San Jose; Sacramento; Portland, Oregon; Tucson (which voted for fluoridation in 1992); and Honolulu.

ly important, the dentist or hygienist should have you demonstrate your technique periodically so he or she can

T I P

Fluoride Check
To find out if your community has fluoridated water, ask a dentist or call the local or state board of health.

suggest improvements. If your dentist doesn't do this automatically, ask him or her to do so.

The Qualities to Seek

Because many aspects of prevention require regular office visits, you want a dentist who notifies you when you need to come in for regular checkups and care. For example, one key to prevention is regular "scaling" by a dentist or hygienist to remove the calculus (hardened plaque) that accumulates on your teeth. Another is diagnosis and treatment of decay and gum disease at an early stage.

In addition, you want a dentist who:

- Takes a thorough medical history at the first exam and updates the history at each subsequent visit;
- Gives you complete, up-to-date instructions on how to care for your teeth;
- Asks you questions and carefully inspects your mouth during each exam;

How Often?

Not everyone needs to visit the dentist with equal frequency. If you have healthy gums and accumulate plaque and calculus slowly, once a year might be enough. Six months is common, and a few people need a checkup and cleaning every three months. Ask your dentist to recommend the best interval for you and to explain why. Ask what notices you will receive when it's time for your next appointment.

FINDING A DENTIST

The best way to start looking for a dentist is to consult friends, especially those with dental-care needs similar to yours. When you identify a few dentists who seem right, press your friends for more details and check out the dentists yourself.

Ask your friends:
- Does the dentist discuss any symptoms you have, such as loose teeth, bleeding gums, pain when eating, or a continual bad taste in your mouth?
- Does the dentist instruct you on prevention?
- Does the dentist check your technique in flossing and brushing?
- Is the dentist gentle?
- Does the dentist explain diagnosis, treatment plans, and costs?
- Does the dentist offer alternatives?
- If a treatment fails, does the dentist volunteer to re-do it at no charge?
- Does the dentist encourage second opinions in complex cases?
- Does the dentist have a pleasant, clean office and pleasant staff?
- How long do you wait in the waiting room? In the dental chair?
- Does the dentist arrange an appointment quickly when needed?

- Explains your options and provides a written treatment plan before major procedures;
- Shows concern for your safety and comfort by wearing gloves to prevent the spread of infection and uses lead aprons to protect you during X-rays;
- Works efficiently and gently;
- Leaves you with a comfortable bite and nicely finished tooth surfaces; *and*
- Tailors care to each individual—for example, by scheduling different intervals between visits depending on each patient's risk for dental disease.

Dentists often vary on these and other items of concern to consumers, although this variation doesn't necessarily translate directly into important differences in quality. Most consumers consider their dentists adequate or better. In all cases, the relationship between you and your dentist is very personal, and a dentist others don't like might be just right for you. Nonetheless, asking questions may prove a useful aid as you begin your search.

A Thorough Diagnosis

Good diagnosis is essential to good treatment. A flawless technician is of little use if he or she misses the problem requiring treatment.

As a central aspect of diagnosis, your dentist should keep a written record of your dental history, beginning with a complete history taken at the first examination. Knowledge of your past toothaches, swelling, bleeding gums, and other problems will help alert the dentist to possible trouble. In addition, knowledge of drug allergies and other medical factors may affect your treatment. A new dentist should request copies of recent X-rays and possibly other records from your previous dentist.

At each visit, a thorough dentist inspects the soft tissues of your mouth, tongue, lips, cheeks, and salivary glands. This can reveal oral cancers and other problems. Next, the dentist checks for cavities and has you close your mouth and move your jaw from side to side to check your bite. Finally, the dentist checks your gums, measuring the depth

14

Signs of Trouble

At each visit, a good dentist looks for and asks you if you have noticed any of the following signs of disease:

- Bleeding, swollen, or inflamed gums;

- Loose teeth;

- Continual bad breath;

- Bad taste in your mouth;

- Pain when eating sweets or drinking hot or cold liquids; *and*

- Pain when chewing.

of the pocket between your gums and your teeth with a metal probe.

Explaining Your Choices

If the exam reveals disease, you may have a choice among several alternatives. For example, a dentist might treat a large cavity in a tooth with a filling, a crown, extraction, or root-canal therapy. You want a dentist who explains the pros and cons of a wide range of old and new approaches.

To help you decide on a treatment, ask the dentist to fully describe the condition of your mouth and the corrections needed. It's a good idea to ask for a written treatment plan. Almost all dentists will do this, although some charge an extra fee for it and the written explanations of diagnosis and treatment might be less than clear.

Unfortunately, diagnosis is replete with conflicts of interest. A specialist has an interest in recommending complex treatment that only he or she can provide. A general practitioner may favor a simplistic approach rather than pass up the opportunity to treat you. Bear in mind that different treatments require more or less of the dentist's time, affecting your bill. Although extensive treatment may be appropriate, be especially cautious if a new dentist recommends far more work than other dentists have suggested in the past.

If a dentist proposes extensive treatment, consider getting a second opinion, perhaps from a specialist. Good dentists often refer patients to an *endodontist* for difficult root-canal treatment, a *periodontist* for gum surgery, an *orthodontist* for moving multiple teeth, or an *oral surgeon* to remove impacted teeth. Discussing treatments with the specialist as well as your general practitioner might give you a balanced view.

Get the second opinion from someone who is independent of your own dentist. Tell this dentist in advance that you won't be using him or her for treatment. Your dentist should be willing to forward X-rays and exam results for review.

X-Rays

Your dentist should take a full set of X-rays (14 to 20 films) or a panoramic film every three to five years. X-rays help reveal cavities, some remote deposits of calculus, bone loss around the teeth, abscesses of the tooth tip, impacted teeth, retained roots, cysts, and jawbone tumors. A more limited set of X-rays called bitewings (two to four films) should be taken more frequently to reveal cavities. Always protect yourself during X-rays with a lead apron.

PART II: OBTAINING QUALITY TREATMENT

Once you and your dentist agree on a plan, the dentist sets to work—with greater or lesser care. Don't assume that any governmental or professional body holds dentists accountable for the quality of their work. The vast majority of dentists practice in their own offices with poor accountability and little or no peer review.

Even if a dentist's peers observe low-quality work, they're unlikely to tell you about it. As recently as two decades ago, the dental code of ethics prohibited dentists from "referring disparagingly, orally or in writing, to the services of another dentist, to a member of the public." The code now states that a "dentist has an obligation to report to the appropriate agency of his component or constituent dental society instances of gross and continual faulty treatment by another dentist." Local dental societies have established patient-relations and peer-review systems, but few dentists are ever disciplined.

Look...and Look Again

Credentials don't indicate much about a dentist's skill either. All practicing dentists must be licensed, but that's no guarantee a dentist will practice good dentistry over the years. Renewing the license every few years requires only paying a nominal fee, and most states grant licenses to practice for life. Nor should a dentist's membership in professional societies and associations impress you. Generally, these groups only require a dentist to have a license and pay dues, although membership does give a dentist a chance to share up-to-date information with colleagues.

However, several factors might suggest a commitment to high-quality dental care:

• *Membership or fellowship in the Academy of General Dentistry:* This indicates a dentist's commitment to continual learning. The academy requires 75 hours of courses every three years for membership and even more training for fellowship.

• *Membership in a dental school's faculty:* Teaching experi-

Deciding What's Right for You

Treatments for the same condition differ in cost, comfort, convenience, and implications for your long-term health. Only you, with the advice of your dentist, can decide what is right for you. You would expect an auto body shop to fully explain the pros and cons of hammering out dents versus replacing fenders. Demand as much from a dentist—in language you can understand.

ence proves nothing about skill, but a teaching dentist is likely to be up-to-date on scientific developments.

• *Membership on a hospital staff:* Being a staff member exposes a dentist to the knowledge of other dentists and physicians.

• *Certification:* Certification indicates that a dentist once took advanced training and passed a difficult exam. A dental specialist should be certified by the appropriate body, such as the American Board of Endodontics for root-canal therapy.

At least as important as any data you can collect on a dentist's skills is your own judgment or that of friends. Here are a few points to check after receiving treatment:

• How does your bite feel?

• Is the tissue around the tooth healthy? Bleeding may signal gum disease or indicate that a crown or other restoration is irritating your gum.

• Does a treated tooth look like a tooth?

• Does dental floss or your tongue catch on the tooth? If dental floss catches, so will food particles.

• Did the dentist take the time to polish your fillings? This improves the appearance *and* extends the life of the filling.

• Do you feel pain when drinking hot or cold liquids? Some temporary discomfort may be normal after treatment; continuing pain or extreme sensitivity may indicate remaining decay or an improperly sealed filling.

• Did the dentist leave debris in your mouth?

• How long does your dental work last? Silver fillings generally last ten years or more, and crowns at least that long.

• Does the dentist use a water spray to cool your teeth while drilling? Keeping the tooth cool helps avoid possible nerve death.

Referral Source

One indicator of quality is the judgment of another dentist. If possible, ask other dentists where they send their own children. For recommendations that at least help you avoid poor practitioners, call dental schools and hospital dental programs, both of which will recommend their faculty or affiliated staff. You can also call the oral-health program of your state or local health department. And a dental society will recommend its members.

T I P **Four-Handed Dentistry**
The less time in the dental chair, the better. One common time-saver is a chair-side dental assistant, allowing for "four-handed dentistry." The assistant hands the dentist the proper instruments and tends to the patient's needs. Ask a prospective dentist whether he or she uses a dental assistant.

Your Safety

Like any medical procedure, dental care carries a risk of complications or medical emergency. Your dentist should be ready and equipped to handle such situations. In addition, the dentist should expose you to as few risks as possible during treatment.

To protect both you and the dentist from infection, especially from hepatitis B and AIDS, a good dentist wears rubber gloves and a mask when treating you and puts on new gloves for each patient. For the dentist's protection, goggles are also recommended for procedures that spray particles or fluid. In any case, the possibility of contracting HIV/AIDS from a dentist is extremely small.

X-rays present another safety concern. Although the exact extent of X-ray risk is uncertain, the benefits almost surely greatly outweigh the risk in most cases. Nonetheless, you want a dentist who takes reasonable steps to minimize any risk, such as offering you a lead apron. This is particularly important because the harmful effects of low doses of X-rays, such as those you receive in the dental chair, are now considered greater than was once thought.

A dentist can also minimize other risks of dental treatment, such as anesthesia mishaps and complications related to infections. The best prevention in these cases is the dentist's taking a careful

T I P	**X-Ray Guard**
	By far the most important and easiest X-ray protection comes from leaded aprons and collars. When you get an X-ray, always ask for a lead apron.

medical history that notes allergies, any history of rheumatic fever, and other danger signals.

Cleanliness is critical. A dentist who cares about the cleanliness of his or her office, especially the lab, will most likely show the same care with his or her instruments and hands. Proper sterilization of equipment will kill all organisms that can cause serious medical problems. An excellent sterilization technique is the use of a steam autoclave. For instruments that can't go in the autoclave, the usual alternative is dry heat, which kills living organisms much more slowly.

THE PAIN FACTOR

From 10 to 14 percent of Americans shun dental treatment because of fear, often living with discomfort because they feel that the cure is worse than the disease. Avoiding the dentist's chair for this reason is silly. Modern anesthetics and equipment can minimize discomfort for even the most sensitive people.

Your dentist should offer you a choice of anesthesia and explain the effects of each one. A person who is extremely sensitive may request nitrous oxide ("laughing gas") or use pre-medication. For others, a local painkiller such as lydocaine or xylocaine suffices. Still others may want no painkiller. In any case, a dentist concerned about your comfort will arrange a way for you to signal if pain becomes severe.

Some dentists use stereo headphones to help patients relax. Patients can listen to their choice of music rather than the sound of a drill. Waiting-room distractions, including video games and video-taped movies, also make the trip to the dentist less frightening.

PART III: FIXING THE DAMAGE

The standard procedures for repairing and replacing teeth have changed little for many years: root-canal therapy, crowns, drilling and filling cavities, inserting fixed bridges or partial dentures, and complete dentures. But advances continue on most of these fronts.

Although your regular dentist will handle routine tasks like cleanings and most restorations, consider a specialist for complex bridges and dentures, oral surgery, periodontal therapy, implants, difficult root-canal therapy, and other extensive procedures. If your dentist offers these services, consider her or him in addition to the specialists. What's key is how often a dentist has performed the procedure in question.

Get names of specialists by asking your general-care dentist or other dentists for sug-

> **TIP**
>
> **Don't Pull That Tooth**
> *Not if you can help it. Extracting a tooth is generally one of several remedies—and almost always the least desirable.*

gestions. Ask specialists about their training and how frequently they perform the procedure you need. Ask for the names of patients you can call for references. To ensure that dentists don't simply refer you to their most enthusiastic clients, specify that you want to talk with people who fit in a fairly narrow category, such as patients who are similar to you in age, sex, and required treatment.

Dental Implants

As a treatment of last resort, dental implants are an alternative to complicated dentures or failed bridge work. In this procedure, a dentist inserts a fixed device below the gum. From this device, one or more posts extend up through the gum. A bridge or other prosthetic device attaches to the posts. Implants are generally made of titanium, often with a ceramic coating. Bone heals directly to a proper implant, and gum tissue forms a biological seal around the posts.

Implants overcome some disadvantages of dentures. Dentures can move when you speak, eat, or yawn. Also, pressure on the gums when you chew and food particles that sometimes lodge between dentures and gums can make dentures uncomfortable. And the bone supports may shrink, making dentures difficult to wear.

However, implants are expensive—$10,000 or more. And success depends heavily on the type of implant, the patient's health, the skill of the person who performs the implant, the patient's motivation for follow-up self-care, and other factors.

If you want to pursue an implant, carefully select a dentist or dentists to perform the procedure. Implants have increased dramatically in popularity, from just a few thousand per year in the late 1970s to several hundred thousand per year today. They represent a lucrative opportunity for dentists whose income may be suffering from stiff competition and reduced demand for treatment of cavities. As a result, thousands of dentists now do implants, and some may lack adequate training. Implant rejection, stress from the attached appliance, and other problems require specific knowledge and experience. In addition, the new entrants into the implant field include many general-care dentists. Some have studied implants; others have not. A few "learn" the technique at quickie courses in hotels.

Get more than one opinion on whether you are a good candidate for an implant and on the plan that best suits your case. A single dentist with good experience might suffice, but a team represents the safest approach. You can

The Eight Dental Specialties

Dental specialists typically receive two to four years training in their field beyond the normal training for all dentists. The American Dental Association recognizes eight specialties:

- *Endodontists* perform root canals and treat diseases of the pulp and nerves on the inside of teeth.

- *Oral and maxillofacial surgeons* treat injuries and defects of the mouth and jaw.

- *Oral pathologists* examine, identify, and diagnose diseases of the mouth.

- *Orthodontists* straighten teeth and correct the position of jaws.

- *Pediatric dentists* provide comprehensive dental care for children and adolescents, as well as for special patients who have mental, physical, or emotional problems.

- *Periodontists* treat diseases of the gums and the underlying bone that holds teeth.

- *Prosthodontists* replace missing teeth by designing and fitting dentures and bridgework.

- *Public health dentists* design and administer public or private education, treatment, and prevention programs for entire communities or organizations.

have a periodontist certified by the American Board of Periodontology or an oral surgeon certified by the American Board of Oral and Maxillofacial Surgery place the implant. Next, a specialist in dentures and other restorations certified by the American Board of Prosthodontics can prepare and mount the artificial teeth.

T I P

Consider the Options
Before getting an implant, thoroughly consider whether conventional dentures or a bridge might satisfy your needs.

Implants and References

Ask any dentist you approach about an implant how many procedures he or she has done. Get references from dentists and other clients. Discuss the particular technique the dentist plans to use. Has the American Dental Association approved it? And consult your regular dentist.

Bonding

Bonding places veneers on cracked, chipped, or stained front teeth. It's an alternative to traditional capping, but, unlike capping, it doesn't significantly alter the natural tooth.

Bonding generally costs about one-third less than a conventional crown. And the process is quicker and less painful. For example, a dentist might treat four front teeth with bonding in a single visit, while one crown might require several trips. In addition, some bonding procedures are reversible: if the result is unsatisfactory, the dentist can remove bonded material. Ask about this.

Bonding can also secure bridgework. In the traditional approach to holding a false tooth, the dentist files down the natural teeth around the gap and places a device over them, with the replacement tooth built into the middle of this device. The bonding alternative extends "wings" at each side of a false tooth and bonds the wings to the surrounding teeth. This requires no grinding of the natural teeth, but it only works if the adjacent teeth are relatively strong and there's no biting force to withstand.

The Dentist's Portfolio

If you are interested in bonding, ask about the dentist's training and experience. Review pictures of the dentist's past work so you can judge his or her sense of style.

Still another application of bonding is to secure orthodontic appliances to teeth. Bonding makes for braces that are less conspicuous.

Root Canal Therapy

In root-canal therapy, a dentist removes the infected nerve and blood supply of a tooth and replaces it with filling material. Success rates are very high, and techniques have changed little in recent years. Some dentists now use lasers to prepare roots for filling.

One debate is whether materials that contain paraformaldehyde, specifically a material called Sargenti paste, should be the root filler. Sargenti paste kills bacteria, so infection is less likely. But Sargenti paste is poisonous and can damage nerves and other tissues in the unlikely event that it leaks out of the root. U.S. dental schools don't teach use of the paste, and associations of root-canal specialists oppose its use.

If you are concerned, ask for a written treatment plan specifying that Sargenti paste won't be used.

Dental Tips for Parents and Children

Teeth are susceptible to decay as soon as they appear in the mouth. Take steps to protect your infants' and toddlers' teeth from the start.

From birth to six months:

• Clean the child's mouth with gauze after feedings and at bedtime.

• Ask your pediatrician or dentist about fluoride supplements.

• Regulate feeding habits.

Between six months and one year:

• The first tooth should appear, signaling the time to see the pediatric dentist for an exam.

> **T I P**
>
> **Seal Those Teeth**
> *Although sealants are an extraordinarily valuable preventive measure, a 1986 survey indicated that fewer than 10 percent of children had them.* Parents should insist that a dentist apply sealants unless there are compelling arguments to the contrary.

• Begin to brush the child's teeth after each feeding and at bedtime with a small, soft-bristled brush. Don't use a fluoride toothpaste that the baby can swallow, which could cause tooth discoloration later on.

• As the baby begins to walk, be alert to dental injuries.

• By the first birthday, wean the baby from breast or bottle feeding.

Should You Agree to Gum Surgery?

You should only agree to gum surgery after thoroughly examining alternatives and perhaps by seeking a second opinion. In most cases, non-surgical approaches cost less, hurt less, and are less likely to disfigure the gum line.

From one to two years:

• Follow schedule of exams and cleanings recommended by pediatric dentist.

• Start using pea-sized portions of fluoridated toothpaste when a child can rinse, but make sure he or she doesn't eat the toothpaste.

Babies are susceptible to what is known as "baby bottle tooth decay." You and others who take care of your baby must know about proper bottle-feeding practices. The National Institute of Dental Research recommends two preventive measures:

• If your baby needs a bottle at bedtime for comfort, use only plain water. Don't fill the bottle with milk, formula, fruit juice, soft drinks, or any other sweetened liquids. All these liquids contain sugar.

• Close to your child's first birthday, teach your child to drink directly from a cup.

For older children, ask your dentist about topical-fluoride treatment to prevent tooth decay. Many dentists apply this with a cleaning. The charge tends to be small, only about $15 per treatment. The value of treatment is less clear for adults, especially those with no recent decay.

Plastic sealants are also an excellent option. Placed on the chewing surfaces of your child's teeth, they prevent caries in any permanent teeth that have no perceptible decay or fillings. Plastic sealants can protect the pits and fissures of the chewing surfaces of molars, where most decay occurs. It's surprising and disappointing that sealants aren't applied as standard practice. The best time to do sealants is just after new teeth emerge, requiring two applications—first at 6 to 8 years and then again at 12 to 14 years.

Presumably, sealants protect adults' teeth as well. On the other hand, a cavity-free adult probably runs little risk of incurring decay even without sealants.

PART IV: MONEY MATTERS

A dentist who helps you maintain the health of your mouth has a strong claim to your patronage—but not if

---

Sealant Service

If you're searching for a dentist for your son or daughter, ask the ones you are considering if they do sealants for children.

the cost is excessive. In fact, some dentists charge more than twice as much as others.

As you select a dentist, ask the candidates about their fees for a few common procedures, such as an initial exam, cleaning, X-rays, a topical-fluoride treatment, and a simple extraction. In particular, ask specialists about their charges. Most dentists readily provide such information, but don't be surprised if you find big differences. You may also want to ask if the dentist accepts credit cards or offers senior citizen discounts.

By far, good preventive care is the best way to save money. Regular brushing with a fluoride toothpaste, proper flossing, and professional cleanings will help you avoid expensive treatments.

T I P	**Second Opinions**
	A second opinion, probably the most underused consumer tool in dentistry, can help you get appropriate, reasonably priced care. Getting a second opinion before agreeing to costly treatment can also provide some leverage if a dispute arises later.

If you do require treatment, ask dentists to describe alternatives. For example, you might be just as well off with a non-precious metal instead of gold in a restoration.

You can hold down dental care costs in several other ways as well:

• Get a written estimate before beginning an expensive treatment. Some dentists charge for estimates, but many provide them free. Even a modest fee is worthwhile if a

Cost and Quality

What a dentist charges doesn't necessarily correlate with the results of patient surveys on satisfaction or with any credentials that might indicate service quality, such as membership in the Academy of General Dentistry.

In other words, you can pay relatively low fees and still get the very best care.

Prevailing Charges for General Dentists, 1993

Preventive Visit with Topical Fluoride Application
Adult: $43.21
Child: $36.00

Topical Fluoride Application
Adult: $17.60
Child: $17.08

Diagnostic Oral Examination
Initial: $25.43
Periodic: $18.54

Source: American Dental Association

written estimate helps prevent surprises after the work is done.

• Check out discounts, special offers, and lower-priced packages that include exams, cleaning, and X-rays.

• Some dentists offer discounts for cash up front because it saves them time and money in collecting unpaid bills.

• Some dentists offer discounts to special groups, such as senior citizens, certain types of professionals, students, people on limited incomes, even newly engaged couples.

It's Your Record

You can save money if a new dentist or a dental specialist gets records and X-rays from your previous or regular dentist. Unless the new dentist has reason to take new ones, full-mouth X-rays are usually good for three to five years.

Your former dentist is ethically bound to pass along copies of X-rays and other records. Check with your state department of health on the legal obligation to do so. You might be charged for the copies.

Warranties

Ask dentists about warranties for restorations. For example, some dentists may guarantee a porcelain crown with non-precious metal or a silver filling for a certain length of time. Don't expect this, however.

A warranty should describe your needs, the proposed treatment, expected costs, expected results, and a specified period during which the dentist will replace defective work free of charge.

It won't be easy to find a dentist who'll offer such a warranty, especially in writing. But even if a dentist won't give you a written warranty, ask for a free replacement if a restoration doesn't last as it should.

Insurance, Prepaid Dental Plans, and Dental HMOs

You might want to find out whether a dentist participates in an insurance or HMO plan. Participation could mean that a dentist accepts as payment in full an

Overtreatment

A written treatment plan and consultation with an independent dentist will safeguard your wallet as well as your mouth. Regardless of a dentist's charges, the cost is too high if you are overtreated.

Both the treatment plan and your bill should itemize costs. A dentist shouldn't make you uncomfortable discussing money and should be willing to work out a payment plan or an alternative treatment if the costs exceed your means.

amount set in the insurer's fee schedule. If you have insurance, be sure the dentist will help you get proper reimbursement. And if you are eligible for Medicaid, you will want a dentist who participates in that program.

Insurance benefits vary greatly from policy to policy, so learn about your dental benefits—and their limitations. You may decide to spread out extensive treatment over several years to bypass an annual maximum benefit. Or your plan may tie you to a group of participating dentists who agree to accept a specified fee schedule.

In some areas, a number of prepaid dental plans are available. Typically these plans cover you completely for routine exams and cleanings and give you lower-than-average fees for more expensive treatments—if you use participating dentists.

Whether these plans are appropriate for you depends on how much dentistry you expect to use. Consider the average local fees for services, how much you'd have to pay under a prepaid plan, the annual premium for the plan, and the gain (or loss) to your family as a result of enrolling in the plan.

You'll want to be sure a dentist doesn't treat you hastily because your case pays less than a regular fee-for-service case. Also, if your employer provides dental insurance, you almost certainly won't want a separate prepaid plan.

Dental School Clinics

Many dental schools have clinics where students treat patients under faculty supervision. The fees are invariably low for the local area. Schools also offer more comprehensive treatment and care during a routine visit so that students receive more training.

These clinics have drawbacks. Because

> **TIP**
>
> **Hygiene Schools**
> For routine dental care—X-rays, cleanings, and exams—consider a dental-hygiene school. They offer a combination of low cost and high quality.

students are learning, your visits will be longer—and your mouth will be open longer. This means some additional discomfort. And you run a small risk if a new student treats you. For more complicated problems, you might prefer a more advanced student—but then your dentist might graduate before you get follow-up care. In sum, they are a good resource for a person with a limited income and the time to spend at the clinic.

RESOURCES

Organizations

American Academy of Pediatric Dentistry
211 East Chicago Ave.
Chicago, IL 60611
(312)337-2169
Call or write for a free pamphlet, "The Pediatric Dentist."

American Association of Orthodontists
401 North Lindbergh Blvd.
St. Louis, MO 63141
(800)424-2841
For information on orthodontics and a list of local orthodontists: (800)222-9969.
Call or write for a free orthodontics planning kit and several pamphlets, including "Facts About Orthodontists: A Special Kind of Dentistry," "Adult Orthodontics: The best Smile

for Your Best Years," and "Good Beginnings: A Head Start for Healthy Smiles."

American Association of Public Health Dentistry
10619 Jousting Lane
Richmond, VA 23235
(804)272-8344
Call or write for a free pamphlet on fluoridation.

American Dental Association
211 E. Chicago Ave.
Chicago, IL 60611
(312)440-2500
(800)621-8099
Provides consumer information on how often you need dental procedures. Call or write for free pamphlets, including "Pregnancy and Oral Health" and "Dental Decisions: Making the Right Choices."

Centers for Disease Control and Prevention
Division on Oral Health
1600 Clifton Rd., F10
Atlanta, GA 30337
(404)639-8375.
Call for information on infection control in dentistry, fluoridation, oral cancer, sealants, and baby bottle tooth decay.

National Institute of Dental Research
P.O. Box 54793
Washington, DC 20032
Write for free pamphlets and posters in English and Spanish on such topics as fluoride for children and adults, tooth decay, gum diseases, and plaque removal.

Eyeglasses and Contact Lenses

15

By Robert Krughoff

O ver half the people in the United States wear eyeglasses or contact lenses, and all Americans should get their eyes checked regularly. For these basic medical needs, you can choose from a multitude of excellent individual and group practitioners and a variety of national and local chains.

Unfortunately, many forms of medical insurance don't cover eyeglasses or contact lenses, so price is a critical factor. Moreover, the differences in both quality and cost among the different types of eyecare providers, let alone the providers of a single variety, are difficult to determine. To a large extent, you must rely on your own initiative as you seek the best place to buy your eyeglasses or contact lenses.

> **T I P**
> **One-Source Shopping**
> When you get your exam and buy your lenses at the same office, you benefit from accountability as well as convenience: If the lenses don't work out—and many times contact lenses don't—it's clear who is responsible.

PART I: THE EYE EXAM

Get your eyes checked every one to two years; less often if you have no eye problems. A thorough vision exam takes 30 to 60 minutes.

The examiner should:

> **T I P**
> **Children's Eyes**
> For a free pamphlet, "Your Child's Eyes," send a self-addressed stamped envelope to the American Academy of Pediatrics, Department C, P.O. Box 927, Elk Grove, IL 60009.

- Begin with a complete health history;
- Inspect the exterior and interior of your eyes for signs of possible diseases;
- Test your ability to see sharply and clearly at all distances;
- Test your eye's ability to focus light rays exactly on the retina;
- Check eye coordination and eye muscle control;
- Test your eyes' ability to change focus; *and*
- Conduct a glaucoma test.

The exam may also include tests for color perception, depth perception, field of vision, and other vision skills.

---

139 Million

That's the number of Americans who wear some type of corrective lenses. Most wear eyeglasses. About 24 million people wear contacts.

Robert Krughoff directs the Center for the Study of Services, based in Washington, DC, and San Francisco. The center publishes Checkbook *magazine, from which this chapter is adapted.*

The Choice: Glasses or Contacts

If you have a recent prescription from an ophthalmologist or optometrist, your next step may be determined largely by your preference: Do you want eyeglasses or contact lenses?

If you prefer glasses, you can go to any optician or optometrist. Many opticians and optometrists dispense contact lenses as well, as do many ophthalmologists.

Although most practitioners dispense contact lenses based on a recent prescription you've gotten elsewhere, some insist on doing their own exam. They argue that providing contact lenses is a professional service in which the exam, the supplying of lenses, and follow-up care must go together to produce a consistently safe and satisfactory result. Other practitioners dispute this view—especially opticians, who can't do exams.

If you do take a prescription to a different location to be filled, a prescription from the past year is usually considered new enough; some practitioners let you go back further, particularly for glasses, depending on your age and eye-care history.

If you don't have a current prescription, you can get one at many places. While opticians can't give an exam, you can

15

THE THREE Os

Ophthalmologists are physicians who specialize in eye disorders. They check eyes for vision problems, diseases, abnormalities, and symptoms of such general bodily disorders as diabetes and hypertension. They treat eyes with drugs, surgery, and other means, and they prescribe corrective glasses and contact lenses. Most ophthalmologists expect you to get eyeglasses elsewhere, but quite a few dispense contacts.

Optometrists are not medical doctors but are properly called doctors. Like ophthalmologists, they give eye exams, looking for a wide range of eye problems as well as symptoms of general health problems. They are limited in the range of drugs they can prescribe. Some use visual therapy to counter certain eye problems, and most prescribe and dispense eyeglasses and contact lenses.

Opticians have less training than ophthalmologists or optometrists, with the exact amount depending on state regulations. Opticians can't write prescriptions. They fit, supply, and adjust glasses and, sometimes, contacts, using a prescription from an ophthalmologist or optometrist. A few opticians grind eyeglass lenses to the correct prescription, but most buy the lenses from a wholesaler and fit them into a frame.

get one at some opti-
cian practices and chain
outlets if an optometrist
works in the office or an
affiliated office nearby.
Even in states that pro-

> **T**
> **I**
> **P**
>
> **Certification Check**
> *You can easily determine if an*
> *ophthalmologist is certified. Call*
> *the American Board of Medical*
> *Specialties Certification Line at*
> *(800)776-2378.*

hibit optician firms from employing an optometrist, he or
she can be a door away.

Medications

Certain drugs or com-
binations of drugs can
impair your vision and
affect the results of
diagnostic tests. Tell
your eye-care provider
the names of any med-
ications you are taking.

PART II: BUYING EYEGLASSES

An important aspect of buying glasses is the selection of
a frame. In picking a frame, consider positioning, comfort,
durability, appearance, and price.

Also take advantage of professional advice. Opticians
and optometrists can be a valuable source of information
when selecting frames. They can suggest models that might
eliminate comfort or positioning problems you have previously experienced, and they can steer you away from models that might cause other problems. But always ask the
professionals to explain their recommendations. Be suspi-
cious if all of the suggestions are for higher-priced frames.

Positioning: Eyeglass frames should position the lenses to
give you the sharpest vision. Some frames may position the
lenses too far from your eyes or too high or low. If the
frames slide down your nose, you won't get the full benefit
from the lenses.

The stronger your prescription, the more critical positioning becomes. If you use glasses for driving, sports, or

COMMON VISION PROBLEMS

Astigmatism: Objects
appear blurry or distorted
at all distances because the
front part of your eye, the
cornea, is slightly irregular
in shape.

Cataracts: A clouding of
the clear lens of your eye,
causing blurred or hazy
vision. Can lead to blind-

ness if not treated.

*Farsightedness (hyper-
opia):* You see far objects
more clearly than close
ones.

Glaucoma: A build-up of
pressure in your eye. Can
result in severe vision loss
and even blindness.

*Nearsightedness
(myopia):* You see close
objects more clearly than
distant ones.

Presbyopia: A natural
part of aging that begins to
blur your reading and near
vision about age 40 or 45
and gradually worsens.

other activities requiring peripheral vision, make sure the sides of the frame are located above or below your eye level.

Comfort: The key comfort points are your ears and the bridge of your nose, the places where glasses rest. Unfortunately, trying on a frame for a minute or two doesn't always reveal discomfort that might occur with extended wear. Getting new glasses similar to your old ones helps limit your risk. All else being equal, lighter glasses are more comfortable than heavier ones. Lighter glasses usually have optyl-plastic or thin metal frames with smallish plastic lenses.

If you are considering metal frames, keep several points in mind. Metal frames usually have a nosepiece of rocking pads. These small adjustable plastic pads are easily adjusted and unlikely to slip. This is an advantage over plastic frames, which usually have a rigid nose support that varies in shape among different manufacturers. On the other hand, rocking pads concentrate the weight on a small surface of the nose. This makes them uncomfortable to some people. If this is a problem for you, consider a model with an inserted molded plastic nosepiece instead of rocking pads. Metal frames are also more likely than plastic ones to irritate your ears. Many models avoid this problem by covering the ends of the temples with plastic or rubber pads.

Durability: Handled with care, most glasses last three or four years, and many people want to change style at least that often. Strength and durability are especially important

Judging Quality

The quality of eyeglass care can reveal itself in:

◆ The kind of advice the provider gives you on selecting frames and lens materials to fit your face and your prescription;

◆ The fitting of lenses in frames and the positioning of lenses to match the position of your eyes;

◆ The adjustment of frames to fit your face, nose, and ears; *and*

◆ The quality of lenses and frames supplied.

15

EYEGLASSES VS. CONTACTS

Eyeglasses are usually cheaper than contact lenses. They don't irritate the eye's surface and can require less care. Eyeglasses are also harder to lose. You can get them in special frames that protect your eyes against many industrial accidents. Some people even wear eyeglasses as a fashion accessory.

Contact lenses have several major advantages of their own. In the first place, they are virtually invisible. They also provide a wider field of vision, and they don't irritate the nose bridge and ears. Contacts are relatively secure and safe to wear during sports. And they distort your vision less than glasses because they are closer to, and move with, your eyes.

Contacts can be a godsend if you are extremely nearsighted or farsighted or have had cataracts removed.

Some people who have preferred glasses may want to reconsider. Because of recent improvements, contacts can now provide a better combination of comfort, safety, and visual acuity than in the past.

if you plan to keep the frames longer or if you knock the frames around a lot in sports, bar fights, or other vigorous activities. The durability of frames depends on the materials used, the thickness of the materials, and the craftsmanship.

The strongest metal frames are usually moderately thick, with a double bar or a single wide bar above the nose. They have smooth welding wherever two pieces of metal join, and they have heavy hinges. Some of the strongest plastic frames are made of nylon, but these tend to be thick, heavy, and plain. Among other plastics, the strongest are usually at least moderately thick and have metal reinforcing for the full length of the temple (unnecessary in nylon or optyl-plastic frames), heavy hinges, and hinges that are secured to the temple with a backing plate of metal on the outside of the temple. However, these are general guidelines. Some frames of other types may be quite durable, and some meeting these standards may be rather frail.

Appearance: Most eyeglass wearers are concerned about style. Indeed, some frames are sold with clear, non-prescription lenses and worn solely for effect.

The popular concern about fashion and brand names gives optometrists and opticians extra leverage if they wish to guide you to high-priced frames. Your best approach is to try on a variety of frame styles to decide for yourself which few look best. Then look at the price tags. Chances are some will be relatively inexpensive. If not, ask if there is another cheaper frame that looks similar to one you like.

Price: The prices of frames vary tremendously. Decent quality frames range in price from less than $40 to more than $400.

Choosing Eyeglass Lenses and Features

As with frames, you face many decisions in choosing eyeglass lenses.

One choice is glass or plastic. The lighter weight of plastic is a particular plus when the lenses are for large frames or a strong prescription that requires a thick lens. The scratch resistance of glass is important if you remove your glasses frequently, slipping them into your pocket, purse, or briefcase. Federal regulations require both glass and plastic lenses to resist breakage from moderate impacts, but no lens is unbreakable.

T I P

For the Very Nearsighted

If you are very nearsighted, you may want lenses made of materials that have a strong capacity to refract light. Such materials permit a thinner, lighter lens but cost extra.

An increasingly popular choice for people who need bifocals or trifocals and don't want others to be aware of this sign of aging is a "progressive," or "no-line," lens. However, such lenses are much more expensive than regular bifocals or trifocals and require special care in fitting.

Several types of lens treatments have grown in popularity in recent years. One of the most popular options treats the lens to filter out the ultraviolet light that may contribute to cataracts or retina damage. This treatment may interest you if you expose your eyes heavily to ultraviolet radiation—for example, by working outdoors or spending a lot of time mountain climbing or at the beach.

Antireflective coatings are rapidly gaining in popularity. This option reduces reflection from your side—an especially helpful feature if you do a lot of night driving. It also reduces the reflection others see when they look at or photograph you.

Chain Stores and Quality

When *Checkbook* magazine surveyed Washington, DC, consumers, chains and franchise operations generally received fewer "superior" ratings than traditional eye-care practices on "doing service properly." But there was substantial variation among the chain and franchise operations.

15

Eyeglass Prices

In *Checkbook* magazine's Washington, DC, survey, For Eyes outlets stood out for lower prices, with quotes on several types of glasses about 60 percent of the average. However, not all chains and franchise operations had low prices. And prices differed from outlet to outlet for all the major chains, although most tended to relatively uniform pricing.

Many independents charged low prices—substantially below the average for any of the chains except For Eyes. Outlets that offered exams in the office (and therefore had optometrists available) were neither more nor less expensive, on average, than other places. Even practices identified as optometrists' offices (with "Dr." in the name) had roughly average prices. And some optometrists beat the all-outlet average handily.

In other words, prices vary a great deal. Call or shop around.

Optometric Management magazine reports annually on optometrist charges for eyeglass lenses. In 1993, the price for lenses made of glass averaged $54.93 nationally for single-vision lenses and $83.55 for bifocals. For plastic lenses, the national average was $51.31 for single-vision lenses and $80.54 for bifocals.

Sunglasses

When choosing sunglasses, seek lenses that meet your eyes' needs for comfort and protection. All sunglasses screen out or absorb some harmful ultraviolet radiation, but the amount varies considerably. For maximum protection, look for those absorbing from 290 to 380 nm, if that information is on the label. Lightly tinted lenses and plastic light-sensitive lenses screen out too little light to be considered sunglasses.

There are four types of sun lenses:

• *Standard tinted* lenses are made of glass or plastic. Dark gray is best: It doesn't affect your ability to see colors. However, some people prefer green or brown.

• *Polarizing lenses* reduce reflected glare.

• *Light-sensitive (photochromic)* glass lenses darken and lighten with the amount of light exposure.

• *Mirror* lenses, designed to wear under intense glare from snow or water, have a thin metallic coating over a tinted lens.

PART III: BUYING CONTACT LENSES

Most outlets supply two basic types of contacts—soft lenses and gas-permeable rigid lenses. In addition, some contact wearers still have old-fashioned hard lenses.

Introduced in 1971, soft contact lenses are made of a gelatin-like substance containing a great deal of water. Most people adapt to soft contacts quickly and easily. The high water content lets oxygen pass through the lenses to the cornea, the tissue covering the eye. This oxygen supply is crucial.

Rigid gas-permeable lenses, which appeared in 1978, also allow oxygen to pass through easily. This means the lenses can be larger than old-fashioned hard contact lenses, which had to be small enough for oxygen to pass around them. The larger size makes for relative comfort because your eyelid doesn't have to pass over the edge of the lid with each blink. The newest gas-permeable lenses are made with special plastics that are very slick, allowing comfortable movement under the eyelid and minimizing the buildup of various deposits.

Soft lenses have several advantages over rigid lenses:

• You can wear soft lenses comfortably almost immediately, and you can stop wearing them for days or months and restart without an extended period to readapt.

• They are easy to fit. Opticians and optometrists generally have many soft lenses in stock and can send you home with a pair in one visit. The softness permits some tolerance of variations in a cornea's shape, making skilled fitting less critical.

• Because soft lenses cover a large part of the eye's surface, they prevent dust from getting to the eye in dusty conditions.

• Soft lenses are hard to dislodge, making them ideal for contact sports.

On the other hand, rigid gas-permeable lenses have important plusses:

> **T I P**
>
> ### Back Ups
> *If you get contacts, it's a good idea to have glasses available as a backup. You'll be glad you did if you lose a contact or must contend with eye infections, allergies, or other problems.*

• They provide clearer vision. Their rigidity allows precise shaping. Until recently, that also meant they could help with serious astigmatism beyond the scope of conventional soft lenses.

• They tend to be easier than soft lenses to clean because they are less prone to collect protein deposits.

• Because rigid gas-permeable lenses can be kept clean, they're less likely than soft lenses to scrape the eye surface or to harbor microorganisms that can infect the eye.

• Since they don't absorb moisture, people with relatively dry eyes can wear rigid gas-permeable lenses.

• They last longer than soft lenses. While soft lenses typically are good for a year or less, rigid lenses generally last twice that long.

Contact Lens Options

There are many variants on the two basic types of contact lenses. Two of the most important are extended-wear lenses and disposable lenses.

More Contact Options

Contact-lens options include bifocal lenses, lenses for astigmatism, tinted lenses, and ultraviolet filtering lenses. New lenses coming on the market have a soft perimeter for comfort and a gas-permeable rigid center to allow oxygen transfer and sharp vision. You can expect all these options to cost more than basic single-correction lenses.

Comparing Prices

While all the variations in contact-lens service packages mean that prices aren't exactly comparable from firm to firm, you can determine the main elements of cost by getting prices that include at least a basic exam and prescription as well as a follow-up visit. You'll find that some places may charge more than three times as much as others.

Extended-Wear Lenses: While you remove regular lenses each night, you can wear extended-wear lenses for longer periods of time. Both soft and rigid gas-permeable extended-wear lenses are available.

However, wearing any soft lenses for a long period may weaken and scratch the cornea's surface, as the oxygen supply is restricted and protein deposits develop. This weakened, scratched surface, in turn, is more likely than the cornea of someone who removes contacts daily to contract an infection called ulcerative keratitis. If not treated immediately, this infection can result in partial or complete loss of sight. Although one study indicates that individuals who use extended-wear lenses have only about 1 chance in 500 of getting corneal ulcers, that possibility may be reason enough for you to steer clear of this option.

If you do decide on extended-wear lenses, don't leave them in for longer than seven days at a time. And follow the instructions for care and cleaning conscientiously.

Disposable Lenses: These are simply soft lenses that are produced at low-enough cost that you can afford to throw them away. The most widespread plan costs $300 per year for soft lenses that you get in six-packs and wear for two weeks before throwing them away. Disposables spare you the trouble of cleaning your lenses and reduce the risk that you'll damage your cornea with built-up deposits.

Since they eliminate the need for cleaning chemicals, disposable lenses might not cost much more per year than regular extended-wear lenses. But wearing lenses for a week still involves risks, even if they are new each week, because your eyes get less oxygen than they otherwise would. If you decide on disposable lenses, don't assume you can cheat and keep them in a few extra days. That might save you money but cost you the health of your eyes.

Contact Lens $$$

Comparing prices for contact lenses can be a puzzling experience. Since most people who buy contact lenses pay a package price that includes an exam and some amount of follow-up care, the lens price is only part of the picture.

And differences in the amount of service firms include in a package add to the confusion.

Sometimes the stated price for contacts includes a thorough eye exam. Sometimes it includes just a quick exam with a refraction test and measurements of the size and shape of the eyeball. Sometimes no exam is included. At some firms, the price covers as many follow-up visits as you wish within a stated period of time (such as three months or a year), but at others it covers only one or two visits.

Refund policies and warranties also vary. Most dispensers will give you some or all of your money back if your eyes do not adapt to the contacts within a specified time. A few have no refund policy but promise to make many adjustments to get a satisfactory fit.

Neither arrangement provides you with foolproof protection. Dispensers with refund policies may give up quickly if you are hard to fit and then give you only a partial refund. On the other hand, promises to make extensive adjustments are worth little if the work isn't skillful. Remember, each adjustment requires your time.

A final element of variation arises with replacement policies for lost contacts. Some dispensers promise to replace lost contacts at prespecified prices for a year or two after the initial purchase. With others, you are on your own.

PART IV: PICKING UP YOUR GLASSES OR CONTACTS

You will rarely get your glasses or contacts on the day you select them. Usually you'll return two to ten days later. This second visit is as important as the first. Check the glasses or contacts carefully when you come to pick them up.

New glasses may have to be adjusted to fit your face or to allow for a difference in the height of your ears. After the adjustment, check positioning and comfort. Be sure there isn't too much pressure on your ears or nose, that the frames don't slip down your nose, and that both lenses are the same height and an equal distance from your eyes.

When you pick up new contact lenses, the practitioner should carefully check their fit on your eyes using a

---

Save Now or Later

Soft contact lenses tend to represent a smaller *initial* investment than gas-permeable lenses, but the long-term price may be higher. In *Checkbook's* Washington, DC, price survey, soft-lens package prices ranged from about $80 to $260 for exam, lens, and follow-up care, with an average of about $140. Prices for a rigid gas-permeable package ranged from $160 to $340, averaging about $240.

The ease of cleaning and relatively long life of rigid gas-permeable contact lenses mean that the long-range cost is likely to be lower than the cost of soft lenses. You might save from $75 to $350 per year on cleaning chemicals alone.

15

Check the Fit

Check new eyeglasses realistically. Turn your head sideways, up, and down several times. Turn sideways while looking down. Chew for 15 seconds. Do the glasses work for their intended purposes? If they are for general use, can you see clearly at a distance and read comfortably? Do they stay in place as you walk?

Go Back

Return to your practitioner if you experience:

◆ Substantial discomfort with glasses;

◆ Mild discomfort for more than a few days;

◆ Dizziness;

◆ Blurred vision;

◆ A tendency to tilt your head when driving or working; *or*

◆ Any other unusual reaction.

slitlamp biomicroscope. He or she should also use a standard eye chart to test how well you see. If these checks indicate no problems, do your

> **T I P**
>
> **Practice Makes Perfect**
> *Practice putting your new contact lenses in and taking them out while the practitioner watches. Before leaving the office, make sure you know how to do it.*

own tests of fit: look left, right, up, and down several times while holding your head in different positions. And try blinking, squinting, and closing your eyes several times. If contacts don't fit perfectly, you may need new lenses, or a rigid lens may need alterations.

Proper follow-up is an important part of buying contacts and choosing a practitioner. Once contacts seem to fit, most practitioners will ask you to return at least once for an additional check. You may have to make several visits before the fit is perfect, and sometimes a good fit requires a change in basic lens design or material.

When you get the lenses, you should receive thorough instructions on how to insert and remove them, on adaptation (how long to wear them each day during the first few weeks), and on care and cleaning. Listen carefully. Get written instructions, and read them right away. Remember, all contacts can cause permanent eye damage if mishandled.

After You Go Home

If new eyeglass frames feel uncomfortable after a few hours, return to your optician or optometrist and ask for further adjustments. This service should be free.

Wait a few days if discomfort seems to be from lenses—either glasses or contacts—and is in the form of mild eyestrain or things appearing closer than before. Often your eyes and brain need time to adjust to new lenses.

The practitioner should check the lenses to determine if their actual correction coincides with your prescription. For glasses, he or she should check the positioning of the lenses in the frame and the positioning of the frame on your face. In the case of contacts, expect a little discomfort as you adapt to them, particularly to rigid lenses, but there should be no real pain. If there is, remove the lenses immediately and return to the practitioner as soon as possible.

If someone who has sold you uncomfortable glasses checks the lenses and then claims that the refractive power and positioning match the prescription, ask for an explanation of the cause for your complaints. If the explanation doesn't satisfy you, it could be that the seller is right and the original prescription was wrong, or perhaps the seller is wrong and doesn't recognize his or her mistake.

As a first step toward resolving such a problem, take the prescription and the glasses to an optician. Explain your problem and offer to pay to have the refractive power and (in the case of glasses) positioning of the lenses measured. Compare these new measurements to your prescription. The measurements will take only a minute or two. If the refractive power and positioning match the prescription, go back to the optometrist or ophthalmologist who wrote the prescription and explain the problem. Your practitioner should check the glasses and might re-test your eyes. Sometimes this is free, but check.

As an alternative, you may decide to get another eye exam from a different optometrist or ophthalmologist, explaining your recent difficulties. This will always cost you an additional examination fee. Do it as a last resort.

Getting Satisfaction

Will an optometrist or ophthalmologist who wrote an erroneous prescription pay for a new set of lenses? Will an optician who incorrectly filled a proper prescription pay for the second visit you made to an optometrist or ophthalmologist? If the party at fault refuses a fair settlement, explain that you will file a complaint.

File complaints against optometrists at the board of optometry of the state in which the practitioner's office is located. File complaints against ophthalmologists at the state board of medical examiners.

15

RESOURCES

American Academy of Ophthalmology
P.O. Box 7424
San Francisco, CA 94120
(415)561-8500
Write for free patient-information brochures on various eye diseases and disorders. Send a self-addressed stamped envelope and state the eye topic on which you desire information.

American Optometric Association
243 N. Lindbergh Blvd.
St. Louis, MO 63121
(314)991-4100

Write for free pamphlets on "Family Guide to Vision Care," "Your Baby's Eyes," "Your Preschool Child's Eyes," "Your School-Age Child's Eyes," "Do Vision Problems Cause Adult Reading Problems?" and others. To receive a copy of any of these pamphlets, send a stamped, self-addressed business envelope.

Better Vision Institute
P.O. Box 77097
Washington, DC 20013
(800)424-8422
Call or write for free brochures on eye care, eye disorders, aging concerns, and choosing eyeglass frames.

National Eye Care Project
P.O. Box 429098
San Francisco, CA 94142
(800)222-EYES
Operated by the American Academy of Ophthalmology, the NECP is a nationwide outreach program to provide medical eye care to disadvantaged senior citizens. Qualified patients receive treatment at no out-of-pocket expense.

Workplace Illness and Injury

By Nancy Lessin and Laurie Stillman

Work can endanger your health. Nationwide, about 10,000 people are killed on their jobs every year; occupational diseases kill another 100,000 Americans. Millions more suffer daily from injuries and illnesses sustained from their employment. And workplace injury and illness are occurring more and more frequently due to the rapid pace and repetitive nature of many of today's jobs and the widespread use of toxic chemicals.

You *don't* have to endure unhealthy conditions, however. Working to support yourself and your family doesn't have to mean compromising your health. This chapter will help you learn about some of your options in addressing harmful workplace conditions, find assistance when you confront risks to your health and safety, and actively work with your health-care providers to get the best treatment.

PART I: OCCUPATIONAL HAZARDS AND YOUR RIGHTS

The causes of many workplace *injuries* are usually obvious—and almost always preventable. Proper guards and maintenance for machinery, adequate rest periods, and good training programs go a long way toward preventing calamities.

Unfortunately, it's usually much harder to recognize when *illnesses* result from work. In the first place, most occupational illnesses closely resemble those that result from other causes. A bakery worker with occupational asthma may wheeze and cough pretty much the same as another asthma victim. In addition, symptoms can show up long after a person is exposed to hazardous materials. Cancers and other diseases may appear many years later, perhaps well after the victim has left the job. Even the patient can easily fail to connect his or her illness to workplace origins.

Your Rights to Workplace Hazard Information

Knowledge helps you and your health-care providers detect and treat occupational illness. In fact, you have a

Untrained Docs?

Few health-care providers receive enough training in occupational health to recognize possible connections between illness and work. Only half of U.S. medical schools offer courses on occupational health, and the typical curriculum lasts about four hours. That makes it all the more important for you as a health-care consumer to better understand how your work conditions affect your health.

Lost Time

Americans miss about 65 million days of work to occupational illness and injury each year, according to the Health Insurance Institute of America.

Laurie Stillman directs the Massachusetts Coalition for Occupational Safety and Health. Nancy Lessin is MassCOSH's senior staff member for strategy and policy.

legal right to obtain a lot of the information—on chemicals and other hazardous conditions—that's crucial to diagnosing work-related disease.

Many of your legal rights come via "OSHA"—the Occupational Safety and Health Administration. This federal agency sets workplace health and safety standards and regulations, inspects workplaces, and cites and fines employers who violate the law. OSHA applies to most private employers, as well as to public employers in some states. These employers must provide a workplace "free of recognized hazards."

Employers also are required to provide some health and safety information to unions under the National Labor Relations Act. And some states have "right-to-know" laws for state and local government employees not covered by OSHA. Right-to-know laws give workers legal rights to written data on the hazards of chemicals to which they are exposed, plus training and information on necessary precautions.

If OSHA covers your workplace, you have the legal right to:

• Read and get a copy of your employer's *OSHA 200 Log*, a record of work-related injuries and illnesses in your workplace;

• Learn the results of any hazard tests, such as noise levels or the amounts of chemicals in the workplace air;

• Read and get a copy of any medical records your employer maintains on you; *and*

• Read and get a copy of chemical fact sheets—so-called Material Safety Data Sheets—for the chemicals to which

BACK INJURIES

Musculoskeletal disorders of the back, arms, and legs occur more often than all other types of disabling work-related injuries and illnesses in the United States, accounting for 40 percent of the cases that require time away from work.

Risk factors for these disorders include working in an awkward posture, use of force, repeated motions, and lack of rest. Reducing these disorders requires redesigning workstations and tools so they "fit" workers and redesigning

jobs to reduce the pace of work and increase the amount of rest so that one body part isn't overtaxed. Quick fixes—such as the use of back belts—may cause more problems than they solve.

you may be exposed at work.

OSHA also requires employers to ensure that their workers receive training about such hazards as noise, asbestos, and blood-borne disease-causing agents (specifically, those for HIV and Hepatitis B). Unfortunately, many employer-sponsored training programs are inadequate or nonexistent. OSHA's most frequently violated regulation is its "Hazard Communications Standard" that requires training on dangerous chemicals.

Rights and Recourses

Some employers resist giving out hazard information, despite the law. If you pursue your right to information under the Occupational Safety and Health Act, it's illegal for your boss to discriminate against you or retaliate in any way. In addition, "whistleblower" protections in some states offer a recourse for people who face repercussions for speaking out about workplace health or safety hazards. The National Labor Relations Act can also protect workers from unfair employer actions: this protection for activities related to health and safety is strongest when two or more workers act together.

Be careful, however: all these protections are weak, and they aren't always effective. Unions offer the most protection for workers who request Material Safety Data Sheets, contact government agencies, speak out about health and safety concerns, or refuse unsafe work. If you are a union member, ask your steward to help you get health and safety information.

PART II: GETTING CARE

Ideally, your physician and other health-care providers routinely ask you about your exposure to possible workplace hazards. The diagnosis and treatment of many diseases would improve tremendously if every medical history included such simple questions as:

- Where do you work?
- What do you do on your job?
- Have you ever worked with dusts, fumes, or chemicals

Material Safety Data Sheets

For almost every chemical used in the United States, there is a Material Safety Data Sheet (MSDS) describing related health effects, physical properties, flammability, emergency procedures, and protective measures to control hazardous or toxic exposure.

The quality of these documents varies enormously. The "Pocket Guide to Chemical Hazards," published by the National Institute for Occupational Safety and Health, and other references can help you check the accuracy of an MSDS. To obtain a copy of the guide, contact NIOSH at (800)35-NIOSH.

16

Shock Un-Therapy

Over half of reported occupational illnesses result from repeated physical stresses. Constant loud noises, repetitive lifting and movement, and vibrating machinery or hand tools can lead to deafness, numbness, and other problems.

that might be dangerous?

If your health-care provider fails to ask these questions, raise the issue yourself. It will also help if you bring your provider the Material Safety Data Sheets for the chemicals to which you are exposed. If you think that asking your employer for these documents may put your job at risk, your health-care provider can request the information on your behalf, without divulging your name.

If an illness or injury could possibly relate to your work, it may be best to seek the opinion of a specialist in occupational medicine. These physicians and nurses are specifically trained and skilled at diagnosing, treating, and preventing work-related diseases and injuries. Unfortunately, there are only about 800 certified occupational physicians in the United States. The Association of Occupational and Environmental Clinics can refer you to an occupational health clinic in your area: call (202)347-4976.

One advantage of reputable occupational-medicine specialists or clinics is that they are better equipped than ordinary providers to advance *your* interests effectively. Besides drawing on their own medical training, specialists can refer you to advocates and help you obtain financial assistance through workers compensation.

More Ways to Get Help

Despite the shortage of trained specialists in occupational health, you're far from alone in your quest for a healthy workplace and for care when your work makes you sick or

---

Company Docs

If you seek a specialist in occupational health, be cautious about "company doctors." They generally work for your employer, whose interests may differ from yours. Be certain any health-care provider you choose is your advocate.

REPRODUCTIVE HAZARDS

In 1977, chemical workers at a plant in California realized that many of the men and their partners couldn't conceive children. Medical tests revealed that many of the men had low sperm counts. Their union, the Oil, Chemical and Atomic Workers, helped the men link this fact with a chemical they manufactured known as DBCP.

In 1978, OSHA responded to the union's petition and issued a very strict exposure limit. Although many of the workers with long-term exposure to DBCP are permanently sterile, the new regulation benefits many current and future workers. It came about because workers talked with one another about their symptoms, and because they had a strong union to pursue the matter medically and with OSHA.

injures you.

In many states and cities, you'll find a strong advocate in the local committee or coalition on occupational safety and health—a COSH group. These are local organizations of labor unions, other worker advocates, and occupational-health professionals. COSH groups provide training, education, referrals, and medical, technical, and legal assistance.

In addition, many national and international unions have health and safety departments that are excellent sources of information and referrals. Your steward or local union officers can refer you to your union's health and safety department.

At the workplace, many union health and safety committees gather information on specific factories or offices and plan ways to control hazards. Members of these committees may also take part in labor-management health and safety groups that engage in such activities as conducting workplace inspections, investigating accidents and incidents, and recommending hazard controls.

Several government agencies can assist the efforts of workers and unions to improve workplace health and safety and obtain medical care and benefits for people injured or made ill by their jobs. On the federal level:

Vague Symptoms

Many workplace hazards are linked with vague symptoms—fatigue, depression, and mental confusion are a few examples. Although recognizing the connection with work is particularly difficult in such cases, it isn't impossible.

For example, Janice was getting headaches and her throat and eyes were irritated. She spoke with co-workers in her office, and it turned out that they suffered from similar symptoms. This was the key to identifying and correcting the problem. An investigation showed that the illness was caused by the building's ventilation system.

16

You, the Expert

In the pressroom of a large newspaper, several workers discovered they had blood in their urine. With the help of occupational health specialists, the press workers linked this symptom with a class of chemicals common in such workplaces—glycol ethers. The workers' union played an important role in getting management to substitute less toxic chemicals for the glycol ethers.

You and your co-workers are the real experts on occupational safety and health. Armed with experience, suspicions, and the specifics of workplace exposures, you can call upon medical, technical, and legal assistance to confirm the links that you suspect. And in the absence of definitive research and strong legal standards, it's often workers who must make the connections and

force the corrections.

Work with your union if you are a member, or with co-workers in any case. This can provide both protection and opportunities for safeguarding your health on the job. If necessary, you can pinpoint hazards and collect detailed data on work-related symptoms. And the *OSHA 200 Log* can help you identify unsafe areas that need further attention.

CONTROLLING HAZARDS

The best response to a hazard is to *eliminate the danger* altogether by substituting safer substances for toxic chemicals or by changing the work. For example, most dry-cleaning processes now use perchloroethylene, a carcinogen. But an alternative wet-cleaning process uses biodegradable soaps and steam heat instead.

Engineering controls are the second most effective way to control a hazard. Engineering controls include attachments to dampen noise or local exhausts to remove toxic fumes. For example, a process to grind hardened steel tips for tools exposed workers to cobalt, chromium, and other toxic chemicals. The factory installed a special grinding wheel guard that directed air and dust toward a moveable local exhaust duct. This cut worker exposure to the dangerous chemicals to under 1 percent of the original level.

Ear plugs, respirators, special clothing, and other *personal protective equipment* are usually the least effective response to hazardous work. In addition to the fact that such equipment is often uncomfortable, it doesn't fully prevent hazardous exposures.

• *The Occupational Safety and Health Administration* can inspect workplaces and fine employers who violate health or safety standards.

• *The National Institute for Occupational Safety and Health* can check your workplace for health hazards, explore links between particular exposures and ill health, and make recommendations on hazard control.

COSH Number
COSH groups assist workers on all aspects of occupational safety and health. To find the nearest committee or coalition on occupational safety and health, contact the New York City committee (NYCOSH) at (212)627-3900.

• *The National Labor Relations Board* can intervene when employers fail to provide unions with certain health and safety information or when employers fire workers for acting collectively to improve health and safety conditions.

On the state level, your sources of help include the Department of Labor (sometimes called the Department of Labor and Industries), Department of Public Health, Workers Compensation Bureau, Poison Control Center, Rehabilitation Agency, and state OSHA. You can also get help from local public-health schools, work-environment departments at universities, and some other academic departments. To contact any of these, check the phone book, call your local COSH group, or ask your union steward.

PART III: MONEY MATTERS

If a job makes you sick or injures you, you're entitled to *workers compensation.* You can receive partial payment of the wages you lose and payment for rehabilitation, medical costs associated with the injury or illness, and certain "losses of function."

Workers compensation is primarily a legal system—not a medical one. That is, a judge, rather than a health-care professional, generally decides whether your injury or illness is work-related, the degree of your disability, whether you are entitled to remain off the job, and when you can return to work. However, the opinion of the person who treats you is very important, especially if an employer or its insurance company disputes the work-relatedness of your claim to workers comp.

Each state administers its own workers-comp system, imposes its own rules, and sets maximum weekly wage benefits for people injured severely enough to miss work. In many states, this maximum is 66 percent of the average weekly wage. Rarely do "wage replacement" benefits equal your earnings before an injury or illness. And in most cases the system precludes you from suing your employer to recover full damages or any payments for pain and suffering.

This arrangement compensates injured people more effectively than it does people suffering from occupational diseases. The connection between workplace exposure and ill health can be difficult to prove, with the burden of proof on the worker. Employers and their insurance companies contest over 80 percent of all compensation cases for chronic occupational disease, and less than 5 percent of all workers-comp cases are paid out to workers for occupational disease.

Some workers-comp laws require you to see doctors your employer designates for treatment. Other states allow you to select your own health-care providers. If you have this option, an occupational-medicine specialist can benefit your case significantly.

More Sources of Compensation

Workers who suffer serious long-term injuries or illness-

Workers Comp Denials

You may need a lawyer to win a workers-comp case. Whether and when to obtain legal assistance depends on many factors. COSH groups, unions, and some of the other resource organizations listed in this chapter can help you make that decision.

An Injury to One...

A person may develop carpal tunnel syndrome in his or her wrists from typing on a computer. That worker's situation can raise the awareness of improvements in equipment and job design that would help all computer users in his or her workplace. Making such changes would protect the first worker from a recurrence of this painful, sometimes disabling condition, *and* prevent other people from ever suffering it in the first place.

From a prevention perspective, if an injured worker returns to a job that is modified to prevent re-injury, everyone else doing that job should benefit from the same improvements.

For more on Medicaid, turn to Chapters 3 and 8

es can apply for Social Security Disability Insurance. SSDI provides monthly benefits to people whose injuries or illnesses prevent them from engaging in "substantial gainful employment" for a year or longer. After a five-month waiting period, SSDI benefits, when combined with workers-comp benefits, equal 80 percent of your average monthly earnings. Social Security denies most SSDI claims initially, but appeals before a Social Security judge often succeed.

At some point, a person injured or made sick by work might feel ready to return to work but not perform all of his or her previous job tasks. According to the Americans with Disabilities Act, employers of 15 or more workers must provide "reasonable accommodations"

T I P

Disability and Insurance

Check to see if a company or state short-term or long-term disability policy covers your situation. This may supplement your wages while out of work.

that allow disabled workers to perform "essential job functions." Some states have additional protections for disabled workers.

COMMON CAUSES OF OCCUPATIONAL ILLNESS

◆ Workers might inhale dust and fumes that are present in the workplace.

◆ Contaminants that get on your hands, food, or cigarettes may be dangerous if you swallow them.

◆ Contact with solvents, acids, or dusts can injure eyes, cause skin burns or diseases, or enter the body to cause internal damage.

◆ Fumes, dusts, and chemicals can lead to respiratory and lung diseases. About 15 percent of asthma cases may be work-related.

◆ Poisoning from metals, gases, sprays, and solvents can lead to liver and kidney ailments, blood disorders, and cancer.

◆ Extreme heat or cold can result in heat stroke or frostbite.

◆ Radiation can cause cancer.

◆ Repetitive work leads to wear and tear on muscles, tendons, ligaments, nerves, and the vascular system.

◆ Stressful work is associated with diseases of almost every vital organ. Workers cite too little personal control on the job as the major source of stress.

◆ Infectious agents, such as bacteria and viruses, can cause tuberculosis, hepatitis, and many other serious illnesses.

◆ Many substances and conditions can harm your ability to produce healthy children or have a healthy sex life. Reproductive disorders and damage to reproductive organs are among the ten leading work-related injuries and illnesses. Reproductive hazards can affect fertility, decrease sex drive, promote birth defects or miscarriages, and contribute to childhood cancer. Both men and women need to be concerned about this danger.

Reasonable accommodations include adjusting the job environment to permit someone with a disability to perform essential job functions. Examples include:

- Physical changes, such as ramps, lower benches, or special equipment;
- Training to be able to use special equipment or new systems; *and*
- Job restructuring, such as reassignment of non-essential tasks, job redesign, more rest breaks, or lighter duty.

Employers often stop paying your health-insurance premiums if you miss work due to a disability. On the other hand, you usually have a right to stay in your employer's group plan if you pay the full premium yourself. If you can't pay the premium, you may be able to obtain medical coverage through state programs or Medicaid.

RESOURCES

Organizations

AFL-CIO
Department of Occupational Safety, Health, and Social Security
815 16th St., NW
Washington, DC 20006
(202)637-5000
Call or write for information on reaching the health and safety department of any international member union.

Association of Occupational and Environmental Clinics
1010 Vermont Ave., NW
Washington, DC 20005
(202)347-4976
The AOEC can refer you to an occupational health clinic in your area.

Coalition of Trade Union Women
15 Union Sq.
New York, NY 10003
(212)242-0700
Call or write for publications and information on job hazards for working women.

Committees/Coalitions on Occupational Safety and Health
Contact the New York City committee (NYCOSH) at (212)627-3900 to locate the organization nearest you.

National Coalition of Injured Workers
12 Rejane St.
Coventry, RI 02816
(401)828-6520
This is an association of organizations that help injured and ill workers obtain support, medical care, and benefits. The groups advocate for better workers-compensation systems. Contact the NCIW to find the injured-workers group in your area.

National Institute for Occupational Safety and Health
4676 Columbia Parkway
Cincinnati, OH 45226
(513)533-8287
(800)35-NIOSH
NIOSH can check your workplace for health hazards, explore links between particular exposures and ill health, and make recommendations on ways to control hazards.

National Labor Relations Board
1717 Pennsylvania Ave., NW
Washington, DC 20570
The NLRB can intervene when employers fail to provide unions with certain health or safety information or when employers fire workers for acting collectively to improve health and safety conditions. There are regional offices throughout the country.

Occupational Safety and Health Administration
200 Constitution Ave., NW
Washington, DC 20210
(202)219-8148
OSHA can inspect workplaces and fine employers that violate health or safety standards. Call or write for a list of publications and ordering information. There are regional OSHA offices around the country.

Publications

Preventing Occupational Disease and Injury, edited by James L. Weeks, Barry S. Levy, and Gregory R. Wagner. To order, contact the American Public Health Association, 1015 15th St., NW, Washington, DC 20005 (202)789-5636. $28.50 (plus $5.00 shipping and handling).

Is Your Job Making You Sick? A CLUW Handbook on Workplace Hazards. To order, contact the Coalition of Labor Union Women, 1126 16th St. NW, Washington, DC 20036 (202)466-4610. $4.00.

Confronting Reproductive Health Hazards on the Job. To order, contact Massachusetts Coalition for Occupational Safety and Health, 555 Amory St., Jamaica Plain, MA 02130 (617)524-6686.

Death With Dignity

By George J. Annas

A t any given time, millions of Americans are either facing the last stages of their own fatal illness or caring for dying relatives. Almost two million Americans die each year, and a million more have a terminal diagnosis.

Nonetheless, as a culture, we persist in denying death. Dying patients often know better. Even more than death, they fear isolation and pain. We can make our deaths a bit easier—for our families and ourselves—by planning and by requiring health-care professionals to take our humanity, our needs, and our rights seriously.

Probably our first and foremost need, and right, is to know the truth about our situation. When people lack the opportunity to discuss their own impending deaths, they simultaneously lose their dignity as adults. The "survivor knows best" attitude is illustrated by the words of a woman who described the death of her uncle as beautiful: "John died happy, never even realizing he was seriously ill."

This "ignorance is bliss" attitude deprives the dying person of his or her last opportunity to accomplish goals and say things they would want to. For example, a father who knows he's dying of cancer might want to put his business affairs in better order now rather than leave his family with problems later.

PART I: HOSPICE CARE

Hospice care is designed for people with a terminal illness who will probably die within six months. The hospice movement is built around the principle that people should be able to die at home and free from pain but without complex medical invasions of their body. Over 2,000 hospice programs across the United States help make this a reality. Almost all of these have been established since 1974, and the number has increased by about one-third since 1989 alone.

According to the National Hospice Organization, hospice is a special kind of care for dying people and their families that:

George J. Annas is the Edward R. Utley Professor of Health Law at the Boston University School of Medicine and head of the Health Law Department at the Boston University School of Public Health. He is the author of many books, including The Rights of Patients *(Southern Illinois University Press, 1989) and* Standard of Care: The Law of American Bioethics *(Oxford University Press, 1993) and writes a regular feature on law in the* New England Journal of Medicine.

17

- Treats the physical *and* emotional and spiritual needs of the patient;
- Takes place in his or her home or in a home-like setting;
- Concentrates on making the patient as free from pain and as comfortable as possible;
- Supports family members as an essential part of the mission; *and*
- Believes quality of life to be as important as length of life.

Hospice programs serve more than a quarter million patients and families each year in the United States, and about three quarters of all hospice patients die in their own homes. About 80 percent of hospice patients suffer from cancer, 10 percent have heart-related illnesses, and 4 percent have AIDS, with various other diagnoses making up the remainder. About 40 percent of all cancer deaths and 30 percent of all AIDS deaths occur in hospice programs.

Physicians and other primary-care providers are usually the ones who refer patients to hospice programs, but family members, friends, and clergy can do this as well. Hospital discharge planners, nurses, and social workers also refer people to hospice programs, and all these people can help you find one for yourself or a family member.

Hospices provide care through a team of professionals and volunteers. The members of the team range from physicians and nurses to counselors, therapists, and home health aides. Volunteers are at the heart of hospice care. Each year, about 100,000 volunteers donate over 5 million hours. Staff members and volunteers receive specific training to work with people in the last months of life. They also cooperate with the patient's own health-care providers.

The members of a hospice team help keep the patient's environment as free and open as possible. Team members can also help the patient with back rubs and foot massages, matters of personal cleanliness, "being there," open discussions about feelings, household chores, financial matters, favorite foods or music, and pastimes.

Hospice team members administer treatment and drugs to ease pain and provide comfort. Because the focus of hos-

Silence and Death

Leo Tolstoy describes the dehumanizing effect of silence in *The Death of Ivan Ilyich:*

"What tormented Ivan Ilyich most was the deception, the lie, which for some reason they all accepted, that he was not dying but was simply ill, and that he only need keep quiet and undergo a treatment and then something very good would result. . . . This deception tortured him—their not wishing him to admit what they all knew and what he knew. . . . Those lies—lies enacted over him on the eve of his death and destined to degrade this awful, solemn act to the level of their visiting, their curtains, their sturgeon for dinner— were a terrible agony for Ivan Ilyich."

pice is on dying with dignity, treatments to attempt to extend life, such as chemotherapy, are not used. On the

> **TIP**
>
> **Hospice Hotline**
> *For referrals to local hospice programs, contact the National Hospice Organization Helpline at (800)658-8898*

other hand, a person in hospice care doesn't forfeit all access to medical technology: about half of U.S. hospice programs admit patients requiring "high-tech" therapies, and almost all will consider such patients on a case-by-case basis. Hospice patients, of course, have the right to change their minds and be admitted to a hospital for high-tech treatment.

Beyond direct service to patients and families, many hospice programs also offer services to the community at large. These activities range from support groups and memorial services to educational programs, individual and family counseling, crisis counseling, and specific children's services.

Money Matters

When a Medicare-eligible patient receives care from a Medicare-approved hospice, Medicare pays almost the entire cost for all services and supplies. In general, this coverage includes physician services, nursing care, medical equipment and supplies, drugs for managing symptoms and relieving pain, short-term inpatient and respite care, homemaker services and home-health aides, physical and other therapy, and counseling. Hospice coverage replaces your usual hospital coverage under Medicare Part A. You can revoke the hospice benefit at any time to revert to the usual Part A benefits.

About three-quarters of U.S. hospice programs are either Medicare-certified or have certification pending. To receive Medicare certification, a hospice program must provide:

- 24-hour staffing;
- Medical and nursing care;
- Home-health services;
- Access to patient care;
- Social-work services;

The Semi-Right to Die at Home

In theory, you have the right to die in your own home. In practice, it's often difficult to arrange. Fewer than 20 percent of all Americans die at home. To do so requires not only the strong resolve of the dying person but also the cooperation of his or her family or anyone with whom the patient lives.

The cooperation of health-care providers also matters a great deal. Without it, a person can't get prescriptions for pain-relieving drugs and other medication.

Insured Benefit

The health insurance of more than 80 percent of employees in medium and large companies covers hospice care. It's also covered under Medicare nationally and under 33 state Medicaid plans. Three-fifths of all hospice patients receive their care under Medicare or Medicaid.

Hospices will assist families lacking insurance to explore other options for coverage. And most hospices will provide for anyone who can't pay, using money raised from the community or other donations.

Finding the Right Hospice

Look for a Medicare-certified hospice program, advises "Harvard Health Letter." In the absence of any national organization that regulates hospices, the procedures required to qualify for Medicare reimbursement indicate that a program meets basic standards of quality.

Once you are ready to check out the quality and suitability of a particular hospice program, talk with its staff. "Harvard Health Letter" recommends that you ask about:

◆ Hospital affiliations;

◆ Procedures for assuring 24-hour access to staff;

◆ Protocol for managing pain;

◆ Criteria for enrolling;

◆ Payment options; and

◆ Arrangements for residential care, if and when it's needed.

In particular, try to get a sense of the willingness of staff members to help patients and their families. Do they sound caring and competent? Or do they use lots of jargon or lead you to expect that the program involves a great deal of bureaucracy?

- Counseling, including bereavement counseling;
- Medications, medical supplies, and durable medical equipment; *and*
- Physical, occupational, and speech therapy.

If a person's need for hospice care extends beyond the expected six-month limit, Medicare may still cover the bills. If a person is recertified as needing hospice care, the benefit can be extended indefinitely, and a hospice can't discharge a person without good cause. If private insurance is paying for hospice care, the coverage for extended periods varies. Some plans define a dollar limit, while others follow the Medicare rules. If you are paying for hospice care yourself, the admission criteria and other policies and procedures of the hospice govern the situation.

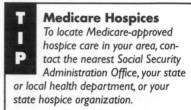

TIP

Medicare Hospices
To locate Medicare-approved hospice care in your area, contact the nearest Social Security Administration Office, your state or local health department, or your state hospice organization.

Pain and Medication

One reason for the growing availability and acceptance of hospice programs is the failure of the U.S. health-care system to alleviate the pain of dying people. Perhaps 90 percent of terminally ill patients don't receive proper relief from pain. This is a major medical scandal.

Even if you refuse medical care that might lengthen your life, physicians can't withhold needed and appropriate pain medications. Physicians have a legal and ethical obligation to give you all the medication you need to be comfortable, even if it shortens your life. Both you and your advocate should demand that your providers meet this obligation. To alleviate pain, doses need not be so high as to distort reality. And terminally ill people and their physicians and nurses have no reason to fear drug addiction or damage to their chromosomes.

The right to pain and comfort medications doesn't extend to marijuana or heroin, although these drugs are used for pain and discomfort in other countries.

PART II: SAYING NO

It's almost incredible that anyone could consider it acceptable to force treatment on a patient. The decision about what treatment options exist is a medical one, but the decision to undergo any particular treatment isn't. It's a personal choice that only you can legitimately make. Specific court cases about refusing treatment have dealt with blood transfusions, mechanical ventilators, kidney dialysis, fluids and nutrition, and chemotherapy, among other things. The point is, you can refuse *any* medical intervention, including lifesaving and life-sustaining treatment and artificial feeding. This even includes cardiopulmonary resuscitation (CPR), which some health-care personnel treat differently from other medical procedures because they administer it under emergency conditions.

Physicians *can* treat patients in emergencies without consent. After all, time is of the essence, and it's often impossible to obtain informed consent in these situations. However, if the emergency can be anticipated and the patient refuses to consent in advance, no one has the legal or ethical right to impose any procedure, even CPR. In a hospital, a person who has refused CPR is designated DNR—do not resuscitate. All other measures to care for you and ensure your comfort are still available unless you specifically refuse them.

Children and Parents

Usually, parents can't refuse potentially life-sustaining care for their children, even for religious reasons. As the U.S. Supreme Court stated in another context, "Parents may be free to become martyrs themselves. But it does not follow they are free . . . to make martyrs of their children."

Parents are legally obligated to provide their children with "necessary medical care." When alternative treatments are available, parents can choose among those that are consistent with generally accepted medical practice. But parents can't legally choose to forgo treatment unless that's consistent with the best interests of the child. To deny a child beneficial treatment may make a parent guilty of

---

Your Pain

When he was dying of cancer, columnist Stewart Alsop wrote eloquently of the experience. He suggested allowing patients "to decide for themselves how much pain-killing drug they will take—it is, after all, they, not the doctors, who are suffering the agonies."

Technology, Life, and Death

Some people claim that the mere existence of medical technology creates an obligation on the part of patients to submit to its use. Such an attitude would make the right to refuse treatment irrelevant.

17

child neglect, in which case a physician or hospital can obtain a court order to treat the child.

PART III: PLANNING AHEAD

While few of us look forward to our own death, we should all take responsibility for making at least some provision for it.

Rather than leave it to chance, designate someone *now* to make health-care decisions for you when you can't decide for yourself. When you are no longer able to give informed consent, your guardian or next-of-kin can make treatment decisions for you. If you don't express your wishes beforehand, the next of kin or guardian must decide what is in your best interest.

The document through which you designate someone to speak for you is called an "advance directive." The term generally applies to two kinds of legal documents: a living will and a durable power of attorney for health care, also called a health-care proxy. These documents let you instruct your family, friends, guardians, health-care providers, and others about your medical care in the event

If You Don't Say Otherwise

Without clear evidence about a person's wishes, health-care providers often continue to treat patients. That's their job. Even if your family believes you'd reject treatment, the medical staff may ask to see proof of your wishes before agreeing to stop treatment.

PHYSICIANS AND ASSISTED SUICIDE

You have no right to insist that a physician end your life by killing you.

All proposals to give doctors legal immunity for helping terminally ill people commit suicide have been rejected. An overwhelming majority of physicians and the public agree that people in severe pain deserve all the medication they need to ease the pain, even if this shortens their lives. But only about 60 percent of the public and 30 per-cent of physicians think it's acceptable to actually take the life of a terminally ill patient even at the patient's request.

This issue is the subject of heated debate. The primary argument in favor of physician-assisted suicide is that only health-care professionals can diagnose a patient's condition, prescribe the appropriate drugs, and administer them. The primary argument against is that medical care relies on trust in healing; adding the act of ending life would radically alter the role of physicians, ultimately erode the public's trust in them, and possibly lead to the killing of patients without their consent. If a family member or friend expresses a desire to kill himself or herself, be sure to explore the reasons for this desire and make sure all efforts to deal with them directly are competently addressed.

that serious illness or some other incapacity prevents you from speaking for yourself.

Forty-five states and the District of Columbia authorize both living wills and the appointment of a health-care agent by statute. Alabama and Alaska only authorize living wills, while Massachusetts, Michigan, and New York laws only deal with appointing an agent.

Some state laws restrict the applicability of living wills and health-care proxies so that, for example, they can't be used to authorize the termination of artificial nutrition and hydration or the refusal of treatment during pregnancy. However, these restrictions simply mean that you can't use the living will or health-care proxy method to attain these ends. Individuals have a *constitutional* right to refuse treatment, and the state can't take this away by statute. There is no constitutional authority for the proposition that women lose their right to refuse treatment when they become pregnant.

Take the time to think carefully about your beliefs and express them fully as you prepare an advance directive. Make sure that it truly reflects your opinions. "Talk openly about your wishes with your family, your friends, and your doctor," advises Choice in Dying, an advocate for people's end-of-life rights. "Don't assume that they know what you would want. . . . Family's and physicians' guesses about a patient's preferences are often mistaken. Talking with the people who may have to act on your behalf ensures that they understand your wishes, gives them a chance to ask questions, and also lets you determine whether they will follow your wishes, even if your choices differ from theirs."

Living Wills

A living will is an advance directive in which you set forth your wishes concerning medical treatment in the event you are incapacitated. A living will is much like a regular will, but it's termed "living" because it takes effect before you die. Living wills usually address only decisions at the end of life, specifying the kinds of treatment you refuse and the conditions under which this refusal applies.

Emergencies and Advance Directives

In any emergency, physicians are privileged to treat you. However, emergency medical technicians in most states can't decide whether your written advance directive applies. Instead, technicians do what is necessary to stabilize you for transfer to a hospital. If you call 911 for another person, expect that person to receive emergency treatment regardless of an advance directive

17

Exercise Your Rights

Almost all Americans approve of living wills—yet only 20 percent actually sign them.

Most people don't want to stay alive in a permanent coma. Even this general statement, included in a living will, is extremely helpful to physicians and families. If you have strong, specific wishes, tell your physician and family how you want to be treated in various situations. In addition, designate one or more people to act on your behalf to decide about your medical care when you can't do so yourself. You may wish to tell this person verbally how you want to be treated, but it's best to write down directions in a letter that your agent can use to document your wishes should the need arise.

The movement to write living wills received a major boost from the case of Karen Ann Quinlan, a young woman who became permanently unconscious after an accident. Her parents had to go to court to get her mechanical ventilator removed. They argued that she wouldn't have wanted to live like that. Almost everyone who heard about the case reacted by thinking, "I'd never want to be like Karen Ann Quinlan, kept alive, in a permanent coma, on a ventilator." To help prevent this from happening, many wrote their wishes down for their relatives and physicians.

> **T I P**
> **Keep It Handy**
> *Advance directives are meant to be read, so keep them handy. Make copies, and keep the original in a safe but easily accessible place. Tell others where you put the original, and note this information on the copies. Give copies to your agent and alternate agent.*

Lawyers and Advance Directives

You may want a lawyer's help as you prepare a living will or a health-care proxy, but this isn't necessary. For advice and state-specific forms and laws at no charge, contact Choice in Dying, 200 Varick St., New York, NY 10014-4810 (212)366-5540 or (800)989-WILL.

Durable Power of Attorney

In addition to preparing a living will, formally designate a friend or relative to make decisions on your behalf through a document called a durable power of attorney or health-care proxy. A durable power of attorney is valid in every state, and some states have specific documents just for health-care decisions. Use this mechanism to designate someone you trust to make health-care decisions for you when you can't make them for yourself.

With any power of attorney, you give someone else the authority to perform certain acts as your agent, consistent with your directions. Ordinarily, powers of attorney cease to be effective when you become incompetent, but a *durable* power of attorney continues in effect. In fact, a durable power of attorney for health care usually goes into effect *only* when and if you become incompetent. It's important that you *talk* to your agent about what you want and make sure your agent is willing to do it.

A health-care proxy is better than a living will because it's impossible to anticipate every circumstance in advance. Moreover, a health-care proxy generally applies in a wider range of situations than those involving the end of your life. For example, an unforeseen decision might be needed while you are unconscious from an accident, even though you are expected to recover and live many years. If specific eventualities worry you, write a detailed letter to your designated agent.

Making Sure
You can best protect your wishes by designating a health-care agent and providing that person with specific written instructions.

If You Don't Designate an Agent

If you don't name someone to make treatment decisions for you, most states have statutes that designate which family member has this authority.

A SAMPLE DONOR CARD

UNIFORM DONOR CARD

Of _____
 (name of donor)

In the hope that I may help others, I hereby make this anatomical gift, if medically acceptable, to take effect upon my death. The words and marks below indicate my desires. I give:

(a) _____ any needed organs or parts

(b) _____ only the following organs or parts: (Specify the organ[s] or part[s])

_____

_____

_____

for the purposes of transplantation, therapy, medical research or education;

_____

(c) _____ my body for anatomical study if needed.
Limitations or special wishes, if any:

_____

The donor should sign this card in the presence of two witnesses.

17

But if you don't have someone you trust implicitly, a living will may be useful for you.

Donating Your Organs

Under the Uniform Anatomical Gift Act, which every state has enacted in some form, anyone eighteen years or older and of sound mind may donate all or any part of his or her body to:

• Any hospital, physician, surgeon, or procurement organization for transplantation, therapy, medical education, dental education, research, or the advancement of medical or dental science;

• Any accredited medical or dental school, college, or university for education, research, therapy, or the advancement of medical or dental science; *and*

• Any specified individual for therapy or transplantation needed by that individual.

You can make such a gift through your will, or you can sign a donor card in the presence of two witnesses. In the latter case, carry the card in your wallet or purse; your driver's license may note your status as a donor as well. In most states, you can revoke the gift either by destroying the card or by saying you revoke it in the presence of two witnesses.

After you die, your next of kin can donate your organs even if you didn't sign a donor card. On the other hand, virtually no physician or hospital will take organs from your corpse without the consent of your next of kin—even if you sign a donor card. This isn't for legal reasons. It simply doesn't seem proper. Also, hospitals must deal with the living, and it's clumsy public relations to take organs unless the next of kin agrees.

PART IV: WHAT IS DEATH?

The determination that a person is dead is a medical decision, and physicians have the legal authority to "declare" a person dead. Traditionally, physicians did so when a person's heart stopped irreversibly and the person stopped breathing.

However, cardiopulmonary resuscitation (CPR) can often restart a heart, and since CPR's introduction in the early 1960s, a stopped heart hasn't necessarily meant irreversible destruction of the brain. However, brain destruction always means death. When CPR either fails or isn't tried, and a person's heart stops beating, the person is dead.

Brain Death

Mechanical ventilators that take over breathing make it feasible to artificially sustain respiration and heartbeat in a body that would otherwise stop functioning because the brain is destroyed. Because of this, brain death is now a widely accepted alternative way to determine death.

Under the current medical and legal definition, an individual is dead when he or she has sustained either:

- Irreversible cessation of circulatory and respiratory functions; *or*
- Irreversible cessation of all functions of the entire brain, including the brain stem.

In either case, the determination of death must accord with accepted medical standards. Note that a permanently unconscious person—such as Karen Ann Quinlan—isn't dead. Among other things, such people can often breathe without mechanical assistance, and so have at least brain-stem function.

Autopsies

An autopsy is a comprehensive study of a corpse performed by a trained physician who employs recognized dissection procedures and techniques. Most commonly, autopsies are used to determine the cause of death, but they also play a valuable role in educating health-care students.

Health-care professionals and students can practice on a corpse only if the person signed a written consent before he or she died, or if the next of kin gives consent after the person is dead. If a hospital doctor requests the autopsy, the hospital almost always absorbs the cost. It shouldn't appear on the hospital bill.

Families and the Determination of Death

A family with reason to doubt that a determination of death accords with accepted medical standards can insist that a qualified neurosurgeon or neurologist confirm the judgment before a ventilator is disconnected.

If the determination is confirmed, the family has no right to insist on further medical care. All treatment should end upon the pronouncement of death and, unless organ donation or autopsy is planned, the body should be released to the family for burial.

17

Brain Death

Brain death is a technical term that applies only to a body attached to a mechanical ventilator. The body's brain must be totally and irreversibly destroyed, and the body can't ever breathe on its own. Brain-dead bodies are dead.

The law protects the personal feelings of the survivors. Unless murder, suicide, or accidental death is suspected, the next of kin must consent before an autopsy can be conducted. While the body isn't "property," the next of kin generally wants to see that the body is treated properly, and if it isn't, a suit for intentional infliction of emotional distress is possible.

RESOURCES

Organizations

Children's Hospice International
700 Princess St.
Alexandria, VA 22314
(703)684-0330
(800)242-4453
Call or write for information about counseling regarding hospice care for terminally ill children. CHI makes referrals to hospice programs, self-help groups, and other local agencies.

Choice in Dying
200 Varick St.
New York, NY 10014-4810
(212)366-5540
(800)989-WILL
Call or write for sample advance directives for every state. Trained professionals answer the toll-free line and provide personal advice, legal assistance, free advance-directive documents, and the latest information on end-of-life laws and regulations in each state. The organization also maintains a network of volunteers in states and a speakers bureau. Publications include *A Good Death* ($11.95), *Questions and Answers: Advance Directive and End-of-Life Planning* ($5.95), and *Medical Treatments and Your Living Will* ($2.95).

Compassionate Friends
P.O. Box 3696
Oak Brook, IL 60522-3696
(708)990-0010
This mutual assistance self-help organization offers friendship and understanding to bereaved parents and siblings through about 650 local chapters. Pamphlets include "Surviving Your Child's Suicide," "When a Brother or Sister Dies," and "Stillbirth, Miscarriage and Infant Death: Understanding Grief." Call or write for a publications list and information on membership and local organizations.

Hospice Education Institute
P.O. Box 713
Essex, CT 06426-0713
(800)331-1620 (HospiceLink)
Call or write for information and referrals on hospice and related care.

National Hospice Organization
1901 North Moore St.
Arlington, VA 22209
(703)243-5900
Hospice Helpline (for referrals):
(800)658-8898
This clearinghouse of information about hospices publishes a national directory and will provide information and referrals to people who write or call.

Publications

"Consumer Guide to Hospice Care." A 32-page booklet available from National Consumers League, 815 15th St., NW, Washington, DC 20005 (202)639-8140. $4.

The Hospice Handbook, by Larry Beresford (Little, Brown, 1993). $12.95.

How We Die, by Sherwin Nuland (Knopf, 1994). $24.

Living Wills and More, by Terry J. Barnett (John Wiley and Sons, 1992). $16.95.

"Medicare Hospice Benefits." Free pamphlet available from Social Security Administration offices and the Health Care Financing Administration, 6325 Security Blvd., Baltimore, MD 21207 (410)966-3000.

Unreformed Health Care

18

By Ron Pollack

You can benefit from being an active and knowledgeable participant in your health care, as *Health Care Choices* clearly demonstrates. Such participation maximizes the likelihood that you will receive—and can pay for—the care you need. Even so, *systemic* failures limit your ability to achieve the health-care security your family deserves. Responding to that situation is one of your greatest challenges as a health-care consumer.

In 1994, with the costs of care rising two to three times faster than inflation over the past two decades, and with more and more people lacking health insurance, most Americans solidly desired meaningful reform. Nevertheless, after a lengthy, sometimes acrimonious, debate, Congress failed to take any steps to improve the U.S. health insurance system. Interest groups spent $300 million to influence the debate in Congress, according to an estimate by *Newsweek,* with the overwhelming portion of this going to defeat reform. Opponents succeeded in delaying true health security for the time being.

What does this mean for the average consumer? What can you expect from the health-care system in the years to come? Unfortunately, the probable answers are:
• Considerably higher costs for everyone;
• Less comprehensive health insurance for most people;
   and
• Increasing insecurity about your family's future health.

Health Insecurity

Health-care costs are the driving engine of the growing crisis in health insurance. For many Americans, these costs are often hidden: some payments do not come *directly* out of your pocket, and others do not *appear* to finance health care. Two methods of paying for health care—employer-paid insurance and taxes—are illustrative. Too few workers fully appreciate that employer-paid health care almost inevitably contributes to stagnant or lower wages, especially when employers face skyrocketing premiums for health insurance. Similarly, rising health-care costs help push up the price tags for Medicare and Medicaid, both of which

Ron Pollack is the Executive Director of Families USA.

are financed by tax dollars.

In fact, if you added up all the different ways that you pay for health care, the sum would undoubtedly create "sticker shock." In 1980, Americans—directly and indirectly—spent $2,590 per family for health care. By 1993, the figure had almost tripled to $7,739. Current projections suggest that the average family will spend over $14,500 in the year 2000.

For working families, higher costs for care are almost inevitable. Already, taken together, employers spend more for worker health benefits than U.S. firms receive in profits. Concerned about ever-mounting health-care bills, businesses will undoubtedly seek to pass much of the growing burden on to their employees, asking them to pay higher shares of the premiums, higher deductibles, and higher copayments—and they will ask their employees to settle for less coverage. In addition, more companies will require workers and their families to join managed-care plans or specific networks of health-care providers, diminishing your opportunities to choose your own doctors and other caregivers.

For beneficiaries of public programs, especially the tens of millions of elders and lower-income Americans who receive care through Medicare and Medicaid, the prospects are especially grim. Because health care is the fastest growing segment of the federal budget, Congress is considering a variety of ways to cut back these programs and apply the savings to reducing the deficit. The bulk of the proposed cuts would reduce payments to health-care providers. As a result, fewer doctors and others will accept and treat Medicare and Medicaid patients, and those who continue to serve program beneficiaries will make up lost revenue by charging people with private insurance more.

For more information on Medicare and Medicaid, turn to Chapters 3 *and* 8

The bottom line? Less health security for almost every family. Already, over 50 million people lose or lack health insurance during at least part of each year. Every month, over 2 million Americans lose their health insurance. Although many people lose insurance "only" temporarily, any lapse in coverage places a family in jeopardy—perhaps leading people to defer necessary diagnoses and treatments. As the price of care continues to skyrocket, and as employers offer diminishing insurance benefits, more and more people will suffer these temporary—and longer-term—losses of insurance.

Holes in the Net

Because the U.S. health system fails so many citizens, millions of American workers *with* health insurance are locked in jobs they do not want. They fear that a switch in jobs means a loss of health insurance. Some states are responding to this "job-lock" phenomenon with insurance reforms, but the results are mixed at best. In the absence of universal coverage and effective cost controls, it is questionable that such insurance reform will reduce the number of people without health insurance.

Moreover, in the absence of reform, even insured people face significant gaps in coverage. For example, over 70 million Americans pay the full cost of prescription drugs out of their own pockets. This number includes most senior citizens: Medicare covers only prescription drugs during a hospital stay, and few private Medigap insurance policies offer cost-effective coverage for these medicines. The costs of prescription drugs have risen even faster than those for health care as a whole, and many seniors today forego filling prescriptions ordered by their doctors.

Similarly, the coverage for long-term care is abysmal. Medicare provides no assistance to people with chronic disabilities requiring long-term care. Only about 6 percent of America's seniors and 1 percent of the overall population have private insurance for long-term care. The only significant protection is Medicaid, but that program will help you only if you spend down your savings to poverty levels—and, even then, the coverage excludes the bulk of home care and community-based care that people want the most. With the costs of a nursing home averaging $35,000 per year—and much more in most urban areas—coverage for long-term care remains a major gap in the U.S. health insurance system. The same situation applies to the often

Delaying Tactics

Inflation in health care has slowed over the past two years while health-care reform remained near the top of the federal agenda, with costs rising at twice, rather than three times, the rate of inflation. Still, price hikes will likely accelerate once again, now that the prospects for reform have diminished. During past debates on health reform, insurance companies and health providers moderated their bills to demonstrate that voluntary, private-sector changes could solve runaway costs. Once the "threat" of health reform diminished, prices again soared.

major expenses involved with home care.

Other serious gaps also persist. For example, private insurers tend to issue "sickness polices" rather than health assurance. That is, they devote far too little attention to preventive care. Fortunately, the proliferation of managed care—and health maintenance organizations in particular—may improve this situation somewhat and lead to more emphasis on primary care, early screening for diseases, and other preventive measures. But there is far less reason for optimism regarding many other gaps. Consider the prospects for the family of someone who experiences a major sickness or injury or requires care for a mental illness:

• Most insurance policies "cap" family coverage. Once the family reaches the cap, the insurer will not pay any more bills. A catastrophic illness or serious accident can easily exceed this cap, causing irreparable, severe financial damage to the entire family.

• Insurance coverage for mental illnesses is but a pale comparison to the protection that's available to those with a physical malady.

The Active Consumer

The unreformed health-care system adds to the costs, and diminishes the security, for consumers. Worsening conditions will only heighten the demand for true health reform.

To hasten the day when the failures of the health-care system are remedied, many consumers are joining with others to achieve reforms that respond to families' needs. While attending to the immediate situation of your own family, you can become active in these efforts in many ways.

How can you play such a larger role? Of course, no answers are uniformly applicable to everyone, but here are a few suggestions:

• If your state has a health-reform coalition, take part in its activities. These consumer and advocacy organizations provide an opportunity for people from many different backgrounds to work together for better health care.

For more information on long-term care and insurance for it, turn to Chapter **12**

For more information on home care, turn to Chapter **13**

Locked In

According to a survey by Lou Harris and Associates for the Henry J. Kaiser Family Foundation, one in five workers feels locked into his or her current job because a family member has a health problem that may prevent their getting coverage from a new insurer.

18

For a list of reform coalitions, turn to the resources at the end of Chapter **19**

• Join a national consumer organization—such as the American Association of Retired Persons, Consumer's Union, and the League of Women Voters. Their staffs keep up with the latest developments related to health reform and can help and often involve members—locally and nationally—in efforts to improve the health-care system. The same is true of the national headquarters of labor unions, various religious organizations, and groups that serve people with specific diseases, such as the Alzheimer's Association, the Epilepsy Foundation, and the National Mental Health Association.

• Contact one of the many organizations of health-care providers that strongly support a system centered on the needs of consumers. A few examples are the American Nurses Association, the American College of Physicians, the American Academy of Family Physicians, the American Academy

For information on contacting provider organizations, turn to the resources at the end of each chapter, especially Chapter ▼**4**

T I P

Take Part
As long as today's many gaps in health insurance persist, consumers will remain insecure. By actively participating in local, state, and federal debates on health-care policy, you can help ensure the creation of a system that meets the needs of your entire family.

of Pediatrics, and the Catholic Health Association. These groups can inform you about initiatives in health-care policy.

• Contact Families USA Foundation. In particular, Families USA operates *a.s.a.p.*, a network of activists who receive timely information about pending health-reform issues, updates on important policy developments at the federal level, notices of key state-level activities, and action alerts that encourage consumer input on congressional deliberations. This is a free service for people who consistently write letters, send telegrams, or make phone calls to public officials and get at least five other people to do likewise. For more information on *a.s.a.p.* or on joining Families USA, write to: Families USA, 1334 G St., NW, Washington, DC 20005.

Partners in
Health

Mutual Help, Going On-Line, and More Resources for the Health Care Consumer

By Martha S. Grover

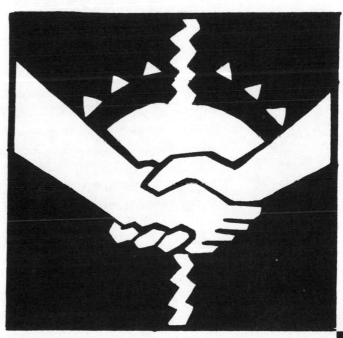

19

One year ago, the *O'Briens* found out that their son Christopher has trachealstenosis, a rare throat disorder that strikes only a few children worldwide. Since then, Christopher, now nine, has been in and out of hospitals and gone through surgery many times. At home, he needs around-the-clock care, sometimes from a visiting nurse but more and more often from his parents. The O'Briens have already fought several battles with their insurance company over Christopher's medical care. Despite everything that has been done, Christopher's doctors remain unsure about his case. They recommend that the family travel 1,500 miles from their home in Oklahoma to a New York hospital, where a doctor has treated children like Christopher—with mixed results. The O'Briens are inclined to do what the doctors suggest, but they are unsure. And how can they cope with caring for Christopher for an indefinite amount of time far from home?

• *Susan Hart* has had a mastectomy for breast cancer and is beginning to think she can't face another medical procedure. Due to start chemotherapy and radiation, she is having second thoughts. She has heard that chemotherapy is awful and makes people really sick. Whenever she tries to discuss her concerns with her husband, he doesn't seem to understand. After all, Hart's oncologist has recommended these treatments and explained them to her. But she fears dying despite the treatments.

• Six months after being diagnosed with genital herpes, *Rob Thompson* is still in shock. The doctor at a clinic for sexually transmitted diseases was comforting and understanding about the initial painful outbreak, but Thompson can't help thinking that he'll have to deal with the virus for the rest of his life. He's had three more outbreaks. The whole experience has paralyzed him, and he can't even talk to his best friend about it.

• *Lillian Rosenberg's* 70-year-old husband has suffered from Alzheimer's disease for 18 months. As his primary caregiver, she has taken care of him day and night, making sure that he doesn't forget to take his medication or leave

Martha S. Grover, MPH, is project associate for Health Care Choices for Today's Consumer.

the house without her. She is exhausted—and she knows his condition will get worse. Mrs. Rosenberg is overwhelmed by all of the tasks that he used to handle—paying the bills, house repairs, planning their future.

• *Florence Allen's* son faces an emergency. Twelve months ago, he was wounded as a bystander to a shooting and received emergency surgery at a Boston hospital through its free-care pool. The hospital told him to return soon for more surgery, but when he did so, he was told to pay up front for the second operation. Because he can't afford to pay, he has gone without the surgery for a year.

Each of these people can improve their situations and relieve some of the stress and isolation they are experiencing. And they can take many of the steps on their own—and with other people like themselves.

PART I: MUTUAL ASSISTANCE

When faced with a personal health-care crisis, over 15 million people every year turn to a support group composed of other people in similar situations. Members of such self-help or mutual-aid groups provide one another with emotional support and practical information far beyond what a physician or professional therapist can offer. The groups are informal and member-run, made up of 10 to 20 people who face a common problem themselves—such as addiction, illness, or a handicap—or who provide care for someone else with such a problem. These groups don't replace standard medical care, but members do benefit from mutual support and advice based on the vast experiential knowledge and practical coping skills each person has acquired. The groups are voluntary and nonprofit, and dues are minimal.

The self-help concept started with Alcoholics Anonymous 50 years ago. Over the past 15 years, it has spread to support people with a wide variety of problems, and national networks have formed out of many local community groups. Some examples include the Well Spouse Foundation for spouses of people with a chronic illness, Compassionate Friends for parents who have lost a child,

19

Food Addicts Anonymous for overeaters, and Us Too for men with prostate cancer.

Members pool information on resources that are available. They also save money as they discover cheaper, more efficient, and more effective ways of treating an illness, getting care, buying medical equipment and other supplies, and avoiding unnecessary procedures. In many cases, members also benefit from the knowledge of professionals by inviting a physician or specialist to speak to the group, rather than each person paying the doctor for an individual consultation.

Almost all self-help groups are controlled by the members themselves rather than professionals or others outside the group. This ensures that the activities of the group address the expressed needs of the members, rather than needs as perceived by others, and it also provides members with a sense of ownership, responsibility, community, and power. Often, members become advocates for improved research and health-care services, increased state and federal funding of programs, and public education about a specific illness or condition.

Groups use different methods to assist people in need. They may hold educational seminars, one-on-one exchanges, or social gatherings. Many offer hotlines for people with immediate needs, as well as outreach programs in which members make unsolicited offers of help. Some groups are more formal than others, with written protocols about how meetings are run. The tight structure and approach of Alcoholics Anonymous are favored by certain groups, while others prefer less formal programs. Many groups have a religious or spiritual focus; others are more secular.

A Remedy That Works

Having someone to turn to for empathy, advice, assistance, and affection can make a big difference in your ability to cope with and survive an illness. People who maintain strong bonds with family and friends have lower death and illness rates, and some researchers believe that social support encourages a positive attitude that helps patients in their fight against illness. This is true for a variety of diseases and health conditions, as a number of preliminary studies show:

• In 1989, the medical journal *The Lancet* published a study by Dr. David Spiegel of Stanford University. He found that social support might help cancer patients live longer. Eighty-six women with advanced breast cancer received standard medical treatment; of these, fifty also participated in weekly group sessions and learned self-hypnosis for controlling pain. The patients who attended meetings regularly for one year lived an average of 18 months longer than patients who attended no meetings. They also experienced less pain and depression.

• In 1992, Duke University Medical Center researchers found that cardiac patients who lacked a spouse or confidant were three times as likely as patients who were married or had a close friend to die within five years of the diagnosis of heart disease. Writing in the *Journal of the American Medical Association,* the researchers concluded that "a support group may be as effective as costly medical treatment. Simply put, having someone to talk to is very powerful medicine."

• A UCLA study published in *The Archives of General Psychiatry* in 1993 found that being part of a support group tripled the chance of survival over a five-year period for patients in the early stages of skin cancer. Patients in the support group experienced fewer deaths and fewer recurrences of the melanoma. The support group met once a week for six sessions to share practical advice about protecting skin from the sun and to learn about coping with anxiety and depression. They also offered one another support during emotional crises. The patients in the comparison group received standard advice from their doctors. All patients were initially treated by surgically removing the cancerous growths. The study also discovered that six months after the group sessions ended, two-thirds of the patients in the support group showed an increase of 25 percent or more of natural cancer-fighting cells in their immune systems. No increase occurred for the members of the comparison group.

Less Depressed, Less Stressed

Older diabetics who learned self-care and attended mutual-support sessions faired better over a two-year study that compared them with diabetics who attended self-care sessions but not the support groups, and with a third group who attended neither. The members of the first group were less depressed and less stressed and rated their quality of life higher than those in the other two groups, according to researchers at the University of Iowa. The study was published in 1992 in the *Journal of the American Geriatrics Society.*

Finding a Group

You can find a mutual-help group in many ways. Start by investigating some of the more common resources listed at the end of this chapter. Call a national office or hotline to get referrals to the local chapter or affiliate. Look in the phone book. Ask your health-care provider for suggestions or contact a hospital social service department, the local health department, mental health department, or United Way office.

National self-help organizations can also refer you to a regional clearinghouse in your state. Regional clearinghouses serve about half the country and can provide detailed information to patients or physicians about available groups. They can usually give better information about smaller, one-of-a-kind community groups than the national clearinghouses can.

Many national, state, and local organizations will assist you in starting a new mutual-help group. These organiza-

---

Visit the Group

"The quality of individual self-help groups will differ, sometimes even among those with the same name. Contact and visit the group to see if it is for you. While initial research reflects the value of self-help groups, the ultimate evaluations and very survival of any self-help group is determined by those who attend it and decide to stay and contribute to it."

—from the *Self-Help Sourcebook*

T I P

National Self Help

Two national clearinghouses have phone numbers and information on groups all over the country. Call the American Self-Help Clearinghouse at (201)625-7101 or the National Self-Help Clearinghouse at (212)354-8525.

STATEWIDE SELF-HELP CLEARINGHOUSES

- ◆ California: (310)825-1799 or (800)222-LINK (in-state only)
- ◆ Connecticut: (203)789-7645
- ◆ Illinois: (312)368-9070
- ◆ Iowa: (515)576-5870 or (800)952-4777 (in-state only)
- ◆ Kansas: (800)445-0116
- ◆ Massachusetts: (413)545-2313
- ◆ Michigan: (517)484-7373 or (800)777-5556
- ◆ Nebraska: (402)476-9668
- ◆ New Jersey: (201)625-7101, (800)367-6274 (in-state only), TDD:(201)625-9053
- ◆ New York: (212)586-5770
- ◆ Oregon and Washington: (503)222-5555
- ◆ Pennsylvania: (717)961-1234
- ◆ Texas: (512)454-3706
- ◆ Washington, DC area: (703)941-5465

tions may provide technical support, how-to materials, advice, contacts, and perhaps even some start-up funds. For instance, the American Self-Help Clearinghouse will assist people who want to start a group that isn't already in existence anywhere. Its publication, *The Self-Help Sourcebook: Finding and Forming Mutual Aid Self-Help Groups,* is a good source of advice on organizing groups. The book also identifies many model groups that can be consulted.

Computerized Self-Help

Electronic bulletin boards and computer on-line services are a popular resource for people who may have difficulty meeting face to face, including some disabled people, people with AIDS, agoraphobics, people living in rural areas, full-time caregivers, and others who may not have the time or means to travel to a meeting. On-line services offer people who have a computer, modem, and telecommunications software the opportunity to meet, share information, and ask and answer questions from home.

Free bulletin board systems (BBSs) are popping up daily. Already, hundreds of them across the country are available with only a local call. Users usually leave messages or post questions that get an answer within a few days. A few examples are HEX (Handicapped Users of Exchange), Easy-Does-It Recovery, Neuropsychology-Bound Bulletin Board (for head injury and stroke victims), and many AIDS bulletin boards.

You can also find self-help through any of a number of national commercial computer networks that charge on a monthly or hourly basis. Some larger self-help organizations have started their own networks as well. For example, the American Self-Help Clearinghouse responds to requests for information on CompuServe's "Self-Help Support" section No. 17 of the Health and Fitness Forum. Also on CompuServe, the National Organization for Rare Disorders maintains the NORD Rare Disease Database.

Many large public libraries and most medical school and hospital libraries have access to Medline, the largest biomedical journal database in the world. Call the National

Network of Libraries of Medicine at (800)338-RMLS (338-7657) to find a library near you.

With your computer, modem, and a database software package, you can access a wealth of information to assist your research. For instance, Grateful Med software helps you search for in-depth articles on any medical subject. For a free Grateful Med demonstration disk and brochure, call (800)638-8480 or (301)496-6308.

Another network software package called CHESS (Comprehensive Health Enhancement Support System) can put you in touch with other patients and 24-hour access to a library of medical information. CHESS can also help people choose among different treatments for AIDS/HIV infections, breast cancer, adult children of alcoholics, stress management, and other conditions. For more information, call Health Decisions Plus at (800)454-4465. CHESS software packages cost $295.

You can "ask" health-related computer-based encyclopedia software packages about symptoms, to depict procedures, to offer possible diagnoses, and to suggest treatment using video clips, text, and anatomical diagrams. Examples of such packages are:

- *Dr. Schueler's Home Medical Advisor Pro* (Pixel Perfect, CD-ROM, $99.95; diskette $87.50);
- *Medical HouseCall* (Applied Medical Informatics, $99.95); *and*
- *Mayo Clinic Family Health Book* (IVI Publishing, $59.95).

A number of consumer-oriented commercial data brokers are available to run searches on health topics. Most use *Medline* and other smaller databases. Searches can be costly, ranging from $25 to $275.

In addition:
- *The Directory of Online Health-Care Databases,* is available for $38, call (503)471-1627. It includes databases on a broad range of health issues.
- *The Health Resource, Inc.,* 564 Locust St., Conway, AR 72032 (501)329-5272 provides clients with in-depth research reports on specific medical problems, including

On-Line Sources

Here's a very brief sampling of health-related organizations with on-line information services:

◆ *Boston Women's Health Book Collective:* E-mail address is bwhbc@igc.apc.org.

◆ *National Association of People With AIDS:* NAPWA-Link. Call (202)898-0141 or write 1413 K St., NW, 10th Floor, Washington, DC 20005-3405.

◆ *New Parents Network:* Call their BBS direct at (602)326-9345, or write to P.O. Box 44226, Tucson, AZ 85733-4226 to receive a local number.

◆ *SeniorNet:* For computer-using older adults. Call (415)750-5030 for more information or write 399 Arguello Blvd., San Francisco, CA 94118.

◆ *World Institute on Disability:* WID Net. For information call (510)763-4100 or write to 510 16th St., First Floor, Oakland, CA 94612.

information on conventional and alternative treatment options, self-help measures, resource organizations, and specialists. It also updates reports annually for a fee, sends out news bulletins on new information, and publishes a newsletter. Reports cost $175 or $275, plus shipping.

- *Medical Information Service,* Palo Alto Medical Foundation, 400 Channing Ave., Palo Alto, CA 94301 (800)999-1999 or (415)853-6000 has a Consumer Guide to Medical Information available for free to assist you in conducting a medical information search. You can also order a search from them for $89.
- *Medical Data Source,* 5959 W. Century Blvd., Suite 1000, Los Angeles, CA 90045 (800)776-4MDS or (310)641-3111 offers easy-to-use information on medical conditions, prescription drugs, and physician backgrounds, as well as referrals to health facilities in your community such as nursing homes, rehabilitation centers, and support groups. Subscription rates vary but are usually under $48 per year.
- *Planetree Health Resource Center,* 2040 Webster St., San Francisco, CA 94115 (415)923-3681, provides an in-depth packet on a particular illness for $100, a basic packet on common conditions for $20, or a Medline search for $35. It will also put you in touch with other organizations as well as with people who have the same condition as you. The center provides information on conventional and alternative treatments.
- *Medical Data Exchange,* 4730 Galice Rd., Merlin, OR 97532 (503)471-1627, offers a search on its own consumer health databases, MDX Health Digest and Per-

> **T I P**
>
> **Finding Bulletin Boards**
>
> *Personal computer newspapers and magazines sometimes have BBS listings. To get a phone listing of over 300 health-related BBSs, send $5 and a legal size self-addressed envelope to Ed Del Grosso, P.O. Box 632, Collegeville, PA 19426, or contact his Black Bag BBS by modem at (610)454-7396 to download the list. Many BBSs carry newsletters, news items, and educational programs, and they also facilitate networking.*

sonal Medical Advisor, for $25. It also offers a Medline search for $48. A more extensive customized search costs $60 an hour.

Mutual Assistance and Consumer Advocacy

Several organizations have formed not around one single issue but around a variety of health issues that affect many diverse individuals. They tend to focus on people who are uninsured or otherwise underserved by the health-care system. One of the largest and oldest of these groups is Health Care For All (HCFA) in Massachusetts. Its experience illustrates the benefits that can result when health-care consumers unite around a common goal.

HCFA reaches people through issues close to their own lives. For example, Dan Sizemore has post-polio syndrome and needs reliable, affordable care; he wanted to know how health-care reform would affect him personally. He joined HCFA's Community Leaders Project and met people with similar concerns. Together, they have learned about the health-care system and come to recognize that their own health-care questions relate to the fragmentation and chaos of the system as a whole. And they are determined to change that system for themselves and others. In the past year, HCFA has:

• Helped over 4,000 callers get needed health care;
• Launched the Boston Health Access Project to allocate more health resources for community-based health services;
• Informed over 2,700 people of their rights to free hospital care; *and*
• Cofounded the Massachusetts Women's Health Care Coalition to ensure that health-care reform responds to the needs of women.

HCFA reaches and serves many victims of the health-care crisis through an "intake and referral" process that centers on the Health Care Access Telephone Helpline. Trained volunteers assist people who call about a wide variety of needs—from finding out about low-cost prescription drugs to advice on applying for free health care to keeping

Anger and Action

The basis of Health Care for All is individuals. People contact the group when the health-care system fails them in a personal way. They are confused about how to get care—and blame themselves for their difficulty.

After they learn more, they become angry. They realize that the fault lies with a system that fails to provide quality, affordable health care to everyone. And they become strong advocates for long-term reforms of that system.

their insurance coverage after losing a job.

However, HCFA does more than respond to phone calls. People served by established health-care programs and institutions generally want to protect their access to care and will fight for a program that provides it. HCFA reaches them through direct mail, organizational networks, leafleting at unemployment offices, and radio ads and newspaper articles.

HCFA also produces and distributes a variety of materials and publications that explain changes in health-care policies and services, translating difficult subjects into language understood by the lay person. These educational and outreach materials keep consumers informed of their rights to health care and help them better understand the issues and contribute to the debate.

Finding Solutions

Self-help groups, computer on-line services, health databases, and consumer health organizations can improve people's lives and even reduce health-care bills. Used wisely, these resources can help you find and decide on the most appropriate care based on the most up-to-date information.

How does all this benefit the O'Briens, Susan Hart, Rob Thompson, Lillian Rosenberg, and Florence Allen?

• On the advice of one of Christopher's nurses, *Mrs. O'Brien* called NORD, the National Organization for Rare Disorders. In a few days, she received a packet of information—including a report on current research and the phone number of a national support group for parents of children with trachealstenosis. Soon she talked with parents in Texas who had taken their own child to New York for surgery, and they shared their experiences with the O'Briens. They offered advice on cutting costs and making Christopher's care at home more efficient, traveling with all of his medical gear, staying cheaply in New York, and knowing what to expect from the surgery and the surgeons. Most importantly, they gave the O'Briens assurance that they had looked at all their options and were doing the right thing.

• *Susan Hart* called the local chapter of the American

A Precious Resource

In 1993, *Financial World* featured HCFA as one of the nation's top non-profit organizations in an article entitled "Finding Gems Among the Rhinestones." According to *Financial World*, "This lobbying and advocacy organization is trying to make health care accessible for those who have had a hard time getting it, particularly those with low incomes and in the minority community."

19

Cancer Society, which referred her to a support group for breast-cancer patients. She went to the next meeting and found a group of people who understood her hesitations and concerns; their support helped Hart work through her depression. The women in the group shared their experiences with chemotherapy and radiation, lessening her fear of the treatment. She learned about various types of chemotherapy drugs and was later able to discuss those options with her oncologist.

• Tired of feeling sorry for himself, *Rob Thompson* dug out pamphlets he had stuffed in a drawer and started to read about the herpes virus. On the back of one pamphlet was the toll-free number of the American Social Health Association. He called and got the number of a herpes support group nearby. Initially, Thompson hesitated. What if he knew someone there? What would they talk about? He hated speaking in public and couldn't imagine talking to strangers about something so personal. Finally, Thompson decided to just go. A little uncomfortable at first, he gradually welcomed the opportunity to talk to others coping with herpes. Group members offered all kinds of practical everyday advice on treatment, managing stress, talking to prospective sexual partners, and preventing herpes from consuming his life. A year later, he is attending meetings every few months to get up-to-date information—and to share his experiences with newcomers to the group.

• Through her computer modem, *Lillian Rosenberg* connected with a caregiver support group she found out about from the local Alzheimer's Association. She could reach it at all hours of the day, particularly at night when she'd become most frustrated. Through the bulletin-board system, she found out about respite care that would give her a break from the 24-hour care she provides for her husband and learned more about what to expect as his disease progresses.

• *Florence Allen* called the Health Care for All helpline. HCFA immediately phoned the hospital, which admitted and treated Florence's son a few days later. Now a board member of HCFA, Allen helps make hospitals better serve the people who live near them.

Families USA: Guiding Your Health Care Choices

Families USA introduces three incomparable guides to health care.
Order one for yourself or a friend!

Health Care Choices for Today's Consumer: The Families USA Guide to Quality & Cost
Marc S. Miller, Editor—Take charge of your family's health care with this step-by-step sourcebook. *Foreword by Hillary Rodham Clinton.*

Plus these companion books!

Health Care Choices in the Boston Area: The Families USA Guide to Quality & Cost
Martha S. Grover & Marc S. Miller, Editors

Health Care Choices in the Washington Area: The Families USA Guide to Quality & Cost
Martha S. Grover & Marc S. Miller, Editors

The first in a series of metropolitan health-care guidebooks, these companions to the national edition provide local facts, listings, regulations, and resources for consumers in the greater Boston and Washington, D.C. areas.

Other Metro Guides being planned for publication include San Francisco, New Orleans, Atlanta, Seattle, and more!

• Stay a step ahead! Place your order for next year's update of
  Health Care Choices for Today's Consumer at 10% off!
• Add your voice to the fight for better health care! Join Families USA Today!
• Talk to us! Send questions and comments to the Families USA address on the attached postcard.

Order Now! Call 1-800-699-6960 or mail the order form on the other side.
(Allow 3–4 weeks for delivery)

NO POSTAGE
NECESSARY
IF MAILED
IN THE
UNITED STATES

BUSINESS REPLY MAIL
FIRST CLASS MAIL   PERMIT NO. 7250   WASHINGTON DC

POSTAGE WILL BE PAID BY ADDRESSEE

HEALTH CARE CHOICES
FAMILIES USA FOUNDATION
30 WINTER ST.
BOSTON MA 02108-9915

☐ Yes! I want to make the best health-care decisions possible! Pease send me:

TOTAL

_____ copies of *Health Care Choices for Today's Consumer*   @ $14.95 ea. $_____

_____ copies of *Health Care Choices in the Boston Area*   @ $10.95 ea. $_____

_____ copies of *Health Care Choices in the Washington Area*   @ $10.95 ea. $_____

Order the two-volume set: *Health Care Choices for Today's Consumer* <u>plus</u> one of the companion guides and get a great deal—*Both for just $23.95!*

_____ set(s) including the *Boston Area* companion   @ $23.95 ea. $_____

_____ set(s) including the *Washington Area* companion   @ $23.95 ea. $_____

_____ I'd like to place an advance order for the 1996 edition of *Health Care Choices for Today's Consumer* at 10% off this year's price!   @ $13.45 ea. $_____

Add $3 for shipping and handling of the first book or set, $.50 for each additional book.   Shipping: $_____

Total: $_____

_____ Please send me information about Families USA.

_____ I'd like to join Families USA! (Use your credit card or mail a check for $25 or more to the address on the attached postcard. Make checks payable to *Families USA Foundation*.)

FOLD HERE AND TAPE CLOSED BEFORE MAILING

NAME

MAILING ADDRESS

CITY

STATE   ZIP

TELEPHONE

PAYMENT

Charge to: ☐ MasterCard   ☐ Visa

Expiration Date: ☐☐☐☐

SIGNATURE

Families USA Foundation is the national consumer advocacy organization working for comprehensive reform of America's health and long term care systems. We issue reports and analyses designed to educate the public, opinion leaders, and policymakers on issues of critical importance to health-care reform. We also work at the grassroots level to give consumers the opportunity to participate in the health-care debate as full partners, armed with a basic understanding of the issues.

RESOURCES

Self-Help Organizations

Most of these are national organiza-tions that can refer you to affiliates in your area. Many are also a good source of information and published materi-als.

AIDS National Hotline
Centers for Disease Control and Prevention
(800)342-AIDS
(800)243-7889 TDD
Call for general information and publications on HIV infections, as well as for referrals to national and local organizations.

Alcoholics Anonymous
P.O. Box 459
Grand Central Station
New York, NY 10163
Write for free copies of publications. For a local group, look in the yellow pages of your phone book.

Alliance of Genetic Support Groups
(800)336-GENE
Call or write for information on genetic illnesses.

Alzheimer's Association
(800)272-3900
Call for referrals to local chapters and support groups and for a list of publications.

American Medical Centers Cancer Information and Counseling Line
(800)525-3777
Professional counselors answer calls from all over about family dynamics, treatment, side effects, support groups, financial assistance, and emotional effects from cancer diag-nosis.

American Association of Suicidology
2459 S. Ash
Denver, CO 80222
(303)692-0985
Call or write for referral to local crisis and suicide prevention centers.

American Cancer Society
1599 Clifton Rd., NE
Atlanta, GA 30329
(404)320-3333
(800)227-2345
Call or write for referrals to pro-grams and local chapters.

American Diabetes Association
1660 Duke St.
Alexandria, VA 22314
(800)232-3472
Call or write for information and publications.

American Foundation for the Blind
15 West 16th St.
New York, NY 10011
(800)AF-BLIND
(212)620-2000
(212)620-2158 TDD
(212)620-2147 (NY residents)
Call or write for publications on blindness and visual impairment.

American Heart Association
National Center
7320 Greenville Ave.
Dallas, TX 75231
(214)706-1220
(800)242-8721
Call or write to connect with a local affiliate and for pamphlets on cardiac health, exercise, nutrition, and classes in cardiopulmonary resuscitation.

American Lung Association
1740 Broadway
New York, NY 10019
(800)LUNG-USA
Call or write for publications and referrals to smoking cessation pro-grams and local chapters.

American Parkinson's
Disease Association
60 Bay St.
Staten Island, NY 10301
(800)223-2732
Call or write for information.

American Self-Help Clearinghouse
St. Clares-Riverside Medical Center
25 Pocono Rd.
Denville, NJ 07834
(800)367-6274 (New Jersey only)
(201)625-7101
(201)625-9053 TDD
Call to locate local self-help groups or to receive help starting your own self-help group if a similar type doesn't already exist. For a copy of *The Self-Help Sourcebook: Finding and Forming Mutual Aid Self-Help Groups,* a national directory of self-help groups, send $10.00.

American Social Health Association
P.O. Box 13827
Research Triangle Park, NC 27709

(800)227-8922
Call or write for comprehensive information on any sexually trans-mitted diseases.

American Trauma Society
8903 Presidential Pkwy.
Upper Marlboro, MD 20772
(800)556-7890
(301)420-4189
Call or write for free information on injury prevention and trauma care.

Arthritis Foundation
1314 Spring St., NW
Atlanta, GA 30309
(404)872-7100
(800)283-7800
Call or write for referrals to providers and local chapters.

Candlelighter Childhood
Cancer Foundation
7910 Woodmont Ave.
Bethesda, MD 20814
(301)657-8401
(800)366-2223
Call for referral to a local support group for families of cancer patients. The foundation will do a search for protocols, treatment options, and literature on childhood cancers. Ask for a publications list.

Multiple Sclerosis Society
733 Third Ave.
New York, NY 10017
(800)LEARN-MS
(202)986-3240
Call or write for brochures and referrals to local chapters of the society.

National Association of Anorexia
Nervosa and Associated Disorders
P.O. Box 271
Highland Park, IL 60035
(312)831-3438
Call or write for information, publi-cations, and referrals.

National Bone Marrow
Donor Program
(800)654-1247
Call for information on transplants, a directory of bone-marrow donors, where to get tested to be a donor, and what donating bone marrow involves.

19

National Cancer Institute
National Institutes of Health
Building 31, Room 10A24
Bethesda, MD 20892-3100
(800)4-CANCER (422-6237)
Call or write for general information on treatments, services, and provider referrals. A list of treatment centers and about 1,500 experimental programs, physicians, and organizations is available through their Physician Data Query (PDQ). It's set up on a computer bulletin board accessible through Grateful Med software *(see page 322)*, or you can request a free PDQ search from the institute.

National Clearinghouse for
Alcohol Information
P.O. Box 3245
Rockville, MD 20852
(301)468-2600
Call or write for free publications.

National Clearinghouse for
Infants with Disabilities and
Life-Threatening Conditions
Center for Developmental Disabilities
Department of Pediatrics
University of South Carolina
Columbia, SC 29208
(800)922-9234
Call or write to find out about services for infants with disabilities, including referrals.

National Mental Health
Consumers' Self-Help
Clearinghouse
311 South Juniper St.
Philadelphia, PA 19107
(800)553-4539
(215)735-6082
The clearinghouse handles inquiries from consumers, family members, professionals, and others about locating mental health self-help groups. It also offers technical assistance for developing self-help groups. Call or write for a publications list on a wide variety of mental health topics.

National Organization for Rare
Disorders (NORD)
P.O. Box 8923
New Fairfield, CT 06812-1783
(800)999-NORD
(203)746-6518
Call for one of 950 reports on lesser

known diseases. The reports, written in lay terms, cover symptoms, therapies, current research, and support groups. The first two reports are free, and subsequent reports cost $3.75 each.

National Self-Help Clearinghouse
25 West 43rd St.
New York, NY 10036
(212)354-8525
This information runs research projects and provides technical assistance to people wishing to start a group. It also provides referrals to self-help regional clearinghouses and self-help groups around the country. Send a stamped, self-addressed envelope for a list of support group information. The clearinghouse publishes a quarterly newsletter, "The Self-Help Reporter" ($10 for an annual subscription).

National Sexually Transmitted
Disease Hotline
(800)227-8922
Call for written information about preventing and treating STDs and for referrals to local health clinics.

Y-ME Breast Cancer Information
and Support Hotline
(800)221-2141
Call for referrals to local chapters, information on health-care facilities, general information on treatment choices, and opportunities to talk with a survivor of breast cancer.

Other National Resources

American Institute for
Preventive Medicine
30445 Northwestern Hwy.
Farmington Hills, MI 48075
(800)345-2476
(313)539-1800 (in Michigan)
Call or write for free information on stress reduction, weight control, smoking cessation, and health education.

American Medical Radio News
(800)448-9384
Call for a recorded message on a current health topic or feature story in medicine.

Ask-A-Nurse
Call (800)535-1111 for the toll-free number of the Ask-A-Nurse closest

to you. This advice line sponsored by hospitals and managed-care companies provides help and reassurance from nurses on a broad range of questions.

Center for Medical Consumers
237 Thompson St.
New York, NY 10012
(212)674-7105
The center's medical library is open to the public. Call and ask for a publications list on surgical treatments. A monthly newsletter, "Health Facts," provides clear, in-depth, referenced discussions of key health issues. Write for a subscription ($21 per year).

Center for Science in
the Public Interest
1501 16th St., NW
Washington, DC 20036
(202)332-9110
This resource center on nutrition and health publishes "Nutrition Action" a monthly newsletter on health ($24 per year).

Center for the Study of Services
733 15th St., NW
Washington, DC 20005
(202)347-9612
(800)475-7283
A nonprofit organization, the center publishes *Consumers' Checkbook* magazines for the Washington, DC and San Francisco, CA metropolitan areas. The magazines include consumer ratings and information on dentists, hospitals, HMOs, physicians, and many on non-medical consumer services and products. The cost is $30 for a two-year subscription (4 issues).

Consumer Health Information
Resource Institute
3521 Broadway
Kansas City, MO 64111
(800)821-6671
(816)753-8850
Call or write for referrals to local, regional, and national organizations; information about a patient education library; sources of health information on various conditions, procedures, and medications; and information about health fraud and quackery.

RESOURCES

Consumer Information Center
P.O. Box 100
Pueblo, CO 81002
Write for a free catalog of consumer-information booklets on such subjects as generic drugs, the new food labels, and food and drug interactions.

Consumer Nutrition Hotline
American Dietetic Association
(800)366-1655
Call with questions about nutrition and diet.

Consumers Union/
Consumer Reports
P.O. Box 56356
Boulder, CO 80322
(513)860-1178
Call or write to subscribe to "On Health Newsletter" ($24 per year), a monthly source of practical advice for health consumers on a variety of issues. *Consumer Reports* magazine ($22 per year for 12 issues) also contains much valuable health-care information. Consumers Union's newest books on health care are *Complete Drug Reference* (1994—$39.95) and *The Patient's Guide to Surgery* (1994—$16.95). Call or write for a complete publications list. Reprints of *Consumer Reports* articles on many health topics are available for $3 each. Also, issues of *Consumer Reports* are available for one year after publication. To receive a copy, send $5 to Consumer Reports Back Issues, 101 Truman Ave., Yonkers, NY 10703.

Harvard Medical
School Publications
P.O. Box 420235
Palm Coast, FL 32142
(800)829-9080
Call or write for an annual subscription to any of the following newsletters: *Harvard Health Letter* ($24), *Harvard Heart Letter* ($24), *Harvard Mental Health Letter* ($48), and *Harvard Women's Health Letter* ($24).

International Association for
Medical Assistance for Travelers
417 Center St.
Lewiston, NY 14092
(716)754-4883
Call or write for information on health and travel and for referrals to about 500 physicians in 120 countries, excluding the United States.

Medic Alert Foundation
P.O. Box 1009
Turlock, CA 95381
(209)668-3333
(800)ID-ALERT
Contact the foundation to order emergency medical identification bracelets for a one-time fee or at no cost to those who are qualified.

Medical Data Source
5959 W. Century Blvd., Suite 1000
Los Angeles, CA 90045
(310)641-3111
(800)776-4MDS
Call for an annual membership to receive comprehensive, easy-to-use information on medical conditions, prescription drugs, and physician backgrounds, as well as referrals to health facilities in your community, such as nursing homes, rehabilitation centers, and support groups. Subscription rates vary but are usually under $48 per year.

National Consumer League
815 15th St., NW
Washington, DC 20005
(202)639-8140
Call or write for a list of consumer-oriented publications, including "When Medications Don't Mix" and "Guide to Warning Labels on Non-prescription Medicine" ($1 each).

National Emergency
Medicine Association
(800)332-6362
Call for referrals for emergency medical services, as well as booklets, brochures, free transcripts of radio programs, and basic information on handling emergencies.

National Health
Information Center
U.S. Public Health Service
P.O. Box 1133
Washington, DC 20013-1133
(800)336-4797
(301)565-4167 (in Maryland)
This national toll-free service puts people with health questions in touch with organizations best able to provide answers. Call or write for free literature on such topics as AIDS, cancer, Medicare, Medicaid, health insurance, asthma, allergies, and drug and alcohol abuse. Ask for a publications list and the "Health Finder" list of toll-free numbers.

National Library of Medicine
8600 Rockville Pike
Bethesda, MD 20894
(800)638-8480
Call or write about searches of medical literature on health-related topics.

Office of Minority Health
Resource Center
(800)444-6472
(301)587-1938
Call for free information on minority health-related topics in Spanish and English.

People's Medical Society
462 Walnut St.
Allentown, PA 18102
(215)770-1670
(800)624-8773
Call or write for an extensive catalog of consumer health books on issues ranging from pediatrics to aging. Among many other things, the society publishes: a monthly newsletter ($20 per year); *Dial 800 for Health* ($5.95) listing toll-free health information numbers nationwide; *Getting the Most for Your Medical Dollar*, by Charles B. Inlander and Karla Morales (1991—$15.95), *Your Medical Rights*, by Charles Inlander (1990, 14.95); and *150 Ways to Be a Savvy Medical Consumer* ($4.95).

Prologue
Consumer Health Services, Inc.
(800)DOCTORS
(800)DENTISTS
Call for free physician and dentist referrals in Chicago, Dallas/Fort Worth, Denver, Houston, Kansas City, Miami/Ft. Lauderdale, Philadelphia, Pittsburgh, and Washington, DC. Prologue matches patient needs and doctor specifications on over 500 variables.

Public Citizen Health
Research Group
2000 P. St., NW
Washington, DC 20036
(202)833-3000
HRG publishes many reports about consumer health issues and rights. "Health Letter," published monthly, costs $18.00 per year. Other publications include *Medical Records: Getting Yours* ($10) and *Women's Health Alert*, by Sidney M. Wolfe ($8).

19

RESOURCES

Total Health Foundation
P.O. Box 5
Yakima, WA 98907
(800)348-0120
Call or write for health information on medical topics 24 hours a day.

U.S. Department of Health and Human Services
Agency for Health Care Policy and Research
Publications Clearinghouse
P.O. Box 8547
Silver Spring, MD 20907
(800)358-9295
Call or write for free booklets on common health problems including pain control after surgery, unstable angina, cancer pain, urinary incontinence, enlarged prostate, pressure ulcers, depression, cataracts, sickle cell anemia, and HIV. Pamphlets are available in English and Spanish.

U.S. Food and Drug Administration
Drug Quality Reporting System: (800)332-1088
FDA Drug Hotline: (800)336-4797 to report mislabeled or defective medication.
Medication Errors: (800)233-7767 to report abuses and medication errors.

U.S. Pharmacopoeia Practitioner's Reporting Network
(800)638-6725
(301)881-0256 in Maryland
Call to report problems with medical devices.

Wheaton Regional Library Health Information Center
11701 Georgia Ave.
Wheaton, MD 20902
(301)929-5520
(301)929-5524 TDD
(301)929-5485 Senior Health Info-Line
The library is a leading national resource for health information. It has an extensive walk-in and telephone referral service for a variety of health topics and organizations as well as access to on-line information.

Statewide Health Consumer Organizations
Several states and many communities have consumer health organizations. If your state isn't listed here, contact the Community Health Action Center of Families USA Foundation, 30 Winter St., Boston, MA 02108 (617)338-6035.

California Health Access
1535 Mission St.
San Francisco, CA 94103
(415)431-3430

Health Care For All
30 Winter St.
Boston, MA 02108
(617)350-7279

Louisiana Health Care Campaign
P.O. Box 2228
Baton Rouge, LA 70821
(504)383-8518

Maine People's Alliance
P.O. Box 2490
Augusta, ME 04338
(207)622-7045

Montana People's Action
208 East Main St.
Missoula, MT 59802
(406)728-5297

North Carolina Health Access Coalition
975 Walnut St.
Cary, NC 27511
(919)469-1116

North Carolina Fair Share
530 North Pearson St.
Raleigh, NC 27604
(919)832-7130

Oregon Health Access Project
840 Jefferson St., NE
Salem, OR 97303
(503)581-6830

Tennessee Health Care Campaign
1103 Chapel Ave.
Nashville, TN 37206
(615)227-7500

Texas Alliance for Human Needs
2520 Longview
Austin, TX 78705
(512)474-5019

Vermont Public Interest Group
43 State St.
Montpelier, VT 05602
(802)223-5221

Washington Citizen Action Education and Research Fund
100 South King
Seattle, WA 98104
(206)389-0017

Publications
American Medical Association Family Medical Guide ($29.95) and the *American Medical Association Encyclopedia of Medicine* ($45). Call the AMA at (800)621-8335 to order these books.

Better Health Care for Less, by Neil Shulman and Letitia Schweitzer (Hippocrene Books, 1993). $14.95. A newsletter of the same name is also available for $24 per year. Contact Better Health Care for Less, P.O. Box 15369, Atlanta, GA 30333-0369 (404)816-6548.

The Best Medicine: How to Choose the Top Doctors, the Top Hospitals, and the Top Treatments, by Robert Arnot (Addison-Wesley, 1992). $14.95.

Confronting Life-Threatening Illness. Order from Consumers Index, Pierian Press, P.O. Box 1808, Ann Arbor, MI 48106 (800)678-2435. $12.95.

Consumers Guide to Free Medical Information by Phone and by Mail, by Arthur Winter and Ruth Winter (Prentice Hall, 1993). Call (800)288-4745 for a copy. $14.95.

Consumer Health Information Source Book, by Alan M. Rees and Catherine Hoffman (Oryx Press, 1990). Consult a library for this collection of information sources, clearinghouses, hotlines, and organizations focusing on health issues.

Directory of National Helplines: A Guide to Toll-Free Public Service Numbers, 1994. Order from Consumers Index, Pierian Press, P.O. Box 1808, Ann Arbor, MI 48106 (800)678-2435. $6.00.

RESOURCES

A Doctor's Guide to the Best Medical Care, by Michael Oppenheim (Rodale, 1992). $14.95.

Encyclopedia of Health Information Sources, edited by Alan M. Rees (Gale Research). Check your library for the latest edition.

The Gift of Life. Order from Consumers Index, Pierian Press, P.O. Box 1808, Ann Arbor, MI 48106 (800)678-2435. $12.95. This book covers organ donations.

Health Pages magazine. Consumer health magazines for the St. Louis, Boston, Atlanta, and Pittsburgh metropolitan areas. To subscribe, contact Health Pages at 36 West 15th St., 12th Floor, New York, NY 10011 (212)505-0103. $9.95 for three issues per year.

Healthwise Handbook ($14.95) for children, adolescents and adults to age 50 and *Healthwise for Life* ($14.95) for adults over age 50. These self-care manuals contain comprehensive information on a wide range of illnesses and emergencies as well as dental care, nutrition, stress reduction, mental health and fitness. For copies, contact Healthwise, P.O. Box 1989, Boise, ID 83701, (208)345-1161.

The PDR Family Guide to Prescription Drugs (Medical Economics Data Production Company, 1994). Call (800)331-0072 to order. $24.95.

Prescription Drug Handbook, by AARP Pharmacy Service (Harper, 1992). $17.95.

Smart Patient, Good Medicine: Working With Your Doctor to Get the Best Medical Care, by Richard L. Sribnick and Wayne B. Sribnick (Walker and Co., 1994). $8.95.

Wellness Letter, University of California at Berkeley, Subscription Department, P.O. Box 420163, Palm Coast, FL 32142 (904)445-4662. Features stories and advice on health and wellness, including buying guides on food and exercise programs. Call or write for a one-year subscription, 12 issues for $24.

What to Do When You Can't Afford Health Care, by Matthew Lesko (Info USA, 1993). $24.95.

Your Good Health: How to Stay Well and What to Do When You're Not, by William I. Bennett (Harvard University Press, 1987). $14.95.

19

APPENDIX A: EMERGENCY HEALTH CARE PHONE NUMBERS

As a visitor to any of these cities, you can go to the hospitals listed here for emergency health care. You can also call the hospitals for referrals to local doctors and other health-care practitioners and for the phone number of pharmacies open 24 hours a day.

The list includes one large general medical and surgical hospital in each of the 50 largest metropolitan areas of the United States. No attempt was made to endorse any hospital as the best one in the area. Rather, any hospital listed here should certainly serve many of your needs for emergency care and other general medical information.

Albany, NY, Albany Medical Center Hospital (518)262-3125

Atlanta, GA, Crawford Long Hospital (404)686-4411

Boston, MA, Massachusetts General Hospital (617)726-2000

Buffalo, NY, Buffalo General Hospital (716)845-5600

Charlotte, NC, Carolinas Medical Center (704)355-2000

Chicago, IL, Cook County Hospital (312)633-6000

Cincinnati, OH, University of Cincinnati Hospital (513)558-1000

Cleveland, OH, Metrohealth Medical Center (216)398-6000

Columbus, OH, Riverside Methodist Hospitals (614)566-5000

Dallas, TX, Baylor University Medical Center (214)820-0111

Dayton, Ohio, Miami Valley Hospital (513)558-1000

Denver, CO, Saint Joseph Hospital (303)837-7111

Detroit, MI, Henry Ford Hospital (313)876-2600

Grand Rapids, MI, Butterworth Hospital (616)774-1774

Greensboro, NC, Moses H. Cone Memorial Hospital (919)574-7000

Hartford, CT, Hartford Hospital (203)524-3011

Honolulu, Hawaii, Queens Medical Center (808)538-9011

Houston, TX, Methodist Hospital (713)790-3311

Indianapolis, IN, Methodist Hospital of Indiana (317)929-2000

Jacksonville, FL, St. Vincent's Medical Center (904)387-7300

Kansas City, MO, St. Luke's Hospital (816)932-2000

Las Vegas, NV, Sunrise Hospital and Medical Center (702)731-8000

Los Angeles, CA, Cedars-Sinai Medical Center (310)855-5000

Los Angeles, CA, University of Southern California Medical Center (213)226-2622

Louisville, KY, Norton Hospital of Alliant Health System (502)629-8000

Memphis, TN, Baptist Memorial Hospital (901)227-6550

Miami, FL, Jackson Memorial Hospital (305)585-6754/325-7429

Milwaukee, WI, St. Luke's Medical Center (414)649-6000

Minneapolis, MN, Fairview Riverside Medical Center (612)672-6300

Nashville, TN, Vanderbilt University Hospital and Clinic (615)322-5000

New Orleans, LA, Medical Center of Louisiana at New Orleans (504)568-3201

New York, NY, New York Hospital/Cornell Medical Center, (212)746-5454

Norfolk, VA, Sentara Norfolk General Hospital (804)628-3000

Oklahoma City, OK, Baptist Medical Center of Oklahoma (405)949-3011

Orlando, FL, Florida Hospital Medical Center (407)896-6611

Philadelphia, PA, Thomas Jefferson University Hospital (215)955-6000

Phoenix, AZ, Good Samaritan Regional Medical Center (602)239-2000

Pittsburgh, PA, Allegheny General Hospital (412)359-3131

Pittsburgh, PA, St. Francis Medical Center (412)622-4343

Portland, OR, Providence Medical Center (503)230-1111

Providence, RI, Rhode Island Hospital (401)444-4000

Raleigh, NC, Wake Medical Center (919)250-8000

Richmond, VA, Medical College of Virginia Hospitals (804)786-9000

Rochester, NY, Strong Memorial Hospital (716)275-2644

Sacramento, CA, University of California Davis Medical Center (916)734-3096

St. Louis, MO, Barnes Hospital (314)362-5000

Salt Lake City, UT, LDS Hospital (801)321-1100

San Antonio, TX, Santa Rosa Health Care Corporation (210)228-2111

San Diego, CA, Mercy Hospital and Medical Center (619)294-8111

San Francisco, CA, San Francisco General Hospital Medical Center (415)206-8000

Seattle, WA, Harborview Hospital (206)223-3000

Seattle, WA, University of Washington Medical Center (206)548-3300

Tampa, FL, Tampa General Hospital (813)251-7000

Virginia Beach, VA, Virginia Beach General Hospital (804)481-8000

Washington, DC, George Washington University Medical School (202)994-3321

West Palm Beach, FL, St. Mary's Hospital (407)844-6300

This glossary covers some of the more common terms you'll encounter in health care. While many of these terms have other meanings in the everyday world, the explanations presented here apply to their use in health care.

Activity of Daily Living (ADL): A basic task such as dressing or eating that can be used as part of a formal measure of the severity of a disability.

Acute illness: An illness that has occurred suddenly and may be serious.

Admitting privileges: The authorization a hospital gives to a health-care provider to admit a patient to that facility.

Adult day care: A variety of health, social, and related support services provided on an outpatient basis for adults who have functional impairments and need supervision.

Advance directive: A document in which a person designates someone to make health decisions when he or she is no longer able to make those decisions.

Allopathic physician: A medical doctor.

Ambulatory care: Health services that are provided without an overnight stay in a health-care facility.

Ancillary services: Miscellaneous tests such as laboratory or radiologic exams.

Assignment: See *Medicare assignment.*

Assisted living facility: Living quarters in which aides help a disabled person cope with ordinary chores, routines, and responsibilities.

Attending physician: The physician who is primarily responsible for the care of a particular patient in a hospital.

Balance billing: When health-care providers charge and collect more for a medical service than an insurance plan will cover. The individual who received the service pays the additional amount.

Board certified: A medical provider who has passed a national examination in a particular field such as anesthesiology, family practice, or surgery.

Board eligible: A medical provider who is preparing for a certification exam and has the training to take it.

Capitation: A payment system in which the insurer pays a provider a set fee per person signed up with that provider to cover all medical services the person receives from the provider.

Care coordination: See *case management.*

Case management: The process of having a person's health-care needs coordinated by using an on-going plan.

Certificate of coverage: The document that describes the benefits, providers, and general rules and regulations of an insurance policy.

Certificate of insurance: See *certificate of coverage.*

Certified: See *board certified.*

Certified nurse midwife: A nurse with specialized training to care for pregnant women and deliver babies.

Chronic illness: A condition that can't be cured, can last a lifetime, or reoccurs and may result in a need for long-term care.

Clinic: A part of a hospital that deals chiefly with outpatients or a health-care facility with several collaborating practitioners.

Clinician: A health-care professional who is directly involved with patient care.

Coinsurance: A percentage (often 20 percent) that an insured person pays for a visit to a physician or other health-care provider, a hospital stay, or treatment.

Community health center: A clinic that serves the surrounding community with accessible and affordable health care, including primary care.

Community hospital: A hospital that primarily serves the needs of its local area with general medical and surgical services.

Community rating: A method of setting insurance premiums for people in a given geographic area based on the expected use and costs of health-care services by all people in that area. An adjusted community rating reflects certain characteristics of the people in the area.

Concurrent review: A review by an insurer at the time of service to verify that a patient needs continued inpatient care.

Continuity of care: Care that is coordinated as a patient moves from one setting or one health-care provider to another.

Conversion: Process by which a policyholder shifts his or her health insurance.

Convertible term insurance: Insurance that a policyholder can exchange for another plan of insurance without evidence of insurability.

Copayment: A fixed dollar amount the recipient pays for health-care services at the time of receiving the service.

Credentialing: The review process for health-care providers that examines such items as their license, certification, malpractice insurance, and history.

Custodial care: Institutional care for basic physical and emotional needs.

Daily living skills: Tasks, such as bathing, eating, and grooming, done each day to meet a person's basic needs.

Deductible: The amount of money an insured person pays for services before the insurer starts paying the bill.

Diagnosis: Identification of a disease producing a specific condition.

Diagnostic services: Procedures to determine the presence of a health condition.

Disability: An impaired physical or mental ability.

Discharge planning: The planning process before a patient leaves a hospital or nursing facility to determine the patient's needs at the time of discharge.

Discharge status: A person's health condition when leaving a hospital or nursing facility.

Durable medical equipment (DME): A long-lasting medical supply, such as a wheelchair.

Durable power of attorney: A document in which a person designates someone to make decisions on his or her behalf.

Elective procedure: A procedure that isn't an emergency and that a patient and doctor plan in advance.

Emergency: An injury or acute medical condition likely to cause death, disability, or serious illness if not attended to very quickly.

Exclusions: Health conditions that an insurance policy specifically doesn't cover.

Extended-care facility: A nursing home or other institution that provides long-term care for patients.

Family practitioner: A medical doctor with special training in a variety of fields to handle primary health care for individuals and families.

Fee-for-service plan: A policy under which an insurer reimburses hospitals and physicians each time the policyholder receives care; often called an indemnity plan.

Gatekeeper: The person who controls a patient's access to health-care services, whether as a case manager or a primary-care provider. Typically, this person must approve all uses of health-care services.

Geriatrics: The special knowledge and skills applied through medicine, nursing, social work, and other professions to helping elders stay independent.

Group model HMO: An HMO that contracts with physicians in established group practices to provide health services.

Group insurance: Policies offered to an individual through his or her present or past employer or through his or her membership in a union or other organization.

Health-care power of attorney: A document in which a person authorizes someone to control his or her medical care when the person becomes unable to do so.

Health maintenance organization (HMO): An entity that provides, offers, or arranges for coverage of designated health services needed by plan members for a fixed, prepaid premium.

Health plan: The set of services in an insurance policy for health care.

History: The record of a person's medical background.

Holistic medicine: Medical care that considers the physical, social, emotional, and spiritual needs of the patient.

Home care: Care, ranging from everyday tasks to advanced medical care, that takes place in a home setting.

Home health agency: An organization that makes skilled nurses and other therapists available to provide services in a patient's home.

Home health care: Home care administered by health-care professionals.

Hospice: Facility or program for terminally ill people that includes counseling and health-care services that comfort a dying patient and his or her family.

Iatrogenic illness: An illness caused by a physician.

Indemnity plan: See *fee-for-service plan.*

Independent Provider Association (IPA): An HMO that contracts directly with physicians in independent practice to provide health services.

Informed consent: A person's agreement to undergo specific medical treatment while understanding what that treatment entails and implies.

Inpatient: A patient who stays in a hospital overnight.

Intermediate care facility (ICF): Nursing home that provides supervised care on a 24-hour basis but is less intense as found in a skilled nursing facility.

Internist: A medical doctor who specializes in the non-surgical diagnosis and treatment of adults.

Licensed practical nurse (LPN): A graduate of a formally approved program of practical nursing who is licensed by the appropriate state authority.

Lifetime maximum: The total amount that an insurance policy will pay out for medical care during the lifetime of the policyholder.

Living will: An advance directive in which a person sets forth his or her wishes concerning medical treatment in the event he or she is incapacitated.

Long-term care: Care provided over the long term to people who can't take care of themselves without assistance.

Malpractice: The basis for a lawsuit for injuries a patient suffers due to a health-care provider's mistake or carelessness.

Managed care: A term used to describe strategies of health-care plans to control costs by monitoring services and providers used or fees charged.

Mandated benefit: A specific benefit that an insurer must offer by law.

Mandated provider: A type of health-care provider a plan must cover by law .

Maximum out-of-pocket cost: The maximum amount of money a member will have to pay from his or her own funds for deductibles, copayments, or other expenses.

Medicaid: A federally aided, state-operated program that provides health-insurance benefits for certain low-income people.

Medical record: The documentation of a person's medical care.

Medically necessary: Services required to prevent harm to the patient or to the patient's quality of life.

Medicare: A national health-insurance program for older Americans, the blind, and disabled.

Medicare assignment: An agreement between a health-care provider and Medicare that he or she will accept the amount Medicare approves as full payment for Medicare-covered services.

Medicare certified agency: A health-care provider that Medicare will reimburse for providing Medicare-covered services.

Medicare risk contract: An arrangement between a health plan and Medicare in which the plan acts like an HMO for providing Medicare and supplemental benefits.

Medicare supplemental insurance (Medigap insurance): Insurance policies that cover the costs of some health-care services not covered by Medicare.

Mortality rate: The proportion of deaths within a population in a given period of time.

Mutual-help group: A support group composed of people in a similar situation.

Nocosomial infection: An infection acquired in a hospital.

Non-participating provider: A provider who isn't part of a specific health plan.

Nongroup plan: Insurance policy sold directly to an individual; also referred to as an individual policy.

Nurse practitioner: A registered nurse with advanced training to assume many of the responsibilities of physicians, including some primary care.

Nursing home: See intermediate care facility or skilled nursing facility.

Occupational medicine: Medicine that focuses on diseases and injuries associated with the workplace.

Ombudsman: A person responsible for investigating and seeking to resolve consumer complaints.

Open enrollment period: A time during which employees of a company can change health plans or during which members of a plan can change coverage.

Outcome: The results of treatment.

Out-of-pocket costs: All the health expenses that a policyholder pays himself or herself.

Outpatient: A patient who visits a hospital or another health-care facility for a specific treatment, procedure, or test but doesn't stay overnight.

Participating providers: Providers who are under contract with a health plan to provide services to plan members.

Patient-care plan: A written program of care for a patient that is based on the assessment of needs and that identifies the role of each service in meeting those needs.

Physician assistant (PA): A health-care worker with at least three years of college education, additional specialized schooling, and on-the-job training to work under the supervision of a physician. Some PAs deliver parts of primary care.

Point-of-Service Plan: A health plan that allows the policyholder to receive a service from either a participating or a non-participating provider, with lower benefit levels associated with the use of non-participating providers.

Pre-admission review: A review undertaken by a health plan that happens before a patient enters a hospital to determine if the admission is necessary and appropriate.

Pre-certification: Similar to pre-admission review but requires a certificate or authorization from the patient's health plan.

Pre-existing condition: A health condition that a person has that an insurance policy specifically excludes from coverage or that prevents the person from qualifying for insurance.

Preferred Provider Organization (PPO): A form of managed care in which medical providers contract with an insurer to provide services at pre-negotiated fees. Subscribers may use providers outside this provider network by paying more out-of-pocket.

Premium: The regular charge, usually monthly, that a policyholder or his or her employer pays to an insurer for health coverage, regardless of the policyholder's use of service.

Prepaid health plan: A health plan in which the member pays a premium for health-care services provided later at minimal additional charge. Many providers are also prepaid for their services.

Preventive care: Health care that stresses healthy behavior, regular testing, screening for diseases, and other services that detect diseases early on or prevent them from occurring.

Primary care: First-level or generalist care that a person receives outside a hospital.

Primary-care physician or *primary-care provider:* The health-care provider a person most commonly calls first when a problem arises.

Prior authorization: A cost-control procedure in which an insurer requires a service or medication to be approved in advance for coverage.

Peer Review Organization (PRO): A physicians' group responsible for assuring that patients are getting services they need in the appropriate place and that the services meet professional standards.

Prognosis: An explanation by a health-care provider to a patient of the likely course of an illness.

Provider: A person or an institution that delivers a service.

Quality assurance: A process that examines the services a provider offers to see that they are provided with high standards.

Reasonable and customary charge: The maximum amount an insurer will reimburse a provider for a given service or procedure.

Referral: When one health-care provider suggests you visit another one for the purpose of further evaluation and treatment.

Registered nurse (RN): A nurse with a degree from a formal program of nursing education and a license from the appropriate state authority.

Rehabilitation: Services and facilities patients use as a part of recovering from an accident or illness.

Respite care: Temporary relief for a caregiver from some tasks.

Risk factor: A characteristic or behavior that entails possible damage to a person's health.

Screening test: A procedure to determine if a person has a certain medical condition.

Secondary care: Care, often provided in hospitals and long-term facilities, that makes more use of caregivers with specialized training than does primary care.

Self-help group: See *mutual-help group.*

Self-referral: When a health-care provider stands to benefit financially from referring a patient to another provider for care.

Service area: The geographic area a health plan serves.

Social HMO (SHMO): An HMO that provides some coverage for long-term care, such as for home-care services.

Skilled nursing facility: A long-term-care facility that offers extensive professional nursing services twenty-four hours a day, but not acute care.

Specialist: A physician whose training focuses on a particular area beyond the general training for all physicians.

Specialty hospital: A hospital that treats patients with a specific type of disease or condition.

Staff model HMO: A prepaid health-care system in which a salaried physician group employed by the HMO delivers health services.

Subspecialist: A specialist with additional training in a particular clinical subject.

Supplemental Security Income (SSI): A national income-maintenance program for older Americans that guarantees a minimum income to those with insufficient resources.

Teaching hospital: A hospital that is affiliated with a medical school and has a teaching program for medical students, interns, and residents.

Tertiary care: Highly specialized care for severe health problems.

Usual and Customary Rates (UCR): See *reasonable and customary.*

Utilization management: The process health plans and insurers use to make sure the kind of treatment and care recommended for a patient is necessary and appropriate.

Veterans Affairs, Department of: A division of the federal government that, among other things, offers certain forms of health care to veterans of the armed forces.

Wellness: A program to keep a person healthy.

Workers compensation: A program paid by employers and managed by states to provide financial assistance to workers who lose wages or incur health-care bills due to workplace injuries and work-related health problems.